DATA IN DOUBT

DATA IN DOUBT

An Introduction to Bayesian Statistical Inference
for Economists

John D. Hey

Martin Robertson

First published in 1983 by Martin Robertson &
Company Ltd., 108 Cowley Road, Oxford OX4 1JF.

British Library Cataloguing in Publication Data
Hey, John D.
  Data in doubt.
  1. Economics—Statistical mathematics
  I. Title
  519.5′02433   HB137
  ISBN 0-85520-559-8

Typeset by Santype International Ltd., Salisbury
Printed and bound in Great Britain by
T. J. Press Ltd., Padstow

To Brian, David and Thomas

CONTENTS

Preface   xi

Acknowledgements   xiii

1   INTRODUCTION   1

2   ELEMENTARY PROBABILITY THEORY   5
    2.1   Introduction   5
    2.2   Distribution, probability and probability density
          functions   6
    2.3   Summaries   17
    2.4   Some specific distributions   25
    2.5   The basic probability laws   34
    2.6   Summary   38
    2.7   Exercises   39

3   FURTHER PROBABILITY THEORY   43
    3.1   Introduction   43
    3.2   Bivariate probability distributions   44
    3.3   Marginal distributions   50
    3.4   Conditional distributions   58
    3.5   Multivariate probability distributions   66
    3.6   Summaries   71
    3.7   Summary   74
    3.8   Exercises   75

4   INFORMATION   79
    4.1   Introduction   79
    4.2   The incorporation of new information:
          simple examples   80
    4.3   The incorporation of new information:
          Bayes' theorem   83
    4.4   Some applications of Bayes' theorem for events   88
    4.5   Some applications of Bayes' theorem for variables   96
    4.6   Some preliminary notions of 'non-existent'
          prior information   105

4.7	Summary	106
4.8	Exercises	106

5 PROPORTIONS   110
5.1	Introduction	110
5.2	The representation of beliefs about a proportion	112
5.3	The nature of (sample) information	116
5.4	The incorporation of sample information	118
5.5	The case of 'non-existent' prior information	125
5.6	'Confidence intervals' and 'significance tests'	129
5.7	Summary	130
5.8	Exercises	131

6 MEANS AND VARIANCES   135
6.1	Introduction	135
6.2	Inference with an unknown mean and known variance	137
6.3	Inference with an unknown variance and known mean	152
6.4	Inference with an unknown mean and unknown variance	160
6.5	'Confidence intervals' and 'significance tests'	168
6.6	Summary	173
6.7	Exercises	175

7 ELEMENTARY REGRESSION ANALYSIS   179
7.1	Introduction	179
7.2	Inference with unknown coefficients and known variance	185
7.3	Inference with known coefficients and unknown variance	195
7.4	Inference with unknown coefficients and unknown variance	198
7.5	'Confidence intervals' and 'significance tests'	205
7.6	Comparison of theories and 'goodness of fit'	209
7.7	Examples of regression	213
7.8	Prediction	222
7.9	Summary	224
7.10	Exercises	225

8 FURTHER REGRESSION ANALYSIS   228
8.1	Introduction	228
8.2	The linear multivariate normal model	230
8.3	Various 'tricks of the trade'	247
8.4	The validity of the assumptions	260
8.5	An example of econometrics in action	268

8.6   Summary   276
8.7   Exercises   277

9   ANALYSIS OF SIMULTANEOUS EQUATION
    MODELS   281
9.1   Introduction   281
9.2   The use of 'single equation' methods   282
9.3   The identification problem   291
9.4   Inference in simultaneous equation models   296
9.5   A simple example   299
9.6   Summary   300
9.7   Exercises   301

APPENDIX   304
A1   Notation for sums and products   304
A2   Calculus: some important notation and results   305
A3   Sketches of proofs of results of chapter 7   305
A4   Sketches of proofs of results of chapter 8   308
A5   Bayesian computer programs   310
A6   Table of the unit normal distribution   312
A7   Table of the t-distribution   313
A8   Table of the χ-square distribution   314

FURTHER READING   316

INDEX   317

PREFACE

For more years than I care to recall, I have been teaching introductory statistics and econometrics to economics students. As many teachers and students are all too aware, this can be a painful experience for all concerned. Many will be familiar with the apparently never-ending quest for ways of reducing the pain – by redesigning courses and by using different texts or writing new ones. But the changes all too often turn out to be purely cosmetic, with the fundamental problem left untouched. So the quest continues.

In retrospect, it is clear that I was aware of the real problem for some time, but it was not until about three years ago that I finally admitted it to myself. The fundamental malaise with most statistics and econometrics courses is that they use the *Classical* approach to inference. Students find this unnatural and contorted. It is not intuitively acceptable and does not accord with the way that people assimilate information (statistical or otherwise) in their everyday life. In practice, people hold (whether consciously or not) probabilistic views about uncertain theories, hypotheses and phenomena, and they update these views in the light of new information. This is precisely the view of statistics adopted by the Bayesian approach.

I first taught a Bayesian course two years ago. Naturally, there were teething problems at first, but these were relatively minor. To my delight, I discovered that the 'fundamental problem' had disappeared. (Though there were problems with some students who had (half-) done a Classical course previously, and found it difficult to shake off past habits of thought.) I am now more than convinced, in the light of the experience of these two years, that the Bayesian approach is the 'correct' one to adopt. (Though this is not to assert that the Bayesian approach is free from all problems; indeed, it is clear that it is not, but these are problems common to all approaches.)

The only real difficulty in teaching a Bayesian course was the lack of a suitable text. Hence this present volume. Draft material was used in courses at York in 1981/82 and 1982/83 and I am grateful to those students who acted as guinea pigs and who offered constructive comments. I am also very grateful to Brian Hillier for his perceptive comments on draft chapters.

This book may well not have seen the light of day if it had not been for the splendid judgement and constant encouragement of Michael Hay. I am grateful to him for attaching more weight to my opinion that a Bayesian book would be an academic and commercial success than to the apparently conflicting opinion evidenced by a textbook market saturated with Classical books. To him, my thanks.

Special thanks go once again to Jo Hall, who produced a beautiful typescript with her usual calm efficiency. The quality of her work shines through in the finished product.

Unlike previous books of mine, this has not benefitted from the literary scrutiny and expertise of my wife, Marlene. Indeed, as far as I know, she has been blissfully unaware that I have been writing this book. This speaks volumes for her qualities as a wife and mother, particularly with two very active young children to care for. To her, my thanks and love.

This book is dedicated to three splendid gentlemen: my father (an actuary and a statistician amongst numerous other things), my brother (although many things not a statistician) and my son (not yet a statistician but could be many other things). While it is a little early for Thomas to care about the difference between Bayesian and Classical statistics, and while David is too busy doing the important things in life to worry about the differences, I hope that this book will prompt Brian to find the time to ponder on the difference.

JOHN D. HEY
York, January 1983

ACKNOWLEDGEMENTS

I am indebted to the Literary Executor of the late Sir Ronald A. Fisher, FRS, to Dr Frank Yates, FRS, and to Longman Group Ltd, London, for permission to reprint Table III from their book *Statistical Tables for Biological, Agricultural and Medical Research* (6th edition, 1974).

1 INTRODUCTION

Statistics are an aid to decision-making under uncertainty. This book is a statistics text aimed primarily at economists. Therefore, the purpose of the book is to show how statistics may be used to aid economic decision-making under uncertainty.

It goes almost without saying that all economic theories, statements, predictions and policy recommendations are subject to some degree of uncertainty. Naturally, the amount of uncertainty varies from area to area within the subject; for example, aggregate consumer spending is fairly well understood, though aggregate investment spending remains fairly difficult to explain. This variability depends partly on the area, and partly on the quantity and quality of the research effort expended in that area. As a general rule, it seems to be the case that the more effort expended, and the more information assimilated, the more economists have learnt about a particular area, and thus the smaller the amount of residual uncertainty that remains. (However, this is not always the case – if, for example, there are structural changes in the way people behave. Then economists have to begin learning afresh.)

Knowledge in economics is accumulated in much the same way as in any other discipline, or indeed in everyday life. One's views about some uncertain theory or phenomenon are continually updated or revised in the light of new information. Hopefully, the end product of this process is the convergence of knowledge onto 'The Truth' about the particular phenomenon under study. Ideally, in economics, we will eventually be able to explain and predict economic behaviour (in aggregate?) with complete certainty – though, at the moment, this ideal looks a long way off.

It is clear from this description of the accumulation of knowledge in economics that there are two key components in this process: the *description* of one's views about some particular theory or phenomenon as they exist at some point in time; and the process of the *revision* of these views in the light of new information relevant to the theory or phenomenon. In essence, this book is concerned with a discussion of these two components.

1

The natural way to *describe* one's views about some theory or phenomenon is to use probabilistic statements. For example, one might say that, on the basis of the available information and in the light of the various economic theories, the monetarist explanation of inflation is more likely to be correct than the cost-push explanation; or, that it is highly unlikely that the naive accelerator model is an adequate explanation of investment behaviour; or, again, that there is a less than 1 in 4 chance that the permanent income hypothesis is the correct explanation of aggregate consumption. More narrowly, one might state that the available evidence suggests that it is almost certain that the aggregate marginal propensity to consume lies between 0.5 and 0.7; or, that there is a relatively small chance (say less than 20 per cent) that the interest-elasticity of the demand for money is greater than 1 (in magnitude); or, again, that there is a very high chance (say more than 95 per cent) that the labour supply curve is backward bending for advanced industrial countries.

Probability, then, plays a crucial role. This book starts with two chapters devoted to probability, showing formally how uncertain views about theories, phenomena or variables can be expressed and characterized in probabilistic terms. Chapter 2 introduces the essential ideas of probability, set in the relatively simple context of statements about simple events and single variables. Since much of the subsequent material in the book will be concerned with variables, most of this chapter is concerned with the characterization and summarization of probabilistic views about single variables, though the chapter also introduces three basic probability laws, which underlie most of the material which follows. In particular, these laws imply Bayes' theorem, which, as we shall see, is the key to the 'correct' revision, or updating, of one's views in the light of new information. Chapter 3 extends the ideas introduced in chapter 2 to more complex situations, specifically the characterization and summarization of probabilistic views about several variables.

The rest of the book is devoted to the second of the two key components discussed above – namely, the process of *revising* one's views in the light of new information. Chapter 4 begins by looking at some relatively simple examples, and continues by formalizing this process through Bayes' theorem, which we met for the first time in chapter 2. Chapter 4 then concludes by giving some relatively simple examples of the use of Bayes' theorem, two of which are studied in greater detail in chapters 5 and 6.

Chapters 2, 3 and 4 contain all the basic conceptual and technical apparatus that we need. The remaining chapters of the book are concerned with applying this apparatus in different contexts and to different problems. As we progress through these remaining chapters, our applications become more and more realistic and more and more relevant to the needs of the economist. In this latter respect, chapters 7, 8 and 9 contain most of the material of direct relevance – being concerned with the empirical investigation of one or more economic relationships. However, this increased realism brings with it an increased algebraic and technical (though not conceptual) complexity of analysis, so that as we progress through the remaining chapters, the algebra becomes more and more complex. For this reason, we interpose two chapters (5 and 6) which, although not of frequent direct interest to economists, are relatively simple illustrations of the application of the apparatus of chapters 2, 3 and 4. The idea behind the inclusion of these chapters is to give you, the reader, confidence in the basic apparatus, and intuitive understanding of its application, so that when we come to chapters 7, 8 and 9 we may increasingly omit the algebraic detail (relegating it, where possible, to the Appendix). After all, it is *not* important that you can prove the results, but it *is* important that you can apply them.

Chapter 5, then, is devoted to one of the simplest possible applications of the basic apparatus of this book – namely, the problem of learning about some unknown proportion. This chapter shows how some beliefs in some proportion can be updated in the light of new information. I also discuss what might be meant by a state of total prior ignorance.

Chapter 6 examines a rather more complicated application of the same methodology – namely, the problem of learning about an unknown mean and/or an unknown variance. As will become apparent, this application is part way (and hence a bridge) between the simple application of chapter 5 and the more complicated (but more relevant) applications of the subsequent chapters.

As already noted, the final three chapters of the book apply the same methodology to the economists' major interest – the empirical investigation of economic relationships. The main ideas are introduced in chapter 7, which considers the simplest of such relationships: a single-equation, bivariate, linear relationship with a normally distributed residual. The chapter shows how one can use economic data on the relevant variables to learn about the (economic) parameters of the relationship. This knowledge can then be used in a variety of ways: for example, to make probabilistic statements about economic parameters of the type discussed above, or to make predictions about future values of economic variables.

Chapter 8 extends the methods introduced in chapter 7 to more complicated relationships – in particular, to multivariate and non-linear relationships – though the analysis stays within the single-equation framework. This chapter also discusses various 'tricks of the trade' that the econometrician (a statistician specializing in the investigation of economic relationships) typically employs during empirical research. Finally, chapter 9 looks briefly at simultaneous-equation models.

Various appendices complete the volume. These consist of a summary of some important notation and results from the calculus, sketches of some of the proofs omitted from chapters 7 and 8, a guide to Bayesian computer programs, and a set of tables of frequently encountered statistical distribution. Finally, the list of references also includes some suggestions for further reading for those who wish to take their study further. I hope that many will.

Each chapter contains a number of examples and concludes with a set of exercises. The reader is strongly urged to work through these exercises after completing each chapter: only by reinforcing your reading by successfully completing some associated exercises can you ever hope to become proficient and confident at a subject like statistics. Be selective, however – some of the exercises are rather repetitive. If your knowledge of calculus is weak or non-existent, omit those exercises (or part of exercises) marked with an asterisk: all the other exercises can be completed without any calculus.

It only remains for me to remind you that this is a *Bayesian* text, and, as such, differs fundamentally in its conceptual approach from *Classical* texts (such as Hey, 1974). Because it is Bayesian, I believe you will find it much easier to understand, and much more intuitively acceptable, than a Classical text. Nevertheless, because the Classical approach remains dominant, I have provided in chapters 5, 6 and 7 material which will enable you to converse with a Classical statistician, to read and understand statistical analyses conducted in the Classical mode, and to present your (Bayesian) results in a Classical mode if the need arises. (As will become apparent, the Classical approach *can* be interpreted as a *special case* of the Bayesian approach; thus, in addition to its other advantages, the Bayesian approach is much more general.) So, do not fear, you will not be at a disadvantage compared with someone who has followed a Classical course. On the contrary, you will end up knowing more, you will understand it better, and above all I hope, you will have enjoyed it more.

2 ELEMENTARY PROBABILITY THEORY

2.1 INTRODUCTION

Probability plays a key role in statistics. Statistical statements about economic parameters and economic hypotheses are expressed in probabilistic terms. For instance, the conclusions of a study of income-consumption data designed to shed light on the value of the marginal propensity to consume (the mpc) might be expressed in the following form: 'in the light of the evidence there is a probability of 0.95 that the mpc lies between 0.59 and 0.63'; or, 'the probability that the mpc lies between 0 and 1, as the theory requires, is 0.9995'.

This chapter introduces the basic ideas of probability. It begins with a brief discussion of what is meant by probability. It then discusses (in sections 2.2 and 2.3) various ways of describing, communicating and summarizing probability statements. In section 2.4, some specific illustrations are given. Then, in section 2.5, it is shown how three basic probability laws may be used to deduce further consequences of some initial probability statements. Finally, section 2.6 presents a summary and section 2.7 some exercises.

Central to this book is the idea that *probability is subjective;* that is, that *probability statements are expressions of subjective belief.* Thus, for example, I might express my view about the various parties' prospects in the next general election by saying: 'I think there is a 50:50 chance that the Conservative Party will form the next Government.' Similarly, you might express your views about the next World Cup by saying: 'I think England's chances of winning are 1 in 10.' Of course, the fact that such probabilities are subjective does not preclude us from agreeing over something: thus, for example, we might both agree that 'there is a 50:50 chance that a coin will land heads'. In general, one might expect that people's probability assessments depend upon the amount of information that they have, and upon the way they process it. Thus, one might expect increasing agreement between people as the amount of shared information increases. Indeed, we will see that if several 'rational' (a

5

term we shall clarify shortly) people are all confronted with the same *large* amount of information, then, irrespective of their subjective beliefs *prior* to this information, they will tend to have similar beliefs *after* receiving the information.

An individual's probability assessment of some uncertain variable or event will depend upon his or her accumulated information relevant to that variable or event. In general, one might quite reasonably expect this assessment to vary as new information is obtained. We delay a discussion of how such new information is incorporated into a probability assessment until chapter 4; and also delay until then a discussion of the determinants of the initial or 'prior' probability assessments. This chapter is confined to the much simpler task of discussing how some given probability assessment, as it exists at some given point in time (and given a certain body of evidence), is described, communicated and summarized.

Before we begin, we must draw an important distinction, namely that between *variables* and *events*. Most of the time in economics we are interested in *variables*, which are things that can be quantified, such as income or price or investment. Indeed, most of the book will be concerned with variables. However, on occasion, and mostly for expositional reasons, we will need to refer to *events*; these are things that can be described, such as 'a coin landing heads' or 'England winning the World Cup' or 'the Conservative Party forming the next Government'. (Though, in practice, the distinction is blurred as one can always 'quantify' a set of events, or describe a variable in terms of events.) In the material that follows, section 2.5 is concerned with events while sections 2.2 to 2.4 are concerned with variables. Moreover, the exposition in sections 2.2 to 2.4 is simplified further by restricting attention to the *univariate* case; this is a situation in which we are interested in just a single variable at a time. The general, *multivariate* case (a situation in which we are interested in many variables) will be examined in chapter 3.

2.2   DISTRIBUTION, PROBABILITY AND PROBABILITY
       DENSITY FUNCTIONS

Suppose, then, that we are interested in describing and summarizing someone's probability assessment of some single variable. Let us call this variable X. We now introduce a very important notational convention which will be used throughout the book, and which will be an important aid to understanding: in referring to variables, we will use *upper-case* letters to denote the *name* of some variable, and the corresponding *lower-case* letter to denote a *specific value* of that variable. For example, if we are interested in the mpc, then X (say) will denote the mpc, while x will denote a specific value, such as 0.59 or 0.63. Again, if we are interested in a person's weekly income (in £s), then X might be used to denote this income, while x will be used to denote a specific value, such as 120 or 150.

Probability statements will be expressed in the shorthand '$P(\ )$' where the bracket contains some statement about the variable. Thus, for example,

$$P(0.59 \leq X \leq 0.63) = 0.9,$$

is shorthand for 'the probability is 0.9 that X lies between 0.59 and 0.63' (where, of course, this statement is taken to be the subjective assessment of whoever is making the statement). Likewise,

$$P(120 \leq X) = 0.5,$$

is shorthand for 'there is a 50:50 chance that X is at least 120'. More generally,

$$P(x_1 \leq X \leq x_2) = a$$

is shorthand for 'the probability is a that X lies between x_1 and x_2'. Clearly, to make sense, a must lie between 0 and 1 (i.e. $0 \leq a \leq 1$).

We now introduce the *distribution function*, which is one of several ways of describing an individual's probability assessment concerning some variable X. The distribution function of X, denoted by $F_X(.)$, is defined by:

$$F_X(x) \equiv P(X \leq x). \tag{2.1}$$

Thus, $F_X(x)$ expresses the probability that X is less than or equal to x. Usually, when no ambiguity is likely to result, the X subscript is omitted, and $F_X(.)$ is simply written $F(.)$. Clearly, $F_X(.)$ takes a value (between 0 and 1 inclusive) for all values of x between $-\infty$ and $+\infty$. Moreover, the following properties of the function $F_X(.)$ must hold irrespective of what X is:

(a) $F_X(-\infty) = 0$
(b) $F_X(+\infty) = 1$ $\qquad\qquad$ (2.2)
(c) $F_X(x)$ is non-decreasing in x.

(You should satisfy yourself that you are happy with these: (a) says that the probability of X taking a value less than or equal to $-\infty$ is zero; (b) says that the probability of X taking a value less than or equal to $+\infty$ is 1; (c) says that as x increases, the probability that X is less than or equal to it cannot decrease.) These properties are all immediate consequences of the fact that $F_X(x)$ measures the *cumulative probability*, up to and including the value x.

To illustrate the use of this function, we give three simple examples. In the first example, the variable X is defined as the number showing when a die is rolled once. The possible values for x are thus 1, 2, 3, 4, 5 and 6. In general, the probability assessment may vary from individual to individual, but let us consider the case of someone who regards the die as fair, and thus feels that each of the six outcomes is equally likely. This individual's assessment could thus be represented by:

$$P(X = x) = \begin{cases} \frac{1}{6} & x = 1, 2, 3, 4, 5, 6 \\ 0 & \text{otherwise.} \end{cases} \tag{2.3}$$

We now determine $F_X(x)$ for all possible values of x. Clearly, $F_X(x) = 0$ for $x < 1$, since X cannot take values less than 1. Also $F_X(1) = \frac{1}{6}$ since the probability that X is less than or equal to 1 is the same as the probability that X equals 1, which is $\frac{1}{6}$. Moreover, $F_X(x) = \frac{1}{6}$ for $1 \leq x < 2$, since there are no values between (but excluding) 1 and 2 that X may take. (Thus, for example, $F_X(1.8) = P(X \leq 1.8) = P(X = 1) = \frac{1}{6}$.) Also, $F_X(2) = \frac{2}{6}$ since the probability that X is less than or equal to 2 is the same as the probability that X equals 1 or 2, which is $\frac{2}{6}$. Moreover, $F_X(x) = \frac{2}{6}$ for $2 \leq x < 3$, since there are no values between (but excluding) 2 and 3 that X may take. Continuing in this fashion, we get the following (rather clumsy, though nevertheless straightforward) expression for $F_X(.)$:

$$F_X(x) = \begin{cases} 0 & x < 1 \\ \frac{1}{6} & 1 \leq x < 2 \\ \frac{2}{6} & 2 \leq x < 3 \\ \frac{3}{6} & 3 \leq x < 4 \\ \frac{4}{6} & 4 \leq x < 5 \\ \frac{5}{6} & 5 \leq x < 6 \\ 1 & 6 \leq x \end{cases} \tag{2.4}$$

A graph clarifies the situation considerably: examine figure 2.1. (Purists will note that I have been rather sloppy in joining together the various horizontal segments, and not making clear the precise functional values at the integer points; however, as we shall see, such 'imprecisions' are of no consequence.)

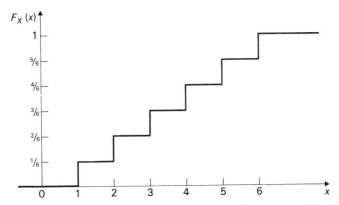

Figure 2.1 The distribution function of the number showing on a 'fair' die

The graph looks like a set of steps. Indeed, the distribution function in this example is what is called a *step-function*, for obvious
reasons. The vertical sections occur at the integer values 1, 2, 3, 4, 5
and 6 (which are the values that X takes), while everywhere in
between (the values that X does not take) the graph is horizontal. In
addition, the *height* of the jump at each integer value is equal to $\frac{1}{6}$,
the probability of X taking the value. This is an important general
property which we shall explore in more detail later in the chapter.

In the meantime, let us consider a second example; in this, as we
shall see, the variable is of a rather different kind. Imagine a horizontal disc, at the centre of which is pivoted a horizontal pointer which
rotates freely. Suppose further that the circumference of the disc is
uniformly and *continuously* calibrated from 0 to 1 (see figure 2.2(a)).
Now define the variable X as the value that the pointer indicates,
having come to rest after being spun. As before, the probability
assessment concerning X may vary from individual to individual
(depending upon the information they may have accumulated), but,
as before, let us consider the assessment of an individual who regards
the pointer as unbiased, and thus equally likely to come to rest at
any position. For such a case, the distribution function is easy to
derive: for example, $F_X(0.5) = 0.5$, since there is a 1 in 2 chance that
the pointer will stop in the right-hand hemisphere; similarly,
$F_X(0.25) = 0.25$ since there is a 1 in 4 chance that it will come to rest
in the first quadrant; similarly, $F_X(0.75) = 0.75$. There is an obvious
pattern here which can be summarized in the general rule:

$$F_X(x) = x \qquad \text{(if } 0 \leq x \leq 1\text{).}$$

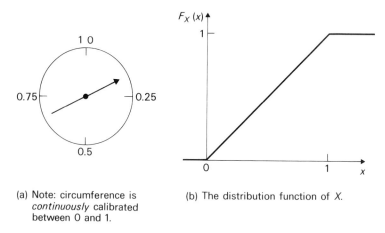

(a) Note: circumference is
continuously calibrated
between 0 and 1.

(b) The distribution function of *X*.

Figure 2.2   A pointer experiment

(If you are not sure about this, try some more specific examples yourself.) To complete the description of $F_X(.)$ note that X cannot take a value less than 0, so that $F_X(x) = 0$ for $x < 0$; and X cannot take a value greater than 1, so that $F_X(x) = 1$ for $x > 1$. (Be sure that you follow why this latter result holds: it is simply because for any $x > 1$, X is certain to be less than it.) Gathering these results together, we have

$$F_X(x) = \begin{cases} 0 & x < 0 \\ x & 0 \le x \le 1 \\ 1 & 1 < x \end{cases} \qquad (2.5)$$

(See figure 2.2(b).)

If you compare the distribution functions in our two examples, you will notice an important similarity: they both have horizontal segments. These segments indicate values of x that X does not take (namely, values other than the integers from 1 to 6 in the first example, and values outside the interval $[0, 1]$ in the second example). You will also notice an important difference: in the first example, the horizontal segments are joined together by vertical jumps; while in the second example, the horizontal segments are joined together by a smoothly increasing curve. This difference reflects an important difference between the variables themselves: in the first example, the variable X is *discrete*; while in the second example, the variable X is *continuous*. (Notice that in the second example, X can take values *continuously* between 0 and 1, while in the first example, possible X values occur only at *discrete* points. If you are unclear about the distinction between discrete and continuous variables, you should consult a mathematics text.) As we will see, discrete and continuous variables require somewhat different treatments.

You will notice that in both our examples, there are several possible values for X, and there is necessarily uncertainty as to which values of X will be observed in any particular case (roll of the die or spin of the pointer). Most of this book will be concerned with problems in which uncertainty is present. Indeed, if uncertainty is absent there is really no problem to consider. But, clearly, certainty is a special case of uncertainty, and thus our methods can also be applied to the special, degenerate case of certainty. Consider the variable X defined as my age on 26 September 1984. In the absence of any information about me your assessment of X would be uncertain. (What would your distribution function look like?) If I told you that I was born during the Second World War, this might narrow down your uncertainty somewhat. (What would your distribution function look like now?) But if I then told you that I was born on 26 September 1944, all residual uncertainty would disappear: you would know for a fact that X equalled 40. Your (everybody's) distribution function would look like that shown in figure 2.3(a): there would be a single jump from 0 to 1 at the value $x = 40$.

Incidentally, when I asked my students about their assessment of X in this example (my age), a typical response, before I gave them any information, was as follows: 'Well, I'm sure he's older than 36, but he's definitely not over 42; as for ages in between, I don't really

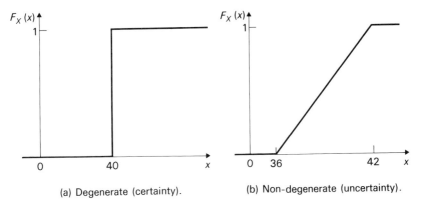

(a) Degenerate (certainty). (b) Non-degenerate (uncertainty).

Figure 2.3 Two distribution functions for the author's age

know, so I'll assume they're all equally likely.' This assessment is encapsulated in the distribution function shown in figure 2.3(b).

The distribution function is just one of several ways of representing someone's probability assessment concerning some variable. Its great advantage is that it can be used for both discrete and continuous variables. There is, however, another representation which appeals rather more to intuition, particularly when a graphical portrayal is required. But separate treatments are required for discrete and continuous variables. Consider first the former.

As we noted above, the distinguishing feature of the distribution function of a *discrete* variable is that it consists of a series of horizontal segments joined together by vertical jumps (or steps). These jumps occur at the discrete values that the variable takes, and the magnitude of the jump at any particular value equals the probability of the variable taking that value. This should be apparent from figure 2.1. More formally, suppose there is a jump at $X = x$; at the foot of the step, the value of the function is $P(X < x)$, while at the top of the step, the value is $P(X \leq x)$; the difference is $P(X \leq x) - P(X < x)$ or $P(X = x)$. In the light of this discussion, let us define a new function, denoted by $f_X(.)$, as follows

$$f_X(x) = \begin{cases} 0, \text{ at all points where } F_X(x) \text{ is horizontal} \\ \text{height of jump, where } F_X(x) \text{ has a vertical jump.} \end{cases} \quad (2.6)$$

It is clear that

$$f_X(x) = P(X = x) \qquad \text{for all } x, \qquad (2.7)$$

which is why $f_X(.)$ is termed the *probability function* of X. The probability function of X in our first example is given in figure 2.4(a). As

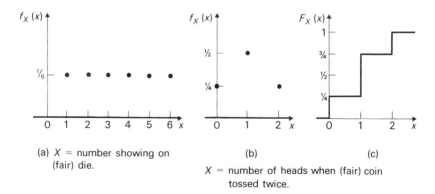

(a) X = number showing on (fair) die.

(b)

X = number of heads when (fair) coin tossed twice.

(c)

Figure 2.4 Introducing the probability function

a further example, figure 2.4(b) shows the probability function of the variable X defined as the number of tosses obtained when an (agreed fair) coin is tossed twice; figure 2.4(c) shows the corresponding distribution function. You should note crucially that the probability function is zero everywhere except at the discrete values taken by the variable (the integers 1 to 6 in the first example, and the integers 0, 1 and 2 in the further example).

If we tried to apply the above definition to a *continuous* variable, we would run into trouble. To begin with, there are no jumps in the distribution function of a continuous variable (cf. figures 2.2(b) and 2.3(b)), so definition (2.6) is rather difficult to apply. Could we use (2.7) instead? Consider our second example – that portrayed in figure 2.2. What is, for example, $P(X = 0.1)$? A moment's reflection will reveal the answer: *zero*! (Clearly, $P(0.1 \leq X \leq 0.9) = 0.8$; $P(0.1 \leq X \leq 0.5) = 0.4$; and, more generally, $P(0.1 \leq X \leq 0.1 + a) = a$. Therefore, putting $a = 0$, we get $P(0.1 \leq X \leq 0.1) = 0$; that is, $P(X = 0.1) = 0$.) Indeed, a similar argument shows that $P(X = x) = 0$ for all x! (This comes from the general result that $P(x \leq X \leq x + a) = a$.) Thus, the probability function as defined in (2.7) is identically zero for all x (which is just another way of saying that there are no jumps in the distribution function). Clearly, the probability function is of precious little use for telling us anything about the probability assessment in our second example.

The problem, of course, is that the variable X in our second example is *continuous*. As x goes from 0 to 1, probability is accumulated *continuously*: there are no big 'lumps' of probability as there are in the discrete case. Thus, there is no point asking *how much* probability there is at a particular x value: more sensible is to ask at *what rate* is probability accumulating at each x value. (An analogy may help here: there is no point in asking how far a car moves *at* a precise moment in time; more sensible is to ask at what rate is the car moving at that moment.) The rate of accumulation is simply given by the *slope* of the distribution function: the steeper it is, the faster is probability accumulating; the shallower it is, the slower is probability accumulating. Such considerations lead us to define a new function, denoted by $f_X(\cdot)$, as follows

$$f_X(x) = F'_X(x) \equiv \mathrm{d}F_X(x)/\mathrm{d}x \quad (\equiv \text{slope of } F_X(x) \text{ at } x). \qquad (2.8)$$

Full insight into this function really requires some elementary knowledge of calculus. If you do not have this knowledge, you could refer to the Appendix, or take the following results on trust (they are not really essential to your subsequent understanding). If you *are* familiar with calculus, you will recall the following definition of the slope of a function: from (2.8) (using (2.1)) we have

$$f_X(x) = \underset{\Delta x \to 0}{Lt} \left[\frac{P(X \le x + \Delta x) - P(X \le x)}{\Delta x} \right] \tag{2.9}$$

The numerator of the expression in square brackets in (2.9) is the probability that X lies in the interval $[x, x + \Delta x]$; the denominator is the width of the interval. Thus the term in square brackets is the *density* of the probability in the interval $[x, x + \Delta x]$. It follows, therefore, that $f_X(x)$ measures the *density* of the probability *at the point x*. It is for this reason that $f_X(.)$ is called the *probability density function* of X. (You should note that, although we have used the same letter, f, to denote the probability function in the discrete case, and the probability density function in the continuous case, no confusion should result, despite their being quite different functions, as the context will clearly specify which is the appropriate one.)

To obtain the probability density function of a continuous variable from its distribution function, we simply differentiate the latter (see (2.8)). Thus, the probability density function in our second example (the pointer experiment, as portrayed in figure 2.2) is given by (from (2.5))

$$f_X(x) = \begin{cases} 1 & 0 \le x \le 1 \\ 0 & \text{elsewhere.} \end{cases} \tag{2.10}$$

(See figure 2.5(a).) As is clear from this, the density function is the same at all values in the interval $[0, 1]$; this encapsulates the fact that the pointer is equally likely to come to rest anywhere in this interval.

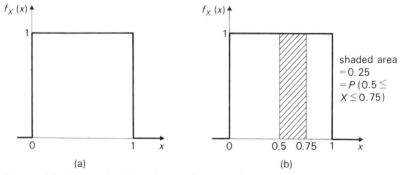

Figure 2.5 The probability density function for the pointer experiment

Since integration and differentiation are the reverse of each other, and since $f_X(.)$ is the derivative of $F_X(.)$, it follows that $F_X(.)$ must be the integral of $f_X(.)$. To be precise, we have

$$F_X(x) = \int_{t=-\infty}^{x} f_X(t)\, dt. \tag{2.11}$$

In geometric terms, this simply means that $F_X(x)$ is the *area* under $f_X(.)$ to the left of x. It immediately follows from (2.11) that

$$F_X(x_2) - F_X(x_1) = \int_{t=x_1}^{x_2} f_X(t)\, dt. \tag{2.12}$$

Now the left-hand of (2.12) is $P(X \leq x_2) - P(X \leq x_1)$, which is $P(x_1 < X \leq x_2)$; thus (2.12) can be written

$$P(x_1 < X \leq x_2) = \int_{t=x_1}^{x_2} f_X(t)\, dt. \tag{2.13}$$

In geometric terms, this simply says that the probability that X lies between x_1 and x_2 is given by the area under the density function between x_1 and x_2. Thus, and this is a very important property, *areas under the probability density function are probabilities*. It immediately follows from this that the *total area under any probability density function must equal one*, since the total probability is always one.

To illustrate these important results, consider figure 2.5 again – the probability density function of the X in our pointer experiment. It is obvious that the total area under $f_X(.)$ is 1. Moreover, areas are probabilities as is instanced in figure 2.5(b): the shaded area equals 0.25 (it is a rectangle of height 1 and width 0.25), which is the same as the probability that X lies between 0.5 and 0.75 (that is, that the pointer comes to rest in the south-west quadrant of the disc). You should verify other areas yourself.

Returning to generalities, note that for a continuous variable it is unnecessary to distinguish between, say, $P(X \leq x)$ and $P(X < x)$, since the difference, $P(X = x)$, is zero as we have already discussed. If this worries you, think of the following heuristic argument: 'Since there are an infinite number of possible values X may take between 0 and 1, the probability that it *exactly* equals any one of them is $1/\infty$ or zero.'

As already noted, lack of knowledge of calculus is not an obstacle to understanding the material of this section; all you really need to know is that $f_X(.)$, the probability density function, is the *slope* of

$F_X(.)$, the distribution function, and that $F_X(.)$ is the area under $f_X(.)$. An analogy may make things clear: $f_X(.)$ and $F_X(.)$ bear the same relationship to each other as do marginal and total cost, or marginal and total revenue. (The marginal-cost curve is the slope of the total-cost curve, while total cost is given by the area under the marginal-cost curve.) If you like, think of $F_X(x)$ as total probability up to x, and $f_X(x)$ as marginal probability at x.

This section is completed with a final example of a continuous variable. Consider the pointer experiment as illustrated in figure 2.2(a); but suppose that the circumference, instead of being calibrated as illustrated, it is calibrated as follows: in the north-east quadrant, the circumference is continuously and uniformly calibrated from 0 to 2; in the southern hemisphere, it is continuously and uniformly calibrated from 2 to 3; and in the north-west quadrant, it is uniformly and continuously calibrated from 3 to 5 (see figure 2.6(a)). Let X be defined as before, and let us suppose we continue to agree that the pointer is fair (that is, equally likely to come to rest anywhere). First, we derive the distribution function: this can be done by trying a number of specific values until a pattern emerges, or by more general reasoning. You should verify that figure 2.6(b) is indeed correct. (Some specific values are $F_X(1) = 0.125$, $F_X(2) = 0.25$, $F_X(2.25) = 0.375$, $F_X(2.5) = 0.5$, $F_X(2.75) = 0.625$, $F_X(3) = 0.75$, $F_X(4) = 0.875$, $F_X(5) = 1$.)

From this, we obtain the density function by differentiation. It is clear from figure 2.6(b) that $F_X(.)$ has a slope of $\frac{1}{8}$ in the interval 0 to 2, a slope of $\frac{1}{2}$ in the interval 2 to 3, a slope of $\frac{1}{8}$ in the interval 3 to 5, and a slope of 0 elsewhere. Thus, $f_X(.)$ takes the value $\frac{1}{8}$ in the interval 0 to 2, the value $\frac{1}{2}$ in the interval 2 to 3, the value $\frac{1}{8}$ in the interval 3 to 5, and the value 0 elsewhere (see figure 2.6(c)). It is clear

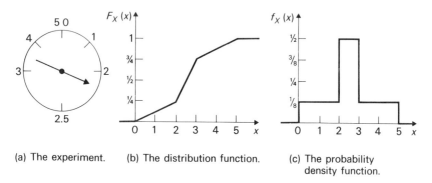

(a) The experiment.   (b) The distribution function.   (c) The probability density function.

Figure 2.6 A modified pointer experiment

from figure 2.6(c) that the total area under $f_X(.)$ is indeed 1 as must be the case if $f_X(.)$ is derived correctly. (This is a useful consistency check you should always apply yourself.) You should verify that areas under $f_X(.)$ do indeed give the corresponding probabilities. For example, the area under $f_X(.)$ between 1 and 2 is $\frac{1}{8}$, which is the probability that the pointer will stop in that arc (which constitutes one-eighth of the total).

This section has introduced three important functions which are used for describing probability assessments in the univariate case; first, the *distribution function*, which is applicable for both discrete and continuous variables, and which measures *cumulative probability*; second, the *probability function*, which is used only for discrete variables, and which measures *probability*; third, the *probability density function*, which is used only for continuous variables, and which measures *marginal probability*.

2.3   SUMMARIES

It is clear that the distribution function (or the probability function or the probability density function as appropriate) contains *all* the information about an individual's probability assessment in the univariate case: it is a *complete characterization*. Sometimes this completeness is helpful; sometimes it is a hindrance, in that it is too difficult to assimilate; other times it is unnecessary, in that only certain features of the assessment are relevant to the problem in hand. There are thus occasions when it is useful to *summarize* key features of the assessment, and to communicate these summaries rather than the complete characterization. This section is concerned with such summaries (though the need for them may not become apparent until later in the book).

The summaries considered in this section fall into two broad groups: (smallest width) *probability intervals*, and the more familiar *measures of central tendency and dispersion*. Let us begin with the former.

Often it is useful to know the range which, in the individual's view, contains most of the probability. For example, we might be interested in knowing that an individual thinks that 'X will almost certainly (that is, with probability 0.95) lie between 120 and 132'. We thus introduce the concept of a α *per cent probability interval*: this is simply an interval $[x_1, x_2]$ for which $P(x_1 \leq X \leq x_2) = \alpha/100$ – that is, for which there is a α per cent chance that X will lie in the interval. Consider the pointer experiment of figure 2.2(a) and the probability assessment as encapsulated in the distribution function of figure 2.2(b). It is clear from this, for example, that an 80 per cent probability interval is [0.1, 0.9], a 90 per cent probability interval is [0.05, 0.95] and a 100 per cent probability interval is [0, 1]. Note that I have said repeatedly *a* α per cent probability interval, rather than *the* α per cent probability interval, as there are clearly lots of them. To cut down the number of possible candidates, one could report the *symmetric* probability interval (as I have done above). More generally, though this does not reduce the number of possibilities in this particular example, one could report the *smallest width* α per cent probability interval. As the italicised phase implies, this is that α per cent probability interval with the smallest width; formally:

> The smallest width α per cent probability interval for X is the interval $[x_1, x_2]$ such that $P(x_1 \leq X \leq x_2)$ $= \alpha/100$ and such that $x_2 - x_1$ is as small as possible. $\qquad$ (2.14)

To illustrate, consider the probability density function portrayed in figure 2.7. For this, the smallest width 95 per cent probability

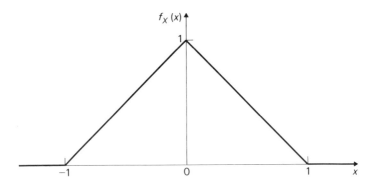

Figure 2.7 A triangular probability density function

interval is from -0.7764 to $+0.7764$ (that is, from $-1 + \sqrt{0.05}$ to $1 - \sqrt{0.05}$). You should check this result, as well as the result that another 95 per cent probability interval is from -1 to $+0.6838$ (that is, from -1 to $1 - \sqrt{0.1}$. You should also note that this second interval is wider (it has width 1.6838) than the smallest width interval (which has width 1.5528). You may have noticed that in this particular example, the smallest width interval is symmetric about zero; this reflects the fact that the probability density function is also symmetric about zero. This result generalizes: it can be shown that for any symmetric probability density function (with a single peak), the smallest width probability intervals are centred on the point of symmetry. More generally still, for continuous variables, if

$$P(x_1 \leq X \leq x_2) = \alpha/100,$$

then $[x_1, x_2]$ is the smallest width α per cent probability interval if and only if $f_X(x_1) = f_X(x_2)$. The proofs of these results are left as exercises for the reader.

From now on, all our probability intervals will be smallest-width intervals, though the phrase 'smallest width' will usually be omitted.

For continuous variables, it will always be possible to find any desired α per cent probability interval. However, for discrete variables, this may not always be possible, because of the inevitable existence of 'lumps' of probability at the discrete points. Consider, for instance, the die example, whose distribution function is portrayed in figure 2.1, and whose probability function is portrayed in figure 2.4(a). Clearly, the interval [3, 4] is a $33\frac{1}{3}$ per cent probability interval, [2, 5] is a $66\frac{2}{3}$ per cent probability interval, and [1, 6] is a 100 per cent probability interval. But it is not possible to find, for instance, a 90 per cent or a 80 per cent probability interval; the problem being, of course, is that the probability comes only in 'lumps' of $\frac{1}{6}$ at each of the six points. However, this is unlikely to cause any problems in practice.

Let us now move on to our second group of summary measures: this group consists of the more familiar *measures of central tendency* and *measures of dispersion*. We begin with the former. The idea of a measure of central tendency is to present, in a single number, some notion of the 'typical' or 'average' or 'representative' value of the variable. Obviously, this can be done in a number of ways, depending upon how one interprets, and what one means by, 'typical', 'average' or 'representative'. Let us consider some popular candidates. One obvious candidate is the value of X that is the *most likely* (relative to a particular individual's probability assessment). This value of X, if it is unique, is called the *modal value* of X, or simply the *mode* of X. Formally, it is defined, both for discrete and continuous variables, by:

Mode of X, M_X, is such that $f_X(M_X) \geq f_X(x)$ for all x.   (2.15)

Thus, for a discrete variable, the mode is the value for which the probability is greatest, while for a continuous variable, it is the value for which the probability density is greatest. In two of the examples in this chapter, the mode is unique: in figure 2.4(b) (the probability function of the number of heads when a fair coin is tossed twice), the mode is 1; in figure 2.7, the mode is 0. In the other examples, the mode is not unique: in figure 2.4(a), all values are equally likely, thus they are all modal values; in figure 2.5(a) as well, all values are modal values; while in figure 2.6(c) all values in the range [2, 3] are modal values.

A second candidate for a 'representative' value is that value of X that is 'in the middle' in the sense that values above it are just as likely as values below it. This value of X, if it exists and is unique, called the *median value* of X, or simply the *median* of X. For continuous variables, it is very simply defined by

Median of X, m_X, is such that $F_X(m_X) = 0.5$.   (2.16)

Thus, $P(X \leq m_X) = P(X \geq m_X) = 0.5$; that is, there is a 50:50 chance that X will lie above, or below, the median. The median in figure 2.5(a) is 0.5; in figure 2.6(c) it is 2.5; and in figure 2.7 it is 0. For discrete variables, definition (2.16) might not lead to a unique solution for m_X: for example, in figure 2.1, it is clear that $F_X(x) = 0.5$ for all x such that $3 \leq x \leq 4$. In such a case, one can either say that all values between 3 and 4 are median values, or one can adopt the usual convention that the median is in the middle of the range – at 3.5. In other cases, (2.16) can be applied directly: for example, in figure 2.4(c), the median is clearly 1.

The third and final candidate for an 'average' value that we shall consider is the familiar *arithmetic mean*. For discrete variables, this is simply the weighted average of the possible X values, where the weights are the probabilities. Formally, it is defined by:

The arithmetic mean of X, EX,
is given by $EX = \sum x f_X(x)$.   (2.17)

In this, the summation is over all values of x (either over all values from $-\infty$ to $+\infty$, or all *possible* values – the difference being immaterial since $f_X(x)$ is zero for all *impossible* values of x). The reason for the notation, EX, will be explained shortly. Let us give two illustrations. The first is the die example portrayed in figure 2.4(a); in this X can take the values 1, 2, 3, 4, 5 and 6 each with probability $\frac{1}{6}$. Applying the definition (2.17), we find that the mean EX is given by

$$EX = 1 \times \tfrac{1}{6} + 2 \times \tfrac{1}{6} + 3 \times \tfrac{1}{6} + 4 \times \tfrac{1}{6} + 5 \times \tfrac{1}{6} + 6 \times \tfrac{1}{6} = 3.5.$$

The second example is the double-coin-toss example portrayed in figure 2.4(b); in this X, which is the number of heads in the two tosses, can take the values 0, 1 and 2 with respective probabilities $\frac{1}{4}, \frac{1}{2}$ and $\frac{1}{4}$. Applying the definition (2.17), we find that the mean EX is given by

$$EX = 0 \times \tfrac{1}{4} + 1 \times \tfrac{1}{2} + 2 \times \tfrac{1}{4} = 1.$$

Now consider the intuition behind this latter result: it states that, on average, the number of heads obtained when a fair coin is tossed twice is 1. This is eminently sensible. Another way of viewing it is to regard 1 as the *expected* number of heads in two tosses. It is for this reason that the mean is denoted EX: the E stands for *Expected*, and thus EX stands for the *Expected value of X*. Returning to the die example, it may seem a bit odd to say that the expected number of spots showing on a (fair) die is 3.5 – after all, no side has $3\frac{1}{2}$ spots on it! But suppose you were to get paid 1p for each spot showing: then you would *expect* (on average) to get paid $3\frac{1}{2}$p per roll.

Equation (2.17) defines the expected value for a discrete variable; for a continuous variable, the definition is as follows:

The arithmetic mean of X, EX, is given by $EX = \displaystyle\int x f_X(x) \, \mathrm{d}x.$

$$(2.18)$$

In this, the integration is over all values of x (either over all values from $-\infty$ to $+\infty$, or all *possible* values – again the difference being immaterial since $f_X(x)$ is zero for all *impossible* values of x). In essence, (2.18) states that EX is a weighted average of the various X values, where the weights are the probability densities. Readers familiar with the calculus will recognize (2.18) as the obvious counterpart of (2.17). Let us give two illustrations. First, the pointer experiment, whose probability density function is given in (2.10) and portrayed in figure 2.5(a). Applying the definition (2.18), we find that the mean EX is given by

$$EX = \int_{-\infty}^{\infty} x f_X(x) \, \mathrm{d}x = \int_{0}^{1} x \, \mathrm{d}x = \left[\frac{x^2}{2}\right]_0^1 = \frac{1}{2}.$$

That is, the expected value of X in the pointer experiment is $\frac{1}{2}$; an intuitively sensible result. Our second illustration is the probability density function portrayed in figure 2.7; its equation is given by:

$$f_X(x) = \begin{cases} x + 1 & -1 \leq x \leq 0 \\ 1 - x & 0 \leq x \leq 1 \\ 0 & \text{elsewhere.} \end{cases} \qquad (2.19)$$

Applying the definition (2.18), we find that the mean EX is given by

$$EX = \int_{-\infty}^{\infty} x f_X(x)\, dx = \int_{-1}^{0} x(x+1)\, dx + \int_{0}^{1} x(1-x)\, dx$$

$$= \left[\frac{x^3}{3} + \frac{x^2}{2} \right]_{-1}^{0} + \left[\frac{x^2}{2} - \frac{x^3}{3} \right]_{0}^{1} = 0.$$

Thus, the expected value, rather unsurprisingly, is zero!

(Before proceeding, let us reassure those readers whose calculus is weak or non-existent. As we shall see below, many important results can be derived using common sense, rather than calculus; only a few results will have to be taken 'on faith', and this will not be an obstacle to the understanding of the statistics.)

Actually, it may prove helpful *not* to get too involved with technical details: those readers who have concentrated on generalities rather than details will have noticed an important result. *For those distributions which are symmetric, the expected value always equals the point of symmetry. Moreover, for such distributions, when the mode and median are unique they also equal the point of symmetry.* (By a distribution being symmetric, we mean, of course, that the probability function or probability density function, as appropriate, is symmetric.) Thus, for symmetric unimodal distributions, all three candidates for the 'typical', 'average' or 'representative' value all yield the same answer. This is an intuitively satisfying result. You may like to show that it does *not* hold for non-symmetric distributions. (Consider, for example, the variable X defined as the *square* of the number of heads obtained when a fair coin is tossed twice. This takes values 0, 1 and 4 with respective probabilities $\frac{1}{4}$, $\frac{1}{2}$ and $\frac{1}{4}$; its expected value is 1.5 and its median and mode are both 1.)

In addition to knowing something about the 'average' or 'typical' value of a probability assessment, it may be useful to know something about the 'spread' or 'dispersion' of the assessment. Just as there are numerous measures of the 'average', there are also numerous *measures of dispersion*. Here, we will consider just a few. One obvious candidate, particularly in the light of our discussion of probability intervals, is to measure the width of some α per cent probability interval. For example, if the 95 per cent probability interval of variable X had width 10.0, while the 95 per cent probability interval of variable Y had width 5.0, it seems natural to conclude that the variable X is 'more dispersed' than Y in some sense. Of course there would be a different measure of dispersion for each value of α, but this would simply reflect the non-uniqueness of the concept of 'dispersion'.

An alternative approach is through the notion that the deviations of the variable about its mean tell us something about its dispersion: if one variable has greater deviations on average than a second, it seems reasonable to call the first more dispersed than the second. However, taking a simple weighted average of the deviations, namely $\sum (x - EX) f_X(x)$ for a discrete variable, does not work, as this measure is identically zero. (Why? Examine (2.17) and remember that $\sum f_X(x) = 1$.) To get round this problem, one can either take the average of the *absolute* deviations, or the average of the *squared* deviations. The latter solution is usually followed, since the resulting expression is more amenable to mathematical analysis. The resulting measure of dispersion is known as the *variance* of X. Formally, for a discrete variable, it is defined by:

The variance of X, var X, is given by var X
$$= \sum (x - EX)^2 f_X(x). \quad (2.20)$$

Here the summation is over all values of X. Unfortunately, since squared deviations are used, this means that the units of the variance are the square of the units of X; that is, if X is in inches, then the variance is in square inches. To get a measure of dispersion which is in the original units, the square root of the variance is taken; the result is called the *standard deviation* of X. Formally, it is defined by

The standard deviation of X, sd X, is given by sd X
$$= \sqrt{\text{var } X}. \quad (2.21)$$

To give an illustration, consider again the fair die example whose probability function is portrayed in figure 2.4. The values taken are 1, 2, 3, 4, 5 and 6 each with probability $\frac{1}{6}$. It will be recalled that the expected value of X is 3.5. Thus, the respective deviations from the mean are

$$-2.5, \; -1.5, \; -0.5, \; 0.5, \; 1.5 \text{ and } 2.5.$$

(Note that the weighted average of these is zero, as stated above.) The respective squared deviations are thus

$$6.25, \; 2.25, \; 0.25, \; 0.25, \; 2.25 \text{ and } 6.25.$$

Applying the definition (2.20) it follows that the variance of X is given by

$$\text{var } X = 6.25 \times \tfrac{1}{6} + 2.25 \times \tfrac{1}{6} + 0.25 \times \tfrac{1}{6}$$
$$+ 0.25 \times \tfrac{1}{6} + 2.25 \times \tfrac{1}{6} + 6.25 \times \tfrac{1}{6}$$
$$= 2.91\dot{6}.$$

Thus, from (2.21), the standard deviation is given by

$$\text{sd } X = \sqrt{\text{var } X} = 1.7078.$$

There is no obvious intuition behind either of these results.

Equation (2.20) defines the variance for a discrete variable; for a continuous variable, the definition is as follows:

The variance of X, var X, is given by

$$\text{var } X = \int (x - EX)^2 f_X(x) \, dx. \qquad (2.22)$$

Again, the integration is over all values of X. Note that (2.20) and (2.22) bear the same relationship to each other as do (2.17) and (2.18): where $\sum$ appears for discrete variables, $\int$ appears for continuous variables; and where $f_X(x)$ appears for discrete variables, $f_X(x)$ dx appears for continuous variables. Again, the standard deviation is given by the square root of the variance, as in (2.21). To give an illustration, consider again the pointer experiment whose probability density function is given in (2.10) and portrayed in figure 2.5(a). It will be recalled that the expected value of X is 0.5. Thus, applying the definition (2.22), it follows that the variance of X is given by

$$\text{var } X = \int_{-\infty}^{\infty} (x - EX)^2 f_X(x) \, dx = \int_{0}^{1} (x - \tfrac{1}{2})^2 \, dx = [\tfrac{1}{3}(x - \tfrac{1}{2})^3]_{0}^{1}$$
$$= \tfrac{1}{12}.$$

Hence, from (2.21), the standard deviation is given by

$$\text{sd } X = \sqrt{\text{var } X} = 0.2887.$$

Again, there is no obvious intuition behind either of these results.

There are several measures of dispersion other than those discussed above, but as we shall not be needing them in this book, we will not mention them here. Also, in addition to measures of central tendency and measures of dispersion, there are numerous other summary measures relating to other features of a probability assessment – such as its skewness. Again, as they will not be needed in this book, we will not discuss them here. The summary measures that we *will* be using in the rest of the book are those discussed above – most notably, probability intervals, means and variances (and standard deviations). These will be sufficient for our purposes.

2.4 SOME SPECIFIC (CONTINUOUS UNIVARIATE)
DISTRIBUTIONS

In economic statistics, there are several standard probability assessments that are frequently encountered. It is useful, therefore, to give these standard distributions names, so that they may be briefly described, and to derive some of the frequently used summary measures for these variables. In this section we do this for five standard forms which we shall encounter frequently during the rest of this book. In order of appearance, they are the *uniform* (or *rectangular*) distribution, the *beta* distribution, the *normal* distribution, the *gamma* distribution and the *t* distribution. Their usefulness will not become apparent until later in the book, however, so you should regard this section partly as an application of some of the general ideas of the previous sections of this chapter, but mainly as a collection of results for future use.

All five of these standard forms are for *continuous* variables; accordingly, we will usually define and illustrate them in terms of their *probability density functions*. Before proceeding, you should make sure that you are familiar with the properties of such functions: most notably that they are non-negative everywhere, that *areas* underneath the function *are probabilities*, and that the *total area* underneath *any* probability density function *is* 1.

Let us begin with the *uniform* (or *rectangular*) distribution, an example of which we have already encountered in the (unmodified) pointer experiment of figure 2.2; its probability density function was portrayed in figure 2.5. Note that the function is uniform (constant) everywhere in the range [0, 1]. Accordingly, X in this example is said to have a *uniform* (or *rectangular*) *distribution over the range* [0, 1]. This reflects the unbiasedness of the pointer, and the fact that the circumference was *uniformly and continuously* calibrated from 0 to 1. If, instead, the calibration was from some number a to some other (greater) number b, then X would have a *uniform* (or *rectangular*) *distribution over the range* [a, b]. As you should be able to verify, its probability density function would then be

$$f_X(x) = \begin{cases} 1/(b-a) & a \leq x \leq b \\ 0 & \text{elsewhere.} \end{cases} \quad (2.23)$$

This is portrayed in figure 2.8(a); again it is uniform over the relevant range, in this case [a, b]. Note that its height is now $1/(b-a)$, so that the total area remains 1: remember, that this *must* be the case for *all* probability density functions.

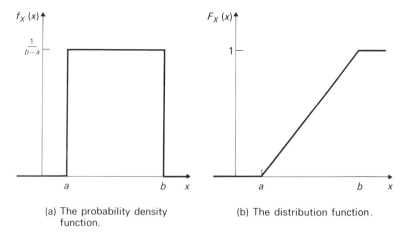

(a) The probability density function.

(b) The distribution function.

Figure 2.8 The uniform distribution over [a, b]

The associated distribution function is given by

$$F_X(x) = \begin{cases} 0 & x < a \\ (x - a)/(b - a) & a \le x \le b \\ 1 & b < x \end{cases} \qquad (2.24)$$

This is portrayed in figure 2.8(b). You should verify that $f_X(.)$ and $F_X(.)$ bear the correct relationship to each other, in that the former is the slope of the latter, and that the latter is the area under the former.

Actually, we have already encountered a second example of the uniform distribution, namely that portrayed in figure 2.3(b): this represents a probability assessment of the author's age that is uniform over the range [36, 42]. Furthermore, figure 2.3(a) represents a degenerate uniform distribution – one uniform over the 'range' [40, 40].

As we have already repeatedly emphasized, the total area under *any* probability density function must be 1. From now on, we will use this important property to simplify many of our algebraic expressions, and to reduce 'algebraic clutter'. In particular, we will use this important property to simplify the way we write the formulae for probability density functions. Thus, for example, in future we will not write the probability density function for the uniform in the 'full' form of (2.23), but rather in the following 'abbreviated' form:

$$f_X(x) \propto \begin{cases} 1 & a \le x \le b \\ 0 & \text{elsewhere.} \end{cases} \qquad (2.25)$$

The symbol '$\propto$' means 'proportional to': for example, if $y = 2x$, or $y = 5.3x$ or, more generally, $y = kx$, then y is proportional to x, that is, $y \propto x$. *The factor of proportionality in* (2.25) *must, of necessity, be chosen so that the total area under* $f_X(.)$ *is one.* Because of this important property, there is no need for us actually to state what the factor of proportionality is.

It is clear from figure 2.8(b) that the distribution is symmetric about its mid-point, which is $(a + b)/2$; this is, therefore, its mean. Also, it can be shown (using (2.22) and (2.23)) that its variance is $(b - a)^2/12$. (If you like integrating things you could verify this result; otherwise you can take it on trust, after convincing yourself that the dispersion must depend upon $(b - a)$.) Collecting results together, and using the shorthand 'X is $U[a, b]$' for 'X has a uniform distribution over the range $[a, b]$', we have

If X is $U[a, b]$ then $EX = (a + b)/2$ and var $X = (b - a)^2/12$.

$$(2.26)$$

We now turn to the *beta* distribution, though we make no attempt at this stage to justify its usefulness. Let us begin by simply stating its definition. A variable X is said to have a *beta distribution with* parameters α and β (in shorthand, 'X is $B(\alpha, \beta)$') if its probability density function is given by

$$f_X(x) \propto \begin{cases} x^{\alpha - 1}(1 - x)^{\beta - 1} & 0 \leq x \leq 1 \\ 0 & \text{elsewhere,} \end{cases} \tag{2.27}$$

(where, of course, the factor of proportionality is chosen to make the area under $f_X(.)$ equal to 1). Note that X takes values only in the range $[0, 1]$; outside this range the density is zero. As for the shape of the function in the range $[0, 1]$, this clearly depends upon the values of the parameters α and β. Some special cases are immediate: first, if $\alpha = \beta = 1$ then (2.27) reduces to (2.10), and so it follows that if X is $B(1, 1)$ then X is also $U[0, 1]$; thus the uniform over the range $[0, 1]$ is a special case of the beta. Second, if $\alpha = 2$ and $\beta = 1$, then the probability density function is 'right-triangular' as in figure 2.9(a). Third, and similarly, if $\alpha = 1$ and $\beta = 2$, then the probability density function is 'left-triangular' (not illustrated). You may like to try other examples yourself. One feature which emerges is that if α is greater than β, then the distribution has its bulk towards the right (as in figure 2.9(c)), while if α is less than β, the bulk is towards the left (not illustrated). The intermediate case is when α equals β, in which case the distribution is obviously symmetrical, as in figure 2.9(b).

These features are reflected by the mean, which can be shown to

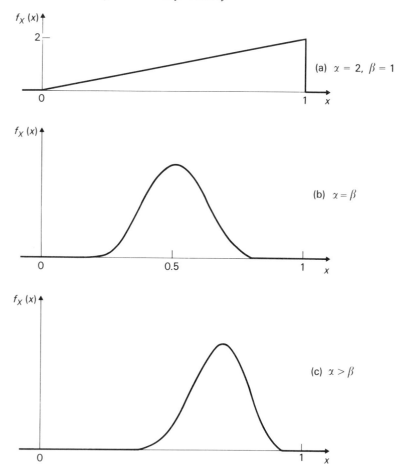

Figure 2.9 *Some examples of the beta distribution*

be given by $\alpha/(\alpha + \beta)$; this is clearly less than, equal to or greater than 0.5 according as α is less than, equal to or greater than β. You may like to verify this expression for the mean; alternatively, you can take it on trust, as you are advised to do for the result on the variance which is included in the following summary.

If X is $B(\alpha, \beta)$ then $EX = \alpha/(\alpha + \beta)$ and var X
$$= \alpha\beta/[(\alpha + \beta)^2(\alpha + \beta + 1)]. \qquad (2.28)$$

You should note, however, that as $(\alpha + \beta)$ increases then the variance decreases: thus the *relative* sizes of α and β determine the position of the mean, while the *absolute* sizes of α and β determine the magnitude of the variance. We shall return to explore these properties in more detail in a subsequent chapter.

Let us now move on to a rather more familiar distribution, namely the *normal* distribution, and we begin by stating its definition. A variable X is said to have a *normal distribution with mean* μ *and variance* σ^2 (in shorthand 'X is $N(\mu, \sigma^2)$') if its probability density function is given by

$$f_X(x) \propto \sigma^{-1} \exp\left[\frac{-(x - \mu)^2}{2\sigma^2}\right] \quad -\infty < x < \infty \quad (2.29)$$

(where, once again, the factor of proportionality is chosen to make the area under $f_X(.)$ equal to 1). The density function is graphed in figure 2.10(a). From this or equivalently from (2.29), a number of features are apparent. First, X can take all values from $-\infty$ to $+\infty$, though the density approaches 0 as x approaches $-\infty$ or $+\infty$. Secondly, the distribution is symmetric about the mean μ. Thirdly, it is 'bell-shaped'. Fourthly, the function has points of inflexion at $\mu - \sigma$ and $\mu + \sigma$. (Points of inflexion occur where the second derivative $f_X''(.)$ equals zero; these are points where the slope of the function is at a maximum (at $\mu - \sigma$) or a minimum (at $\mu + \sigma$).) The variance is σ^2 (which can be found by using (2.29) in (2.22)), and thus the standard deviation is σ. It follows, therefore, that the points of inflexion lie one standard deviation either side of the mean. This is a useful property to remember when sketching the normal probability density function (2.29).

An important special case of the normal distribution is when μ is zero and σ is 1. In this case, the variable is said to have the *unit* (or standard) *normal* distribution, and the letter Z is usually reserved for this special case. We would then write: 'Z is $N(0, 1)$'. The probability density function of Z, which is just a special case of (2.29), is graphed in figure 2.10(b). Note that it is centred on 0, and has points of inflexion at ± 1.

Note that the horizontal scales in the two graphs in figure 2.10 differ, as do the vertical scales. However, both graphs have the same area, namely 1, as must all density functions. Moreover, since both functions have the same shape, it follows that corresponding areas must be equal: for example, the area between $\mu - \sigma$ and μ under $f_X(.)$ must equal the area between -1 and 0 under $f_Z(.)$; similarly, the area to the right of $\mu + \sigma$ under $f_X(.)$ must equal the area to the right of 1 under $f_Z(\cdot)$. Since areas under density functions are probabilities, it follows that, for example

$$P(\mu - \sigma \le X \le \mu) = P(-1 \le Z \le 0);$$

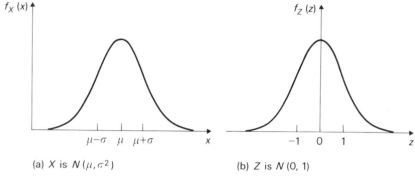

(a) X is $N(\mu, \sigma^2)$ (b) Z is $N(0, 1)$

Figure 2.10 Two normal distributions

similarly

$$P(\mu + \sigma \le X) = P(1 \le Z).$$

This relationship can clearly be generalized. Indeed, a few moments thought (combined perhaps with a few more examples) will show that the following general relationship holds:

$$P(X \le \mu + z\sigma) = P(Z \le z).$$

Alternatively, this can be written (putting $z = (x - \mu)/\sigma$)

$$P(X \le x) = P(Z \le (x - \mu)/\sigma).$$

As this is a very important result, which we shall use on numerous occasions, let us express it in full, using our distribution function notation:

If X is $N(\mu, \sigma^2)$ and Z is $N(0, 1)$ then $F_X(x) = F_Z\left(\dfrac{x - \mu}{\sigma}\right)$ (2.30)

(Although we have derived this result intuitively, it can be proved formally: using (2.29) and (2.11) we have

$$F_X(x) \propto \sigma^{-1} \int_{-\infty}^{x} \exp\left[\frac{-(t - \mu)^2}{2\sigma^2}\right] dt \propto \int_{-\infty}^{(x - \mu)/\sigma} \exp\left(\frac{-v^2}{2}\right) dv$$

$$\propto F_Z\left(\frac{x - \mu}{\sigma}\right),$$

where the middle step is carried out using the change of variable technique, with $v = (t - \mu)/\sigma$; and where the final step makes use of the fact (from (2.29)) that if Z is $N(0, 1)$, then $f_Z(z) \propto \exp(-z^2/2)$.)

The distribution function of the normal distribution cannot be explicitly obtained (that is, it is not possible to find the explicit integral of the probability density function (2.29)). It is, therefore, necessary to use numerical (as distinct from analytical) methods to find areas under the density function, and hence to make probability statements about normally distributed variables. It is for this reason that result (2.30) is so important: it enables any probability statement about *any* normally distributed variable to be expressed as a probability statement about the *unit* normal distribution. Thus one set of numerical results (concerning areas under the unit normal density function) is sufficient to calculate all areas under all normal probability density functions. In the Appendix of this book (and, indeed, in the appendices of most statistical texts) you will find a table of areas under the unit normal probability density function. The particular form of the table presented in this book (in Appendix A6) gives areas between 0, the mean, and any desired z value. For example, suppose you wished to find the area under the curve between 0 and $z = 1.96$; then you would look down the left-hand column until you found 1.9 and then move across that row until you got to the column headed 0.06; the entry in that row and column, 0.4750, gives you the required area. Similarly, the area under the curve between 0 and 0.62 is 0.2324. Areas other than those between 0 and some positive z value are found from these areas using the facts that the function is symmetric about 0 and that total area underneath it is 1. Thus, for example,

$$P(Z \leq -1.96) = P(Z \geq 1.96) = 1 - P(Z < 1.96)$$
$$= 1 - [P(Z < 0) + P(0 \leq Z < 1.96)]$$
$$= 1 - (0.5 + 0.4750) = 0.0250.$$

(The first step uses symmetry, the second the fact that the total area is one, the third is just an identity, and the fourth uses the result obtained above combined with the fact that half the area lies each side of 0.) To make sure you fully understand the use of this table, you should verify the following examples.

$$P(0 \leq Z \leq 1) = 0.3413$$
$$P(-2 \leq Z \leq 0) = 0.4772$$
$$P(-1 \leq Z \leq 1) = 0.6426$$
$$P(-1 \leq Z \leq 2) = 0.8185$$
$$P(-2 \leq Z \leq 1) = 0.8185$$
$$P(2 \leq Z) = 0.0228$$

To find areas, and hence make probability statements, for some other normal distribution, we make use of (2.30). For example, suppose X is $N(4, 9)$, that is, it is normally distributed with mean $\mu = 4$ and variance $\sigma^2 = 9$. Its standard deviation is thus $\sigma = 3$. Now to find, say, $P(X \leq 7)$ we use (2.30) to write this as

$$P(Z \leq (7 - 4)/3)) = P(Z \leq 1),$$

which from Appendix A6 is 0.8413. Similarly,

$$\begin{aligned} P(-2 \leq X \leq 7) &= P((-2 - 4)/3 \leq Z \leq (7 - 4)/3) \\ &= P(-2 \leq Z \leq 1) \\ &= 0.8185. \end{aligned}$$

To make sure you fully understand the use of this table, you should verify the following examples.

If X is $N(24, 16)$	then	$P(24 \leq X \leq 28) = 0.3413$
If X is $N(10, 100)$	then	$P(-10 \leq X \leq 10) = 0.4772$
If X is $N(-1, 4)$	then	$P(-3 \leq X \leq 1) = 0.6426$
If X is $N(9, 9)$	then	$P(6 \leq X \leq 15) = 0.8185$
If X is $N(10, 25)$	then	$P(0 \leq X \leq 15) = 0.8185$
If X is $N(0, 4)$	then	$P(4 \leq X) = 0.0228$

(You may have already noted that the transformation $(x - \mu)/\sigma$ simply calculates how many standard deviations x is away from the mean: the result (2.30) makes use of the fact that a value z standard deviations away from the mean is in the same relative position of the distribution irrespective of μ and σ^2.)

As we shall see, the normal distribution is frequently encountered in economic statistics: many probability assessments of continuous variables take a form identical or similar to that of the normal distribution. For example, if X is the height of a student picked at random, most individuals' assessment of X would look approximately normal. Similarly when X is IQ, and perhaps when X is income. Furthermore, the normal distribution is often a useful approximation to more complicated probability distributions. For example, if α and β are 'large enough' (the meaning of which we shall clarify in due course), then a variable with a beta distribution with parameters α and β can be approximated by the normal distribution (in the sense that the beta density function and the normal density function, with the same mean and the same variance, are approximately the same). These issues will be explored in more detail later in the book.

In the meantime, let us conclude our brief catalogue of distributions with the *gamma* and t distributions. As with the beta distribution, these are distributions whose usefulness will not become apparent until later in the book. Here we confine ourselves to the definitions and the statement of a few properties. First, a variable X is said to have a *gamma distribution* with parameters α and β (in shorthand, 'X is $G(\alpha, \beta)$') if its probability density function is given by

$$f_X(x) \propto \begin{cases} x^{\alpha-1}e^{-\beta x} & x \geq 0 \\ 0 & \text{elsewhere,} \end{cases} \tag{2.31}$$

(where, of course, the factor of proportionality is chosen to make the area under $f_X(.)$ equal to 1). Note that X takes only positive values; for negative x the density is zero. The mean and variance are as follows:

If X is $G(\alpha, \beta)$ then $EX = \alpha/\beta$ and var $X = \alpha/\beta^2$. (2.32)

An important special case of the gamma occurs when $\alpha = k/2$ and $\beta = \frac{1}{2}$ where k is a positive integer; in this case the variable is said to have a *chi-square* (χ^2) *distribution with k degrees of freedom* (a phrase whose meaning will not be apparent until later); in shorthand, 'X is $\chi^2(k)$'. Finally, a variable X is said to have a t distribution with k *degrees of freedom* (or, in shorthand, 'X is $t(k)$') if its probability density function is given by

$$f_X(x) \propto (1 + x^2/k)^{-(k+1)/2} \quad -\infty < x < \infty \tag{2.33}$$

(where, of course, the factor of proportionality is chosen to make the area under $f_X(.)$ equal to 1). Note that X can take all values between $-\infty$ and ∞, though the density approaches zero as x approaches $-\infty$ or $+\infty$. The mean and variance are as follows:

If X is $t(k)$ then $EX = 0$ and var $X = k/(k - 2)$. (2.34)

It is apparent from (2.33) that the density function is symmetric about zero and bell-shaped. Indeed, in many ways it is similar to that of the unit normal, except that it is more spread out (its variance is greater than that of the unit normal, which is, of course, 1). However, as k approaches infinity the density function of the t distribution approaches that of the unit normal; so the latter is a limiting case of the former.

This concludes the brief catalogue of standard distributions. Their use will become apparent later in the book.

2.5 THE BASIC PROBABILITY LAWS

So far, the discussion of probability has been almost exclusively in terms of *variables*. In this section, the final substantive one of this chapter, we continue the discussion in terms of *events*. This, as you will see, is purely for expositional reasons: the material of this section is equally applicable, and indeed will soon be applied, to variables. However, by concentrating upon events, we can simplify our notation.

This section begins by formally stating two probability laws which we have been implicitly assuming throughout our earlier discussion. It then goes on to introduce the important concept of *conditional probability*, and express, in a third law, the relationship between conditional and unconditional probabilities. Finally, this third law is used to introduce *Bayes' Theorem* – the foundation stone of all our remaining analyses.

We state these laws and definitions in terms of events, which we shall denote by E and F. Think of these as events such as 'the Conservative Party forming the next Government' or 'England winning the World Cup' or 'a "6" showing on a die'. The first two laws are as follows.

> *First law*   If E is any event then $0 \leq P(E) \leq 1$
> If E is certain to happen then $P(E) = 1$.   (2.35)

(Continue to think of these as individual subjective assessments; thus, for example, by 'certain to happen' we mean that the individual whose assessment we are describing thinks that E is certain to happen. It is possible, of course, that the individual is wrong in his assessment; but that is irrelevant to the fact that if the individual thinks E is certain to happen, then he or she *must* assign probability 1 to E.) It is clear that we have been using this first law throughout sections 2.2 to 2.4 above; its 'validity' is essentially definitional.

> *Second law* If E and F are mutually exclusive events (that is, they cannot *both* happen), then
> $$P(E \text{ or } F) = P(E) + P(F)   (2.36)$$
> where 'E or F' denotes the event that either E or F happens.

Again, this is a law whose validity we have been implicitly taking for granted during the discussion of sections 2.2 to 2.4. An example will illustrate its obvious appeal. Consider the next World Cup, and let E be 'England will win' and F 'Scotland will win'. Clearly, they cannot *both* win, and so E and F are mutually exclusive events. Now, suppose your assessment says $P(E) = 0.1$ and $P(F) = 0.2$ (surely Scotland's luck will improve next time!); then the second law requires that

$$P(E \text{ or } F) = 0.1 + 0.2 = 0.3.$$

In other words, you assess the chances of *either* England *or* Scotland winning as 3 in 10. As a second example, consider drawing *one* card out of a well-shuffled pack of cards; let E be 'drawing a spade' and F 'drawing a club'. Clearly E and F are mutually exclusive events as one card cannot simultaneously be a spade and a club. Now suppose that you think that the shuffling and drawing mechanism are 'fair', so that $P(E) = P(F) = \frac{1}{4}$; then the second law requires that

$$P(E \text{ or } F) = \frac{1}{4} + \frac{1}{4} = \frac{1}{2}.$$

In other words, you assess the chances of drawing a black card as 1 in 2. This is an obviously sensible result.

Up till now, all the probabilities that we have been examining have been *unconditional* probabilities; we now introduce the important concept of *conditional* probability. This concept, as we shall show, is of crucial importance for describing how new information is incorporated into probability assessments. First, some new notation: by '$P(F \mid E)$' we shall denote 'the probability of event F given event E', or equivalently, the 'conditional probability of event F given event E'. It is a *conditional probability* statement. The symbol $\mid$ is read 'given' or 'conditional on'; thus '$\mid E$' means 'given E' or 'conditional on E' – it *conditions* the probability statement on F.

So much for notation; what does $P(F \mid E)$ *mean?* Simply: the probability of F in the light of the 'information' E. An example will help. Suppose a die (which is agreed fair) is rolled twice. Let E be the event that the first roll produces a number greater than 4; and let F be the event that the total on the two rolls is 10 or less. By $P(F \mid E)$ is meant the probability of getting a total of 10 or less given that the first roll is greater than 4. To evaluate this conditional probability, we can proceed as follows: given that the first roll is greater than 4, then the following pairs are possible:

(5, 1)	(5, 2)	(5, 3)	(5, 4)	(5, 5)	(5, 6)
(6, 1)	(6, 2)	(6, 3)	(6, 4)	(6, 5)	(6, 6),

where the first (second) number in parentheses represents the outcome on the first (second) roll. Of these twelve pairs, nine have a total of 10 or less, namely:

(5, 1)   (5, 2)   (5, 3)   (5, 4)   (5, 5)
(6, 1)   (6, 2)   (6, 3)   (6, 4).

If, as we said earlier, the die is agreed to be fair, then all twelve pairs are equally likely, and thus the probability of getting one of the nine in which the total is 10 or less is simply $\frac{9}{12}$. Thus, in this example, $P(F \mid E) = \frac{9}{12}$. A similar argument shows that $P(E \mid F) = \frac{9}{33}$, a result you should verify yourself. (There are thirty-three possible pairs in which the total is 10 or less; of these nine have a number greater than 4 on the first roll.)

To recapitulate: $P(F \mid E)$ gives the probability of F in the light of the 'information' E; the conditioning statement, $\mid E$, gives information which may modify the probability of F happening.

In the die example above, the conditional probability $P(F \mid E)$ is different from the unconditional probability $P(F)$ – the former being $\frac{9}{12}$ and the latter being $\frac{33}{36}$. Thus, in this example, the 'information' E changes the assessment of the probability of F happening. Similarly, the conditional probability $P(E \mid F)$ is different from the unconditional probability $P(E)$ – the former being $\frac{9}{33}$ and the latter being $\frac{12}{36}$. Thus, again, the 'information' F changes the assessment of the probability of E happening. However, this is not always the case. Consider a second example, in which one card is drawn from a well-shuffled pack of cards. Let E in this example be the event drawing a heart, and F be the event drawing an ace. If we agree that the shuffling and selecting are fair so that each card in the pack has an equal $\frac{1}{52}$ chance of being drawn, then the following probabilities can be derived. (You should verify these yourself.)

$$P(F \mid E) = \tfrac{1}{13} \qquad P(F) = \tfrac{4}{52} \qquad P(E \mid F) = \tfrac{1}{4} \qquad P(E) = \tfrac{13}{52}.$$

In this example, the conditional probability $P(F \mid E)$ and the unconditional probability $P(F)$ are equal. Thus, the 'information' E does not affect the probability assessment of F. Similarly, the conditional probability $P(E \mid F)$ and the unconditional probability $P(E)$ are equal. Thus, the 'information' F does not affect the probability assessment of E. A moment's reflection will reveal why this is so: if the drawing mechanism is fair, knowledge of the suit of the card does not help to decide its face value, nor does knowledge of the face value help to decide its suit. In this case, the 'information' is uninformative.

However, in the die example, the information *was* informative:

knowledge that the first roll produces a high outcome reduces the chances of the total being small; similarly, knowledge that the total is small reduces the chances of the first roll having a high outcome. We must introduce some terminology to distinguish between these two cases (that is, when 'information' is informative and when it is uninformative). This we do as follows:

Two events, E and F are said to be *independent* if and only if $P(F \mid E) = P(F)$ and $P(E \mid F) = P(E)$. (2.37)

(Shortly you will be able to show that one half of this condition is redundant, in that either half implies the other. This reinforces the intuitive notion that independence is a *symmetrical* property; that is, it is impossible to have E dependent on F but F independent of E.) If the condition in (2.37) does not hold, then E and F are said to be *dependent* events.

In our die example, E and F were dependent; in the card example, E and F were independent. Using this terminology, we can conclude that 'information' E is *uninformative* about F if E and F are *independent*, and is *informative* if E and F are *dependent*. This confirms the intuitive notion that 'information' is only of value if that information is dependent upon the thing in which you are interested. It is no use knowing the going is good at Sandown Park when filling in your Australian pools coupon!

We have discussed what is meant by conditional probability and have given a few examples, but have not yet given a general definition. Let us do this now, proceeding rather obliquely, by first introducing a third probability law:

Third law $P(E$ and $F) = P(F \mid E)P(E) = P(E \mid F)P(F)$
where 'E and F' denotes the event that (2.38)
both E and F happen.

There are two parts to this law, though they effectively say the same thing. The equality of the first two terms in (2.38) says: the probability of *both E and F* happening equals the probability of E happening times the conditional probability of F happening given E. An example should clarify the situation: suppose you assess $P(E) = \frac{1}{2}$, that is, you think there is a 50 : 50 chance of E happening; suppose also you assess $P(F \mid E) = \frac{1}{4}$, that is you think that if E happens there is a 1 in 4 chance of F happening. Then (2.38) says that you must conclude that there is a 1 in 8 chance of them *both* happening. For example, consider picking one student at random from a university in which 50 per cent are male, and in which 25 per cent of the men are economists. Then, if you feel that the selection process is fair, then the chances of picking someone who is both male *and* an economist is 1 in 8. (Here, the event E is being male, and the event F is being an economist.)

The equality of the first and last terms in (2.38) says the same thing 'the other way round': the probability of *both E and F* happening equals the probability of F happening times the conditional probability of E happening given F. Thus, *in toto*, (2.38) simply says that for two events to happen, one must happen, and then given that the other must happen.

The third law can now be rearranged to give a general result on conditional probability. From (2.38) we have

$$P(F \mid E) = P(E \text{ and } F)/P(E). \tag{2.39}$$

You may like to verify that the conditional probabilities found 'intuitively' in our two examples above agree with this formula. For instance, in the card example, $P(E) = \frac{13}{52}$ and $P(E \text{ and } F) = \frac{1}{52}$ (that is, the probability of drawing the ace of hearts is $\frac{1}{52}$). Thus, using (2.39),

$$P(F \mid E) = \tfrac{1}{52}/\tfrac{13}{52} = \tfrac{1}{13},$$

the same as that derived above.

Finally, note that the last two terms in the third probability law (2.38) can be re-arranged to give:

$$P(F \mid E) = \frac{P(E \mid F)P(F)}{P(E)} \tag{2.40}$$

In essence this is *Bayes' Theorem*. We will use this important result repeatedly throughout the rest of the book.

2.6 SUMMARY

This chapter has been exclusively concerned with *probability*. It began by focussing attention on probability assessments about variables, and, in particular, on showing how such assessments can be described, communicated and summarized. Section 2.2 introduced three important functions which are used for encapsulating probability assessments in the univariate case: first, the distribution function, which is used for both discrete and continuous variables, and which measures cumulative probability; second, the probability function, which is used only for discrete variables, and which measures probability; third; the probability density function, which is used only for continuous variables, and which measures marginal probability. We then showed, in section 2.3, how probability assessments may be summarized: most crucially, we introduced the notion of (smallest width) probability intervals, and various measures of central tendency and of dispersion, most notably the mean and variance. Section 2.4 then presented a catalogue of standard distributions, specifically the uniform, beta, normal, gamma and t distributions. Then, in section 2.5, we turned our attention to probability assessments about events, and introduced three important probability laws, as well as the key concept of conditional probability. The relationships of dependence and independence were also introduced, and related to the informativeness of 'information'. Finally, but briefly, Bayes' Theorem made its first appearance.

Throughout the whole chapter, it has been repeatedly emphasized that probability, as used in this book, is a subjective concept. Thus, probability statements are viewed as expressions of subjective belief. This philosophical standpoint is the essence of Bayesian statistics in general and this book in particular.

2.7 EXERCISES

* These questions should be tackled only by those familiar with calculus.

2.1   Draw, in the form of a distribution function, your answers to the questions.
(a) What age is ____ ? (Fill in the blank with the name of your statistics lecturer, or some other similar person.)
(b) What is the value of the aggregate marginal propensity to consume in ____ ? (Fill in the blank with the name of your country.)

2.2   Now do the following.
(a) Ask the person whose name you put in the blank in 2.1(a) above which decade he or she was born in.
(b) Find aggregate data on consumption and income for your country annually for the past ten years; draw a scatter diagram of consumption against income.
In the light of this information, redraw the distribution functions of exercise 2.1.

2.3   Derive the associated probability density functions (of the distribution functions drawn in exercises 2.1 and 2.2). (Note that both age and the mpc are continuous variables.) If you find this difficult, you may find it helpful to do exercises 2.7 to 2.10 below, and then return to this question.

2.4   Let X be the (discrete) variable defined as the total obtained when two (agreed fair) dice are rolled; note that X takes the integral values 2, 3, ..., 12. Draw the distribution function of X. Draw the probability function of X. Relate the two.

2.5   Verify that figures 2.4(b) and 2.4(c) do indeed give the distribution function and probability function of the variable X defined as the number of heads obtained when an (agreed fair) coin is tossed twice.

2.6   Let X be the (discrete) variable defined as the number of heads obtained when an (agreed fair) coin is tossed three times. Draw the distribution and probability functions of X. Relate the two.

2.7   Consider an (agreed fair) pointer, on which the circumference is uniformly and continuously calibrated from 0 to 4. Let X be the (continuous) variable defined as the value to which the pointer points after being spun. Draw the distribution function of X. Derive the probability density function of X. Show that the area under the latter between 1 and 3 is $\frac{1}{2}$; between 2 and 3 is $\frac{1}{4}$. Interpret these areas.

2.8   Consider the distribution function given in figure 2.11(a). Derive the probability density function. How should the cir-

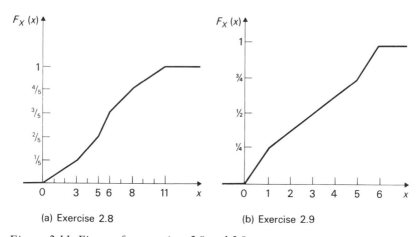

(a) Exercise 2.8   (b) Exercise 2.9

Figure 2.11 Figures for exercises 2.8 and 2.9

cumference of an (agreed fair) pointer be calibrated to generate such a distribution?

2.9 Repeat exercise 2.8 for the distribution function given in figure 2.11(b).

2.10 Consider the probability density function given in figure 2.7. Work out the value of the associated distribution function at values of x from -1 to 1 in steps of 0.1. Graph these points (on graph paper) and join them up with a freehand curve. Now, from your graph, calculate the slope of the distribution function at values of x from -1 to 1 in steps of 0.1. Graph these values and join up the points. Does the end-product look like figure 2.7? Why or why not? [* Find the functional form $f_X(x)$ of figure 2.7. Integrate it to get $F_X(x)$. Differentiate this and verify that you get back to $f_X(x)$.]

2.11 Trace the probability density function of the unit normal (given in figure 2.10(b)) on to a sheet of graph paper. Repeat exercise 2.10 with respect to this density function.

2.12 Is Figure 2.3(a) the distribution function of a discrete or continuous variable?

2.13 List all the properties of the distribution function.

2.14 List all the properties of the probability function (discrete variables) and the probability density function (continuous variables). Relate these to the properties of the distribution function.

2.15 Find (smallest width) 90 per cent probability intervals for the distributions in exercises 2.1, 2.2, 2.7, 2.8, 2.9, 2.10 and 2.11. (For the last of these you may use Appendix A6.)

2.16 Find the mean of the distributions in exercises 2.4, 2.5, 2.6, 2.7, 2.8, 2.9, 2.10 and 2.11. Find the variance of the distributions in exercises 2.4, 2.5 and 2.6. By using equation (2.26) find the variance of the distribution in exercise 2.7. What is the variance of the distribution in exercise 2.11?

2.17* Verify equation (2.26).

2.18* Prove that if $[x_1, x_2]$ is a smallest width α per cent probability interval for a continuous variable X, then $f_X(x_1) = f_X(x_2)$.

2.19 Find the factor of proportionality for the beta distribution in the following four cases: (a) $\alpha = \beta = 1$; (b) $\alpha = 2$, $\beta = 1$; (c) $\alpha = 1$, $\beta = 2$; (d)* $\alpha = \beta = 2$.

2.20 If Z is $N(0, 1)$, find (using Appendix A6) the probability that Z; (a) lies between 0 and 1.5, (b) lies between -1.5 and 1.5, (c) lies between -1.5 and 0.5, (d) equals 1.5.

2.21 If X is $N(2, 4)$, find (using Appendix A6) the probability that X; (a) lies between 2 and 5, (b) lies between -1 and 5, (c) lies between -1 and 3, (d) equals 1.5.

2.22 Two urns are filled with balls: urn 1 has 25 per cent white and 75 per cent black balls; urn 2 has 75 per cent white and 25 per cent black balls. If an urn is selected at random, and one ball selected at random, what is your assessment of the probability that it will be white? (You should state what you are assuming is meant by 'selected at random'.)

2.23 A scientist about to conduct an experiment figures there is about a 0.9 chance of observing result X if Theory A is true, and about a 0.3 chance of observing X is Theory B is true. He feels that Theory A is about twice as likely to be true as Theory B. If Theories A and B are the only reasonable contenders, what probability does the scientist attach to the possibility that he will observe X when he carries out the experiment?

2.24 Suppose a new breath-testing device has a 0.95 chance of detecting an individual whose alcohol level is over the limit, and a 0.95 chance of clearing an individual whose level is below the limit. If 5 per cent of the population are over the limit at a particular time, what is the probability that a randomly selected individual is over the limit given that the device says he or she is? (The answer will amaze/frighten you!)

3 FURTHER PROBABILITY THEORY

3.1 INTRODUCTION

All the central ideas and concepts of probability have now been introduced. To simplify the exposition in chapter 2, we focused attention exclusively on probability assessments about *events* and about *single variables*, though the basic ideas and concepts can obviously be extended to more complicated situations. In economics, the usual case of interest is the *multivariate* case, which is a situation in which many variables are involved. An important special case is the *bivariate* case, in which just two variables are involved. It is the purpose of this chapter to extend the apparatus of chapter 2 to cover the multivariate case in general and the bivariate case in particular. To simplify the exposition and the notation, we begin with the bivariate case.

The basic concept of a bivariate probability distribution is introduced in section 3.2. As we shall see, bivariate probability statements are statements about *joint* probabilities; thus, the values taken by *both* variables are relevant. Often it is also useful to know about each variable in isolation; to this end we introduce, in section 3.3, the concept of a *marginal* probability distribution. Then, in section 3.4 we introduce the *conditional* probability distribution, which is the distribution of one variable give some information about the other. This is obviously the natural extension of the conditional probability concept for events introduced in section 2.5. The generalization of all these concepts (joint, marginal and conditional probability distributions) to the multivariate case is then sketched in section 3.5. Penultimately, section 3.6 extends the material of section 2.3, on summary measures for univariate distributions, to the bivariate and multivariate cases. Finally, section 3.7 provides a summary, and section 3.8 a set of exercises.

3.2   BIVARIATE PROBABILITY DISTRIBUTIONS

In this and the following two sections, we will be exploring the *bivariate* case – a situation in which there are *two* variables of interest. As an obvious extension of the notation of chapter 2 we call these variables X and Y, using upper case letters, as before, to denote names of variables. Lower case letters, x and y, will, as before, be used to denote specific values of these variables.

Suppose, then, we are concerned with a situation in which there are two variables of interest, X and Y, each of which may take a range of values. As in the univariate case, we can encapsulate an individual's probability assessment about X and Y in the form of a distribution function, or a probability function or a probability density function as appropriate. Let us extend the definitions of these functions, as given in chapter 2, to the bivariate case. Begin with the distribution function, which, you will recall, can be used for both discrete and continuous variables. The definition in the univariate case is given by (2.1); it simply says that the distribution function measures *cumulative* probability. The following extension to the bivariate case should be immediate. We denote the *bivariate* (or joint) *distribution function* of X and Y by $F_{XY}(.,.)$, and define it by

$$F_{XY}(x, y) = P(X \leq x \text{ and } Y \leq y). \tag{3.1}$$

As in the univariate case, we will drop the subscripts XY if no confusion results by so doing. As can be seen from (3.1), $F_{XY}(x, y)$ measures the cumulative probability for X up to x and Y up to y. Note that it is a probability statement about *both* X and Y; that is why it is called a *bivariate* (or *joint*) distribution function.

In chapter 2, we frequently used graphs to illustrate the various functions. On a two-dimensional sheet of paper it is straightforward to graph a function of one variable: with the variable plotted along the horizontal axis and the value of the function up the vertical axis. However, to illustrate a function of two variables, one ideally needs three dimensions: one for each of the variables and one for the value of the function. Since it is rather difficult to draw a three-dimensional diagram on a two-dimensional sheet of paper, we are forced in this chapter to make considerably less use of graphical representations. Instead, we shall make rather greater use of tabular and algebraic representations, though occasionally we shall use two-dimensional representations of three-dimensional objects. (Economists are, of course, familiar with this procedure through the use of indifference curves and isoquants.)

Let us now give two examples of (3.1). In the first example, suppose two (agreed fair) coins are tossed, and suppose X and Y are defined as follows: X equals 1 if the first coin gives a head, and zero otherwise; and Y equals the number of heads obtained in the two tosses. Figure 3.1(a) illustrates schematically the various possible outcomes and the associated values of X and Y. If the coins are agreed to be fair, then all four points are regarded as equally likely. We thus get

$$P(X = 0 \text{ and } Y = 0) = P(X = 0 \text{ and } Y = 1)$$
$$= P(X = 1 \text{ and } Y = 1)$$
$$= P(X = 1 \text{ and } Y = 2) = \tfrac{1}{4}.$$

From this, we get the following rather clumsy but nevertheless straightforward expression for $F_{XY}(., .)$:

$$F_{XY}(x, y) = \begin{cases} 0 & x < 0 & y < 0 \\ \tfrac{1}{4} & & 0 \le y < 1 \\ \tfrac{1}{2} & 0 \le x < 1 & 1 \le y \\ \tfrac{3}{4} & 1 \le x & 1 \le y < 2 \\ 1 & 1 \le x & 2 \le y. \end{cases} \qquad (3.2)$$

You should verify this yourself. If you imagine this graphed in three dimensions, you will see that it looks like a series of steps. As in the univariate case, the discrete bivariate distribution function is a step-function. (If you are an expert at three-dimensional drawing, you might like to try drawing this function. You will swiftly realize that it is rather difficult, and adds little to one's understanding of the distribution.)

Our second example is schematically portrayed in figure 3.1(b): consider the square of size 1 by 1 drawn on this figure. Suppose that there is a selection mechanism which selects a point either within or on the boundary of the square in such a way that all points have an equal chance of being selected. Thus, the probability that the point selected is in some region such as the shaded region A is simply determined by the *area* of the region and not by its position in the square. Let X and Y be the x and y co-ordinates of the point

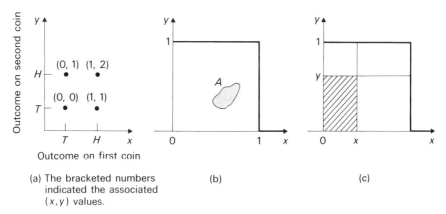

(a) The bracketed numbers   (b)   (c)
indicated the associated
(x, y) values.

Figure 3.1   Two examples of the bivariate case

selected. Then it follows that the bivariate distribution function $F_{XY}(.,.)$ is given by:

$$F_{XY}(x, y) = \begin{cases} 0 & x < 0 & y < 0 \\ x & 0 \le x < 1 & 1 \le y \\ xy & 0 \le x < 1 & 0 \le y < 1 \\ y & 1 \le x & 0 \le y < 1 \\ 1 & 1 \le x & 1 \le y. \end{cases} \quad (3.3)$$

(The first and last components of this are obvious; the middle part comes from the fact that if (x, y) lies within the square, then

$$F_{XY}(x, y) = P(X \le x \text{ and } Y \le y)$$
$$= \text{the shaded area in figure 3.1(c)} = xy$$

since the area is a rectangle of width x and height y; the remaining parts are now immediate.) If you imagine (3.3) graphed in three dimensions, you will see that it has two flat sections (all the negative region, and the region where both x and y are greater than one) joined together by a smoothly increasing plane. As in the univariate case, the continuous bivariate distribution function is smooth, and does *not* have jumps in it.

It is clear from both these examples, that the distribution function is not a particularly useful characterization in the bivariate case. Let us therefore explore the alternative characterizations, the probability function for the discrete case and the probability density function for the continuous case. We begin with the former.

In the univariate case, the probability function was defined by (2.7) (or equivalently (2.6)). The obvious counterpart for the bivariate case is as follows. We denote the (bivariate) probability function of X and Y by $f_{XY}(., .)$ (dropping the subscripts if no confusion results by so doing) and define it by:

$$f_{XY}(x, y) = P(X = x \text{ and } Y = y). \tag{3.4}$$

Thus, $f_{XY}(x, y)$ simply measures the probability that $X = x$ *and* $Y = y$. For the first of our two examples, it can be seen that $f_{XY}(., .)$ is given by

$$f_{XY}(x, y) = \begin{cases} \frac{1}{4} & \text{for } (x, y) = (0, 0), (0, 1), (1, 1) \text{ and } (1, 2) \\ 0 & \text{elsewhere.} \end{cases} \tag{3.5}$$

This function is graphed in figure 3.2(a). An alternative representation is in the tabular form of table 3.1; in this the entries in the

Table 3.1 The probability function for the two coin example

$X = 1$ if first coin shows a head, 0 if tail.
$Y =$ number of heads showing on two coins.
The table entries give $f_{XY}(x, y)$.

y \ x	0	1
0	$\frac{1}{4}$	0
1	$\frac{1}{4}$	$\frac{1}{4}$
2	0	$\frac{1}{4}$

table represent the probabilities of X and Y taking the values indicated in the margins.

Let us give one further discrete example before moving on to the continuous case. Suppose two (agreed fair) dice are rolled. Define X as the number showing on the first die and Y as the absolute magnitude of the difference between the numbers on the two dice. By drawing a diagram illustrating all thirty-six possible (and equally probable) outcomes, and their associated (x, y) values, you should be able to verify that the probability function is as given in table 3.2. (For example, consider the case of $x = 3$, $y = 2$; this arises if and only if the two dice show (3, 1) or (3, 5). Thus, out of the thirty-six possible outcomes, two give rise to $x = 3$ and $y = 2$; hence the probability is $\frac{2}{36}$. Thus, $f_{XY}(3, 2) = \frac{2}{36}$, as the table indicates.)

We will return to this example in section 3.3. In the meantime, we turn to the continuous case, and introduce the bivariate probability

Table 3.2   The probability function for the two dice example

X = number showing on first die.
Y = absolute magnitude of difference between the two numbers.
The table entries give $f_{XY}(x, y)$ *multiplied by 36.*

x \\ y	1	2	3	4	5	6
0	1	1	1	1	1	1
1	1	2	2	2	2	1
2	1	1	2	2	1	1
3	1	1	1	1	1	1
4	1	1	0	0	1	1
5	1	0	0	0	0	1

density function, which, for two variables X and Y, we denote by $f_{XY}(.\,,.)$ (dropping the subscripts if no confusion results by so doing). As in the univariate case, and as its name indicates, $f_{XY}(.\,,.)$ measures the *density of the probability*. Specifically, $f_{XY}(x, y)$ measures the density of the probability at the point (x, y). To derive this, we first find the density of the probability over a rectangular region based on the point (x, y), and then calculate what happens to this density as the region shrinks to the point (x, y). More precisely, consider the rectangle bounded by x and $x + \Delta x$ in the x-direction, and by y and $y + \Delta y$ in the y-direction. The area of this rectangle is $\Delta x \cdot \Delta y$ (since it has width Δx and depth Δy); thus, since the probability of (X, Y) lying in this rectangle is definitionally

$$P(x \leq X \leq x + \Delta x \quad \text{and} \quad y \leq Y \leq y + \Delta y)$$

it follows that the density of the probability in this rectangle is

$$\frac{P(x \leq X \leq x + \Delta x \quad \text{and} \quad y \leq Y \leq y + \Delta y)}{\Delta x \cdot \Delta y}.$$

We then define the probability density *at the point* (x, y) as the limit of this as Δx and Δy shrink to zero. Formally,

$$f_{XY}(x, y)$$
$$= \underset{\Delta x \to 0}{Lt} \; \underset{\Delta y \to 0}{Lt} \; \frac{P(x \leq X \leq x + \Delta x \quad \text{and} \quad y \leq Y \leq y + \Delta y)}{\Delta x \cdot \Delta y}. \quad (3.6)$$

If you are familiar with calculus (particularly partial differentiation), you could combine (3.1) and (3.6) to show that

$$f_{XY}(x, y) = \partial^2 F_{XY}(x, y)/\partial x \, \partial y. \quad (3.7)$$

This is the natural extension of (2.8). As an illustration, let us apply (3.7) to the example of figure 3.1(b), whose joint distribution function was given by (3.3); we can show immediately that its joint probability density function is given by:

$$f_{XY}(x, y) = \begin{cases} 1 & 0 \leq x \leq 1 \quad 0 \leq y \leq 1 \\ 0 & \text{elsewhere.} \end{cases} \tag{3.8}$$

This is graphed in figure 3.2(b). As can be seen either from this figure,

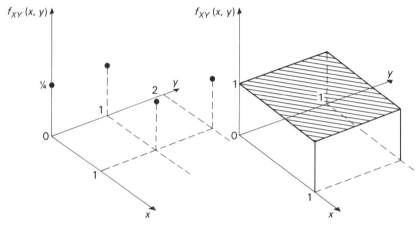

(a) The probability function in the two coin example (the function is zero except at the 4 points marked).

(b) The probability density function in the example of Figure 3.1(b) (the function is zero except where marked).

Figure 3.2 A probability function and a probability density function

or directly from (3.8), this density function is *uniform* over the square $0 \leq x \leq 1$, $0 \leq y \leq 1$. This reflects the initial assumption that the selection mechanism was 'fair' in the sense that all points within or on the boundary of the square had an equal chance of being selected. In a way, our discussion has come full circle.

The material of this section has been rather difficult, and you would be forgiven if you found it rather tough-going. Essentially, all we have done is to extend the univariate definitions of distribution functions, probability functions and probability density functions to the bivariate case. However, the notation has necessarily become more complicated, and it has been less easy to illustrate the various concepts diagrammatically. But do not worry if you have not understood all the details; in a sense, this material has been included only for the sake of completeness. We will very rarely be drawing directly on this material in the coming pages. In particular, we will have virtually no occasion to refer to the joint distribution function.

What you *do* need to know, and feel confident about, are the following. First, in the discrete case, you need to know what a *probability function* is; that is, you should know that $f_{XY}(x, y)$ measures the *joint* probability that X equals x and Y equals y. Second, in the continuous case, you need to know what a *probability density function* is; that is, you should know that $f_{XY}(x, y)$ measures the *joint* probability density at the point where X equals x *and* Y equals y.

The reason why you do not need to worry too much about the material of this section is that, although we will be examining the bivariate case in some detail in the coming pages, we will very rarely be interested in *joint* probability statements about the two variables. Most of the time, we will be interested in probability statements either about one variable in isolation or about one variable given some information about the other. The next two sections discuss such issues.

3.3   MARGINAL DISTRIBUTIONS

As mentioned above, there are often situations where, although we are dealing with a bivariate case, we may wish to restrict attention for a while to just one of the two variables, and thus ignore, for the time being, the other. That is, we may wish to make probability statements about X ignoring Y, or about Y ignoring X.

It should be clear that this can be done simply by employing the apparatus of chapter 2, since by ignoring one variable and concentrating on the other we are effectively returning to the univariate case. Thus, we can use the univariate functions, as appropriate, to describe the probability assessments about X ignoring Y, or about Y ignoring X.

Consider the simple (discrete) example which formed our first illustration in section 3.2. In this, two (agreed fair) coins are tossed; X is defined as 1 if the first coin shows a head, and zero otherwise; and Y is defined as the number of heads obtained on the two tosses. Although two variables are involved, we can easily find the distribution of each variable by itself. Consider first X; it takes values 1 and 0. If the coin(s) are agreed to be fair, then the probability assessment about X can be expressed as follows, in terms of the probability function of X:

$$f_X(0) = f_X(1) = \tfrac{1}{2}. \tag{3.9}$$

Similarly, the probability assessment about Y (which takes values 0, 1 and 2) can be expressed in terms of *its* probability function, as follows:

$$f_Y(0) = \tfrac{1}{4} \qquad f_Y(1) = \tfrac{1}{2} \qquad f_Y(2) = \tfrac{1}{4}. \qquad (3.10)$$

(Note that $Y = 0$ if the outcome is TT, that $Y = 1$ if the outcome is either TH or HT, and that $Y = 2$ if the outcome is HH.)

This is all very straightforward: $f_X(.)$ and $f_Y(.)$ can each be separately obtained without any reference to the other variable. But what is the relationship of these two functions to the *joint* probability function, as given in table 3.1? Consider first the *columns* of this table: the first column represents all the possible ways that X may equal zero; the second column represents all the possible ways that X may equal 1. By adding all the entries in the first column, one simply gets the overall probability that X equals zero; similarly, by adding all the entries in the second column, one gets the overall probability that X equals 1. Rather long-windedly, we could write

$$
\begin{aligned}
f_X(0) &= P(X = 0) \\
&= P(X = 0 \text{ and } Y = 0) + P(X = 0 \text{ and } Y = 1) \\
&\quad + P(X = 0 \text{ and } Y = 2) \\
&= f_{XY}(0, 0) + f_{XY}(0, 1) + f_{XY}(0, 2) \\
&= \tfrac{1}{4} + \tfrac{1}{4} + 0 = \tfrac{1}{2}.
\end{aligned}
$$

Similarly,

$$
\begin{aligned}
f_X(1) &= P(X = 1) \\
&= P(X = 1 \text{ and } Y = 0) + P(X = 1 \text{ and } Y = 1) \\
&\quad + P(X = 1 \text{ and } Y = 2) \\
&= f_{XY}(1, 0) + f_{XY}(1, 1) + f_{XY}(1, 2) \\
&= 0 + \tfrac{1}{4} + \tfrac{1}{4} = \tfrac{1}{2}.
\end{aligned}
$$

There is a general pattern here, which we can express as follows:

$$f_X(x) = \sum_y f_{XY}(x, y). \qquad (3.11)$$

In this the summation is over all values of y (or over all possible values of y – the difference being immaterial, since $f_{XY}(x, y)$ is zero for impossible values of y).

By an exactly parallel argument, we see that if we add up the *rows* in the table, we arrive at the probability function of Y. Thus,

$$
\begin{aligned}
f_Y(0) &= P(Y = 0) \\
&= P(X = 0 \text{ and } Y = 0) + P(X = 1 \text{ and } Y = 0) \\
&= f_{XY}(0, 0) + f_{XY}(1, 0) \\
&= \tfrac{1}{4} + 0 = \tfrac{1}{4};
\end{aligned}
$$

Table 3.3   Joint and marginal probabilities for the two coin example

$X = 1$ if first coin shows a head, 0 if tail.
$Y = $ number of heads showing on two coins.
The entries in the main body of the table give $f_{XY}(x, y)$.

y \ x	0	1	$f_Y(y)$
0	$\frac{1}{4}$	0	$\frac{1}{4}$
1	$\frac{1}{4}$	$\frac{1}{4}$	$\frac{1}{2}$
2	0	$\frac{1}{4}$	$\frac{1}{4}$
$f_X(x)$	$\frac{1}{2}$	$\frac{1}{2}$	1

and so on. More generally,

$$f_Y(y) = \sum_x f_{XY}(x, y), \tag{3.12}$$

where the summation is over all values of x. This is illustrated in table 3.3. In this, the probability function of X is in the bottom 'margin', and the probability function of Y is in the right-hand 'margin'. It is for this reason that the distributions of X and Y *by themselves* are called the *marginal* distributions of X and Y respectively. Formally, $f_{XY}(., .)$ is called the *bivariate* (or *joint*) probability function, and $f_X(.)$ and $f_Y(.)$ are called the *marginal* probability functions of X and Y respectively.

The relationship between marginal and joint probability functions should now be clear: to find the marginal probability function of X one sums the joint probability function over all values of y (equation (3.11)), and to find the marginal probability function of Y one sums the joint probability function over all values of x (equation (3.12)). Effectively, by adding up over y (or x) you are saying that you are not interested in what Y (or X) is.

To reinforce these ideas, consider the second discrete example introduced in this chapter. In this example, two (agreed fair) dice are rolled; X is defined as the number showing on the first die, and Y as the absolute magnitude of the difference between the numbers on the two dice. Table 3.2 gave the joint probability function. To find the marginal probability functions of X and Y we employ (3.11) and (3.12); that is, the columns and rows of table 3.2 are added to find the marginal totals. This is done in table 3.4. (Note that, as in table 3.2, we multiply all the entries by 36, to save clutter; otherwise all the entries would have '/36' after them. We trust no confusion results.)

Table 3.4   Joint and marginal probabilities for the two dice example

X = number showing on first die.
Y = absolute magnitude of the difference between the two numbers.
The entries in main body of the table give $f_{XY}(x, y)$ *multiplied by 36.*

x \ y	1	2	3	4	5	6	$f_Y(y) \times 36$
0	1	1	1	1	1	1	6
1	1	2	2	2	2	1	10
2	1	1	2	2	1	1	8
3	1	1	1	1	1	1	6
4	1	1	0	0	1	1	4
5	1	0	0	0	0	1	2
$f_X(x) \times 36$	6	6	6	6	6	6	36

From table 3.4 we see that the marginal probability function of X is given by:

$$f_X(1) = f_X(2) = f_X(3) = f_X(4) = f_X(5) = f_X(6) = \tfrac{6}{36} = \tfrac{1}{6}.$$

This is clearly correct: it says that for an agreed fair die, the probability of it taking any one of the six possible values is $\tfrac{1}{6}$. The marginal probability function of Y is given by the right-hand 'margin'; it is as follows:

$$f_Y(0) = \tfrac{6}{36} \qquad f_Y(1) = \tfrac{10}{36} \qquad f_Y(2) = \tfrac{8}{36}$$
$$f_Y(3) = \tfrac{6}{36} \qquad f_Y(4) = \tfrac{4}{36} \qquad f_Y(5) = \tfrac{2}{36}.$$

You may like to verify these yourself. (Consider, for example, $Y = 0$: this occurs when the numbers on the two dice are the same, which happens for six of the possible thirty-six pairs. Thus the probability is $\tfrac{6}{36}$. Again, $Y = 5$ happens on two occasions: when the first is a '1' and the second a '6', and vice versa. Thus the probability is $\tfrac{2}{36}$.)

The above discussion has concentrated on the *discrete* case. For the *continuous* case, similar arguments hold (appropriately modified to reflect the differences between discrete and continuous variables). Thus, the marginal probability density functions of X and Y respectively are related to the bivariate (or joint) probability density function as follows:

$$f_X(x) = \int_y f_{XY}(x, y)\, \mathrm{d}y \tag{3.13}$$

and

$$f_Y(y) = \int_x f_{XY}(x, y) \, dx. \tag{3.14}$$

In (3.13) the integration is carried out over all values of y, and in (3.14) the integration is carried out over all values of x. Equation (3.13) is the continuous counterpart of (3.11); similarly, equation (3.14) is the continuous counterpart of (3.12). As we remarked in chapter 2, where $\sum$ appears in the discrete case, $\int$ appears in the continuous case; and where f appears in the discrete case, $f \, dx$ (or $f \, dy$) appears in the continuous case.

Let us give two illustrations of these relationships ((3.13) and (3.14)) between marginal and joint probability density functions. Our first illustration is the continuous example already used in this chapter, and introduced schematically in figure 3.1(b). Recall that a point in the square is selected at random, and that X and Y are simply defined as the x- and y-coordinates of the point selected. Recall also that the joint probability density function is given by (3.8), and illustrated in figure 3.1(b): it is, quite naturally, uniform over the unit square. To find the marginal probability density functions of X and Y we apply (3.13) and (3.14). Thus,

$$f_X(x) = \int_y f_{XY}(x, y) \, dy = \int_0^1 1 \cdot dy = [y]_0^1 = 1,$$

if x is between 0 and 1; otherwise $f_X(x)$ is zero. Similarly,

$$f_Y(y) = \int_x f_{XY}(x, y) \, dx = \int_0^1 1 \cdot dx = [x]_0^1 = 1,$$

if y is between 0 and 1; otherwise $f_Y(y)$ is zero. Note that, when deriving $f_X(x)$, for example, for $0 \le x \le 1$, the joint density is 1 for $0 \le y \le 1$, but zero elsewhere; that is why

$$\int_y f_{XY}(x, y) \, dy = \int_0^1 1 \cdot dy.$$

Note also that $f_X(x)$ is zero for x outside [0, 1] and $f_Y(y)$ is zero for y outside [0, 1] since $f_{XY}(x, y)$ is zero in such cases (reflecting the fact that points outside the unit square cannot be selected).

Collecting results, we have

$$f_X(x) = \begin{cases} 1 & 0 \le x \le 1 \\ 0 & \text{elsewhere} \end{cases} \quad \text{and} \quad f_Y(y) = \begin{cases} 1 & 0 \le y \le 1 \\ 0 & \text{elsewhere,} \end{cases} \tag{3.15}$$

and thus the marginal distributions of X and Y are both uniform over $[0, 1]$. A moment's reflection should convince you that this is indeed correct.

Consider now a second example, illustrated schematically in figure 3.3(a). In this, a point is selected from the shaded triangle, using the by-now-familiar 'fair' selection mechanism. The variables X and Y are defined as the x- and y-coordinates of the point selected. We will find the joint distribution and probability density functions, and the marginal density functions. Begin with the joint distribution function. Consider a point within the triangle, such as A. To find $F_{XY}(x, y)$ for this point, we need to find the area of the cross-hatched region to the south-west of A as a proportion of the total area of the triangle; this gives the probability that the point selected will fall in the cross-hatched region, and hence $P(X \leq x$ and $Y \leq y)$. Elementary geometry shows that the total area of the triangle is $\frac{1}{2}$, and that the area of the cross-hatched region is $xy - y^2/2$ (that is, the area of the rectangle $0xAy$ less the area of the little triangle above the hypotenuse of the triangle). Therefore, we have

$$F_{XY}(x, y) = 2xy - y^2$$

if (x, y) lies in the triangle. Similarly, if (x, y) is above the triangle (that is if $0 \leq x \leq 1$ and $x \leq y$), then

$$F_{XY}(x, y) = x^2;$$

if (x, y) is to the right of the triangle (that is, $1 \leq x$ and $0 \leq y \leq 1$), then

$$F_{XY}(x, y) = 2 - y^2;$$

if (x, y) is north-east of the triangle (that is $1 \leq x$, $1 \leq y$), then

$$F_{XY}(x, y) = 1;$$

and, finally, if (x, y) is anywhere else then

$$F_{XY}(x, y) = 0.$$

Collecting these results, we have:

$$F_{XY}(x, y) = \begin{cases} 0 & x \leq 0 & y \leq 0 \\ x^2 & 0 \leq x \leq 1 & x \leq y \\ 2xy - y^2 & 0 \leq x \leq 1 & 0 \leq y \leq x \\ 2 - y^2 & 1 \leq x & 0 \leq y \leq 1 \\ 1 & 1 \leq x & 1 \leq y. \end{cases} \qquad (3.16)$$

As you will probably have gathered by now, this is *not* a particularly helpful, or intuitively obvious expression!

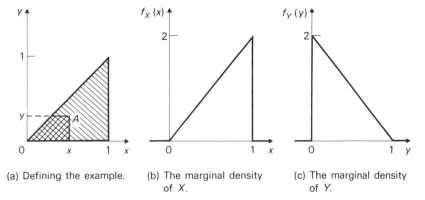

(a) Defining the example. (b) The marginal density of X. (c) The marginal density of Y.

Figure 3.3 A second example of a continuous bivariate distribution

Consider, however, the joint probability density function; formally, it can be derived by applying (3.7) to (3.16). This yields

$$f_{XY}(x, y) = \begin{cases} 2 & 0 \le x \le 1 \quad 0 \le y \le x \\ 0 & \text{elsewhere.} \end{cases} \tag{3.17}$$

(To verify this, note that (3.7) says that, to get the density function, you differentiate the distribution function twice; first with respect to x and then with respect to y. For the first component of (3.16), namely 0, this gives 0; for the second, namely x^2, also 0; for the third, namely $2xy - y^2$, this gives 2; for the fourth, namely $2 - y^2$, this gives 0; and for the fifth, namely 1, also 0.)

Equation (3.17) states that the probability density is uniform over the triangle. This intuition behind this result should be immediate. (Note that the density is uniform at the value 2, because the total probability must still equal 1, and the area of the triangle is $\frac{1}{2}$. Note also that we could have stated (3.17) directly, rather than approach it through the distribution function. Indeed, as we have said before, distribution functions are not particularly helpful in the bivariate case.)

Let us now find the marginal probability density functions. There are two ways of doing this: either directly from the statement of the example, or indirectly from the joint probability density function. You should try the direct method yourself, so that you may verify the following results based on the indirect method. First, we find the density function for X. Applying (3.13) to (3.17), we get

(a) for $0 \leq x \leq 1$:

$$f_X(x) = \int_y f_{XY}(x, y)\, dy = \int_0^x 2\, dy = [2y]_0^x = 2x. \qquad (3.18)$$

(b) for x outside $[0, 1]$:

$$f_X(x) = \int_y f_{XY}(x, y)\, dy = 0.$$

Note, *very carefully*, in the third term of (3.18), that the integration is from $y = 0$ to $y = x$; this is since the joint density is zero for $y < 0$ and $y > x$, that is, for a point outside the triangle.

Similarly, applying (3.14) to (3.17), we get the marginal probability density function for Y:

(a) $0 \leq y \leq 1$:

$$f_Y(y) = \int_x f_{XY}(x, y)\, dx = \int_y^1 2\, dx = [2x]_y^1 = 2(1 - y). \qquad (3.19)$$

(b) for y outside $[0, 1]$:

$$f_Y(y) = \int_x f_{XY}(x, y)\, dx = 0.$$

Note, again, *very carefully*, in the third term of (3.19), that the integration is from $x = y$ to $x = 1$; this is since the joint density is zero for $x < y$ and $x > 1$, that is, for a point outside the triangle.

Collecting results together, we have

$$f_X(x) = \begin{cases} 2x & 0 \leq x \leq 1 \\ 0 & \text{elsewhere.} \end{cases}$$

$$f_Y(y) = \begin{cases} 2(1 - y) & 0 \leq y \leq 1 \\ 0 & \text{elsewhere.} \end{cases} \qquad (3.20)$$

These are illustrated in figures 3.3(b) and (c). As can be seen from these, the distribution of X is 'right-triangular' and that of Y 'left-triangular'. Further, recalling the terminology of section 2.4, we note that X is $B(2, 1)$ and that Y is $B(1, 2)$. Note that the area under each of the density functions is one, as must be the case if we have derived the functions correctly. I hope that your results using the direct method are the same as (3.20); if they are not, exercise 3.7 may help you to discover where you went wrong.

This completes our treatment of marginal distributions. Again, you may have found this section rather difficult; but again, you do not need to worry unduly if you have not mastered all the details. In most instances, you will be able to find the marginal distributions of the variables of interest directly – that is, without recourse to the joint distribution. In such cases, all you need to know is the material of chapter 2. However, in those few instances where you need to travel the indirect route via the joint distribution, all you need to know is that: *in the discrete case, the marginal probability function of X (Y) is obtained by summing the joint probability function over all values of y (x)* (see (3.11) and (3.12)); *in the continuous case, the marginal probability density function of X (Y) is obtained by integrating the joint probability density function over all values of y (x)* (see (3.13) and (3.14)).

3.4   CONDITIONAL DISTRIBUTIONS

Marginal distributions are distributions of one variable, *ignoring the other*. In contrast, conditional distributions, which are the subject of this section, are distributions of one variable *given some information about the other*. To be specific, the conditional distributions examined in this section, are distributions of one variable *given a particular value of the other*. Thus, for example, one might be told that Y equals 3; this section investigates how this affects, if at all, the probability assessment of X.

As might be already apparent, conditional distributions are generalizations of the conditional probability concept introduced for events in section 2.5. Recall the general result (2.39) for the conditional probability of event F given event E:

$$P(F \mid E) = P(E \text{ and } F)/P(E). \tag{3.21}$$

Consider the numerator and denominator of the right-hand side of (3.21): in the terminology of this chapter, the numerator is a *joint* probability statement, and the denominator is a *marginal* probability statement. Clearly (3.21) is ripe for generalization to variables, using the concepts and notation introduced in this chapter.

Consider first the discrete case; suppose that E is the 'event' that

X equals x, and that F is the 'event' that Y equals y. Then (3.21) gives

$$P(Y = y \,|\, X = x) = P(X = x \text{ and } Y = y)/P(X = x). \tag{3.22}$$

The two components on the right-hand side of this expression are familiar: the numerator is simply the joint probability $f_{XY}(x, y)$; the denominator is simply the marginal probability $f_X(x)$. The left-hand side, which is a probability statement about Y *given* a specific value of X, is a *conditional* probability statement. Let us introduce the notation $g_Y(y \,|\, x)$ to represent this conditional statement. Thus,

$$g_Y(y \,|\, x) \equiv P(Y = y \,|\, X = x). \tag{3.23}$$

Notice three important things about the notation '$g_Y(. \,|\, x)$': first, the subscript 'Y' which signals that it is a statement about the variable Y; second, the conditioning '$| \, x$' which signals that it is a statement conditional on X taking the value x; third, the use of the lower- (rather than upper-) case 'g' which signals that it is a probability (as distinct from a distribution) function. Using this new notation (3.22) can be written

$$g_Y(y \,|\, x) = f_{XY}(x, y)/f_X(x). \tag{3.24}$$

This is a general, and very important, result which shows how conditional probability statements about Y may be derived. An exactly parallel argument yields the following result, which shows how conditional probability statements about X may be derived:

$$g_X(x \,|\, y) = f_{XY}(x, y)/f_Y(y). \tag{3.25}$$

In this, of course, $g_X(. \,|\, y)$ denotes the probability function of X given that Y equals y; it is a conditional probability function.

To illustrate the concept of conditional probability assessments, consider the two discrete bivariate examples introduced earlier in this chapter. The first example, you will recall, is the two-coin example, in which X equals 1 (0) if the first coin shows a head (tail) and Y equals the number of heads on the two coins. Table 3.3 gives the joint and marginal probability functions for X and Y. Now consider the various conditional probability distributions for Y. As there are two possible values for X (namely 0 and 1), there are two conditional distributions for Y – one conditional on $X = 0$ and the other conditional on $X = 1$. To derive the respective conditional probability functions, we apply (3.24). You will note from this that, to find $g_Y(. \,|\, 0)$ for example, we simply divide the $f_{XY}(0, y)$ values by $f_X(0)$. In terms of the tabular presentation of table 3.3, we simply divide the entries in the column headed $x = 0$ by the column total, which is $f_X(0)$. Similarly, to find $g_Y(.\,|\,1)$ we simply divide the entries in the column headed $x = 1$ by the column total, which is $f_X(1)$. The results of carrying out this process are given in table 3.5(a).

Table 3.5 *Conditional probability functions for the two coin example*

(a) Conditional distributions of Y

y	$g_Y(y\,|\,0)$	$g_Y(y\,|\,1)$
0	$\frac{1}{2}$	0
1	$\frac{1}{2}$	$\frac{1}{2}$
2	0	$\frac{1}{2}$
sum	1	1

(b) Conditional distributions of X

x	$g_X(x\,|\,0)$	$g_X(x\,|\,1)$	$g_X(x\,|\,2)$
0	1	$\frac{1}{2}$	0
1	0	$\frac{1}{2}$	1
sum	1	1	1

Let us check that our intuition agrees with table 3.5(a). Consider first the distribution conditional on $X = 0$. According to the table, when $X = 0$, Y is equally likely to take the values 0 and 1 (but can *not* take the value 2). In terms of the two coins, this means that when the first coin shows a tail (that is, $X = 0$), the total number of heads on the two coins is equally likely to be 0 or 1 (but can *not* be 2). This is clearly sensible. Similarly, according to the table, when $X = 1$, Y is equally likely to take the values 1 and 2 (but can *not* take the value 1). In terms of the two coins, this means that when the first coin shows a head (that is $X = 1$), the total number of heads on the two coins is equally likely to be 1 or 2 (but can *not* be 0). Again, this is clearly sensible.

To find the conditional distributions of X, we proceed in an entirely analogous manner. As (3.25) says, we divide the various row entries in table 3.3 by the corresponding row total. The results of carrying out this process are given in table 3.5(b). Again, let us check that our intuition agrees with the results. According to the table, when $Y = 0$, X is certain to take the value 0. In terms of the two coins, this means that when the total number of heads is zero, the first toss must be a tail. This is obvious. Similarly when $Y = 2$, X must be 1. Finally, when $Y = 1$, X is equally likely to be 0 or 1; you should verify this final result yourself.

Let us now turn to the second of our discrete examples, namely the two dice example. In this, X is the number showing on the first die, and Y is the absolute magnitude of the difference between the numbers on the two dice. Table 3.4 gives the joint and marginal probability functions for X and Y. To find the conditional distributions of $Y(X)$, we proceed exactly as before – by dividing the various column (row) entries in table 3.4 by the corresponding column (row) totals. Table 3.6 shows the results of carrying out this procedure for Y; you should carry out the procedure for X yourself.

Table 3.6   Conditional probability functions for Y in the two dice example

y	$g_Y(y\vert 1)$	$g_Y(y\vert 2)$	$g_Y(y\vert 3)$	$g_Y(y\vert 4)$	$g_Y(y\vert 5)$	$g_Y(y\vert 6)$
0	$\frac{1}{6}$	$\frac{1}{6}$	$\frac{1}{6}$	$\frac{1}{6}$	$\frac{1}{6}$	$\frac{1}{6}$
1	$\frac{1}{6}$	$\frac{2}{6}$	$\frac{2}{6}$	$\frac{2}{6}$	$\frac{2}{6}$	$\frac{1}{6}$
2	$\frac{1}{6}$	$\frac{1}{6}$	$\frac{2}{6}$	$\frac{2}{6}$	$\frac{1}{6}$	$\frac{1}{6}$
3	$\frac{1}{6}$	$\frac{1}{6}$	$\frac{1}{6}$	$\frac{1}{6}$	$\frac{1}{6}$	$\frac{1}{6}$
4	$\frac{1}{6}$	$\frac{1}{6}$	0	0	$\frac{1}{6}$	$\frac{1}{6}$
5	$\frac{1}{6}$	0	0	0	0	$\frac{1}{6}$
sum	1	1	1	1	1	1

This table shows, for example, that when X equals 1, then Y is equally likely to take any of its six values: 0, 1, 2, 3, 4 and 5. This is clearly sensible: the possible values of the second die are 1, 2, 3, 4, 5 and 6, which, when combined with a first die value of 1, give Y values of 0, 1, 2, 3, 4 and 5 respectively. Again, for example, the table shows that when X equals 3, Y takes the values 0, 1, 2 and 3 with respective probabilities $\frac{1}{6}, \frac{2}{6}, \frac{2}{6}$ and $\frac{1}{6}$. Again, this is clearly sensible: the possible values of the second die are 1, 2, 3, 4, 5 and 6, which, when combined with a first die value of 3, give Y values of 2, 1, 0, 1, 2 and 3 respectively.

You may have noticed by now that sometimes a conditional probability distribution and the corresponding unconditional distribution are the same, and sometimes they are different. For example, in the two-coin example, the marginal distribution of X (see table 3.3) is:

$$f_X(0) = \tfrac{1}{2} \qquad f_X(1) = \tfrac{1}{2},$$

while the various conditional distributions (see Table 3.5) are:

$$g_X(0\,|\,0) = 1 \qquad g_X(1\,|\,0) = 0;$$
$$g_X(0\,|\,1) = \tfrac{1}{2} \qquad g_X(1\,|\,1) = \tfrac{1}{2}; \quad \text{and}$$
$$g_X(0\,|\,2) = 0 \qquad g_X(1\,|\,2) = 1.$$

Thus, $f_X(.)$ and $g_X(.\,|\,1)$ are the same, but $f_X(.)$ and $g_X(.\,|\,0)$ are different, as are $f_X(.)$ and $g_X(.\,|\,2)$. You may recall a similar situation being discussed in section 2.5: to be specific, we said that when the conditional probability $P(F\,|\,E)$ and the unconditional probability $P(F)$ differed, then E was 'informative' as far as F was concerned. Consider the situation in the two-coin example: if you are told that Y equals zero, is this informative as far as X is concerned? Clearly it is. But, if you are told that Y equals 1, is *this* informative as far as X is concerned? Clearly not. (Knowing that one of the two coins shows a head, does not help to determine whether the first coin shows a head or not; but knowing that neither coin shows a head immediately tells you that the first coin does not show a head.) As our examples show, $f_X(.)$ and $g_X(.\,|\,y)$ are the same when knowledge that Y equals y is uninformative as far as X is concerned, and $f_X(.)$ and $g_X(.\,|\,y)$ differ when knowledge that Y equals y *is* informative.

In section 2.5, we defined two events as being *independent* if $P(E\,|\,F) = P(E)$ and $P(F\,|\,E) = P(F)$, that is, if the conditional and the corresponding unconditional probabilities are equal. In an entirely analogous manner, we define two variables X and Y as being independent if the conditional and corresponding unconditional probability functions are equal for all values of X and Y. Formally:

> Variables X and Y are said to be *independent* if and only if $g_X(x\,|\,y) = f_X(x)$ and $g_Y(y\,|\,x) = f_Y(y)$ for all x and y. (3.26)

Clearly, if X and Y are independent then knowledge of the value of Y (X) is *always* uninformative as far as X (Y) is concerned. If two variables are not independent (that is, if the condition in (3.26) does *not* hold), then the variables are said to be *dependent*. In such cases, knowledge of the value of Y (X) *may* be informative as far as X (Y) is concerned. In both of our (discrete bivariate) examples, X and Y are dependent, though occasionally specific values of X or Y are uninformative. (For example, $Y = 1$ in the two-coin example, and $Y = 0$ in the two-dice example. Can you find any more?)

If we combine the condition for independence (3.26) with the general results for conditional probabilities (3.24) and (3.25), we get the following very important implication:

$$\left.\begin{array}{l} \text{Variables } X \text{ and } Y \text{ are independent if and only if} \\ f_{XY}(x, y) = f_X(x)f_Y(y) \text{ for all } x \text{ and } y. \end{array}\right\} \quad (3.27)$$

Thus, two variables are independent if and only if their joint probability function is the product of the marginal probability functions. In terms of a tabular representation (such as in tables 3.3 and 3.4), this requires that each entry in the main body of the table equals the product of the corresponding row and column totals (or marginal entries). This is clearly not true for *all* entries in tables 3.3 and 3.4, which is another reflection of the fact that X and Y are dependent in these examples. (However, it is true sometimes: for example, consider the entries in the $y = 1$ row in table 3.3, and those in the $y = 0$ row in table 3.4. Is there anything familiar about these examples?)

This completes our introduction to conditional probability distributions in the discrete case. The crucial results are equations (3.24) and (3.25) which express the conditional probability functions in terms of the joint and marginal probability functions. We now turn to the continuous case. As it happens, equations (3.24) and (3.25) remain the crucial results as long as the various functions are reinterpreted appropriately. Specifically, in the continuous case, $f_{XY}(., .)$, $f_X(.)$ and $f_Y(.)$ are *probability density* functions, as must be the two new functions, $g_Y(. \,|\, x)$ and $g_X(. \,|\, y)$. To be precise, $g_Y(. \,|\, x)$ is the conditional probability density function of Y given that X equals x, and $g_X(. \,|\, y)$ is the conditional probability density function of X given that Y equals y. As we have already noted, they are defined, as in the discrete case, by equations (3.24) and (3.25). For convenience, we repeat these two equations here:

$$g_Y(y \,|\, x) = f_{XY}(x, y)/f_X(x)$$

and

$$\left.\begin{array}{l} \\ \\ \end{array}\right\} \quad (3.28)$$

$$g_X(x \,|\, y) = f_{XY}(x, y)/f_Y(y).$$

Thus, to find the conditional density function of Y (X) given x (y), one simply divides the joint density function by the marginal density function of X (Y).

Let us give two examples, namely the two examples of continuous bivariate distributions introduced earlier in this chapter. The first example was defined schematically in figure 3.1(b): a point is selected at random from the unit square, and X and Y are defined as the x- and y-coordinates of the point selected. To find the various conditional distributions, we need (cf. (3.28)) to know the joint and marginal distributions. The joint probability density function is given by (3.8); this states the obvious fact that the joint density is uniform over the unit square. The marginal density functions of X and Y are given by (3.15); this states the equally obvious fact that the densities of X and Y are each uniform over the unit interval [0, 1]. Substituting (3.8) and (3.15) into (3.28), we arrive at the following expressions for the various conditional density functions:

$$\left.\begin{array}{l} g_Y(y \mid x) = \begin{cases} 1 & 0 \leq y \leq 1 \\ 0 & \text{elsewhere} \end{cases} \quad (\text{if } 0 \leq x \leq 1) \\[2em] g_X(x \mid y) = \begin{cases} 1 & 0 \leq x \leq 1 \\ 0 & \text{elsewhere} \end{cases} \quad (\text{if } 0 \leq y \leq 1). \end{array}\right\} \quad (3.29)$$

(Note that the conditional distribution of Y (X) for x (y) outside the range [0, 1] is undefined and meaningless. From now on, we take for granted that the conditioning value of x or y is not an impossible value.) Thus, all the conditional distributions of Y, irrespective of the value of x, are uniform over the unit interval [0, 1]. Similarly, all the conditional distributions of X, irrespective of the value of y, are uniform over the unit interval [0, 1]. Do these results agree with your intuition?

Our second example of a continuous bivariate distribution was introduced schematically in figure 3.3(b). In this, a point is selected at random from the shaded triangle, and X and Y are defined as the x- and y-coordinates of the point selected. The joint density function of X and Y is given by (3.17); this states the obvious fact that the density is uniform (at the value 2) over the triangle. The marginal density functions of X and Y are given by (3.20); these state that the distribution of X is 'right-triangular' on [0, 1], and that the distribution of Y is 'left-triangular' on [0, 1]. To find the conditional distributions of X and Y, we substitute (3.17) and (3.20) into (3.28). This gives:

$$\left.\begin{array}{l} g_Y(y \mid x) = \begin{cases} 1/x & 0 \leq y \leq x \\ 0 & \text{elsewhere} \end{cases} \quad (\text{if } 0 \leq x \leq 1) \\[2em] g_X(x \mid y) = \begin{cases} 1/(1-y) & y \leq x \leq 1 \\ 0 & \text{elsewhere} \end{cases} \quad (\text{if } 0 \leq y \leq 1). \end{array}\right\} \quad (3.30)$$

Let us interpret these results. The conditional density of Y (given $X = x$) does not depend upon y: indeed, it is constant at the value

$1/x$ over the range $[0, x]$. Thus, the conditional distribution of Y given $X = x$ is uniform over the range $[0, x]$. If you refer back to figure 3.3(a), you will see that this makes sense: given the information that X equals x (and given the random selection mechanism), it follows that Y is equally likely to be anywhere between 0 (the x-axis) and x (the value of Y on the diagonal corresponding to $X = x$). Similarly (3.30) states that the conditional distribution of X given $Y = y$ is uniform over the range $[y, 1]$. Again, if you refer back to figure 3.3(a), you will see that this makes sense: given the information that $Y = y$ (and given the random selection mechanism), it follows that X is equally likely to be anywhere between y (the value of X on the diagonal corresponding to $Y = y$) and 1 (the right-hand boundary of the triangle).

You will have noticed an important difference between the two examples. In the first example, the conditional distribution of Y given $X = x$ does not depend upon x; moreover, each conditional distribution is exactly the same as the marginal distribution (that is, $g_Y(y \mid x) = f_Y(y)$ for all y and x). Similarly, in the first example, the conditional distribution of X given $Y = y$ does not depend upon y; moreover, each conditional distribution is exactly the same as the marginal distribution (that is, $g_X(x \mid y) = f_X(x)$ for all x and y). It is clear, therefore, that in this first example, X and Y are *independent* variables (cf. (3.26)). In other words, knowledge of the value of X is uninformative as far as Y is concerned, and knowledge of the value of Y is uninformative as far as X is concerned.

In contrast, in the second example, X and Y are *dependent*: it is clear from (3.30) that the conditional distribution of Y *does* depend upon x, and that the conditional distribution of X *does* depend upon y. Moreover, the conditional distributions and corresponding unconditional (that is, marginal) distributions *are* different. Clearly, in this second example, knowledge of the value of X *is* informative as far as Y is concerned, and knowledge of the value of Y *is* informative as far as X is concerned. For example, if you are told that x is 0.5, then your assessment of Y is $U(0, 0.5)$, whereas if you are told that x is 0.1, your assessment of Y is $U(0, 0.1)$.

As the above discussion illustrates, the conditions for independence and dependence are the same in the continuous case as in the discrete case. Thus (3.26) is the definition of independence in both cases. Moreover, (3.27) is an implication of independence in both cases. To illustrate this latter point, consider again the two continuous examples. In the first example, the joint density function is given by (3.8) and the marginal density functions by (3.15); from these it can be seen that $f_{XY}(x, y) = f_X(x)f_Y(y)$ for all x and y. This reflects the independence of X and Y in this example. In contrast, in the second example, $f_{XY}(x, y)$ (given by (3.17)) is *not* equal to the product of $f_X(x)$ and $f_Y(y)$ (given by (3.20)). This reflects the dependence of X and Y in this example.

This completes our introduction to conditional distributions. The key elements of the material of this section are the definitions of the conditional probability functions (for the discrete case) and the conditional probability density functions (for the continuous case). Algebraically, these are equivalent, and are given by (3.24) and (3.25) (repeated in (3.28)). These show how the conditional distributions are defined in terms of the joint and marginal distributions. This section also generalized the key concept of independence (introduced in section 2.5 with respect to events) to cover independence between variables. As shown, independence between two variables is synonymous with uninformativeness (of each variable about the other).

3.5 MULTIVARIATE PROBABILITY DISTRIBUTIONS

Sections 3.2 to 3.4 examined the bivariate case – a situation in which there are two variables of interest. This section briefly extends the concepts introduced in sections 3.2 to 3.4 to the multivariate case. This case, as the terminology indicates, is when there are many variables of interest.

For a variety of reasons, which will become apparent shortly, it is useful to use *vector notation* in this section. If you are familiar with vector notation, you will recognize that the use of it in this section is merely a form of *shorthand*: it facilitates an enormous reduction in the length of the various algebraic expressions. Of course, the benefit of this reduction of algebraic clutter is a marked increase in the clarity of the exposition. Moreover, it enables us simply to carry over results from the bivariate case to the multivariate case. By so doing, the whole of the extension to the multivariate case is drastically shortened, and becomes merely a matter of appropriate reinterpretation of already familiar results.

Let us begin by introducing vector notation for those readers who are unfamiliar with it. Suppose we are interested in a set of m variables, called $X_1, X_2, \ldots, X_m$. To save writing '$X_1, X_2, \ldots, X_m$' repeatedly, we use the notation $\mathbf{X}$ as a shorthand for the set $(X_1, X_2, \ldots, X_m)$. Thus, the *vector* $\mathbf{X}$ is defined by

$$\mathbf{X} \equiv (X_1, X_2, \ldots, X_m). \tag{3.31}$$

Note that **X** is in **bold face**; this is a generally accepted notational convention for **vectors**. Of course, m could just be 1; that is, we could be interested in just 1 variable. In such a case X consists of the one element X_1, and is called a *scalar*. Thus, a scalar is a special (degenerate) case of a vector. Up to now (that is, in chapter 2 and in sections 3.1 to 3.4 of this chapter) we have been dealing solely with scalars; as we shall see, all this material can be straightforwardly generalized to vectors as well.

If we wish to refer to a specific set of values of the variables X_1, $X_2, \ldots, X_m$ – say $x_1, x_2, \ldots, x_m$ – then again we can use this vector shorthand. Thus, we write **x** as shorthand for the set $(x_1, x_2, \ldots, x_m)$. Furthermore, we can write equations using vectors. For example, the vector equation:

$$\mathbf{X} = \mathbf{x}$$

is shorthand for the set of m equations:

$$X_1 = x_1 \qquad X_2 = x_2 \qquad \ldots \qquad X_m = x_m.$$

Similarly, the expression

$$\mathbf{X} \leq \mathbf{x}$$

is shorthand for the set of m expressions

$$X_1 \leq x_1 \qquad X_2 \leq x_2 \qquad \ldots \qquad X_m \leq x_m.$$

Thus, '$P(\mathbf{X} \leq \mathbf{x})$' denotes 'the probability that X_1 is less than x_1, that X_2 is less than x_2, …, and that X_m is less than x_m'. It should be clear by now that this vector notation is indeed a very powerful shorthand.

In our discussion of the bivariate case, we considered two (scalar) variables X and Y. In order to draw as many parallels as possible with that discussion, we consider in this section two (vector) variables **X** and **Y**. We suppose that **X** consists of m variables, $X_1, X_2, \ldots, X_m$, and that **Y** consists of n variables, $Y_1, Y_2, \ldots, Y_n$. The total number of variables under discussion is thus $m + n$. Of course, m and n can take any (integer) values greater than or equal to 1. In the special case when both m and n are 1, then both **X** and **Y** are scalars, and the material of this section collapses to the bivariate case, as discussed in sections 3.2 to 3.4.

In this section, we are, therefore, discussing the most general case possible: a case in which we have a total of $m + n$ variables, $X_1, X_2, \ldots, X_m$ and $Y_1, Y_2, \ldots, Y_n$, where m and n can take any (integral) values greater than or equal to 1. In our shorthand notation the variables of interest are the vectors **X** and **Y**. Our concern in this section will be to extend the material of sections 3.2 to 3.4 to cover this vector case. Specifically, we will introduce and define the joint distribution of **X** and **Y**, the marginal distributions of **X** and **Y**, and the conditional distributions of **X** (given **Y** = **y**) and **Y** (given **X** = **x**).

As should be obvious by now, the only difference between this situation and the one faced at the beginning of section 3.2 is that now we are dealing with two *vectors* **X** and **Y**, whereas before we were dealing with two *scalars* X and Y. The obvious question to ask is: *can we carry over all the previous results on the bivariate scalar case to the bivariate vector case simply by changing the notation from scalars to vectors?* If we can, then, because the multivariate case and the bivariate vector case are one and the same, we will have completed the multivariate extension.

The answer, as you will probably have guessed by now, is that we can. Consider first the *discrete case*, and begin as usual with the joint distribution. In the bivariate scalar case, the joint (or bivariate) probability function is given by (3.4); the vector equivalent of this is:

$$f_{\mathbf{XY}}(\mathbf{x}, \mathbf{y}) = P(\mathbf{X} = \mathbf{x} \text{ and } \mathbf{Y} = \mathbf{y}). \tag{3.32}$$

In longhand, this states that the joint probability function of the $m + n$ variables, $X_1, X_2, \ldots, X_m, Y_1, Y_2, \ldots, Y_n$ at the value $x_1, x_2, \ldots, x_m, y_1, y_2, \ldots, y_n$ is given by the probability that $X_1 = x_1$, $X_2 = x_2, \ldots, X_m = x_m, Y_1 = y_1, Y_2 = y_2, \ldots$, and $Y_n = y_n$. From now on, we will omit the longhand interpretation, though you are recommended to do the interpretation yourself until you become thoroughly familiar with the shorthand notation.

Equation (3.32) is the multivariate probability function. It is a joint probability statement about the two vectors **X** and **Y** (or, equivalently, the $m + n$ variables $X_1, X_2, \ldots, X_m, Y_1, Y_2, \ldots, Y_n$). In a manner entirely analogous to the bivariate (scalar) case, the marginal distributions of **X** and **Y** can be defined and related to the joint distribution. In the bivariate (scalar) case, the relationships between the marginal and joint distributions is given by (3.11) and (3.12); the vector equivalents of these are:

$$f_{\mathbf{X}}(\mathbf{x}) = \sum_{\mathbf{y}} f_{\mathbf{XY}}(\mathbf{x}, \mathbf{y})$$

and

$$f_{\mathbf{Y}}(\mathbf{y}) = \sum_{\mathbf{x}} f_{\mathbf{XY}}(\mathbf{x}, \mathbf{y}). \tag{3.33}$$

In the first of these, the summation is over all values of (the vector) **y**, and in the second, the summation is over all values of (the vector) **x**.

Of course, $f_X(x)$ and $f_Y(y)$ have the familiar interpretation: the first measures the probability that $X = x$, and the second measures the probability that $Y = y$.

Similarly, conditional distributions can be defined and related to the joint and marginal distributions. In the bivariate (scalar) case, these relationships are given by (3.24) and (3.25); the vector equivalents of these are:

$$g_Y(y \mid x) = f_{XY}(x, y)/f_X(x)$$

and $\qquad\qquad\qquad\qquad\qquad\qquad\qquad$ (3.34)

$$g_X(x \mid y) = f_{XY}(x, y)/f_Y(y).$$

Once again, these distributions have the familiar interpretations. Thus, $g_Y(y \mid x)$ measures the conditional probability that Y equals y given that X equals x; similarly, $g_X(x \mid y)$ measures the conditional probability that X equals x given that Y equals y.

As before, we can define *independence* between (vector) variables. The scalar definition is given by (3.26); the vector equivalent of this is:

(Vector) variables X and Y are said to be *independent* if and only if $g_X(x \mid y) = f_X(x)$ and $g_Y(y \mid x) = f_Y(y)$ for $\qquad$ (3.35) all x and y.

As before, there is an important implication of independence: in the scalar case this is given in (3.27); the vector equivalent of this is:

(Vector) variables X and Y are independent if and only if $f_{XY}(x, y) = f_X(x)f_Y(y)$ for all x and y. $\qquad$ (3.36)

The extension to the multivariate (or bivariate vector) case in the *continuous case* goes through just as easily, *mutatis mutandis*. Thus, $f_{XY}(x, y)$ denotes the multivariate (or joint) probability density function of X and Y at the value $X = x$ and $Y = y$. The marginal density functions $f_X(.)$ and $f_Y(.)$ are related to this joint density function in a manner entirely analogous to the relationship in the bivariate scalar case (namely (3.13) and (3.14)). To be specific, the relationships are:

$$f_X(x) = \int_y f_{XY}(x, y)\, dy$$

and $\qquad\qquad\qquad\qquad\qquad\qquad\qquad$ (3.37)

$$f_Y(y) = \int_x f_{XY}(x, y)\, dx.$$

In the first of these the integration is carried out over all values of (the vector) **y**, and in the second the integration is carried out over all values of (the vector) **x**.

In the bivariate scalar case, the relationship between the *conditional* distribution and the joint and marginal distributions is the same whether the variables are discrete or continuous. The same is true in the multivariate (or bivariate vector) case. Thus (3.34) appropriately relates the conditional probability density functions of **Y** (given **X** = **x**) and **X** (given **Y** = **y**) to the joint and marginal density functions. It follows, therefore, that the conditions and implications of independence are also the same in the continuous case. Thus, (3.35) and (3.36) apply equally well to both discrete and continuous variables.

Note that (3.36) says that if two (vector or scalar) variables are independent then their joint probability (density) function can be expressed as the product of their marginal probability (density) functions. It should be clear that repeated application of this result can be used to show that if a *set* of scalar variables are all mutually independent, then their joint probability (density) function can be expressed as the product of all their individual marginal probability (density) functions. As this is an important result, which we shall use on a number of occasions in the following chapters, let us express it formally.

$$
\left.
\begin{aligned}
&\text{If } \mathbf{X} \equiv (X_1, X_2, \ldots, X_m) \text{ is such that } X_1, X_2, \ldots, X_m \\
&\text{are all independent of each other, then} \\[2mm]
&f_{\mathbf{X}}(\mathbf{x}) = f_{X_1}(x_1) f_{X_2}(x_2) \cdots f_{X_m}(x_m) \equiv \prod_{i \equiv 1}^{m} f_{X_i}(x_i) \\[2mm]
&\text{for all } \mathbf{x} \equiv (x_1, x_2, \ldots, x_m).
\end{aligned}
\right\} \quad (3.38)
$$

(If you are not familiar with the '$\prod$' shorthand, see Appendix A1.)

For example, suppose that $X_1, X_2, \ldots, X_m$ are independent of each other and all have beta distributions (see section 2.4); specifically, suppose that X_i is $B(\alpha_i, \beta_i)$ $(i = 1, 2, \ldots, m)$. Then (see (2.27)),

$$
f_{X_i}(x_i) \propto x_i^{\alpha_i - 1}(1 - x_i)^{\beta_i - 1} \qquad (i = 1, 2, \ldots, m),
$$

and hence the joint probability density function of $\mathbf{X} \equiv (X_1, X_2, \ldots, X_m)$ is given by (using (3.38)):

$$
f_{\mathbf{X}}(\mathbf{x}) \propto \prod_{i \equiv 1}^{m} x_i^{\alpha_i - 1}(1 - x_i)^{\beta_i - 1}.
$$

This concludes our treatment of multivariate distributions for the time being. As should be apparent, if we use vector notation, there is nothing 'new' in the multivariate case as compared with the bivariate case. Thus, repeated application of the ideas and results in the bivariate scalar case is sufficient to cover the most general multivariate case.

3.6 SUMMARIES

Throughout the whole of the above discussion, we have been dealing with *complete characterizations* of probability assessments. Thus, for discrete variables we have been concerned with the form of various probability *functions*, while, for continuous variables, we have been concerned with the form of various probability density *functions*. However, as in the univariate case discussed in chapter 2, such complete characterizations may be excessive for our purposes. We might prefer, or it might be simpler, to deal with a few summary measures.

In section 2.3, we discussed such summaries in so far as they related to univariate distributions. In particular, we examined (minimum width) probability intervals, and various measures of central tendency and of dispersion. Clearly, such measures can be applied to any univariate distribution. It follows that they can be used to provide summaries of the marginal and conditional distributions in the bivariate scalar case, and in the bivariate vector case where the appropriate one of m or n is 1.

Generally, such summaries of univariate distributions will be sufficient for our purposes. But there will be a few occasions in which we will require summary measures of a bivariate (scalar or vector) distribution. It is the purpose of this section to introduce some of the appropriate summary measures.

What we are looking for, then, are summary measures of the *joint* distribution of two variables. For simplicity, we will confine attention to the case of two scalar variables, but the material can be straightforwardly extended to the vector case. Two such measures will be examined: the first being the natural generalization of the (minimum width) probability interval concept used in the univariate case; the second being a *measure of association* closely related to the main measure of central tendency and measure of dispersion used in the univariate case.

You will recall that, in the univariate case, the α per cent (minimum width) probability interval was defined as that interval

$[x_1, x_2]$ for which $P(x_1 \leq X \leq x_2) = \alpha/100$ and for which $x_2 - x_1$ was as small as possible. The natural generalization of this to the bivariate case is the α *per cent* (*minimum area*) *probability region*. By this we mean a region R in (X, Y) space such that $P[(x, y)$ is in R] $= \alpha/100$ and such that the area of R is as small as possible. If the bivariate distribution is unimodal, it can be shown that the boundary of the region R is given by $f_{XY}(x, y) = $ constant. (You may recall that in the unimodal univariate case, the end-points of the minimum width probability interval satisfied $f_X(x_1) = f_X(x_2)$. The condition stated above is the natural generalization of this.) Readers familiar with economics will recognize this condition as a typical indifference curve, or isoquant, definition. To be specific, the condition, $f_{XY}(x, y) = $ constant, defines the (*constant*) *probability density isoquants* of the joint distribution. If you imagine the joint probability density function as a (single-peaked) hill in three-dimensional space, then these probability density isoquants are simply the contour lines of the hill. An illustrative contour map is shown in figure 3.4 (the precise values of $f_{XY}(., .)$ associated with each isoquant are not

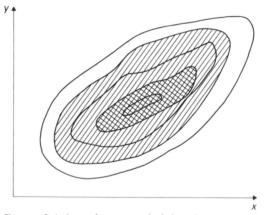

Figure 3.4 Introducing probability density isoquants

shown). Also illustrated in this figure are two examples of (minimum area) probability regions: the cross-hatched region showing the 50 per cent (minimum area) probability region, and the larger shaded region the 90 per cent (minimum area) probability region.

The precise form of the isoquant map depends crucially, of course, on the form of the joint distribution. One particular distribution which we shall encounter from time to time later in the book is the *bivariate normal distribution*. This is the natural bivariate extension of the (univariate) normal distribution introduced in section 2.4. The general form of the bivariate normal probability density function is given in exercise 3.12; here we look at a special case which is useful for illustrative purposes. Suppose X and Y have the joint probability density function

$$f_{XY}(x, y) \propto \exp\left\{-(x^2 - 2\rho xy + y^2)/[2(1 - \rho^2)]\right\}. \tag{3.39}$$

(You may be able to show that both the marginal distributions are unit normal.) Then the probability density isoquants are given by:

$$x^2 - 2\rho xy + y^2 = \text{constant}. \tag{3.40}$$

The shape of these depends critically on ρ: if ρ is zero, (3.40) represents a set of concentric circles centred on the origin, as in figure 3.5(a); if ρ is positive, (3.40) represents a set of concentric ellipses with positive main diagonals, as in figures 3.5(b) and (c). Moreover, the larger is ρ the longer and thinner are the ellipses. If ρ is negative, then the isoquants are concentric ellipses with negative main diagonals; moreover, the more negative is ρ the longer and thinner are the ellipses. (The case of negative ρ is not illustrated.)

One thing that may have become apparent is that the isoquant map is conveying information about the form of the *relationship between* the two variables. Specifically, in figure 3.5(a) there appears to be no relationship between X and Y, whereas in figures 3.5(b) and (c) there appears to be a *positive* relationship. (Note that when $\rho = 0$, the joint density (3.39) can be written as proportional to $\exp(-x^2/2) \times \exp(-y^2/2)$, which is proportional to the product of the marginal

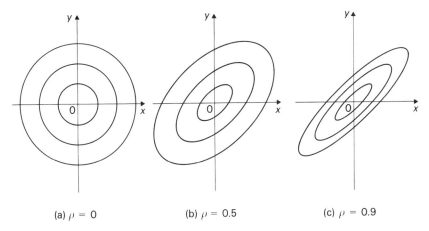

(a) $\rho = 0$ (b) $\rho = 0.5$ (c) $\rho = 0.9$

Figure 3.5 Probability density isoquants for some bivariate normals

densities. Thus, using (3.27), X and Y are independent when $\rho = 0$.) Moreover, the relationship in figure 3.5(c) appears to be stronger than that in figure 3.5(b).

An alternative, and much more succinct, way of summarizing this form of relationship between the two variables X and Y is using the *covariance* summary measure. This is denoted by cov (X, Y), and is defined, for discrete variables by

$$\text{cov } (X, Y) = \sum_x \sum_y (x - EX)(y - EY)f_{XY}(x, y) \qquad (3.41)$$

and for continuous variables by

$$\text{cov } (X, Y) = \int_x \int_y (x - EX)(y - EY)f_{XY}(x, y) \, dx \, dy. \qquad (3.42)$$

A closely related measure is the *correlation coefficient* between X and Y, denoted by r_{XY} (or simply by r if no confusion results from dropping the subscripts), and defined by

$$r_{XY} = \frac{\text{cov } (X, Y)}{(\text{sd } X)(\text{sd } Y)} \qquad (3.43)$$

It can be shown that r_{XY} always lies between -1 and $+1$, and that it is a *measure of the degree of linear association*. Specifically, r_{XY} equals 0 if there is no linear association between X and Y; it equals -1 if there is a perfect negative linear association; and it equals $+1$ if there is a perfect positive linear association. As it happens, in the case of the bivariate normal distribution, r_{XY} equals the ρ in (3.39). We will have more to say about the correlation coefficient later in the book.

3.7   SUMMARY

This chapter has been concerned with generalizing the basic probability concepts introduced in chapter 2 to the bivariate and multivariate cases. We began with the bivariate case, first introducing the notion of a *joint* probability distribution of the two variables, then showing how the *marginal* distributions (of each variable by itself) are related to the joint distribution. We then introduced the vitally important notion of a *conditional* probability distribution – which is the distribution of one variable given some specific information about the other. It was shown how the conditional, joint and marginal distributions are related to each other. The important relationship of *independence* between variables was introduced and defined. All these concepts and ideas were then extended to the multivariate case, by the simple device of using vector notation, and re-writing all our previous scalar results in vector terms. Finally, some possible summary measures for the bivariate case were briefly discussed.

If one feature of this chapter were to be singled out as having supreme importance it would be the concept of a *conditional distribution*. As we shall see in the next chapter, and in the succeeding ones, it is this concept which is crucial for the modelling of the incorporation of new information into probability assessments.

3.8 EXERCISES

* You should tackle these exercises (or parts of exercises) only if you are familiar with basic integral calculus.

3.1 Consider the experiment of tossing an (agreed fair) coin twice. Let X be defined as 1 (0) if a head (tail) occurs on the first toss, and let Y be defined as 1 (0) if a head (tail) occurs on the second toss. Find the joint, marginal and conditional probability functions (in tabular form). (There is one joint, two marginal and a total of four conditional distributions.) Are X and Y independent?

3.2 Consider the experiment of tossing an (agreed fair) coin four times. Let X be defined as the number of heads obtained, and Y as the number of tails observed before the first head (take Y as 4 if no heads at all are observed). Find the joint, marginal and conditional probability functions (in tabular form). (There is one joint, two marginal and a total of ten conditional distributions.) Are X and Y independent?

3.3 Find the conditional probability function of X (in tabular form) for the two-dice example discussed in sections 3.2 to 3.4.

3.4 Show that in the two-dice example, $Y = 3$ is uninformative as far as X is concerned.

3.5 Suppose the joint probability function of the discrete variables X and Y is given by

$$f_{XY}(x, y) = (x + y)/21 \qquad x = 1, 2, 3 \qquad y = 1, 2.$$

Find the marginal and conditional distributions. Are X and Y independent?

3.6   Suppose the joint probability function of the discrete variables X and Y is given by

$$f_{XY}(x, y) = xy^2/30 \qquad x = 1, 2, 3 \qquad y = 1, 2.$$

Find the marginal and conditional distributions. Are X and Y independent?

3.7   Verify (3.20) directly from the definition of the triangle experiment. (Hint: consider first the probability that X lies between x and $x + \Delta x$; by examining the appropriate area in the triangle show that this equals $[x \, \Delta x + \frac{1}{2}(\Delta x)^2]/0.5$. Thus, the probability density of x in the interval $[x, x + \Delta x]$ is $2x + \Delta x$. Hence the probability density at x is $2x$.)

3.8   In the text, two examples of continuous bivariate distributions were given: one based on the unit square and the other based on the bottom right triangle of this square. Consider a third example based on the upper left triangle. For this example find (in algebraic form) the joint, marginal and conditional probability density functions. Are X and Y independent?

3.9*   Suppose a selection mechanism chooses a point in the unit square such that the joint probability density function of the point selected is given by

$$f_{XY}(x, y) = \begin{cases} 4(1 - x)(1 - y) & 0 \le x \le 1 \qquad 0 \le y \le 1 \\ 0 & \text{elsewhere.} \end{cases}$$

Find the marginal and conditional probability density functions. Are X and Y independent?

3.10*   Suppose a selection mechanism chooses a point in the unit square such that the joint probability density function of the point selected is given by

$$f_{XY}(x, y) = \begin{cases} x + y & 0 \le x \le 1 \qquad 0 \le y \le 1 \\ 0 & \text{elsewhere.} \end{cases}$$

Find the marginal and conditional probability density functions. Are X and Y independent?

3.11*   Suppose X is $U(0, 2)$ and suppose that the conditional distribution of Y given $X = x$ is $U(0, x^2)$. Find the joint density function, and the marginal density function of Y. Find the conditional distribution of X, given $Y = y$; hence find the mean of X given $Y = y$.

3.12* The variables X and Y are said to have a bivariate normal distribution if their joint probability density function is given by:

$$f_{XY}(x, y) = \exp \left\{ -\frac{1}{2(1 - \rho^2)} (z_X^2 - 2\rho z_X z_Y + z_Y^2) \right\}$$

$$\div \{ 2\pi \sigma_X \sigma_Y (1 - \rho^2)^{1/2} \}$$

where $z_X = (x - \mu_X)/\sigma_X$ and $z_Y = (y - \mu_Y)/\sigma_Y$.
Show that marginal density function of X is given by

$$f_X(x) = \exp \{ -\tfrac{1}{2} z_X^2 \} / \{ (2\pi)^{1/2} \sigma_X \},$$

and hence that X is $N(\mu_X, \sigma_X^2)$.
Similarly show that Y is $N(\mu_Y, \sigma_Y^2)$. Show further that the conditional density function of Y given $X = x$ is:

$$g_Y(y \mid x) = \exp \left\{ -\frac{1}{2(1 - \rho^2)} [z_Y - \rho(\sigma_Y/\sigma_X) z_X]^2 \right\}$$

$$\div \{ [2\pi(1 - \rho^2)]^{1/2} \sigma_Y \}.$$

Interpret this result.
What is the conditional distribution of X given $Y = y$?

3.13* Consider the distribution as given in exercise 3.10. Show that the $66\tfrac{2}{3}$ per cent (minimum area) probability region is the triangle to the north-east of the downward sloping diagonal of the square.

3.14 Suppose the joint probability density function of X and Y is given by

$$f_{XY}(x, y) = \begin{cases} 2e^{-x-y} & 0 \le x \le y < \infty \\ 0 & \text{elsewhere.} \end{cases}$$

* Find the marginal density functions of X and Y. Are X and Y independent?

3.15 Suppose the joint probability density function of X and Y is given by

$$f_{XY}(x, y) = \begin{cases} e^{-x-y} & 0 \le x < \infty \quad 0 \le y < \infty \\ 0 & \text{elsewhere.} \end{cases}$$

  * Find the marginal and conditional density functions. Are X and Y independent?

3.16 Suppose that the joint probability density function of X and Y is given by

$$f_{XY}(x, y) \propto \begin{cases} (xy)^{\alpha - 1} e^{-\beta(x+y)} & 0 < x \quad 0 < y \\ 0 & \text{elsewhere.} \end{cases}$$

Argue that X and Y are independent and that each is $G(\alpha, \beta)$ (see section 2.4).

4 INFORMATION

Up till now, we have been concerned with the description and summarization of probability assessments as they exist at some given
point in time; that is, relative to some given set of information. We
now consider how these probability assessments change in the light
of new information. Thus, this chapter is concerned with examining
how new information is incorporated into existing probability
assessments.

We are interested in how new information affects probability
assessments. To distinguish between the assessment *before* the information is received and the assessment *after* the information is
received and incorporated, the former are termed the *prior beliefs*,
and the latter the *posterior beliefs*. The word 'beliefs' is used to
emphasize that the probability assessments continue to be viewed as
the subjective assessment of some individual. (It should be mentioned that the adjectives 'prior' and 'posterior' are (unfortunately)
accepted usage amongst Bayesian statisticians; '*ex ante*' and '*ex post*'
would be preferred qualifiers, particularly amongst economists, but
convention is too deeply ingrained.)

The posterior beliefs clearly depend partly on the prior beliefs and
partly on the new information. Moreover, the relative weights given
to the prior beliefs and the new information, in determining the
posterior beliefs, clearly depend upon the strength of the prior beliefs
relative to the confidence placed in the new information. It is the
purpose of this chapter to formalize, and make precise, this relationship between posterior and prior beliefs and new information. As we
shall see, this formalization is accomplished through the use of
Bayes' theorem, which we met for the first time in section 2.5.

Bayes' theorem is re-encountered in section 4.3. In the meantime,
in section 4.2, we pave the way by examining some simple examples
of the incorporation of new information. We then formalize these
ideas through the use of Bayes' theorem in section 4.3, before going

on to apply the theorem to several important examples in sections 4.4 and 4.5. The applications in section 4.4 are all concerned with events, while those in section 4.5 are concerned with variables. By this point, we will have become reasonably familiar with the way that new information affects prior beliefs. We will thus be ready for a brief, introductory, discussion of what might be meant by 'non-existent' prior information, or 'total prior ignorance'. This introduction is given in section 4.6; as we will see, this material will prove useful for those situations where it is felt totally incapable of making any prior judgement of any kind (and thus need to rely totally on the new information for our posterior beliefs). The chapter concludes with a summary in section 4.7, and a set of exercises in section 4.8.

4.2   THE INCORPORATION OF NEW INFORMATION:
SIMPLE EXAMPLES

Perhaps the simplest examples of the incorporation of new information are those in which the new information is such that it completely eliminates all uncertainty. To recall an example used in chapter 2, suppose we are interested in the variable X defined as the author's age on 26 September 1984. Since you probably do not know the true value of X, your assessment of X will be subject to some degree of uncertainty. For example, depending on what you know, or are prepared to hazard, about me, your assessment of X may be $U(36, 42)$ or $U(30, 50)$, or $U(20, 80)$ or $N(40, 9)$ or $N(38, 4)$ or whatever. But suppose I now tell you that I was born on 26 September 1944. Assuming that you believe me (that is, that you regard the information as accurate), then all residual uncertainty about X has been eliminated: you know for a fact that X is 40. Thus, whatever your prior beliefs about X, your posterior beliefs are $U(40, 40)$ (or, equivalently, $N(40, 0)$ – both these representing distributions degenerate at the value 40). It is clear in this case that, if the information is regarded as accurate, then there is a 'rational' way of arriving at the posterior beliefs: it would be irrational to hold any posterior beliefs other than that X equals 40. These notions of 'rationality' can be generalized, as we shall see in due course. (We leave for the time being the interesting question of the derivation of the posterior distribution for cases in which the information is not regarded as accurate, but instead is treated with some suspicion. You may like to consider yourself what you would do in such cases.)

A second simple example in which a particular piece of information completely eliminates all uncertainty is as follows. Suppose a rather shady-looking character accosts you on a train, and suggests that you toss for a fiver using a coin he has produced from his pocket, but refuses to let you inspect. According to him, it is a perfectly ordinary (fair) coin; but you, being naturally cautious, fear that it may be double headed. You are, however, open-minded, and prepared to admit that there is (in your mind) a 50 : 50 chance that he is telling the truth. In turn, he is prepared to have a trial toss – to calm your fears. Suppose this trial toss results in a tail; then (relative to your prior beliefs) all residual uncertainty has been eliminated. The coin is clearly not double-headed, and you must thus conclude that the coin is fair. (Note carefully, that this example is rather extreme, in that the prior beliefs allowed only two possibilities – that the coin was fair or that it was double-headed. In practice, you might prefer to consider other possibilities – such as a bias in favour of heads.) Thus, when the new information is 'a tail', all residual uncertainty is eliminated. Note, however, that if the new information was 'a head', then some residual uncertainty would remain (though the odds would now be in favour of the coin being double-headed).

In these two simple examples, a particular piece of information completely *eliminates* all residual uncertainty. These are rather unusual examples: the more usual case is when information *reduces* the amount of uncertainty, rather than eliminates it completely. Consider, once again, the variable X defined as the author's age on 26 September 1984. Imagine that you do not know the author's date of birth, and that your assessment of X is $U(36, 42)$. Suppose I now give you the information that I was born on or after 26 September 1943 (a date forty-one years before the date defining X). What is your posterior assessment about X in the light of this information (assuming that you believe it to be true)? Presumably, $U(36, 41)$. (Before the information, you thought all values of X between 36 and 42 equally likely; the information says that X is less than or equal to 41; thus, it seems right to conclude that all values of X between 36 and 41 should now be regarded as equally likely.) Further, suppose I now told you that I was born on or before 26 September 1946 (a date thirty-eight years before the date defining X). What is your posterior assessment about X in the light of this further piece of information (assuming that you believe it to be true)? Presumably, $U(38, 41)$.

We can generalize these examples. Suppose that someone's prior beliefs about a variable X are $U(a, b)$ where a is less than b. Given the (believed true) information that X is less than or equal to d

(where $a < d < b$), then the posterior beliefs must be $U(a, d)$. Further, given the (believed true) information that X is greater than or equal to c (where $a < c < d$), then the posterior beliefs must now be $U(c, d)$.

This example can also be used to illustrate a phenomenon that we have already encountered in chapters 2 and 3: namely, a situation in which so-called information is uninformative. Suppose that someone's prior beliefs about a variable X are $U(a, b)$. Suppose now that this person is given the 'information' that X is greater than c, *where c is less than a*. Clearly, this 'information' cannot affect the assessment about X, since the prior beliefs already postulated that X was greater than c. Thus, the posterior beliefs remain $U(a, b)$. In this case, the so-called information is uninformative. (Though this is not to deny that it might not be informative to someone else; for example, someone whose prior on X was $U(e, f)$, where $e < c < f$.)

Additionally, recalling the discussion of independence in sections 2.5 and 3.4, information is uninformative about some variable or event if the information is independent of that variable or event. For example, being told the value of some variable Y is uninformative about the variable X if the variables X and Y are independent. Formally, this is expressed by the condition for independence between variables (3.26), namely:

$$g_X(x \mid y) = f_X(x) \qquad \text{for all } x \text{ and } y. \tag{4.1}$$

In terms of the terminology of this chapter, $g_X(. \mid y)$ encapsulates the *posterior beliefs* about the variable X in the light of the information that Y equals y, while $f_X(.)$ encapsulates the *prior beliefs* about X. Equation (4.1) states the obvious fact that if X and Y are independent, then the posterior beliefs (after receiving the 'information' y) are exactly the same as the prior beliefs. Thus, the 'information' has not changed the assessment. Again, this appears to be a perfectly 'rational' reaction. For instance, you are unlikely to change your views about my age by knowing that the FT index closed at 556.5 on Friday, 30 July 1982.

This section has considered two extreme cases: the first in which a piece of information completely eliminates all residual uncertainty; the second in which so-called 'information' has no effect on the prior probability assessment. This section also considered briefly one example of an intermediate case – that is, one in which the information changes the prior assessment, and, in so doing, reduces the amount of uncertainty but does not eliminate it completely. In the next section, we consider this intermediate case in more detail.

4.3 THE INCORPORATION OF NEW INFORMATION:
BAYES' THEOREM

Let us start with one of the simplest applications of Bayes' theorem. Suppose we are interested in the occurrence or non-occurrence of some event F. For illustrative purposes you might like to take a concrete example; for instance, suppose that F is the event that it will rain tomorrow. Let $\bar{F}$ denote the non-occurrence of the event F; thus, in our illustration, $\bar{F}$ is the event that it will not rain tomorrow. Clearly, one and only one of F and $\bar{F}$ must happen: in statistical terminology, they are *mutually exclusive* and *exhaustive* events. Now, based on your general knowledge and experience, and given the state of the weather today, you will be able to form some judgement of the relative likelihood of F and $\bar{F}$. In other words, you will be able to form some assessment of $P(F)$ and $P(\bar{F})$. (It may not be a very 'good' assessment in an 'objective' sense, if that phrase has any meaning, but that is irrelevant. We are interested in *your* assessment and how it changes in the light of new information you receive.) Clearly, for your assessment to be 'rational', the two probabilities must be such that they sum to 1; that is,

$$P(F) + P(\bar{F}) = 1. \tag{4.2}$$

For the moment, we assume that both probabilities are non-zero; that is, $P(F) > 0$ and $P(\bar{F}) > 0$. In due course, we will examine what happens if one of the two probabilities is zero. (Thus, if you live somewhere – the Sahara Desert or Manchester? – where one or other of the two events, $\bar{F}$ and F, looks certain to occur, you should adopt a different illustrative example!)

Now suppose you decide to listen to the weather forecast for tomorrow. That forecast is an item of *information*. In practice, the information obtainable from a typical weather forecast is multi-dimensioned, but let us suppose for the time being that it takes a particularly simple form: either a prediction that it will rain tomorrow or a prediction that it will not rain tomorrow. Let us denote the former by E and the latter by $\bar{E}$. Thus, the event E is (the information) that the weather forecast predicts that it will rain tomorrow; similarly, the event $\bar{E}$ is (the information) that the weather forecast predicts that it will not rain tomorrow.

Suppose now that the forecast is for rain tomorrow. (Using our notation, event E has occurred.) What is your assessment of F now? Presumably, this depends on how much faith you place in weather forecasts, and how much on your own prior beliefs. This can be formalized. What we want to determine is $P(F \mid E)$ – the probability of F given the information E. Using the third law of probability, (2.38), this is given by

$$P(F \mid E) = P(E \text{ and } F)/P(E).$$

The numerator of this can be expanded using the third law of probability a second time. This gives

$$P(F \mid E) = \frac{P(E \mid F)P(F)}{P(E)} \tag{4.3}$$

This equation, which is the simplest form of Bayes' theorem, we have already encountered, as equation (2.40) in section 2.5. It can be interpreted in a number of ways, the simplest being as follows: according to (4.3) the *posterior probability* of F (in the light of the information E) is given by the *prior probability* of F multiplied by the ratio $P(E \mid F)/P(E)$. What is the interpretation of this ratio? In terms of our specific example, the numerator represents the probability of the weather forecast correctly predicting rain when it occurs; the denominator is simply the probability that the forecast predicts rain. Thus, the ratio is the relative likelihood of a correct rain prediction. More generally, the ratio is the relative likelihood of getting the information E when F is to happen. Or, more simply, the ratio is the *relative likelihood of E given F*.

Suppose you are a cynic in that you believe weather forecasts are useless (though not deliberately misleading). Your cynicism could be expressed in the following way:

$$P(E \mid F) = P(E \mid \bar{F}) \tag{4.4}$$

or, equivalently, by

$$P(\bar{E} \mid F) = P(\bar{E} \mid \bar{F}). \tag{4.5}$$

Equation (4.4) says the probability of a forecast of rain is the same whether it is going to rain or not, while (4.5) says that the probability of a forecast of no rain is the same whether it is going to rain or not. Note that (4.4) implies (4.5) and vice versa, since $P(E \mid F) + P(\bar{E} \mid F)$ must equal 1, as must $P(E \mid \bar{F}) + P(\bar{E} \mid \bar{F})$. Note also, very important-ly, that (4.4) also implies that both $P(E \mid F)$ and $P(E \mid \bar{F})$ equal $P(E)$; in other words, the conditional probabilities of E and the unconditional probability are equal. This can be proved as follows. Consider the event E; since this must happen with one and only one of F and $\bar{F}$, we can write

$$E \equiv (E \text{ and } F) \text{ or } (E \text{ and } \bar{F}), \tag{4.6}$$

using the notation of section 2.5. This equation simply states that for E to happen, either E and F must happen or E and $\bar{F}$ must happen. Further, since the events $(E$ and $F)$ and $(E$ and $\bar{F})$ clearly cannot both happen, we can apply the second law of probability (2.36) to (4.6) to get

$$P(E) = P(E \text{ and } F) + P(E \text{ and } \bar{F}).$$

We can now use the third law of probability (2.38) to expand the two terms on the right-hand side of this expression, thus getting

$$P(E) = P(E \mid F)P(F) + P(E \mid \bar{F})P(\bar{F}). \tag{4.7}$$

Equation (4.7) states the rather obvious fact that, for E to happen, either F must happen and then, given that, E must happen or F must not happen and then, given that, E must happen.

Now suppose (4.4) holds; substituting this in (4.7) gives

$$P(E) = P(E \mid F)[P(F) + P(\bar{F})] = P(E \mid F) \text{ since } P(F) + P(\bar{F}) = 1.$$

Thus, the conditional probabilities $P(E \mid F)$ and $P(E \mid \bar{F})$ and the unconditional probability $P(E)$ are all equal, if your cynical view about weather forecasting, as represented by (4.4), holds. In a similar fashion, we can show that (4.5) (which is implied by (4.4)) also implies that $P(\bar{E} \mid F)$ and $P(\bar{E} \mid \bar{F})$ are both equal to $P(\bar{E})$. If we now return to Bayes' theorem, equation (4.3), we see that (4.4) implies that

$$P(F \mid E) = P(F),$$

since the relative likelihood ratio $P(E \mid F)/P(E)$ is 1. Thus, we conclude that the cynical view of the value of forecasting, as represented by (4.4), means that the posterior probability of F is the same as the prior probability: the 'information' E has not changed the assessment.

But, I can hear you saying, this is all familiar stuff; we have heard it all before. All that has been done is to 'rediscover' the implications of independence. This cynicism notion, as embodied in (4.4), is nothing more than independence. All that has been shown is that, if the 'information' is independent of the thing in which we are interested, then the 'information' is uninformative. This is quite true. Indeed, it is clear that we can state this perfectly generally: *if the information is independent of the thing in which we are interested, then* the relative likelihood ratio is one, and the *posterior assessment is identical with the prior assessment.*

Let us now examine another extreme case. Suppose weather forecasts are always perfectly reliable, or, at least, you believe them to be so. This implies that

$$P(E \mid F) = 1 \qquad P(\bar{E} \mid F) = 0 \qquad P(E \mid \bar{F}) = 0 \qquad P(\bar{E} \mid \bar{F}) = 1.$$
(4.8)

In words, the first two of these (each of which implies the other) state that rain is always preceded by a forecast of rain; and the final two (each of which implies the other) state that lack of rain is always preceded by a forecast of lack of rain. Note that the first two do not imply the final two, or vice versa; for example, it could be the case that every rainy day is preceded by a forecast of rain, yet not every not-rainy day preceded by a non-rain forecast. If we substitute (4.8) into (4.7) we see that perfect forecasting, as embodied in (4.8), implies that

$$P(E) = P(F).$$

If we then substitute this, and (4.8) into Bayes' theorem (4.3), we get

$$P(F \mid E) = 1.$$

Thus, with perfect forecasting, the posterior assessment of rain given a forecast of rain is 1, irrespective of the prior assessment. This is an obviously sensible result.

One final extreme case is of interest: suppose you think that the forecast is deliberately and perfectly perverse, as embodied in

$$P(E \mid F) = 0 \qquad P(\bar{E} \mid F) = 1 \qquad P(E \mid \bar{F}) = 1 \qquad P(\bar{E} \mid \bar{F}) = 0.$$
(4.9)

(You should check that this is the appropriate embodiment.) Combining (4.9) and (4.7) in (4.3), this implies

$$P(F \mid E) = 0.$$

Thus, with perfectly perverse forecasting, the posterior assessment of rain given a forecast of rain is 0, irrespective of the prior assessment. Again, this is an obviously sensible result.

Let us now consider the intermediate cases. In between useless forecasts (as encapsulated by (4.4) and/or (4.5)) and perfect forecasts (as embodied by (4.8)) are forecasts which are 'better than nothing, but not perfect'. These are characterized by

$$P(E \mid F) > P(E) > P(E \mid \bar{F})$$
(4.10)

or, equivalently, by

$$P(\bar{E}\,|\,F) < P(\bar{E}) < P(\bar{E}\,|\,\bar{F}). \tag{4.11}$$

(A number of inter-relationships between and among (4.10) and (4.11) should be noted before proceeding. First (4.10) implies (4.11) and vice versa. Second, any two of the inequalities in (4.10) imply the third. Finally, and similarly, any two of the inequalities in (4.11) imply the third.) If (4.10) and (4.11) hold, it follows that the relative likelihood ratio $P(E\,|\,F)/P(E)$ is greater than 1. Thus, from Bayes' theorem (4.3), it follows that

$$P(F\,|\,E) > P(F).$$

Obviously, it must also be the case (see exercise 4.4) that

$$P(\bar{F}\,|\,E) < P(\bar{F}).$$

Thus, with forecasts that are 'better than nothing, but not perfect', a forecast of rain leads to an upward revision in the probability assessment of rain, and a downward revision in the probability assessment of no-rain. These results are obviously sensible. Clearly there is a parallel argument for forecasts that are 'misleading, but not perfectly so'.

We can summarize the above discussion: with perfectly good forecasts, the posterior assessment $P(F\,|\,E)$ is 1 irrespective of the value of $P(F)$; with quite good forecasts, the posterior probability is greater than the prior; with useless forecasts, the posterior is the same as the prior; with partially perverse forecasts, the posterior is smaller than the prior; and with perfectly perverse forecasts, the posterior is 0, irrespective of the value of the prior. Thus, the probability assessment is revised upwards or downwards in the light of the information, the direction and magnitude of the revision depending upon the quality of the forecasts (in the sense of their relationship to the actual outcome). These implications of Bayes' theorem (4.3) all make excellent sense.

One further implication should be noted. It is clear from (4.7) that $P(E)$ is a weighted average of $P(E\,|\,F)$ and $P(E\,|\,\bar{F})$, the weights being $P(F)$ and $P(\bar{F})$ which sum to 1. Thus, for any given pair $P(E\,|\,F)$ and $P(E\,|\,\bar{F})$ for which $P(E\,|\,F)$ is greater than $P(E\,|\,\bar{F})$ ('better than nothing' forecasts), then the greater is $P(F)$ the greater will be $P(E)$. This means that the greater is $P(F)$ the smaller is the relative likelihood ratio $P(E\,|\,F)/P(E)$. It therefore follows from Bayes' Theorem (4.3), that the greater is $P(F)$ the smaller is $P(F\,|\,E) - P(F)$. This embodies the intuitive notion that the more firmly you hold your prior beliefs the less they are revised by any given information.

All of the above analysis is based on the assumption that both F and $\bar{F}$ have a non-zero prior probability; that is, $P(F) > 0$ and $P(\bar{F}) > 0$. For completeness, let us now analyze the case when one of them is zero. (Obviously they cannot both be zero, as their sum must be 1.) Suppose, for example, that $P(\bar{F}) = 0$ and so $P(F) = 1$. If you look at Bayes' Theorem (4.3) you will see that this implies that $P(F \mid E) = P(E \mid F)/P(E)$. But, from (4.7), the same condition implies that $P(E) = P(E \mid F)$. It follows, therefore, that if $P(F) = 1$ then $P(F \mid E) = 1$. Thus, the information does not change the assessment. The same is true when $P(F) = 0$; in which case $P(F \mid E)$ is also zero.

This completes our first analysis of Bayes' theorem. Our purpose in this section has been to explore the theorem in its simplest form. In particular, we have been concerned to show that the way it models the incorporation of new information into existing probability assessments is intuitively acceptable, and that the relationship between the posterior and prior assessments and the new information which it yields conforms with intuition. Of course, this appeal to intuition is not necessary to justify the *logical correctness* of Bayes' theorem (since the theorem is a logical implication of the three simple probability laws introduced in chapter 2), but it is reassuring to verify that logic and intuition march hand in hand.

4.4   SOME APPLICATIONS OF BAYES' THEOREM FOR EVENTS

Although in formal terms, the version of Bayes' theorem for events presented in equation (4.3) is perfectly general, and can be applied to any kind of probability updating problem for events, it is not a particularly *practical* version. This section begins, therefore, by deriving a rather more practical version. We then present a number of applications.

In the previous section, we restricted attention to a case in which only one event F, and its non-occurrence $\bar{F}$, were of interest. In this section we generalize by supposing that there are I events of interest, denoted by F_1, F_2, ..., F_I. We assume that these I events are *mutually exclusive and exhaustive*; that is, that one and only one of the events can occur. (Formally, this means that the event (F_i and F_j) is impossible for $i \neq j$, and that the event (F_1 or F_2 or ... or F_I) encompasses all possibilities.)

The prior assessments of these I events are denoted by $P(F_i)$ ($i = 1, 2, ..., I$), where $\sum_{i=1}^{I} P(F_i) = 1$, of course. We continue to denote the information by E, and thus the posterior assessments of the I events are denoted by $P(F_i | E)$ ($i = 1, 2, \ldots, I$). Since our simplest version of Bayes' Theorem (4.3) is perfectly general, it can be used to find the $P(F_i | E)$. Thus, we get

$$P(F_i | E) = \frac{P(E | F_i)P(F_i)}{P(E)} \qquad (i = 1, 2, \ldots, I). \qquad (4.12)$$

The denominator of this can be expanded in a manner similar to that used in section 4.3. Since E can be written

$$E \equiv (E \text{ and } F_1) \text{ or } (E \text{ and } F_2) \text{ or } \ldots \text{ or } (E \text{ and } F_I),$$

and since the events $(E \text{ and } F_i)$ and $(E \text{ and } F_j)$ are mutually exclusive for $i \neq j$, it follows that

$$P(E) = P(E \text{ and } F_1) + P(E \text{ and } F_2) + \cdots + P(E \text{ and } F_I).$$

To save writing, we can express this as

$$P(E) = \sum_{j=1}^{I} P(E \text{ and } F_j).$$

Finally, we note that we can use (2.38) to write $P(E \text{ and } F_j)$ as $P(E | F_j)P(F_j)$. We thus get

$$P(E) = \sum_{j=1}^{I} P(E | F_j)P(F_j). \qquad (4.13)$$

If we now substitute (4.13) into (4.12), we get

$$P(F_i | E) = \frac{P(E | F_i)P(F_i)}{\sum_{j=1}^{I} P(E | F_j)P(F_j)} \qquad (i = 1, 2, \ldots, I). \qquad (4.14)$$

This is the most commonly used form of Bayes' theorem for events.

Let us apply a quick check to see whether (4.14) makes sense: if the posterior probabilities have been correctly calculated then they should add up to 1. (Remember that $F_1, F_2, \ldots, F_I$ are mutually exclusive and exhaustive events.) From (4.14), summing over $i = 1, 2, \ldots, I$, we get

$$\sum_{i=1}^{I} P(F_i | E) = \frac{1}{\sum_{j=1}^{I} P(E | F_j)P(F_j)} \sum_{i=1}^{I} P(E | F_i)P(F_i) = 1,$$

which is reassuring! Note that in this summation, we can factor out the denominator of (4.14) since it does not depend upon i. More importantly, as our quick check demonstrates, the denominator of (4.14) is simply a *scaling factor* that ensures that the posterior probabilities do indeed sum to 1. Recalling a similar procedure used in section 2.4, we can save writing by expressing (4.14) in the following form:

$$P(F_i | E) \propto P(E | F_i)P(F_i) \qquad (i = 1, 2, \ldots, I), \qquad (4.15)$$

where the factor of proportionality is chosen to make the posterior probabilities sum to 1. This is a particularly useful form of Bayes' theorem, which we will be using repeatedly later in the book.

Equation (4.15) has a simple interpretation. Recall that $P(F_i)$ denotes the prior probability of F_i, that $P(F_i | E)$ denotes the posterior probability, and that $P(E | F_i)$ denotes the probability of getting the information given F_i. More commonly, $P(E | F_i)$ is referred to as the *likelihood of E given* F_i. (It measures how likely you are to get the evidence E if F_i is to occur.) Using this terminology, we can express Bayes' Theorem, as represented by (4.15), as follows:

$$\text{the posterior is proportional to the product of the likelihood and the prior.} \qquad (4.16)$$

This formalizes the intuition notion that the posterior assessment is a blend of the new information and the prior assessment.

Let us consider a simple example (which is chosen for its simplicity not for its realism). Suppose you have three coins: one which you regard as fair; one which you regard as biased in favour of heads (in that a head is three times as likely as a tail); and one which you regard as biased in favour of tails (in that a tail is three times as likely as a head). Suppose someone selects one of the three coins at random (without telling you which it is), and tosses it twice – obtaining a head on each toss. What is your posterior assessment (in the light of the information that two heads were obtained on two tosses) as to which coin was selected?

Let us introduce some notation, and make two key assumptions. Let F_1 denote the event that the coin selected was the one biased in favour of heads, F_2 the event that the fair coin was selected, and F_3 the event that the coin selected was the one biased in favour of tails. Finally, let E denote the information that two heads were obtained in two tosses. To proceed, we need to make some assumptions about two things: first, the selection procedure; secondly, the tossing mechanism. In the absence of any alternative suggestions, we assume that both these are 'fair' in the following sense. First, as far as the selection procedure is concerned, we assume that

$$P(F_1) = P(F_2) = P(F_3) = \tfrac{1}{3}; \qquad (4.17)$$

that is, each of the three coins is equally likely to be selected.

Secondly, as far as the tossing mechanism is concerned, we assume that

$$P(H \mid F_1) = \tfrac{3}{4} \qquad P(H \mid F_2) = \tfrac{1}{2} \qquad P(H \mid F_3) = \tfrac{1}{4}, \tag{4.18}$$

where H denotes getting a head on a single toss. Equation (4.18) embodies the notion that the tossing mechanism preserves and reflects your views about the coins' biases.

We are now in a position to calculate the posterior probabilities. For illustrative purposes, we will first use the full form of Bayes' Theorem as given in (4.14), and then repeat the calculations using the abbreviated form as given in (4.15). First we need to calculate the likelihoods. From (4.18), remembering that E is the information that two tosses resulted in two heads, we have

$$P(E \mid F_1) = P\{[(H \text{ on first}) \text{ and } (H \text{ on second})] \mid F_1\}$$

$$= P[(H \text{ on first}) \mid F_1] P[(H \text{ on second}) \mid F_1]$$

$$= \tfrac{3}{4} \times \tfrac{3}{4} = \tfrac{9}{16},$$

where we assume that the outcomes on the two tosses are independent. Similarly,

$$P(E \mid F_2) = \tfrac{4}{16} \qquad \text{and} \qquad P(E \mid F_3) = \tfrac{1}{16}.$$

It follows from these, and (4.17), that the denominator of the right-hand side of (4.14) is

$$(\tfrac{9}{16} \times \tfrac{1}{3}) + (\tfrac{4}{16} \times \tfrac{1}{3}) + (\tfrac{1}{16} \times \tfrac{1}{3}) = \tfrac{14}{48}.$$

Thus, applying (4.14) repeatedly, we have

$$P(F_1 \mid E) = \frac{\tfrac{9}{16} \times \tfrac{1}{3}}{\tfrac{14}{48}} = \frac{\tfrac{9}{48}}{\tfrac{14}{48}} = \tfrac{9}{14};$$

$$P(F_2 \mid E) = \frac{\tfrac{4}{16} \times \tfrac{1}{3}}{\tfrac{14}{48}} = \frac{\tfrac{4}{48}}{\tfrac{14}{48}} = \tfrac{4}{14}; \text{ and}$$

$$P(F_3 \mid E) = \frac{\tfrac{1}{16} \times \tfrac{1}{3}}{\tfrac{14}{48}} = \frac{\tfrac{1}{48}}{\tfrac{14}{48}} = \tfrac{1}{14}.$$

Thus, the posterior probabilities of F_1, F_2 and F_3 in the light of the information that two tosses resulted in two heads are $\tfrac{9}{14}$, $\tfrac{4}{14}$ and $\tfrac{1}{14}$ respectively. Compared with the prior probabilities of $\tfrac{1}{3}$, $\tfrac{1}{3}$ and $\tfrac{1}{3}$, it is clear that the evidence has tipped the scales in favour of the pro-heads biased coin.

An alternative, less arithmetically tedious, way of calculating these probabilities is to use the abbreviated form of Bayes' theorem (4.15), and to adopt a tabular presentation. Table 4.1 shows the relevant calculations.

Table 4.1   Calculating the posterior probabilities for the 3-coin example

(1)	(2)	(3)	(4) = (2) × (3)	(5) = (4) ÷ sum of column (4) = (4) ÷ $\frac{14}{48}$
i	$P(F_i)$	$P(E \mid F_i)$	$P(E \mid F_i)P(F_i)$	$P(F_i \mid E)$
1	$\frac{1}{3}$	$\frac{9}{16}$	$\frac{9}{48}$	$\frac{9}{14}$
2	$\frac{1}{3}$	$\frac{4}{16}$	$\frac{4}{48}$	$\frac{4}{14}$
3	$\frac{1}{3}$	$\frac{1}{16}$	$\frac{1}{48}$	$\frac{1}{14}$
Sum			$\frac{14}{48}$	1

In this, column (2) contains for each i the prior probability, column (3) the likelihood and column (4) the product of the likelihood and the prior (cf. (4.16)). To find the factor of proportionality, we find the sum of column (4), and divide each entry by this sum; thus getting column (5). In column (5), the entry for each i is proportional to the product of the likelihood and prior; moreover, the sum is 1. Thus, column (5) contains the posterior probabilities.

Actually, it is clear that the calculations can be made even simpler, by dropping all the fractions in columns (2), (3) and (4). Thus, the entries in (2) would be 1, 1 and 1; in (3), they would be 9, 4 and 1; and in (4), they would be 9, 4 and 1. The sum of these is 14, and thus the posterior probabilities are $\frac{9}{14}$, $\frac{4}{14}$ and $\frac{1}{14}$ as before.

The posterior probabilities depend, of course, on the information obtained. The calculations above are based on the information that two heads were obtained in two tosses. It should go without saying that if different information had been obtained, then different posterior probabilities would have been generated. As an exercise, you should verify that if the two tosses had resulted in one head and one tail, the posteriors would have been as in table 4.2(a), and that if two tails had resulted, the posteriors would have been as in table 4.2(b).

We will return to this example in a little while – approaching it by a rather devious route. In the meantime, we examine a slightly simpler example, based on the above example, but in which only one toss of the coin selected is performed. Let us ask a similar question; if the outcome on this one toss is a head, what is the posterior

Table 4.2   The posterior probabilities for the other information possibilities

(a) E = {one head and one tail in two tosses		(b) E = {two tails in two tosses}	
i	$P(F_i \mid E)$	i	$P(F_i \mid E)$
1	$\frac{3}{10}$	1	$\frac{1}{14}$
2	$\frac{4}{10}$	2	$\frac{4}{14}$
3	$\frac{3}{10}$	3	$\frac{9}{14}$

assessment? Under the same assumptions as before, the likelihoods of the information E (namely getting one head in one toss) are given by:

$$P(E \mid F_1) = \tfrac{3}{4} \qquad P(E \mid F_2) = \tfrac{2}{4} \qquad P(E \mid F_3) = \tfrac{1}{4}. \qquad (4.19)$$

Thus, if the priors are still given by (4.17), the posteriors of F_1, F_2 and F_3 are proportional to $\tfrac{3}{12}$, $\tfrac{2}{12}$ and $\tfrac{1}{12}$ respectively. Hence, applying the appropriate scaling factor, we derive the following posterior probabilities:

$$P(F_1 \mid E) = \tfrac{3}{6} \qquad P(F_2 \mid E) = \tfrac{2}{6} \qquad P(F_3 \mid E) = \tfrac{1}{6}. \qquad (4.20)$$

Let us suppose that the coin is now tossed a second time, and the outcome is another head. In the light of *this* information, what are our posteriors now? Clearly, we can apply the same procedure as before. The relevant likelihoods remain as in (4.19) (since, in this particular illustration it is supposed that the outcome on the second toss happened to be the same as the outcome on the first toss). The relevant 'priors' are now the probabilities given in (4.20), since these are the probabilities prior to the second item of information (the outcome on the second toss). Thus, the product of the relevant likelihoods and the relevant priors for F_1, F_2 and F_3 are $\tfrac{9}{24}$, $\tfrac{4}{24}$ and $\tfrac{1}{24}$ respectively. Applying the appropriate scaling factor, we derive the following posterior probabilities (for the situation after two tosses yielded two heads):

$$P(F_1 \mid E) = \tfrac{9}{14} \qquad P(F_2 \mid E) = \tfrac{4}{14} \qquad P(F_3 \mid E) = \tfrac{1}{14}.$$

Are these not familiar? Indeed, they are precisely the same as in the original example – in which the outcome on the two tosses was considered as one item of information. We have shown, therefore, that whether we consider the outcome on the two tosses as one item of information, or whether we consider it as two (updating our assessment after each one), we end up with exactly the same posterior assessment. This is a most reassuring result. (Indeed, it would be rather worrying if it did not hold.) Perhaps you would like to show that it is a perfectly general result?

A few general comments should be made before we conclude this section. First, let us reiterate the point we have made on a number of occasions to the effect that 'information' is uninformative if it is independent of the phenomena in which we are interested. In the context of the material of this section, independence is characterized by $P(E \mid F_i) = P(E)$ for all $i = 1, 2, \ldots, I$. It is clear that if we substitute this in Bayes' Theorem (4.14) we get $P(F_i \mid E) = P(F_i)$ for all $i = 1, 2, \ldots, I$. The assessment is unchanged as a result of the 'information'. We can also generalize an earlier discussion concerning the implication of zero prior probabilities for an event. From (4.14), it is immediate that if $P(F_j) = 0$ then $P(F_j \mid E)$ is also zero. Thus, if you consider an event to be impossible *ab initio*, then no amount of evidence will convince you otherwise.

There is a rather unexpected implication of this last result: namely, that the posterior probability of an event depends *inter alia* upon the set of other events that are deemed possible. In a sense this is implicit in what has gone before, but it is as well to make it explicit. Consider, for illustrative purposes, our first example of this section. Again suppose two tosses had resulted in two heads, but suppose now that only two possibilities concerning the coin are being entertained, say F_1 and F_3. (Thus, the prior on F_2 is zero.) You should be able to verify that if both these are considered equally likely to begin with, then the posteriors after two tosses had resulted in two heads would be

$$P(F_1 \mid E) = \tfrac{9}{10} \quad \text{and} \quad P(F_3 \mid E) = \tfrac{1}{10} \qquad (4.21)$$

These are, of course, different from those calculated earlier for the case when all three possibilities were deemed equally likely; though it should be noted that the *ratio* of the posterior probabilities remains the same (why is this?).

We note also that if E and some single event F_j are *mutually exclusive* (that is, they cannot both happen), then it follows that the occurrence of E automatically rules out F_j. In other words, $P(F_j \mid E) = 0$. This follows from (4.14) since $P(E \mid F_j)$ must be zero if E and F_j are mutually exclusive.

The above paragraph deals with the case when E and *one* event F_j are mutually exclusive. The situation becomes rather difficult if some information E is generated which is such that it and *every* F_i are mutually exclusive. In such a situation we would be taken by surprise! Unfortunately, Bayes' Theorem does not offer us any advice as to what we ought to do. (In (4.14) both the numerator and the denominator of the right-hand side are zero; thus the posterior probabilities are undefined.) The implication is clear: make sure right from the start that the set $F_1, F_2, \ldots, F_I$ contains all conceivable possibilities, even though many of them will have very, very small prior probabilities.

Finally, we ought to illustrate a remark made at the beginning of chapter 2 concerning the convergence of posterior assessments in the light of a large amount of information irrespective of the prior assessments. Consider the example discussed in this section, but restrict attention to just F_1 and F_3 (that is, suppose $P(F_2) = 0$). Let p denote $P(F_1)$; thus $P(F_3) = 1 - p$. Suppose n tosses of the coin selected have been performed and that m of them have resulted in heads. The posterior assessments in the light of this information can be shown to be (see exercise 4.11):

$$P(F_1 \mid E) = \frac{3^m p}{3^m p + 3^{n-m}(1 - p)}$$

$$\quad (4.22)$$

$$P(F_3 \mid E) = \frac{3^{m-n}(1 - p)}{3^m p + 3^{n-m}(1 - p)}$$

Now suppose that the coin selected is indeed the heads-biased one. Then, in the long-run m will tend to $3n/4$. Hence, we can evaluate the limit of $P(F_1 \mid E)$ as n approaches infinity, as follows:

$$\underset{n \to \infty}{Lt}\ P(F_1 \mid E) = \underset{n \to \infty}{Lt}\ \frac{3^{3n/4} p}{3^{3n/4} p + 3^{n/4}(1 - p)}$$

$$= \underset{n \to \infty}{Lt}\ \frac{p}{p + 3^{-(n/2)}(1 - p)}$$

$$= \frac{p}{p}$$

$$= 1$$

Likewise, $P(F_3 \mid E)$ approaches zero as n approaches infinity. Thus, if the coin selected is the heads-biased one, then, in the limit you will come to believe this with certainty, irrespective of the value of p. A similar result holds, *mutatis mutandis*, if the coin selected is the tails-biased one. These are reassuring results. They can be generalized.

4.5 SOME APPLICATIONS OF BAYES' THEOREM FOR VARIABLES

Bayes' theorem for variables is derived in a manner entirely analogous to that used to derive the theorem for events in sections 4.3 and 4.4. Accordingly, we will omit a formal derivation, and simply state the theorem for variables in the abbreviated form analogous to (4.15) above. It is as follows:

$$g_Y(y \mid x) \propto g_X(x \mid y) f_Y(y) \qquad \text{for all } x \text{ and } y. \tag{4.23}$$

To interpret this, consider Y as some variable in which we are interested, and X as some evidence (in the form of a variable) which potentially provides some information about Y. The left-hand side represents the posterior beliefs about Y in the light of the information x. The first term on the right-hand side is the likelihood of getting the information x given y; and the second term on the right-hand side represents the prior beliefs about Y. Once again, Bayes' theorem formalizes the intuitive notion that the posterior assessment is a blend of the new information and the prior assessment.

Bayes' theorem for variables, equation (4.23) above, should be compared with that for events, equation (4.15). The observed value of x in the former corresponds to E in the latter, and the values taken by the variable Y in the former correspond to the events $F_1, F_2, \ldots,$ F_I in the latter. Similarly, the posterior probability statements $g_Y(y \mid x)$ and $P(F_i \mid E)$ correspond to each other; as do the likelihoods $g_X(x \mid y)$ and $P(E \mid F_i)$, and the prior probability statements $f_Y(y)$ and $P(F_i)$.

A number of points about (4.23) should be noted. First, it is valid whether X and Y are discrete or continuous. If X is discrete, then $g_X(. \mid y)$ is the conditional probability function; if it is continuous, then $g_X(. \mid y)$ is the conditional probability density function. Likewise, if Y is discrete, then $g_Y(. \mid x)$ and $f_Y(.)$ are the conditional and unconditional probability functions; if Y is continuous, then $g_Y(. \mid x)$ and $f_Y(.)$ are the conditional and unconditional probability density functions. However, the scaling factor, or the factor of proportionality, *does* depend upon whether Y is discrete or continuous. To be specific, if Y is discrete, then the scaling factor (that is, the factor by which the right-hand side of (4.23) should be divided in order to turn the proportionality into an equality) is $\sum_y g_X(x \mid y) f_Y(y)$. If Y is continuous, then the scaling factor is $\int_y g_X(x \mid y) f_Y(y) \, dy$. In both cases, the summation or integration, as appropriate, is carried out over all values of y.

Further, equation (4.23) is equally valid if we replace the scalar variables X and Y by vector variables $\mathbf{X}$ and $\mathbf{Y}$. Thus, the vector extension allows us to consider both the updating of multivariate probability assessments and the use of multidimensioned information (which could consist of several observations on one variable, or one observation on each of several variables, or several observations on several variables).

Let us now examine a number of applications of (4.23). Our first example is really rather trivial (as it simply rediscovers something we found out in chapter 3), but it is a useful starting point. Consider the two-coin example of chapter 3, in which two (agreed fair) coins are tossed, and in which the variable X is defined as taking the value 1 if the first coin shows a head and zero otherwise, and the variable Y is defined as the total number of heads obtained. Following the notation of (4.23), we shall take Y as the variable in which we are interested, and the observed value of X will be the item of information. The prior assessment of Y (assuming the coins are agreed fair) is (cf. (3.10))

$$f_Y(0) = \tfrac{1}{4} \qquad f_Y(1) = \tfrac{1}{2} \qquad f_Y(2) = \tfrac{1}{4}.$$

To implement (4.23) for any observed value of x, we need to know the values of $g_X(x \mid y)$ for all (possible) x and y. These are (cf. table 3.5)

$$g_X(0 \mid 0) = 1 \qquad g_X(0 \mid 1) = \tfrac{1}{2} \qquad g_X(0 \mid 2) = 0$$
$$g_X(1 \mid 0) = 0 \qquad g_X(1 \mid 1) = \tfrac{1}{2} \qquad g_X(1 \mid 2) = 1.$$

Applying (4.23), we can derive the posterior distributions of Y for each possible value of the information variable X.

(a)   if observed value of $X = 0$

$$g_Y(0 \mid 0) \propto g_X(0 \mid 0)f_Y(0) = 1 \times \tfrac{1}{4} = \tfrac{1}{4}$$
$$g_Y(1 \mid 0) \propto g_X(0 \mid 1)f_Y(1) = \tfrac{1}{2} \times \tfrac{1}{2} = \tfrac{1}{4}$$
$$g_Y(2 \mid 0) \propto g_X(0 \mid 2)f_Y(2) = 0 \times \tfrac{1}{4} = 0.$$

The scaling factor, which applies to all three of these, is $\tfrac{1}{4} + \tfrac{1}{4} + 0 = \tfrac{1}{2}$. Applying this, we get the following posterior assessment:

$$g_Y(y \mid 0) = \begin{cases} \tfrac{1}{2} & y = 0, 1 \\ 0 & \text{elsewhere.} \end{cases}$$

This states the rather obvious result that if a tail is observed on the first coin ($X = 0$), then there is a 50:50 chance that the total number of heads on the two coins is 0 or 1.

(b)   if observed value of $X = 1$

$$g_Y(0 \mid 1) \propto g_X(1 \mid 0)f_Y(0) = 0 \times \tfrac{1}{4} = 0$$
$$g_Y(1 \mid 1) \propto g_X(1 \mid 1)f_Y(1) = \tfrac{1}{2} \times \tfrac{1}{2} = \tfrac{1}{4}$$
$$g_Y(2 \mid 1) \propto g_X(1 \mid 2)f_Y(2) = 1 \times \tfrac{1}{4} = \tfrac{1}{4}.$$

Applying the scaling factor, which is again $\tfrac{1}{2}$ ($= 0 + \tfrac{1}{4} + \tfrac{1}{4}$), we get the following posterior assessment:

$$g_Y(y \mid 1) = \begin{cases} \tfrac{1}{2} & y = 1, 2 \\ 0 & \text{elsewhere.} \end{cases}$$

Again this is a rather obvious result (which you should interpret yourself).

Of course, all we have done is to rediscover the conditional distribution of Y (which we derived in chapter 3). But then this is all that Bayes' theorem really is.

Our second and third examples are more substantive. Indeed, the second example forms the basis for the material in chapter 5, and the third example forms the basis for the material in chapter 6. In turn, the remaining chapters of the book build on the foundations laid in chapters 5 and 6. Thus, these two examples are of particular importance.

In our second example, we suppose we are interested in some *proportion*. This could be anything: the proportion of women in the UK; the proportion of times a particular coin comes down heads; the proportion of SDP voters in Crosby; the proportion of times that a particular die shows a '6'; the proportion of gay vegetarian cyclists amongst *Guardian* readers; the proportion of Socialists in the University of York; the proportion of retired colonels amongst *Daily Telegraph* readers; and so on. These all take the form: 'the proportion of A in B', where A is some *characteristic of interest* (such as: being female; showing a head; being an SDP voter; showing a '6'; and so on), and where B is some *population of interest* (such as: all people in the UK; all tosses of a particular coin; all voters in Crosby; all rolls of a die; and so on). For the purposes of generality and shorthand, we shall refer to the *proportion* with the *characteristic* in the *population*, or, even more simply, the *population proportion*.

In this second example, this population proportion is the thing in which we are interested. In keeping with the notation used above, we shall denote this population proportion by Y. Thus, Y is the proportion with the characteristic in the population; for example, Y is the proportion of women in the UK; or Y is the proportion of times a particular coin comes down heads; and so on. We presume that we do not know (at least to begin with) the value of Y – otherwise there would be no problem to discuss. We might, however, have some quite strong notions about Y from previous experience: for example, we might think that the proportion of women in the UK is most likely to be in the range 0.46 to 0.52. In other cases, we might have only very vague ideas about Y. In all cases, though, we should be able to express our prior views about Y in the form of a prior probability distribution for Y; for example, if we have extremely vague views about Y, these could be expressed by saying that our prior on Y is $U(0, 1)$ (or, equivalently, $B(1, 1)$; see section 2.4) – that is, we regard all values of Y between 0 and 1 as being equally likely. (It should go without saying that Y, and hence our probability assessment, is necessarily restricted to the interval $[0, 1]$; a proportion cannot lie outside this interval.)

In this section, we will assume that our prior views upon Y can be expressed in the form of a *beta distribution*. As we saw in section 2.4, beta distributions take values (only) in the interval $[0, 1]$, and, depending upon the numerical values of the parameters, can take a variety of different shapes. For example, if the parameters α and β are both 1, then the distribution is uniform (over $[0, 1]$); if α is 2 and β is 1, then the distribution is right-triangular; if α is 1 and β is 2, it is left-triangular; for larger α and β values it is unimodal – its bulk lying to the right if α is greater than β and to the left if α is less than β – and its dispersion decreases as the sum of α and β increases. It is obviously a very flexible family of distributions (all on the interval $[0, 1]$). It would appear reasonable to suppose, therefore, that for many prior assessments of Y, one of the beta family would provide a reasonable approximation. In other words, by selecting the parameters α and β appropriately, a beta distribution could reasonably well represent many prior assessments for Y.

We will discuss these issues in more detail in chapter 5. In the meantime, in this section, we will simply restrict attention to those cases in which the prior beliefs about Y can be represented by a beta distribution with appropriately chosen parameters a and b. From now on we suppose, therefore, that the prior on Y is $B(\alpha, \beta)$, where α and β are appropriately selected. From (2.27), it follows that the prior probability density function for Y is given by:

$$f_Y(y) \propto \begin{cases} y^{\alpha-1}(1-y)^{\beta-1} & 0 \le y \le 1 \\ 0 & \text{elsewhere.} \end{cases} \tag{4.24}$$

Now let us turn to the question of updating our assessment of Y in the light of new information. There is an obvious way that information about Y can be gleaned in this example: by inspecting the relevant population. At one extreme, we could look at the entire population and check each member of the population to see whether they had the characteristic or not. Clearly, this would lead to certain knowledge of Y. (The posterior distribution of Y would be degenerate at the true value of Y.) At the other extreme, we could look at just *one* member of the population, and check whether this member had the characteristic or not. Clearly, this would lead to a modest reduction in our uncertainty about Y, though not complete elimination of this uncertainty. In between these extremes, we could look at, say, n members of the population, and check them for the incidence of the characteristic. Clearly, the greater that n is, the larger the reduction in uncertainty about Y that would result.

We will consider the general case in detail in chapter 5. Here, we will simply investigate the implications of looking at one member of the population, and checking whether this member has the characteristic or not. Presumably, we might as well pick this one member at random (though there may be circumstances when a more selective procedure might be more appropriate); thus each member of the population has an equal chance of being the one selected. The information we will gain from this exercise is knowledge of whether the member selected has the characteristic or not. In keeping with the notation used earlier in this section, we will use the variable X to denote this information. To be specific, we shall define X as taking the value 1 if the member selected has the characteristic, and the value 0 otherwise. To apply Bayes' theorem (4.23), we need to find the conditional distribution of X for each y. If our selection procedure is random (in the sense described above) then it follows that

$$g_X(x \mid y) = \begin{cases} 1 - y & x = 0 \\ y & x = 1 \\ 0 & \text{otherwise.} \end{cases} \tag{4.25}$$

You should make sure that you are happy with this before proceeding: what it says is that, if a proportion y of the population have the characteristic, and if each member of the population has an equal chance of being selected, then the probability is y that the member selected *has* the characteristic (i.e. $X = 1$) and the probability is $1 - y$ that the member selected does *not* have the characteristic (i.e. $X = 0$). (For example: if 50 per cent of the population are women, then random selection implies a 50:50 chance of picking a woman; if

95 per cent of *Guardian* readers are gay vegetarian cyclists, then random selection implies a 0.95 chance of picking a gay vegetarian cyclist; and so on.)

We are now in a position to derive the posterior assessment of Y given some observation on X. Combining (4.24) and (4.25) in (4.23), we get:

(a) if observed value of $X = 0$

$$g_Y(y \mid 0) \propto g_X(0 \mid y)f_Y(y) \propto \begin{cases} (1 - y)y^{\alpha - 1}(1 - y)^{\beta - 1} & 0 \le y \le 1 \\ 0 & \text{elsewhere.} \end{cases}$$

Thus,

$$g_Y(y \mid 0) \propto \begin{cases} y^{\alpha - 1}(1 - y)^{\beta} & 0 \le y \le 1 \\ 0 & \text{elsewhere.} \end{cases} \tag{4.26}$$

(b) if observed value of $X = 1$

$$g_Y(y \mid 1) \propto g_X(1 \mid y)f_Y(y) \propto \begin{cases} yy^{\alpha - 1}(1 - y)^{\beta - 1} & 0 \le y \le 1 \\ 0 & \text{elsewhere.} \end{cases}$$

Thus,

$$g_Y(y \mid 1) \propto \begin{cases} y^{\alpha}(1 - y)^{\beta - 1} & 0 \le y \le 1 \\ 0 & \text{elsewhere.} \end{cases} \tag{4.27}$$

These expressions may look of a familiar form. Indeed, if you examine (2.27) you will see that (4.26) is the probability density function of a beta distribution with parameters α and $\beta + 1$, and that (4.27) is the probability density function of a beta distribution with parameters $\alpha + 1$ and β. We thus get the following important result: if the prior on Y is $B(\alpha, \beta)$, then the posterior is $B(\alpha, \beta + 1)$ if $x = 0$ (that is, if the member randomly selected does *not* have the characteristic) and is $B(\alpha + 1, \beta)$ if $x = 1$ (that is, if the member randomly selected *does* have the characteristic). More succinctly, we can say:

> if the prior on Y is $B(\alpha, \beta)$, then the posterior is $B(\alpha + x, \beta + 1 - x)$, where x is the observed value of X. $\left.\right\}$ (4.28)

Recalling our previous discussion of the effect of changes in the parameters on the shape of the beta distribution, it is clear that picking a member *with* the characteristic has the effect of shifting the distribution *rightwards* (that is, towards higher values of y), while picking a member without the characteristic shifts it in the opposite direction. In both cases, the dispersion decreases, since the sum of the parameters has increased by 1, thus, the posterior assessment is more precise than the prior.

Before moving on to our third example, you may like to deduce from (4.28) the effect on the assessment of adding a second observation (that is, a second randomly selected member). You should then be able to move to the most general case of n observations. (This will be discussed in detail in chapter 5, but it is a good test of your understanding to attempt the generalization. It is very straightforward, and requires no further algebra or statistics, once you are thinking along the right lines.)

Our third and final example is, in a sense, a generalization of the above example. Whereas in the above example, we were interested in the incidence of some *characteristic* in some population, in this third example, we will be interested in the incidence of some *variable* in some population. More precisely, we will be interested in the mean value of some variable which is normally distributed in some population. Let us introduce some notation, before turning to some examples. In keeping with the notation of the early part of the section, we shall denote by Y the thing in which we are interested, namely the mean of the variable. Since we will be using observations on the variable itself as our information about Y, we will use X to denote the variable. We assume that X is normally distributed in the population of interest, and we will further assume that its variance s^2 is known. We will refer to Y, quite naturally, as the *population mean*.

One can envisage a variety of situations for which this formulation is appropriate. For example, when we are interested in the mean income of manual workers in the UK; the mean wage rate of trade union members; the mean IQ amongst school-children; the mean mpc (marginal propensity to consume) in the UK; the mean consumption of beer amongst one-parent families; the mean elasticity of demand for tomatoes; the mean failure rate amongst foreign cars; the mean height of children from poor homes; and so on. In each of these examples, there is a well-defined population and variable of interest, with the focus of attention in each instance on the mean value of the variable.

We presume that we do not know the precise value of Y with certainty (otherwise there would be no problem to discuss). However, we suppose we do have some prior, or initial, views about Y (which may be quite precise or rather vague depending upon the particular application). These can be represented in the form of a prior distribution for Y. For the purposes of this example, we will suppose that this prior distribution is *normal*, with mean μ and variance σ^2. That is, the prior on Y is $N(\mu, \sigma^2)$. From section 2.4, equation (2.29), we see that this implies that the prior density function for Y is given by:

$$f_Y(y) \propto \sigma^{-1} \exp\left[-(y - \mu)^2/2\sigma^2\right]. \tag{4.29}$$

Now let us turn to the question of information. As in our second example, there is a natural way of getting information about Y: namely, by inspecting the relevant population. Again, as in our second example, there are two extreme options open to us: either to inspect the whole population, or to inspect just one randomly selected member. In the former, by finding the value of X for every member of the population, we will be able to determine Y (the mean value of X) with certainty; thus all residual uncertainty would be eliminated. In contrast, inspecting just one member of the population would lead to a relatively modest reduction in uncertainty. In between these two extremes, there is again the option of inspecting n members of the population.

We consider the general case in chapter 6. Here we confine attention to the second of the two options mentioned above: namely, the inspection of just one randomly selected member of the population. Since X in the population is normally distributed with mean Y and variance s^2, it follows that the distribution of the value of X for our randomly selected member will also be $N(Y, s^2)$. It follows, therefore, that the conditional probability density function of X given $Y = y$ is given by (cf. (2.29)):

$$g_X(x\,|\,y) \propto s^{-1} \exp\left[-(x - y)^2/2s^2\right]. \tag{4.30}$$

We are now in a position to find the posterior distribution of Y given one observation on X. Combining (4.29) and (4.30) in Bayes' theorem for variables (4.23), and incorporating σ^{-1} and s^{-1} into the scaling factor, we get

$$g_Y(y\,|\,x) \propto g_X(x\,|\,y)f_Y(y)$$
$$\propto \exp\left[-(x - y)^2/2s^2\right] \exp\left[-(y - \mu)^2/2\sigma^2\right]$$

Thus,

$$g_Y(y\,|\,x) \propto \exp\left\{\frac{-(x - y)^2}{2s^2} - \frac{(y - \mu)^2}{2\sigma^2}\right\} \tag{4.31}$$

To simplify this, let us separate out the terms involving y by noting that the expression inside the curly brackets in (4.31) can be written

$$-\frac{(x - y)^2}{2s^2} - \frac{(y - \mu)^2}{2\sigma^2}$$

$$= -\frac{1}{2s^2\sigma^2}\left[(\sigma^2 + s^2)y^2 - 2(\sigma^2 x + s^2\mu)y + (\sigma^2 x^2 + s^2\mu^2)\right]$$

$$= -\frac{1}{2s^2\sigma^2}\left[(\sigma^2 + s^2)\left(y - \frac{\sigma^2 x + s^2\mu}{\sigma^2 + s^2}\right)^2 + \frac{\sigma^2 s^2(x - \mu)^2}{\sigma^2 + s^2}\right]$$

Now recall that we are calculating the posterior density function of Y, and thus all (multiplicative) items not involving y can be ignored, as they will be taken care of by the scaling factor. Thus, using the above simplification in (4.31), we get

$$g_Y(y \mid x) \propto \exp\left\{-\left(y - \frac{\sigma^2 x + s^2\mu}{\sigma^2 + s^2}\right)^2 \Big/ \left[2\left(\frac{\sigma^2 s^2}{\sigma^2 + s^2}\right)\right]\right\} \qquad (4.32)$$

This is the posterior probability density function of Y. Its form may (should?) look familiar. If you compare it with (2.29), you will see that it is the density function of a variable that is normally distributed with mean $(\sigma^2 x + s^2\mu)/(\sigma^2 + s^2)$ and variance $\sigma^2 s^2/(\sigma^2 + s^2)$. (Note that the density function of a normally distributed variable is proportional to $\exp\left[-(x - M)^2/2V\right]$ where M is the mean and V is the variance.) We thus get the following important result:

> if the prior on Y is $N(\mu, \sigma^2)$, then the posterior is
> $$N\left(\frac{\sigma^2 x + s^2\mu}{\sigma^2 + s^2}, \frac{\sigma^2 s^2}{\sigma^2 + s^2}\right)$$
> where x is the observed value of X.

$$(4.33)$$

This completes the technicalities; let us now interpret the result. The first thing to note is that the posterior is normally distributed, as was the prior. The prior was centred on its mean μ; the posterior is centred on *its* mean $(\sigma^2 x + s^2\mu)/(\sigma^2 + s^2)$ – which, you should note carefully, is a weighted average of the prior mean μ and the observation x. The weight attached to μ is s^2 and the weight attached to x is σ^2; thus, the larger is s^2 relative to σ^2 the more weight is attached to μ. To interpret this result, recall that σ^2 is the prior variance of Y, and that s^2 is the variance of X. Thus, a small value for σ^2 implies relatively precise prior knowledge of Y, while a large value implies relatively imprecise prior knowledge. Similarly, a small value for s^2

implies that the observed value of x is likely to be relatively near its mean Y, while a large value implies that it is likely to be relatively far away. The above result on the mean therefore states the intuitively pleasing proposition that the posterior mean is a weighted average of the prior mean and the observation, with the weights depending upon the precision of the prior assessment relative to the accuracy of the observation.

The final point to note about (4.33) is the result for the variance: the prior variance was σ^2; the posterior variance is $\sigma^2 s^2/(\sigma^2 + s^2)$, which is smaller than σ^2 by an amount depending upon the relative sizes of σ^2 and s^2. In other words, the posterior distribution has a smaller variance (that is, it is less dispersed) than the prior distribution – the reduction being small or large depending upon whether s^2 is small or large in relation to σ^2. Again, this is an intuitively pleasing result.

This completes, for the time being, our treatment of this third example. We will return to it in chapter 6, when we will explore it in greater detail. In particular, we will examine the general case involving the inspection of n members of the population. Perhaps you can anticipate the results?

4.6 SOME PRELIMINARY NOTIONS OF 'NON-EXISTENT'
PRIOR INFORMATION

It is possible that the notion of a prior assessment is causing you some concern: our methods obviously rely on some initial or starting point, which is subsequently updated in the light of new information. What, you might be asking, do we do if we do not really have any prior views? In other words, what do we do if we are genuinely and completely ignorant about Y before our information is obtained? How can we update nothing?

At this stage, we cannot give a complete answer to these questions. What we can do, however, is to give two illustrations which should allay your worries until we can give a more complete treatment. Consider first our third example in section 4.5. The prior assessment about Y is assumed to be $N(\mu, \sigma^2)$. In this, the larger is σ^2 the more dispersed is the prior assessment; that is, the less confidently is the assessment held. Suppose we let σ^2 tend to infinity as an expression of total prior ignorance? This appears to encapsulate the idea that we really do not know anything about Y. Consider what happens when we let σ^2 tend to infinity in (4.33); we find that the posterior is

$N(x, s^2)$. In other words, the posterior depends solely and simply on the observed value of X and its variance. This seems to make excellent sense.

Consider now the second example of section 4.5. Recall from (4.28) that, if the prior was $B(a, b)$, then the posterior is either $B(a + 1, b)$ or $B(a, b + 1)$ depending upon whether the member selected had the characteristic or not. Thus an observation has the effect of adding 1 to one of the two parameters. Generalizing, it follows that n observations have the effect of adding a total of n to the two parameters. In a sense, therefore, a prior of $B(a, b)$ is 'equivalent' to $(a + b)$ observations. One obvious way of encapsulating total prior ignorance is thus by putting a and b both equal to zero, so that $(a + b)$ is zero. It is clear from (4.28) that the effect of doing this is to make the posterior assessment a function of the observation(s) alone. Again, this seems to be an intuitively acceptable implication of zero prior knowledge.

4.7   SUMMARY

This chapter has been concerned with new information, and how it is incorporated into probability assessments. After a few simple examples which could be handled informally, we derived Bayes' theorem, which formally characterizes how new information is incorporated into probability assessments. The intuitive notion, that posterior beliefs are a blend of prior beliefs and the new information, finds its formal expression in Bayes' theorem. In essence, this states that the posterior probability (density) (function) is proportional to the product of the likelihood (of getting the information) and the prior probability (density) (function). After a general discussion of its implications, we examined a number of applications, first with respect to events, and then with respect to variables. Two of the latter examples will be discussed in much greater detail in the next two chapters. Finally, the chapter concluded with a very brief introduction to various possible ways of representing 'non-existent' prior information. These ideas will be discussed in more detail later.

4.8   EXERCISES

4.1   Construct an example of your own showing how a particular item of information can lead to the complete elimination of uncertainty.

4.2 Suppose your prior about a certain country's aggregate marginal propensity to consume out of pre-tax income is $U(0, 1)$. Suppose you are then told that all citizens in the country are subject to a minimum national insurance contribution of 5 per cent of pre-tax income. What is your posterior about the country's mpc?

4.3 Prove the statements made in the text after equations (4.10) and (4.11) to the effect that any two of the inequalities in either of them imply all the others.

4.4 Prove the assertion made in the text that (4.10) and (4.11), together with Bayes' theorem, imply that $P(\bar{F}|E) < P(\bar{F})$.

4.5 (a) A gambler has in his pocket a fair coin (with a head and a tail), and a double-headed coin. He selects one of the coins at random, and when he tosses it, it shows heads. What is the probability that it is the fair coin? (b) Suppose that he tosses the coin a second time and again it shows heads. What is now the probability that it is the fair coin? (c) Suppose that he tosses the coin a third time and it shows tails. What is now the probability that it is the fair coin? (d) Repeat (a) to (c) for different sequences with the same overall outcomes: namely, HTH and THH. Comment.

4.6 There are three coins in a box. One is a double-headed coin, another is a double-tailed coin, and the third is a fair coin. When one of the three coins is selected at random and tossed, it shows heads. What is the probability that it is the double-headed coin?

4.7 Two scientists, Jones and Smith, design an experiment to test two hypotheses, H_1 and H_2. Jones assigns a prior probability of 0.8 to H_1, while Smith thinks that H_2 is twice as likely to be true as H_1. Data (D) are collected, and the likelihoods calculated. These are

$P(D|H_1) = 0.0084 \qquad P(D|H_2) = 0.0008.$

Show that the posterior beliefs of the two scientists are closer together than the prior beliefs. Is this always true?

4.8 Suppose that you know that a particular University has 60 per cent of one sex and 40 per cent of the other, but that you have forgotten whether the majority sex is male or female. If the first two people you meet are both female, what probability do

you attach to the hypothesis that the females are in the majority? How do you feel if the next two are male? Does this mean
that information is useless?

4.9   Verify table 4.2. (This contains the posterior assessments for
the three-coin example, given (a) one head and one tail in two
tosses; and (b) two tails in two tosses.) Carry out this verifica-
tion in two separate ways: first, considering the outcome on
the two tosses as one item of information; second, considering
the outcome on the two tosses as two items of information,
updating the assessment after each toss. Show that the posterior assessment is the same, irrespective of the route travelled.

4.10   Consider two (independent) items of information E_1 and E_2.
(a) For any given prior $P(F)$ for some event F, find the poste-
rior $P(F \mid E_1 \text{ and } E_2)$. (b) Now find $P(F \mid E_1)$. (c) Use this to find
$P(F \mid E_1 \text{ and } E_2)$ by a different method from that used in (a) –
namely, by considering $P(F \mid E_1)$ as the prior before information E_2 is received. Show that this method yields the same
answer as that in (a). (d) What modifications to your proof
would be necessary if E_1 and E_2 were *not* independent?

4.11   Verify (4.22). Hint: the prior is $P(F_1) = p$; $P(F_3) = 1 - p$; the
likelihood of obtaining m heads and $(n - m)$ tails in n tosses is
$(\frac{3}{4})^m(\frac{1}{4})^{n-m}$ given F_1, and is $(\frac{1}{4})^m(\frac{3}{4})^{n-m}$ given F_3. Now apply
Bayes' theorem.

4.12   Construct an example (of your own invention) of the incorporation of new information (using or not using Bayes' theorem
as appropriate).

4.13   Suppose you have two urns, each of which contains a large
number of white and black beads: Urn 1 contains 40 per cent
white beads and 60 per cent black, while Urn 2 contains 60
per cent white and 40 per cent black. Suppose one of the two
urns has been selected by a mechanism which implies that the
probability that it is Urn 1 is p. (A 'fair' selection mechanism
gives $p = \frac{1}{2}$.) Now suppose n beads are withdrawn and m are
found to be white (thus $n - m$ are black). Find the posterior
probability that the urn selected was Urn 1. Argue that if the
urn was Urn 1, then this probability would approach 1 as n
approached infinity; whereas if the urn was Urn 2, then this
probability would approach 0. Is this sensible?

4.14 Recall from section 2.4 that a variable Y is said to have a gamma distribution with parameters α and β if its density function is given by:

$$f_Y(y) \propto \begin{cases} y^{\alpha-1}e^{-\beta y} & y > 0 \\ 0 & y \le 0. \end{cases}$$

A (discrete) variable X is said to have a *Poisson* distribution with parameter y if its probability function is given by:

$$g_X(x \mid y) \propto \begin{cases} e^{-y}y^x & x = 0, 1, 2, \ldots \\ 0 & \text{otherwise.} \end{cases}$$

Show that if X is Poisson with parameter Y, and if the prior on Y is gamma with parameters α and β, then after one observation x on X, the posterior on Y is gamma with parameters $\alpha + x$ and $\beta + 1$. What would be the posterior after n observations $x_1, x_2, \ldots, x_n$? (This question is nowhere near as difficult as it appears.)

5 PROPORTIONS

This chapter examines the problem of inference about a proportion. Although the problem itself is not of over-riding interest or significance, it is a relatively simple one, and its solution illustrates well the general principles of inference which we will be applying to more relevant problems later in the book. This chapter is therefore important in that it enables us to discuss the general conceptual ideas of Bayesian inference in a context relatively free from algebraic and technical distractions. Once you have mastered the conceptual ideas of this chapter, you will be well-prepared to tackle the rest of the book: although the applications in the succeeding chapters become more relevant, and the algebra more complicated, no new concepts of inference are introduced.

The basic problem which we will be examining in this and the remaining chapters is as follows: it is supposed that there is some thing (or things) in which we are interested; by definition (for otherwise there would be no problem to examine) we are not certain about this thing (or things) though we may have some prior notions, or beliefs, about it (or them); further, it is supposed that we can obtain some information relevant to this thing (or things); this information enables us to improve our knowledge about the thing (or things). There are thus two elements in this problem: the description of the beliefs at any particular moment; and the updating of the beliefs in the light of new information. In principle, we have all the apparatus we need to tackle both these elements: chapters 2 and 3 discussed the description of beliefs, and chapter 4 discussed the incorporation of new information. All we need to do is to apply this material to particular problems.

The problem of most obvious interest to economists is, of course, the question of the 'validity' of competing economic theories; for example, whether a monetarist explanation of inflation is better than a Phillips' curve explanation. We will be discussing such issues in chapters 7, 8 and 9. More narrowly, given a particular economic theory, economists are interested in the numerical values of certain key economic parameters (such as the marginal propensity to consume, and the interest-elasticity of the demand for money), and thus in the economic significance of one economic variable for the behaviour of another.

In the paragraph above, the 'things of interest' are economic theories generally, and economic parameters more narrowly. Such issues will be the concern of chapters 7, 8 and 9. Special cases of economic parameters will be discussed in the preceding two chapters: to be specific, means and variances will be explored in chapter 6, while in this chapter the case of proportions will be examined.

We have already encountered this problem in chapter 4 – as the second example of the application of Bayes' theorem for variables in section 4.5. Indeed, that section derived the key result (equation (4.28)) that forms the foundation for all the material of this chapter; all we are really doing in this chapter is exploring, extending and interpreting that key result.

Let us recall the basic framework. It is supposed that we are interested in some *proportion*. This proportion could be anything: the proportion of top people who read *The Times*; the proportion of times a black comes up on a particular roulette wheel; the proportion of Asians in Brixton, and so on. The particular context defines two things: the particular *characteristic of interest* (being a top person; a black number on a roulette wheel; being an Asian); and a particular *population of interest* (all readers of *The Times*; all spins of a particular roulette wheel; all people in Brixton). Quite naturally, we refer to the item of interest as the *population proportion*.

In chapter 4, when we first encountered this example, we used Y to denote the population proportion – in keeping with the notation of that chapter. However, this is not a particularly appealing notation; therefore, in this chapter we will use the more natural P to denote the population proportion of interest. Note carefully that we continue to use upper-case letters to refer to *names* of variable, and lower-case letters to refer to *specific values*. It is of the essence of this chapter that the precise value of P is not known, at least to begin with, though, of course, some precise true value of P, call it p, is supposed to exist. The whole purpose of the exercise is to use information to learn more about the value p; the (subjective) distribution of P at any stage expresses the individual's assessment about the value p at that stage. (Later in the book, when we are dealing with several variables or parameters at once, we shall use this notational convention to distinguish between variables or parameters whose values are not known with certainty, and those that are. Thus, for example, if the value of the population proportion is *not* known with certainty, it will be referred to as P; if it *is* known with certainty, it will be referred to as p – where p equals the known value.)

The following section discusses how an assessment about P might be represented, and, in particular, it looks at a specific family of distributions (the beta family) which is especially appropriate for encapsulating assessments about a proportion. Section 5.3 then examines how information about P might be obtained, while section 5.4 shows how this information is incorporated into the prior assessment of P to provide the posterior assessment. Section 5.5 then explores in more detail the ideas introduced in section 4.6 concerning the modelling of 'non-existent' prior information. Although our analysis is now complete, section 5.6 provides a link with the Classical school of inference; in particular, it shows how 'confidence intervals' and 'significance tests' can be interpreted within a Bayesian framework. Finally, section 5.7 provides a summary, and section 5.8 a set of exercises.

5.2 THE REPRESENTATION OF BELIEFS ABOUT A PROPORTION

The value of P must necessarily be some number between and including 0 and 1. If one does not know (or does not think one knows) the value of P with certainty, then the natural way to express one's beliefs about P is in the form of a probability distribution defined on part or all of the interval $[0, 1]$. If one believes that the possible values for P consist of a set of discrete points in $[0, 1]$, then a discrete distribution is appropriate; otherwise a continuous distribution is appropriate. For example, if one's assessment of P is that it is either $\frac{1}{4}$ or $\frac{3}{4}$, and equally likely to be either, then the appropriate representation is the probability function:

$$f_P(p) = \begin{cases} \frac{1}{2} & p = \frac{1}{4}, \frac{3}{4} \\ 0 & \text{otherwise.} \end{cases}$$

Or again, if one believes that p is equally likely to take any one of the $n + 1$ values $0, 1/n, 2/n, \ldots, (n - 1)/n, 1$, then the appropriate representation is the probability function:

$$f_P(p) = \begin{cases} 1/(n + 1) & p = 0, 1/n, 2/n, \ldots, (n - 1)/n, 1 \\ 0 & \text{otherwise.} \end{cases}$$

Or again, if one believes that p may take (only) the values $\frac{1}{4}$, $\frac{1}{2}$ and $\frac{3}{4}$, and that the second of these is twice as likely as each of the other two, then the appropriate representation of one's beliefs is the probability function:

$$f_P(p) = \begin{cases} \frac{1}{2} & p = \frac{1}{2} \\ \frac{1}{4} & p = \frac{1}{4}, \frac{3}{4} \\ 0 & \text{otherwise.} \end{cases}$$

Alternatively, one might feel that P is equally likely to take any of the (infinitely many) possible values in the interval $[0, 1]$; in this case, the appropriate representation is the probability density function:

$$f_P(p) = \begin{cases} 1 & 0 \le p \le 1 \\ 0 & \text{elsewhere.} \end{cases}$$

This, of course, is the density function of a variable which is $U(0, 1)$, that is, uniform over the range 0 to 1. It is also the density function of a beta distribution with parameters $\alpha = 1$ and $\beta = 1$ (cf. (2.27)).

The *methods* that we will be discussing and using later in this chapter *can be applied whatever the form of the probability assessment.* However, we will be restricting attention to cases in which the form of the assessment is that of a beta distribution. In particular, since beta distributions are appropriate only for continuous variables, we will not be explicitly considering cases where the assessment is discrete. However, other cases, including discrete cases, can easily be covered by our general methodology (see, for example, exercises 4.5, 4.6, 4.8, 4.9, 4.11 and 4.13 of chapter 4); you are encouraged to investigate other cases yourself.

It may appear that considering only cases in which the prior assessment can be represented by a beta distribution is unduly restrictive, even for the continuous case. But this is not so. The beta family is a fairly flexible set of distributions, which, by suitable choice of parameters, can represent a wide variety of different prior assessments. We have already noted certain special cases: for example, when $\alpha = \beta = 1$, the distribution is uniform on $[0, 1]$; when $\alpha = 2$ and $\beta = 1$, the distribution is right-triangular, and when $\alpha = 1$ and $\beta = 2$, the distribution is left-triangular. More generally, when α and β are both greater than 1, then the distribution is unimodal, being symmetric if α and β are equal, and with its bulk to the right (left) if α is greater (less) than β. For many assessments, such a unimodal form would be particularly appropriate: consider, for example, your assessment of the proportion of females in the University of York; or your assessment of the proportion of SDP voters in West Huyton.

From section 2.4, we recall that if a variable has a beta distribution with parameters α and β, then its mean is $\alpha/(\alpha + \beta)$ and its variance is $\alpha\beta/[(\alpha + \beta)^2(\alpha + \beta + 1)]$. Moreover, it can be shown that as the sum of the parameters $(\alpha + \beta)$ increases, then the *shape* of the beta distribution becomes increasingly like the *shape* of the normal distribution; this means that for $(\alpha + \beta)$ sufficiently large (say greater than 30) then the beta distribution can be approximated by the normal distribution with the same mean and variance, with the approximation improving as $(\alpha + \beta)$ increases. This is a useful result as it means that probability statements about beta distributions can be approximated by use of the normal distribution.

In practice, of course, it does not come naturally (particularly to the man or woman in the street) to think in terms of beta distributions with specific values of the parameters. It is more natural to express one's beliefs in the following fashion: 'Well, I think that this most likely value for P is $\frac{1}{2}$, and it's almost certainly in the range 0.3 to 0.7.' When pressed further, one might agree that the distribution is symmetrical about $\frac{1}{2}$, and roughly bell-shaped. How can we translate this kind of assessment into an appropriate member of the beta family? That is, how do we select the appropriate parameters α and β?

We use the properties of the beta distribution described above (specifically its mean, variance and approximate shape), combined with the fact that almost all the area under a normal distribution lies within 2 standard deviations of its mean. Thus, from the quoted assessment above, we deduce that the mean is 0.5 and the standard deviation is 0.1 (the range 0.3 to 0.7 is 0.5 ± 0.2; therefore, 2 standard deviations equal 0.2). Hence, the appropriate α and β must satisfy

$$\alpha/(\alpha + \beta) = 0.5 \tag{5.1}$$

and

$$\sqrt{\{\alpha\beta/[(\alpha + \beta)^2(\alpha + \beta + 1)]\}} = 0.1. \tag{5.2}$$

Equations (5.1) and (5.2) are equations in the two unknowns α and β. One way to solve them is as follows: first, denote by v the sum $(\alpha + \beta)$; then (5.1) implies that $\alpha = 0.5v$ and hence that $\beta = 0.5v$; if these are substituted in (5.2) we get

$$\sqrt{\{(0.5v)(0.5v)/[v^2(v + 1)]\}} = 0.1,$$

which gives

$$0.25/(v + 1) = (0.1)^2 = 0.01,$$

and hence

$$v = 24.$$

Thus, the solution to (5.1) and (5.2) is $\alpha = \beta = 12$.

We have shown, therefore, that a beta distribution with parameters $\alpha = 12$ and $\beta = 12$ is a possible representation of beliefs which are unimodal, symmetrical about $p = \frac{1}{2}$, bell-shaped and with the bulk lying between 0.3 and 0.7.

In this example, the mean of the assessment for P was 0.5 and the standard deviation was 0.1. Suppose another assessment had the same mean, but a larger standard deviation – say 0.125; what would be the appropriate values of α and β for this assessment? Clearly equation (5.1) must still hold, and thus if $\alpha + \beta = v$ then $\alpha = \beta = 0.5v$. But now equation (5.2) is replaced by

$$\sqrt{\{\alpha\beta/[(\alpha + \beta)^2(\alpha + \beta + 1)]\}} = 0.125,$$

since the standard deviation is now 0.125. Substituting $\alpha = \beta = 0.5v$ in *this* equation gives

$$0.25/(v + 1) = (0.125)^2,$$

which solves to give $v = 15$. Hence $\alpha = \beta = 7.5$. Thus a beta distribution with parameters $\alpha = 7.5$ and $\beta = 7.5$ has a mean of 0.5 and a standard deviation of 0.125, as required.

In both these examples, the mean of the distribution was 0.5 – that is, the assessment was centred on, and symmetrical about, 0.5. Let us now consider a second pair of assessments, but now ones with a mean of 0.6. This implies that α and β must satisfy

$$\alpha/(\alpha + \beta) = 0.6.$$

Thus, if we put $\alpha + \beta = v$ again, it follows that $\alpha = 0.6v$ and $\beta = 0.4v$. Now let us consider the standard deviation. Suppose the first assessment of our second pair has a standard deviation of 0.1; then α and β must satisfy

$$\sqrt{\{\alpha\beta/[(\alpha + \beta)^2(\alpha + \beta + 1)]\}} = 0.1.$$

If $\alpha = 0.6v$ and $\beta = 0.4v$ are substituted into this, and the resulting expression solved for v, we get $v = 23$. Hence $\alpha = 13.8$ and $\beta = 9.2$. Thus, a beta distribution with parameters $\alpha = 13.8$ and $\beta = 9.2$ has a mean of 0.6 and a standard deviation of 0.1. Finally, suppose the second assessment of our second pair has a standard deviation of 0.05. Using the same method as above, it can be shown that the required parameters are $\alpha = 57$ and $\beta = 38$.

These examples confirm the general properties of the beta distribution: the mean is less than, equal to, or greater than 0.5 according as α is less than, equal to, or greater than β; and the standard deviation falls as the sum $(\alpha + \beta)$ increases.

The above discussion has shown how the appropriate values of α and β are chosen so as to select the appropriate member of the beta family to represent an assessment about P which is unimodal and roughly bell-shaped, with specified values for the mean and standard deviation. It also gives some feel for the impact of differing parameter values on the position, dispersion and shape of the distribution. You are encouraged to try further numerical values yourself.

We will assume throughout the remainder of this chapter that the prior assessment of P takes the form of a beta distribution with appropriately chosen parameters. Thus, the prior probability density function of P is given by (cf. (2.27))

$$f_P(p) \propto \begin{cases} p^{\alpha-1}(1-p)^{\beta-1} & 0 \leq p \leq 1 \\ 0 & \text{elsewhere.} \end{cases} \tag{5.3}$$

Let us now move on to look at the acquisition of new information.

5.3   THE NATURE OF (SAMPLE) INFORMATION

The thing in which we are interested, P, is the proportion of some population with some characteristic. There is, therefore, a natural source for information about P – namely, the population of interest. More precisely, we can look at the *members* of that population. The size of the population will vary from application to application: in some, the population will be of infinite size ('all tosses of a particular coin', 'all spins of a roulette wheel'); in others, the population will be of a finite size ('all readers of *The Times*', 'all people in Brixton'). What constitutes a 'member' will also vary from application to application: it could be a human being, or a physical object, or the outcome of a physical act ('tossing a coin').

Information can be obtained by inspecting members of the population, and checking to see whether they have the characteristic or not. Clearly, the *number* of members selected is a matter for choice: at one extreme, we could just select one member; at the other extreme, we could inspect all members (though that might take rather a long time if the population size was infinite!); in between, we could select say n members. We will begin our analysis by considering the simplest extreme – the selection of just one member – and then show how the results can be generalized to the case of the selection of n members. (After all, a total of n is just made up of n ones.)

We will examine the situation in which we select one member of the population. Our object, of course, is to see how a prior assessment should be updated after the inspection of this one selected member. Consider the possible outcomes of the inspection. By the nature of the problem, there are only two outcomes of interest: either the member selected has the characteristic, or it does not. Let us represent these two possibilities through the variable X: $X = 1$ will denote that the member selected *has* the characteristic; $X = 0$ will denote that the member does *not* have the characteristic. Now recall that we require this inspection to be informative about p (the true, but currently unknown, value of P). Obviously the *values* of X can not depend upon p; but the *distribution* of X *can* depend upon p if we select our member in an appropriate fashion. Clearly the appropriate selection mechanism is one which we have termed 'fair' in earlier chapters; this is one for which there is a probability of p that $X = 1$ and a probability of $1 - p$ that $X = 0$. Formally, this requires that

$$g_X(1 \mid p) = p$$
$$g_X(0 \mid p) = 1 - p. \tag{5.4}$$

This states the simple requirement that, if a proportion p of the population has the characteristic, then the selection mechanism should be such that the probability is p of picking a member *with* the characteristic, and $1 - p$ of picking a member without the characteristic. Thus, if 50 per cent of the population have the characteristic, then the selection mechanism should imply a $50:50$ chance of picking a member with the characteristic; if only 25 per cent of the population have the characteristic, then the mechanism should imply a 1 in 4 chance of picking a member with the characteristic. If the population is a physical one (of people or objects), then the requirement is that each member of the population has an equal chance of being selected: this is known as *random sampling*, the word 'random' implying a 'fair' selection mechanism. If the population consists of physical acts ('tossing a coin') then the particular physical act enacted ('the member selected') must be performed in a 'fair' manner ('a fair toss of the coin').

From now on, we will assume that the *sample* obtained (the 'member selected') was the outcome of a random process, as encapsulated in (5.4) above. It is emphasized that (5.4) implies that the distribution of X depends upon p, and thus that the observed value of X is informative about p.

We can write (5.4) rather more succinctly in the following form:

$$g_X(x \mid p) = \begin{cases} p^x(1-p)^{1-x} & x = 0, 1 \\ 0 & \text{otherwise.} \end{cases} \tag{5.5}$$

We are now in a position to investigate the effect of this information on the prior assessment. This we do in the next section.

5.4   THE INCORPORATION OF SAMPLE INFORMATION

We are assuming that the prior assessment about P takes the form of a beta distribution with parameters α and β, as given by (5.3). We are also assuming that the selection mechanism is such that the likelihood of observing x given p is given by (5.5). We can now combine these two expressions to find the posterior assessment for P in the light of the observed value of x. Substituting (5.3) and (5.5) into Bayes' theorem for variables (4.23), we get

$$g_P(p \mid x) \propto g_X(x \mid p) f_P(p)$$

$$\propto \begin{cases} p^x(1-p)^{1-x}p^{\alpha-1}(1-p)^{\beta-1} & x = 0, 1 \quad 0 \leq p \leq 1 \\ 0 & \text{otherwise.} \end{cases}$$

Thus,

$$g_P(p \mid x) \propto \begin{cases} p^{\alpha+x-1}(1-p)^{\beta+(1-x)-1} & x = 0, 1 \quad 0 \leq p \leq 1 \\ 0 & \text{otherwise.} \end{cases} \tag{5.6}$$

If you compare equations (5.6) and (2.27), you will see that the posterior distribution of P is beta with parameters $\alpha + x$ and $\beta + 1 - x$. We can express this result rather more long-windedly as follows (remembering that $x = 1$ means that the member selected *has* the characteristic, and that $x = 0$ means that the member selected does *not* have the characteristic):

If the prior on P is $B(\alpha, \beta)$, then if a member selected at random turns out to have the characteristic, the posterior on P is $B(\alpha + 1, \beta)$.
If the prior on P is $B(\alpha, \beta)$, then if a member selected at random turns out not to have the characteristic, the posterior on P is $B(\alpha, \beta + 1)$. (5.7)

This is an important result. (You will recognize it as one we derived, rather more briefly, in section 4.5.) The first thing to note about it is that the posterior is of the same form as the prior: that is, the posterior is a beta distribution as was the prior. Thus the assessment stays within the (beta) family. The second thing to note about (5.7) is the simple way the parameters change from the prior to the posterior: 1 is added to the first parameter if the sampled member *has* the characteristic; otherwise 1 is added to the second parameter.

It is clear that these two properties imply that this result can be straightforwardly generalized to the situation in which n members of the population are selected and inspected. *Assuming that the selection mechanism continues to imply* (5.5) (which underlies (5.7)), then it follows that the assessment always stays within the beta family, and that for *each* sampled member which *has* the characteristic 1 is added to the first parameter, while for *each* sampled member which does *not* have the characteristic 1 is added to the second parameter. Formally, we have:

> If the prior on P is $B(\alpha, \beta)$, then if, of n members selected at random, a have the characteristic and b do not (where $a + b = n$), the posterior on P is $B(\alpha + a, \beta + b)$. (5.8)

(Before proceeding, let us insert a brief aside for any readers who have been disconcerted by our rather cavalier jump from (5.7) to (5.8). If you are happy with the derivation of (5.8) you can ignore this aside. Otherwise you may prefer the following formal proof of (5.8). Consider the random selection of n members in such a way that (5.5) applies to each. Define the variable A as the number of members out of the n sampled with the characteristic. Then A takes the values 0, 1, 2, ..., n, and the likelihood function for A given p is (see exercise 5.10):

$$g_A(a \mid p) = \begin{cases} p^a(1 - p)^b & a = 0, 1, \ldots, n \qquad b = n - a; \\ 0 & \text{otherwise.} \end{cases} \qquad (5.9)$$

Here b $(= n - a)$ denotes the number without the characteristic. Now combine (5.3) and (5.9) in Bayes' theorem to get the following posterior assessment for P:

$$g_P(p \mid a)$$
$$\propto \begin{cases} p^a(1 - p)^b p^{\alpha - 1}(1 - p)^{\beta - 1} & \begin{matrix} a = 0, 1, \ldots, n \\ b = n - a \qquad 0 \le p \le 1 \end{matrix} \\ 0 & \text{otherwise.} \end{cases} \qquad (5.10)$$

After simplification, you will recognize this (cf. (2.27)) as the density function of a beta distribution with parameters $\alpha + a$ and $\beta + b$. End of aside.)

Equation (5.8) is a key result in our treatment of proportions. We will devote the rest of this section to a discussion of its implications. We have already noted that it implies that the assessment of P always stays within the (beta) family irrespective of the size of the sample (the value of n). We have also already noted that the incorporation of sample information implies that the first parameter increases by the number in the sample with the characteristic, and that the second parameter increases by the number in the sample without the characteristic. It follows, therefore, that the sum of the parameters increases by n, the sample size.

It is also of interest to explore how the mean and variance of the assessment are affected by the sample information. Consider first the mean. Recalling that the mean of a beta distribution with parameters α and β is $\alpha/(\alpha + \beta)$, it follows from (5.8) that the prior mean is $\alpha/(\alpha + \beta)$ and that the posterior mean is $(\alpha + a)/(\alpha + a + \beta + b) = (\alpha + a)/(\alpha + \beta + n)$. Now note that the posterior mean can be written

$$\frac{\alpha + a}{\alpha + \beta + n} \equiv w\left(\frac{\alpha}{\alpha + \beta}\right) + (1 - w)\left(\frac{a}{n}\right) \quad \text{where } w = \frac{\alpha + \beta}{\alpha + \beta + n}$$

(5.11)

Equation (5.11) states that the posterior mean is a weighted average of the prior mean and the ratio (a/n), with the weights being w and $1 - w$ respectively. The ratio (a/n) is the proportion of members of the sample with the characteristic; or, more succinctly, the *sample proportion*. Thus, from (5.11), we see that the *posterior mean for the population proportion is a weighted average of the prior mean and the sample proportion*. This is intuitively sensible.

Now let us consider the weights attached to the two terms: from (5.11) we see that the weight attached to the prior mean is $w \equiv (\alpha + \beta)/(\alpha + \beta + n)$, while the weight attached to the sample proportion is $(1 - w) \equiv n/(\alpha + \beta + n)$. Clearly, the relative weights depend upon the ratio of $(\alpha + \beta)$ to n, and thus the magnitude of $(\alpha + \beta)$ is of crucial importance. To interpret $(\alpha + \beta)$, consider again result (5.8); since a sample of size n in which there are a members with the characteristic and b without updates the assessment by adding a to the first parameter and b to the second, then we could consider *a prior of $B(\alpha, \beta)$ as 'equivalent to' having observed a sample of size $\alpha + \beta$ in which α have the characteristic and β do not*. Thus the sum ($\alpha + \beta$) represents the 'equivalence' in terms of sample size of the prior assessment. Let v denote this sum ($\alpha + \beta$); then v measures the sample-size-equivalence of the prior assessment. Using this notation and interpretation, it can be seen that the weight w attached to the prior mean in (5.11) is given by $w = v/(v + n)$, while the weight attached to the sample proportion is $1 - w = n/(v + n)$. Thus, the relative weights depend on v relative to n: in other words, the greater is the sample-size-equivalence of the prior the more weight is attached to the prior mean; while the greater the sample size the more weight is attached to the sample proportion. This is again intuitively sensible.

Now consider the variances. Recalling that the variance of a beta distribution with parameters α and β is $\alpha\beta/[(\alpha + \beta)^2(\alpha + \beta + 1)]$ it follows from (5.8) that the prior variance is $\alpha\beta/[(\alpha + \beta)^2(\alpha + \beta + 1)]$ and that the posterior variance is

$$(\alpha + a)(\beta + b)/[(\alpha + a + \beta + b)^2(\alpha + a + \beta + b + 1)].$$

To simplify these expressions, denote the prior mean $\alpha/(\alpha + \beta)$ by m and the posterior mean by m'. Then the prior and posterior variances can be written as

$$\frac{m(1 - m)}{v + 1} \quad \text{and} \quad \frac{m'(1 - m')}{(v + n + 1)} \tag{5.12}$$

respectively. From these it can be seen that the larger is v the smaller is both the prior variance and the posterior variance, and the larger is n the smaller is the posterior variance. Thus, the dispersion of the posterior assessment is smaller the larger is the sample-size-equivalence of the prior and the larger the sample size. Again, these are intuitively sensible results.

Summarizing: the posterior mean is a weighted average of the prior mean and the sample proportion, the weights depending upon the sample-size-equivalence of the prior (or the confidence with which the prior is held) relative to the sample size; the posterior variance is smaller the smaller the prior variance and the larger the sample size.

To give some feel for the orders of magnitude involved, we present in table 5.1 some numerical examples of the use of the key result (5.8).

It is worthwhile your spending a little time studying this. In particular, you should note that different routes can lead to the same posterior assessment. For example, a prior of $B(11, 11)$ combined with sample outcomes $a = 15$ and $b = 5$ leads to the same posterior

Table 5.1   Some numerical examples of (5.8)

Sample *a*	Outcome *b*	Sample proportion *a/n*	Posterior* assessment mean	Posterior* assessment standard deviation
(a) Prior assessment *B*(1, 1)				
0	0	†	0.5*	0.2887*
10	10	0.5	0.5	0.1043
15	5	0.75	0.7273	0.0929
5	15	0.25	0.2727	0.0929
(b) Prior assessment *B*(11, 11)				
0	0	†	0.5*	0.1043*
10	10	0.5	0.5	0.0762
15	5	0.75	0.619	0.0741
5	15	0.25	0.381	0.0741
(c) Prior assessment *B*(16, 6)				
0	0	†	0.7273*	0.0929*
10	10	0.5	0.619	0.0741
15	5	0.75	0.7381	0.0670
5	15	0.25	0.5	0.0762
(d) Prior assessment *B*(6, 16)				
0	0	†	0.2727*	0.0929*
10	10	0.5	0.381	0.0741
15	5	0.75	0.5	0.0762
5	15	0.25	0.2619	0.0670

* Where $a = b = 0$ the entries relate to the prior assessment.
† Undefined.

as a prior of $B(16, 6)$ combined with sample outcomes $a = 10$ and $b = 10$. These examples emphasize the interpretation of a prior of $B(\alpha, \beta)$ as 'equivalent to' having observed a sample in which α have the characteristic and β do not.

In essence, our analysis is complete. Result (5.8) tells us all we need to know: if our prior assessment is beta then our posterior assessment is beta, irrespective of the size of the sample; moreover, the first parameter of our posterior is the sum of the first parameter of our prior and the number in the sample *with* the characteristic; and the second parameter of our posterior is the sum of the second parameter of our prior and the number in the sample *without* the characteristic. If anyone asks us at any stage what our view about P is, we simply report our posterior at that stage. That is, we reply 'our assessment of P at the moment is $B(., .)$' with the blanks filled in appropriately. That is all there is to it. Statistical inference is as simple as that.

Of course, we may wish to summarize the statement 'our assessment of P is $B(., .)$' by presenting some or all of the summary measures discussed in section 2.3. For instance, we may prefer to talk simply in terms of the mean and variance of our assessment, as we have done in the paragraphs above. Alternatively, we may wish to communicate our assessment in terms of *probability intervals*. In principle, there is no problem with this; we simply follow the procedures discussed in section 2.3. In practice, there is a slight difficulty with the beta distribution since its distribution function cannot be found explicitly: one needs to resort to numerical methods. However, the fact that the beta distribution can be approximated by the normal distribution (with the same mean and variance) comes to our aid. Thus, if our assessment of P at some stage is $B(\alpha, \beta)$, and if $\alpha + \beta$ is sufficiently large (say, greater than 30), then we can approximate our assessment by the normal distribution with the same mean and variance. We can say, therefore, that our assessment of P is approximately

$$N\{\alpha/(\alpha + \beta), \alpha\beta/[(\alpha + \beta)^2(\alpha + \beta + 1)]\},$$

and can then construct (approximate) probability intervals for P using the table of the normal distribution given in Appendix A6.

For example, suppose our assessment of P at some stage is $B(25, 25)$. This has mean $25/(25 + 25) = 0.5$ and variance

$$25 \times 25/[(25 + 25)^2(25 + 25 + 1)] = (0.07)^2.$$

Thus, we can say that our assessment of P is approximately $N[0.5, (0.07)^2]$. If we now wish to present a 95 per cent probability interval for P we consult Appendix A6 and note that a normal distribution lies within 1.96 standard deviations of its mean 95 per cent of the time (see also section 2.4). Hence, our approximate 95 per cent probability interval for P is

$$0.5 \pm 1.96 \times 0.07,$$

that is, $(0.3628, 0.6372)$. Similarly, our approximate 99 per cent probability interval for P is $(0.3194, 0.6806)$. (You may like to know that the *exact* 95 per cent and 99 per cent probability intervals for a $B(25, 25)$ – calculated by numerical methods – are $(0.3634, 0.6366)$ and

(0.3229, 0.6771) respectively. As you can see, the approximation is very close.)

A detailed numerical example of result (5.8) will be given in the next section. In the meantime, we conclude this section by discussing one further implication of (5.8), and emphasizing the implications of one of the assumptions underlying it. Consider first the behaviour of our posterior as the sample size n gets larger. To be specific, let us restrict attention to those cases in which the population size is infinite, and consider the limiting behaviour of our posterior as n approaches infinity. It is intuitively obvious (and it can be proved formally) that as n approaches infinity, the sample proportion a/n approaches the (actual) population proportion p. It follows, therefore, from (5.11) that the posterior mean of our assessment of P approaches p. This is true irrespective of our prior assessment since w in (5.11) approaches 0 as n approaches infinity. Moreover, from (5.12) it can be seen that the posterior variance approaches zero. Thus, *as n approaches infinity, our posterior assessment of P approaches a degenerate distribution centred on the actual p, irrespective of our prior assessment.* This is a most reassuring result.

Finally, let us return to (5.5); this, you will recall, is an assumption about the sampling or selection mechanism. The key result (5.8) relies on (5.5) for its validity. Equation (5.5) states that for every member of the sample, the probability is p that it has the characteristic of interest. If we are sampling from a *finite* population, this means that, not only must we be sampling randomly, but we must also be sampling *with replacement*. For consider, with a simple numerical example, what happens if we do not. Suppose the population consists of 100 people, of which 50 per cent have the characteristic of interest, say are male. Suppose we always select so that each (remaining) member of the population has an equal chance of being selected, *but do not replace* sampled members in the 'sampling pool'. Then, on the first selection, the chance of getting a male is $\frac{1}{2}$. On the second selection, the chance of a male is $\frac{49}{99}$ if a male was selected on the first, and $\frac{50}{99}$ otherwise. Neither of these is equal to $\frac{1}{2}$: hence (5.5) is violated. Thus, from a finite population, sampling must be done with replacement for (5.5), and hence (5.8), to be valid. (There is, of course, a result analogous to (5.8) for the without-replacement case; but, as it is rather messy algebraically, we do not consider it here. In practice, if the population, though finite, is large in relation to the sample size, result (5.8) remains approximately valid even if sampling is done without replacement.)

In some situations, one will feel entirely unable to make any prior assessment about P. This section discusses how our methods may cope with such situations. Consider again our interpretation of a prior which is $B(\alpha, \beta)$ as 'equivalent to' having observed a sample of size $(\alpha + \beta)$ in which α have the characteristic and β do not. Given this interpretation, one natural way to represent complete prior ignorance is by putting α and β equal to zero, since a prior which is $B(0, 0)$ is 'equivalent to' having observed a sample of size 0 (in which 0 have the characteristic and 0 do not). Let us explore the implications of putting α and β both equal to zero in our prior assessment.

From (5.8), we see that, if $\alpha = \beta = 0$, then the posterior assessment, based on a sample of size $a + b$ in which a have the characteristic and b do not, is $B(a, b)$. Rather tautologically, this posterior depends solely and simply on the new information. Also the posterior mean is $a/(a + b) = a/n$, which is the sample proportion; thus the posterior mean for the population proportion is the sample proportion. Moreover, the posterior variance is $ab/[(a + b)^2(a + b + 1)]$, or $\hat{p}(1 - \hat{p})/(n + 1)$ if we let $\hat{p}$ denote the sample proportion a/n. Thus the posterior variance depends only on sample information: specifically the sample proportion and the sample size.

The representation of complete prior ignorance, or non-existent prior information, by putting α and β both equal to zero in the prior assessment appears to be appropriate. The only problem is that, in the definition of the beta distribution (2.27), α and β are both supposed to be positive. Indeed, if α and β are put equal to zero in (2.27), the resulting function has an infinite area underneath it for any scaling factor; as such it cannot represent a probability density function (which must have an area of 1 underneath it after suitable scaling). The resulting function is clearly not a *proper* density function. For that reason, the function with α and β both equal to zero is termed an *improper* density function. Nevertheless, it 'works' in the sense that the posterior distribution is perfectly proper, even though the prior is improper. Moreover, it works *well* in the sense that the properties of the posterior distribution all accord with intuition. Accordingly, we will use it as our representation of complete prior ignorance; in so doing, we follow the practice of most Bayesian statisticians.

Let us explore the implications a little further. As has been noted

above, if a sample of size $a + b$ yields a members with the characteristic and b without, and if we start from a position of complete prior
ignorance ($\alpha = \beta = 0$) then the posterior is $B(a, b)$. This has mean $\hat{p}$
and variance $\hat{p}(1 - \hat{p})/(n + 1)$, where $\hat{p}(\equiv a/n)$ is the sample proportion. If $a + b$ is sufficiently large, then we can use the normal approximation to give us the following important result.

> With total prior ignorance, the posterior on P is
> approximately $N[\hat{p}, \hat{p}(1 - \hat{p})/(n + 1)]$ where $\hat{p}$ is the $\qquad$ (5.13)
> sample proportion and n the sample size.

This is a complete characterization of our posterior assessment.
Summaries can be provided in the usual manner. For example, to
obtain the 95 per cent probability interval for P we use the fact that
a normally distributed variable lies within 1.96 standard deviations
of its mean 95 per cent of the time. Thus, from (5.13), an
(approximate) 95 per cent probability interval for P is given by

$$\hat{p} \pm 1.96\sqrt{[\hat{p}(1 - \hat{p})/(n + 1)]}. \qquad (5.14)$$

For example, starting from a position of complete prior ignorance
and obtaining a random sample of size 50 in which 20 are found to
have the characteristic of interest, then $\hat{p} = 0.4$, and the posterior
assessment is approximately $N[0.4, (0.0686)^2]$ (from (5.13)). Hence,
from (5.14), the posterior 95 per cent probability interval is
$(0.4 \pm 1.96 \times 0.0686)$; that is, $(0.266, 0.534)$. Thus, one can conclude
on the basis of this sample information that the probability is 0.95
that P is between 0.266 and 0.534.

From (5.14) it can be seen that the *width* of the 95 per cent prob-
ability interval is $3.92\sqrt{[\hat{p}(1 - \hat{p})/(n + 1)]}$. This is clearly a decreasing
function of n, the sample size, though the precise magnitude depends
also on $\hat{p}$, the sample proportion. This means that one cannot guarantee in advance a specified value for the width by suitable choice of
n, though one *can* guarantee a specified *maximum* width. Consider
the expression $3.92\sqrt{[\hat{p}(1 - \hat{p})/(n + 1)]}$ as a function of $\hat{p}$; it takes the
value 0 for $\hat{p}$ equal to 0 or 1 and is positive for intermediate values;
moreover, it reaches its maximum when $\hat{p} = 0.5$. Thus the maximum
width of the 95 per cent probability interval is

$$3.92\sqrt{[0.5 \times 0.5/(n + 1)]} = 1.96/\sqrt{(n + 1)}.$$

Hence, a specified maximum width can be guaranteed by suitable
choice of n. (For example, for maximum widths of 0.4, 0.2, 0.1, 0.05,
0.02 and 0.01 the requisite values of n are 23, 95, 384, 1536, 9603 and
38 415 respectively. As these examples illustrate, and as is borne out

by the general result, a halving of the maximum width requires a quadrupling of the sample size.)

Let us now give an extended example of the material of this chapter. Suppose you are approached by the local SDP secretary, who wishes to find out whether it might be worth fielding an SDP candidate in the forthcoming election. Clearly this depends on the proportion p of voters who would vote SDP if a candidate stood; if p is large it might be worth fielding a candidate, otherwise it might simply be a waste of party funds. The problem, of course, is that neither you nor the local secretary know the value of p. However, you can get information about p by conducting an opinion poll amongst a sample of local electors. From the local post office you can get the latest electoral register, from which you can obtain a random sample of any desired size. (One way would be to write each voter's name on a separate slip of paper, put the slips into a hat, shuffle them well, and draw out the requisite number of slips, replacing each one after each draw. A less tedious way would be to select one name at random out of the first m/n names, and then pick every (m/n)th name thereafter, where m and n are the population and sample sizes respectively. Would this satisfy (5.5)?) Suppose you decide to be rather cautious to begin with, and just take a relatively small sample – say of 100 voters. (After all, if sampling is costly, a large sample will prove to be rather wasteful if the sample proportion turns out to be very low or very high.) Suppose this pilot sample yields twenty-five people who say they will vote SDP and seventy-five who say they will not. What is your assessment of P, the proportion of the whole electorate who will vote SDP, in the light of this information?

This clearly depends upon your prior assessment. Let us consider two cases, the first in which you start from a position of total prior ignorance, and the second in which you build on your experience of SDP voting patterns elsewhere in the country. In the first case, you feel totally unable to say anything at all about P; thus, your prior on P is $B(0, 0)$. From (5.8), it follows that your posterior on P, in the light of your pilot sample, is $B(25, 75)$. Thus has mean 0.25 and variance $(0.043)^2$, and is approximately normal. Thus, your posterior is approximately $N[0.25, (0.043)^2]$. As the local SDP secretary is unlikely to be able to make sense of this statement, you may find it easier to communicate in terms of probability intervals. The 95 per cent probability interval is $0.25 \pm 1.96 \times 0.043$; that is, $(0.166, 0.334)$. So you can say to the secretary that you think there is a 95 per cent chance that between 16.6 per cent and 33.4 per cent of the electorate will vote SDP. The chances are that the secretary may be moderately encouraged by this, particularly if the election is to be a three-cornered fight, but also may be rather concerned by the large margin of error (that is, the large width of the interval). He may, therefore, encourage you to take a further sample, on the grounds that further investigation may prove worthwhile. Suppose you now decide to take a somewhat larger sample, say of 500 voters, again selected in a random manner from the electoral register. Suppose this larger sample yields 95 people who say they will vote SDP and 405 who say they will not. This information updates your assessment from $B(25, 75)$ (which it was after the pilot sample but before the main sample) to $B(120, 480)$, using (5.8). This has mean 0.2 and variance $(0.0163)^2$, and is approximately normal. Thus, your assessment now is approximately $N[0.2, (0.0163)^2]$, and the corresponding 95 per cent probability interval is $0.2 \pm 1.96 \times 0.0163$; that is (0.168, 0.232). So you can now say to the local SDP secretary that you think there is a 95 per cent chance that between 16.8 per cent and 23.2 per cent of the electorate will vote SDP. The chances are that the secretary will not be particularly pleased by this updated assessment!

Consider now a second case in which your prior assessment of P, before *any* local sampling is carried out, is $B(3, 12)$. This has mean 0.2 and standard deviation 0.1 (with approximate 95 per cent probability interval of (0.004, 0.396)), and may be based on your experience of SDP voting patterns elsewhere in the country. Using (5.8), it follows that your assessment after the pilot sample, but before the main sample, is $B(28, 87)$, and after the main sample is $B(123, 492)$. Thus, the intermediate 95 per cent probability interval is (0.165, 0.322), and the final 95 per cent probability interval is (0.168, 0.232). As you can see from these, your prior assessment is very soon swamped by the sample evidence; this is because your prior beliefs about P were not particularly strong. You may like to investigate the situation if your prior beliefs are stronger, say $B(30, 120)$ or $B(120, 480)$.

This example almost concludes this section. However, one final comment may be helpful, particularly if you are feeling worried with the use of the improper prior $B(0, 0)$ as a representation of total prior ignorance. You may prefer to use $B(1, 1)$ as the appropriate representation. This, you will recall, is the same as the uniform over $[0, 1]$, and captures the idea that all values of P between 0 and 1 are considered equally likely. However, in practice, the difference between a prior of $B(0, 0)$ and one of $B(1, 1)$ is negligible, as the above example shows: a posterior of $B(a, b)$ and one of $B(a + 1, b + 1)$ are almost the same for a and b at all large.

5.6 'CONFIDENCE INTERVALS' AND 'SIGNIFICANCE TESTS'

The essence of Bayesian statistics is the representation of beliefs in the form of probability assessments, and the updating of those assessments in the light of new information. When asked about some parameter(s) or variable(s) at some point in time, the Bayesian statistician simply reports his or her assessment at that point in time (either the complete characterization or some appropriate summary). That is all there is to it.

Classical statisticians, however, do things differently. It is the purpose of this section to relate (as far as is possible) statements made by Classical statisticians with those made by their Bayesian counterparts. This is so that you may read and understand analyses conducted in the Classical mode.

The crucial difference is that Classical statistics regards probability as an *objective* concept, and thus not a statement of subjective belief. This implies, *inter alia*, that probability statements can *not* be made about fixed numbers – such as the *actual* proportion with some characteristic in some population. Thus, a Classical statistician would regard the statement 'the probability is 0.95 that P lies between 0.168 and 0.232' as meaningless: to him or her, P either lies in that interval or it does not. Classical statistics does not allow 'α per cent probability intervals for P'. However, there is a very similar sounding concept in Classical statistics – namely, that of an 'α per cent *confidence interval* for P'. Thus, a Classical statistician may report that, 'on the basis of the sample information, a 95 per cent confidence interval for P is (0.168, 0.232)'. As we have noted above, this *does not* imply that the Classical statistician thinks that the probability is 0.95 that P lies between 0.168 and 0.232. Indeed, to him or her, P either lies between 0.168 and 0.232 or it does not. (So, in a formal sense, the probability is either 1 or 0.) The appropriate interpretation of the phrase '95 per cent confidence interval for P' is that, of all such 95 per cent confidence intervals for (some) P constructed by the Classical statistician, 95 per cent of them *will* contain P while the remaining 5 per cent will not. So the phrases 'α per cent probability interval for P' and 'α per cent confidence interval for P' have quite different interpretations – reflecting the difference between the subjective concept of probability in the Bayesian school and the objective concept in the Classical school. (My own view is that the Classical notion of a confidence interval is highly contorted, and that most students, even when ostensibly operating within the Classical school, implicitly employ the more intuitive Bayesian interpretation.)

One consequence of the Classical view of probability is that it automatically denies any role for *prior* beliefs. Thus, the 'final assessment' must depend solely and simply on the sample information. Classical statistics, therefore, effectively only considers the case of total prior ignorance. This, very small, subset of Bayesian statistics was considered in section 5.5. A key result of that section is the result on the posterior assessment given in (5.13), and the consequent result on the 95 per cent probability interval given in (5.14). This states that with total prior ignorance, the 95 per cent probability interval for P, given a sample of size n and a sample proportion $\hat{p}$, is approximately

$$\hat{p} \pm 1.96\sqrt{[\hat{p}(1 - \hat{p})/(n + 1)]}. \tag{5.15}$$

A Classical statistician, faced with the same evidence, would conclude (see section 4.5 of Hey (1974)) that a 95 per cent confidence interval for P is approximately

$$\hat{p} \pm 1.96\sqrt{[\hat{p}(1 - \hat{p})/n]}. \tag{5.16}$$

Apart from the interpretation, the only difference between (5.15) and (5.16) is that $(n + 1)$ appears in the former where n appears in the latter. Clearly, for large n this difference is immaterial. Thus, apart from the interpretation, *the Classical confidence interval is the same as the Bayesian posterior probability interval based on total prior ignorance.* So, if a Classical statistician reports a 95 per cent confidence interval for P as (0.168, 0.232), it is entirely correct for you *as a Bayesian statistician* to use this as your posterior 95 per cent probability interval if your prior beliefs were non-existent.

Classical statistics also has a procedure called *hypothesis testing*; this has no direct counterpart in Bayesian statistics. A Bayesian interpretation of (a modified version of) Classical hypothesis testing *is* possible, though we prefer to delay this, for expositional reasons, until the next chapter. To attempt an interpretation here would risk confusion.

5.7   SUMMARY

This chapter has examined one of the simplest problems of statistical inference: namely, that of inference about an unknown proportion. Although relatively simple, this problem provides a useful introduction to the basic procedure of Bayesian inference – that of the updating of prior beliefs in the light of new information. For expositional reasons, we restricted attention in this chapter to the case in which the prior beliefs about the proportion could be expressed in the form of a beta distribution, though clearly the *methods* can equally well be applied to other forms of prior assessment. The effect of new information on the prior assessment depends, of course, on the form of the new information and, in particular, on the way that it was obtained. In this chapter, we explored the implications of the 'natural' source of information about the population proportion – namely, the inspection of randomly selected members of that population. In a key result, we showed that, whatever the size of the randomly selected sample, if the prior assessment is a beta distribution, then the posterior assessment is also. In other words, the assessment stays within the (beta) family. Moreover, the parameters of the assessment change in a simple fashion: the first parameter increases by the number in the sample with the characteristic, and the second by the number without the characteristic. We showed how this had intuitively acceptable implications for the way that sample information affected the mean and variance of the assessment. Penultimately, we discussed how total prior ignorance might be characterized, and concluded that a beta prior with both parameters set equal to zero seemed to be an appropriate characterization. Finally, we related the results of this chapter to the Classical analysis of the same problem, and showed that a Classical confidence interval is numerically essentially the same as a Bayesian probability interval based on total prior ignorance (though the interpretations are quite different).

5.8 EXERCISES

(Note that some of these exercises are rather repetitive. You are, therefore, encouraged to be selective once you have gained confidence with your understanding of the material of this chapter.)

5.1 Suppose that your prior on P is not beta, but instead takes the following (discrete) form

$$f_P(p) = \begin{cases} \frac{1}{2} & p = \frac{1}{4}, \frac{3}{4} \\ 0 & \text{otherwise.} \end{cases}$$

Find your posterior assessment of P given that a randomly selected sample yielded a members with the characteristic and b members without. If the true value of p is $\frac{1}{4}$, argue that your posterior will converge to a degenerate distribution at the value $p = \frac{1}{4}$ as n approaches infinity. (A heuristic argument will suffice.) What would happen if the true value was $p = \frac{1}{2}$ (that is, a value considered as impossible by your prior assessment)?

5.2   Suppose that your prior on P is not beta, but instead takes the following (discrete) form

$$f_P(p) = \begin{cases} \frac{1}{3} & p = 0, \frac{1}{2}, 1 \\ 0 & \text{otherwise.} \end{cases}$$

Find your posterior assessment of P given that a randomly selected sample yielded a members with the characteristic and b without. (Care, this is slightly tricky. You should consider separately the three cases: (i) $a = 0$, $b > 0$; (ii) $a > 0$, $b > 0$; (iii) $a > 0$, $b = 0$.)

5.3   Suppose your prior for some unknown proportion P is beta with parameters α and β. Suppose the mean of your prior is 0.5. Find α and β when the standard deviation takes the values: (a) $1/\sqrt{12}$; (b) 0.125; (c) 0.1; (d) 0.05; (e) 0.0625; (f) 0.025.

5.4   Suppose your prior for some unknown proportion P is beta with parameters α and β. Suppose the mean of your prior is 0.3. Find α and β when the standard deviation takes the values: (a) 0.1; (b) 0.05; (c) 0.025; (d) 0.02.

5.5   Suppose your prior for some unknown proportion P is beta with parameters α and β. Suppose the mean of your prior is 0.7. Find α and β when the standard deviation takes the values: (a) 0.1; (b) 0.05; (c) 0.025; (d) 0.02.

5.6   Suppose your prior for some unknown proportion P is beta with parameters α and β. Suppose the mean of your prior is 0.2. Find α and β when the standard deviation takes the values: (a) 0.2; (b) 0.1; (c) 0.05; (d) 0.025.

5.7   Suppose a random sample of size 100 yielded 40 with the characteristic and 60 without. Find, for the priors given in the following exercises, the posterior distribution of P, and the consequent 95 per cent probability interval for P.

(a) exercise 5.3(d);   (b) exercise 5.4(b);   (c) exercise 5.5(b); (d) exercise 5.6(c).

In each case calculate the reduction in the width of the 95 per cent probability interval between the prior and the posterior.

5.8   Repeat exercise 5.7 for the following priors.

(a) exercise 5.3(f);   (b) exercise 5.4(c);   (c) exercise 5.5(c);
(d) exercise 5.6(d).

5.9   Suppose Smith's prior for some unknown proportion P is beta
with mean 0.4 and standard deviation 0.1, and that Jones's
prior for the same P is beta with mean 0.6 and standard
deviation 0.1. Suppose they observe the same evidence –
namely, a random sample of size 50 in which half have the
characteristic of interest. Find the respective posterior distributions, and the implied 95 per cent probability intervals.

5.10   Prove that, if sampling is done according to (5.5) then the
probability that a sample of size n has a with the characteristic
and b without is given by (5.9).

5.11   Suppose you wish to select n items from a list containing a
total of m items. Suppose you select one item at random out of
the first m/n items, and then pick every (m/n)th thereafter. Are
you sampling with replacement? Will (5.5) be satisfied?

5.12   Consider the example discussed at length in section 5.7.
Rework the analysis for the two priors suggested at the end of
the penultimate paragraph of that section.

5.13   Suppose your prior knowledge about some unknown proportion P is essentially non-existent. Find the posterior distribution in the light of a sample of size sixteen that contained
exactly half with the characteristic. Now suppose you obtain a
further eighty observations in which thirty have the characteristic and fifty do not. What is your posterior now? Find the 95
per cent probability intervals at both the intervening and final
stages.

5.14   Suppose your prior for P, the proportion of potential SDP
voters in Bristol North East is beta with mean 0.5 and standard deviation 0.0625. Suppose a gallup poll of thirty voters
yields twenty potential SDP voters; find the posterior 95 per
cent probability interval for P. What would this interval
become after a further thirty observations with the same SDP-
ratio?

5.15   (a) If your prior knowledge about some unknown proportion
P is essentially non-existent, how large a sample size do

you need to ensure that your posterior 95 per cent probability interval has a width less than 0.2?

(b) Suppose you collect the sample of the size recommended in (a), and find that 25 per cent of the sample have the characteristic. What is the width of the posterior 95 per cent probability interval? Is this 0.2? Why or why not?

5.16 (a) If your prior knowledge about some unknown proportion P is essentially non-existent, what is the greatest width that your posterior 95 per cent probability interval would have, based on a sample of size 25?

(b) What would your answer be to (a) above if, instead, your prior on P was β with mean 0.5 and standard deviation 0.0625? In the light of this, assess the 'value' of this prior information.

5.17 Discuss the adequacy of the beta distribution as an encapsulation of beliefs about a proportion. What do *you* feel about $\alpha = \beta = 0$ and $\alpha = \beta = 1$ as characteristics of vague prior knowledge? Give an example of a situation in which the beta distribution would be unsuitable as an encapsulation of prior beliefs; how would Bayesian analysis proceed in this case?

5.18 'Bayesian inference about a proportion requires that the prior assessment be in the form of a beta distribution.' True or False?

6 MEANS AND VARIANCES

In chapter 5, we were concerned with the incidence of some characteristic in some population. Moreover, that was *all* that we were concerned with. Now, given that each member of the population either has the characteristic or does not have it, the incidence of the characteristic in the population is *completely* described by the proportion P with the characteristic. Knowledge of the value of P is thus all we want or need to know.

Of course, in practice, our interest would not normally stop there; being naturally inquisitive, we would probably want to inquire further – into *which types* of members have the characteristic and *why*. But this goes beyond the scope of the problem analysed in chapter 5, and takes us into the realm of economic *relationships*, which is the concern of chapters 7, 8 and 9. Rather obviously, if we are interested in more than just the value of P, we need to set the problem up more generally in the first instance. This we do in the following chapter. Before that, we consider, in this chapter, a rather simpler generalization of the material of chapter 5 – one that will pave the way for the material of chapter 7.

In chapter 5, the thing in which we were interested was of an all-or-nothing nature: members of the population either have the characteristic or they do not. Rather more generally, we may be interested in something which may be had in varying degrees by members of the population. Thus, for example, we may be interested in the incomes of the members of the population, or their consumption expenditures, or their heights, or their weights, or their spending on beer, or their holdings of index-linked stock, or whatever. In other words, we may be interested in the values of some variable, let us call it X, taken by the various members of the population. In general, the value of X will vary from member to member of the population; that is, there will be a *distribution* of X values across the population. Now, depending upon our particular interest in some

135

particular application, we may be interested in learning *everything* about this distribution of X, or we may simply be interested in learning about the value of some *summary measure* (or measures) of the distribution – say its mean or variance (or both).

As in chapter 5, information about the distribution of X can be obtained by inspecting randomly selected members of the population and determining their X-values. This information can be combined with any prior assessment of the distribution of X to yield a posterior assessment, using Bayes' theorem in the manner illustrated in chapter 5. The outcome of this procedure depends, of course, upon the precise form of the prior assessment and, in particular, upon the way that the distribution of X is characterized.

The problem is simplified if one knows the *form* of the distribution of X in the population; for example, if one knows that it is uniform, or beta, or normal or whatever. In such cases, the distribution is completely described by a small number of key parameters: such as a and b in the case of the uniform (see (2.23)); α and β in the case of the beta (see (2.27)); μ and σ^2 in the case of the normal (see (2.29)); and so on. In these cases, knowledge of these key parameters implies knowledge of all aspects of the distribution.

Although the *methods* of this chapter can be applied *whatever the form of the distribution* of X, we will restrict attention to the case when the distribution is *normal*. This is a particularly important case, which is encountered frequently in practice. (Many economic variables are normally distributed, and many others, when suitably transformed, are also normally distributed; for example, weekly consumption expenditure for given income groups is approximately normal, as is the logarithm of weekly income.) If X is normally distributed, then its distribution is completely characterized by its *mean* and *variance* (see (2.29)). Thus, knowledge of the mean and variance implies knowledge of all aspects of the distribution. In this case, therefore, learning everything about the distribution is synonymous with learning about the two summary measures, the mean and the variance of the distribution.

The key parameters of the distribution are the mean and variance; we denote these by M and S^2 respectively. Thus, M denotes the *M*ean and S the *S*tandard deviation of X in the population. In keeping with our notational convention, we use upper-case letters to denote the *names* of these parameters, and the corresponding lower-case letters to denote specific values. Thus the *actual* value of M in the population is denoted by m, and the *actual* value of S in the population is denoted by s (with m and s set equal to the appropriate values, of course). We can distinguish four possible cases, as listed in the following table.

Case	Mean	Variance
1	known	known
2	unknown	known
3	known	unknown
4	unknown	unknown

Case 1 is essentially trivial, and there is no problem to investigate – everything is known about the distribution. In the other three cases, the problem is non-trivial, and information is potentially useful: to reduce uncertainty about the mean in case 2; to reduce uncertainty about the variance in case 3; and to reduce uncertainty about both in case 4.

The appropriate notation varies from case to case depending upon what is known and what is unknown. To be specific, the mean is referred to as m if it is known, and M if it is unknown; likewise, the standard deviation is referred to as s if it is known, and S if it is unknown (with m and s set equal to the appropriate values, of course). In the cases where the mean and/or the variance are unknown, the basic procedure illustrated in chapter 5 is followed: first some prior assessment of the unknown parameter(s) is formed; then a sample of members of the population is obtained and inspected; finally, the information contained in the sample is used to update the prior assessment, and hence obtain the posterior assessment. The purpose of this chapter is to derive the posterior assessments in cases 2 to 4 for certain given prior assessments. To be specific, section 6.2 deals with case 2, section 6.3 with case 3 and section 6.4 with case 4. In each case, the question of vague prior knowledge is explored. Section 6.5 shows how the results of sections 6.2 to 6.4 may be related to a Classical analysis of the same problem. Finally, section 6.6 provides a summary, and section 6.7 a set of exercises.

6.2 INFERENCE WITH AN UNKNOWN MEAN AND KNOWN VARIANCE

In this section we examine case 2. In this, we are concerned with some variable of interest X which is normally distributed in some population of interest. We do not know the value of the mean, M, of

X, though we *do* know the variance s^2. The purpose of this section is to show how observations on X can be used to update a prior assessment about M, the unknown mean.

The assumptions of this section can be summarized as follows:

$$X \text{ is } N(M, s^2). \tag{6.1}$$

We now need to consider two elements: the form of the prior assessment of M, and the source of information about M which can be used to update this prior assessment. We examine these in turn.

Clearly, the form of the prior assessment depends upon the beliefs of the individual making the assessment, and these will generally vary from individual to individual depending upon their previous experience and knowledge. Since X is continuous (implicit in (6.1)) it seems reasonable to suppose that the assessment of M will be continuous, rather than discrete. Although the methods of this section can be applied whatever the form of this prior assessment, we will restrict attention to the case when the prior assessment takes the form of a *normal distribution*. This appears to be a fairly natural form for the prior assessment to take. We suppose, then, that the prior on M is normal with mean μ and variance σ^2, where μ and σ are chosen appropriately. To select the appropriate values for μ and σ, we proceed as in section 5.2. For example, if our assessment of M is such that you regard 100 as its most likely value, and such that you are almost (95.44 per cent) certain that M lies between 80 and 120, then the appropriate values for μ and σ would be 100 and 10 respectively. (Recall that a normally distributed variable lies within 2 standard deviations of its mean with probability 0.9544.) Or again, if your prior 95.44 per cent probability interval for M is (100, 120), then μ, your prior mean, is 110, and σ, your prior standard deviation, is 5.

We can express this assumption, that the prior assessment of M is $N(\mu, \sigma^2)$, in terms of the prior probability density function of M. Thus (cf. (2.29), where we incorporate the σ^{-1} into the factor of proportionality):

$$f_M(m) \propto \exp\left[-(m - \mu)^2/2\sigma^2\right]. \tag{6.2}$$

Now consider the question of information about M. As in chapter 5, there is a natural source for this information, namely the members of the population of interest. To be specific, since M is the mean value of X in the population, it is natural to look at the X-values of members of the population to shed light on M. Again, as in chapter 5, there are two extremes: we could look at *all* members of the population, or we could look at just *one* member of the population. In between, there is the option of inspecting *n* members. We will follow the procedure adopted in chapter 5: that is, we will explore the implications of inspecting just *one* member of the population, and then generalize those implications to the general case of the inspection of *n* members.

As in chapter 5, it is natural to select our one member (our sample of size 1) in a manner which yields information about the parameter of interest. This suggests that we select our sample in a 'fair' manner – so that each member of the population has an equal chance of being selected. This implies that the probability distribution of the *X*-value of the sampled member is exactly the same as the distribution of *X* in the population. Thus, from (6.1), the distribution of the *X*-value of the sampled member must be $N(M, s^2)$. Clearly, this depends upon the unknown value of *M*; the most appropriate way to express this is to state that the *conditional distribution* (of the *X*-value of the sampled member), given that *M* equals *m*, is $N(m, s^2)$. We can write this in terms of the conditional probability density function (cf. (2.29), where we incorporate the s^{-1} into the factor of proportionality):

$$g_X(x \mid m) \propto \exp\left[-(x-m)^2/2s^2\right]. \tag{6.3}$$

This is the likelihood of the sampled member having an *X*-value equal to *x* (or, more succinctly, 'the likelihood of observing *x*'), given that *M* equals *m*.

We are now in a position to apply Bayes' theorem, and hence to obtain the posterior assessment of *M* in the light of an observation *x*. The prior is given by (6.2); the likelihood by (6.3), and hence, using (4.23), the posterior is given by:

$$g_M(m \mid x) \propto g_X(x \mid m) f_M(m)$$
$$\propto \exp\left[-(x-m)^2/2s^2\right] \exp\left[-(m-\mu)^2/2\sigma^2\right]$$

Thus,

$$g_M(m \mid x) \propto \exp\left[-\frac{(x-m)^2}{2s^2} - \frac{(m-\mu)^2}{2\sigma^2}\right] \tag{6.4}$$

Now note that the term in square brackets can be simplified by use of the following algebraic identity:

$$\frac{(x-m)^2}{s^2} + \frac{(m-\mu)^2}{\sigma^2} \equiv \left(\frac{s^2+\sigma^2}{s^2\sigma^2}\right)\left(m - \frac{s^2\mu + \sigma^2 x}{s^2+\sigma^2}\right)^2 + \frac{(x-\mu)^2}{s^2+\sigma^2}.$$

Substituting this in (6.4) we get

$$g_M(m \mid x) \propto \exp\left[-\left(\frac{s^2 + \sigma^2}{2s^2\sigma^2}\right)\left(m - \frac{s^2\mu + \sigma^2 x}{s^2 + \sigma^2}\right)^2\right]$$

$$\times \exp\left[-\frac{(x - \mu)^2}{2(s^2 + \sigma^2)}\right].$$

This can be simplified by incorporating the part which does not depend upon m in the factor of proportionality. This yields:

$$g_M(m \mid x) \propto \exp\left[-\left(m - \frac{s^2\mu + \sigma^2 x}{s^2 + \sigma^2}\right)^2 \Big/ \left(\frac{2s^2\sigma^2}{s^2 + \sigma^2}\right)\right] \tag{6.5}$$

This you will recognize (cf. (2.29)) as the probability density function of a normally distributed variable with mean $(s^2\mu + \sigma^2 x)/(s^2 + \sigma^2)$ and variance $s^2\sigma^2/(s^2 + \sigma^2)$. We thus get the following important result:

If the prior on M is $N(\mu, \sigma^2)$, then after an observation x on X (which is $N(M, s^2)$), the posterior on M is

$$N\left(\frac{s^2\mu + \sigma^2 x}{s^2 + \sigma^2}, \frac{s^2\sigma^2}{s^2 + \sigma^2}\right) \tag{6.6}$$

The first thing to note about this result is that the posterior assessment is normal, as was the prior assessment. Thus, the assessment stays within the (normal) family. The second thing to note is the effect of the new observation on the mean of the assessment: as can be seen from (6.6) the prior mean is μ and the posterior mean is

$$\frac{s^2\mu + \sigma^2 x}{s^2 + \sigma^2} \tag{6.7}$$

It is apparent that this posterior mean is a weighted average of the prior mean (μ) and the observation (x). Moreover, the weight attached to the prior mean is s^2, the variance of X, and the weight attached to the observation is σ^2, the prior variance of M. This means that the smaller is σ^2 the more weight is attached to the prior mean, while the smaller is s^2 the more weight is attached to the observation. Or, in other words, the more confident you are about your prior assessment of M, the less weight you attach to the new information in determining your posterior assessment; and the closer the observation is likely to be to the actual m, the more weight you attach to the observation. All these implications make good intuitive sense.

An alternative way of writing the posterior mean (6.7) is obtained by dividing top and bottom by $s^2\sigma^2$. This yields the following alternative, but algebraically identical, expression for the posterior mean:

$$\frac{(1/\sigma^2)\mu + (1/s^2)x}{(1/\sigma^2) + (1/s^2)} \tag{6.8}$$

In this form, the weight attached to μ is $(1/\sigma^2)$ and the weight attached to x is $(1/s^2)$. Of course, the relative weights remain s^2 to σ^2 as before, but this alternative representation is more 'natural' in the sense that each component is weighted by an indicator of *its own* 'accuracy'. To be specific, the weight attached to the prior mean is $(1/\sigma^2)$, the reciprocal of the prior variance; thus the smaller is the prior variance, the greater is the weight attached to the prior mean. Likewise, the weight attached to the observation is $(1/s^2)$, the reciprocal of the variance of the observation; thus the smaller is the variance of the observation, the greater is the weight attached to the observation. In each case, the weight is the *reciprocal* of a variance. As will become apparent, it will be useful to give this reciprocal a name, and a notation, of its own. Quite naturally, the reciprocal of the variance of a variable is termed the *precision* of that variable. Clearly, the smaller is the variance, the larger is the precision, and the larger is the variance, the smaller is the precision; the word 'precision' is therefore entirely appropriate. We will let π denote the precision of the prior assessment, and p denote the precision of the observation. Thus,

$$\pi \equiv 1/\sigma^2 \quad \text{and} \quad p \equiv 1/s^2. \tag{6.9}$$

Substituting these in (6.8), we get the following expression for the posterior mean of M:

$$\frac{\pi\mu + px}{\pi + p} \tag{6.10}$$

This states that the posterior mean is a weighted average of the prior mean and the observation, the weights being the precision of the prior and the precision of the observation respectively. Thus, the more precise is the prior, the more weight is attached to the prior mean; and the more precise is the observation, the more weight is attached to the observation.

Let us now examine the effect on the variance and on the precision of the assessment of the new information. From (6.6) it is seen that the prior variance in σ^2, and the posterior variance is $s^2\sigma^2/(s^2 + \sigma^2)$. This means that the prior precision is $1/\sigma^2 = \pi$, and the posterior precision is $(s^2 + \sigma^2)/s^2\sigma^2 = (1/\sigma^2 + 1/s^2) = \pi + p$. Thus, the effect of the observation is to increase the precision from π to $\pi + p$: the assessment after the observation is necessarily more precise than that beforehand, with the increase in the precision being equal to the precision of the observation. This is an intuitively sensible result.

Using our new notation, we can express the key result (6.6) in the following alternative, but algebraically identical, form:

$$\left.\begin{array}{l} \text{If the prior on } M \text{ is } N(\mu, 1/\pi), \text{ then after an observation} \\ x \text{ on } X \text{ (which is } N(M, 1/p)), \text{ the posterior on } M \text{ is} \\[2mm] N\left(\dfrac{\pi\mu + px}{\pi + p}, \dfrac{1}{\pi + p}\right) \end{array}\right\} \quad (6.11)$$

Summarizing: the posterior is normal, as was the prior; the posterior mean is a weighted average of the prior mean μ and the observation x, with the weights being the prior precision π and the precision of the observation p respectively; and the posterior precision is the sum of the prior precision and the precision of the observation.

Before generalizing this result, let us give a simple example of its use. Suppose we are interested in a variable X which we know is normally distributed with variance $s^2 = 9$ but unknown mean M in some population. Suppose our prior beliefs about M can be represented by a prior assessment which is normally distributed with mean $\mu = 100$ and variance $\sigma^2 = 16$. Suppose we then obtain a random sample of one member of the population, and find that the X-value for this member is $x = 112.5$. Applying (6.6), or equivalently (6.11), we find that the posterior assessment of M is normally distributed with mean

$$\frac{(1/\sigma^2) + (1/s^2)x}{(1/\sigma^2) + (1/s^2)} = \frac{(\frac{1}{16})100 + (\frac{1}{9})112.5}{\frac{1}{16} + \frac{1}{9}} = 108$$

and precision

$$1/\sigma^2 + 1/s^2 = \tfrac{1}{16} + \tfrac{1}{9} = \tfrac{25}{144}.$$

It follows that the posterior variance is $\frac{144}{25}$, and hence that the posterior standard deviation is $\frac{12}{5} = 2.4$. Thus, the posterior assessment is $N[108, (2.4)^2]$. This, and the prior assessment, are illustrated in figure 6.1.

As can be seen from this figure, the effect of the observation on the assessment of M is to shift it towards the observation (by an amount depending on the relative sizes of the prior precision and the precision of the observation), at the same time reducing its dispersion.

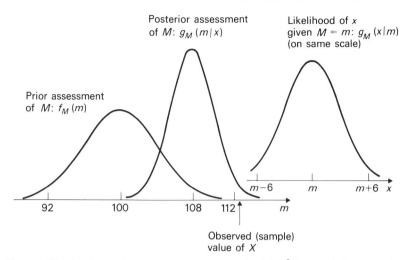

Figure 6.1 A prior and posterior assessment for M*(s² known). Prior on* M *is* M*(100, 16) likelihood of* X *given* M = m *is* N*(m, 9) posterior on* M *is* N*(108, 2.4²).*

This effect is reflected in the various probability intervals. For example, the prior 95 per cent probability interval for M is $100 \pm 1.96 \times 4$, that is, (92.16, 107.84); while the posterior 95 per cent probability interval for M is $108 \pm 1.96 \times 2.4$, that is (103.296, 112.704). Thus, given the prior assessment and the one observation $x = 112.5$, one can conclude that the probability is 0.95 that M lies between 103.296 and 112.704. You will note that the width of the 95 per cent probability interval is reduced from 15.68 to 9.408 as a result of the observation; this reduction is a measure of the 'value' of the information. You will also note that this reduction does not depend upon the actual value of the observation – because the width of a 95 per cent probability interval depends only on the precision (or variance), and the posterior precision is unaffected by the actual value of the observation. Perhaps you would like to reflect on whether this is intuitively sensible?

So far we have considered only the case of a sample of size 1. Let us now generalize our results to the case of a sample of size n. We continue to suppose that our sample is selected in a 'fair' manner – in that all members have an equal chance of being selected. This implies that the conditional distribution of *each* X-value in the sample is given by (6.3). This means that (6.11) remains valid, and can be used to determine the effect of a sample of size n on our prior assessment. What we will do is to consider the incorporation of the n observations (which we shall denote by $x_1, x_2, \ldots, x_n$) sequentially. If the prior is $N(\mu, \sigma^2)$ then after the first observation x_1 the posterior is $N[\pi\mu + px_1)/(\pi + p), 1/(\pi + p)]$, using (6.11). It may be helpful to represent this schematically as follows:

prior $N(\mu, 1/\pi)$ + observation x_1

$$\Rightarrow \text{posterior } N\left(\frac{\pi\mu + px_1}{\pi + p}, \frac{1}{\pi + p}\right). \quad (6.12)$$

Now consider the incorporation of the second observation x_2. Before this is incorporated the assessment is $N[(\pi\mu + px_1)/(\pi + p), 1/(\pi + p)]$, and thus this is the relevant prior to use in (6.11) when considering the incorporation of x_2 into the assessment. Note crucially that (6.11) is valid whatever 'μ' and 'π' are. In particular, 'μ' can take the value $(\pi\mu + px_1)/(\pi + p)$ and 'π' can take the value $\pi + p$. Using these values in (6.11) we get:

prior $N\left(\dfrac{\pi\mu + px_1}{\pi + p}, \dfrac{1}{\pi + p}\right)$ + observation x_2

$$\Rightarrow \text{posterior } N\left(\frac{(\pi + p)\left(\dfrac{\pi\mu + px_1}{\pi + p}\right) + px_2}{(\pi + p) + p}, \frac{1}{(\pi + p) + p}\right) \quad (6.13)$$

In this, the posterior mean is the appropriate weighted average of the relevant prior mean $[(\pi\mu + px_1)/(\pi + p)]$ and the observation x_2, with the weights being the relevant prior precision $(\pi + p)$ and the precision of the observation (p). Also the posterior precision is the sum of the relevant prior precision $(\pi + p)$ and the precision of the observation (p).

Simplifying the expression on the right-hand side of (6.13), we get:

prior $N\left(\dfrac{\pi\mu + px_1}{\pi + p}, \dfrac{1}{\pi + p}\right)$ + observation x_2

$$\Rightarrow \text{posterior } N\left(\frac{\pi\mu + p(x_1 + x_2)}{\pi + 2p}, \frac{1}{\pi + 2p}\right) \quad (6.14)$$

Clearly, (6.12) and (6.14) can be combined to give

$$\text{prior } N\left(\mu, \frac{1}{\pi}\right) + \text{observations } x_1 \text{ and } x_2$$

$$\Rightarrow \text{posterior } N\left(\frac{\pi\mu + p(x_1 + x_2)}{\pi + 2p}, \frac{1}{\pi + 2p}\right) \quad (6.15)$$

This process can be continued. Consider the incorporation of the third observation x_3. Before this is incorporated the assessment is $N[(\pi\mu + p(x_1 + x_2))/(\pi + 2p), 1/(\pi + 2p)]$ (see (6.14) or (6.15)), and thus this is the relevant prior to use in (6.11) when considering the incorporation of x_3 into the assessment. Using (6.11), with 'μ' put equal to $(\pi\mu + p(x_1 + x_2))/(\pi + 2p)$ and 'π' put equal to $\pi + 2p$, we get:

$$\text{prior } N\left(\frac{\pi\mu + p(x_1 + x_2)}{\pi + 2p}, \frac{1}{\pi + 2p}\right) + \text{observation } x_3$$

$$\Rightarrow \text{posterior } N\left(\frac{(\pi + 2p)\left(\dfrac{\pi\mu + p(x_1 + x_2)}{\pi + 2p}\right) + px_3}{(\pi + 2p) + p}, \frac{1}{(\pi + 2p) + p}\right)$$

$$(6.16)$$

In this, the posterior mean is the appropriate weighted average of the relevant prior mean $((\pi\mu + p(x_1 + x_2))/(\pi + 2p))$ and the observation x_3, with the weights being the relevant prior precision $(\pi + 2p)$ and the precision of the observation (p). Also the posterior precision is the sum of the relevant prior precision $(\pi + 2p)$ and the precision of the observation (p).

Simplifying the expression on the right-hand side of (6.16), we get:

$$\text{prior } N\left(\frac{\pi\mu + p(x_1 + x_2)}{\pi + 2p}, \frac{1}{\pi + 2p}\right) + \text{observation } x_3$$

$$\Rightarrow \text{posterior } N\left(\frac{\pi\mu + p(x_1 + x_2 + x_3)}{\pi + 3p}, \frac{1}{\pi + 3p}\right) \quad (6.17)$$

Clearly, (6.12), (6.13) and (6.17) (or, equivalently, (6.15) and (6.17)) can be combined to give:

$$\text{prior } N\left(\mu, \frac{1}{\pi}\right) + \text{observations } x_1, x_2 \text{ and } x_3$$

$$\Rightarrow \text{posterior } N\left(\frac{\pi\mu + p(x_1 + x_2 + x_3)}{\pi + 3p}, \frac{1}{\pi + 3p}\right) \quad (6.18)$$

Without any further ado, we can now proceed to the general case of n observations $x_1, x_2, \ldots, x_n$. It is clear we must have

$$\text{prior } N(\mu, 1/\pi) + \text{observations } x_1, x_2, \ldots, x_n$$

$$\Rightarrow \text{posterior } N\left(\frac{\pi\mu + p(x_1 + x_2 + \cdots + x_n)}{\pi + np}, \frac{1}{\pi + np}\right) \quad (6.19)$$

This can be simplified slightly by using $\bar{x}$ to denote the mean of the sample values, namely:

$$\bar{x} \equiv (x_1 + x_2 + \cdots + x_n)/n \equiv \sum_{i=1}^{n} \frac{x_i}{n}. \quad (6.20)$$

From (6.20) it follows that $(x_1 + x_2 + \cdots + x_n) \equiv n\bar{x}$, and so (6.19) can be written

$$\text{prior } N(\mu, 1/\pi) + \text{observations } x_1, x_2, \ldots, x_n$$

$$\text{posterior } N\left(\frac{\pi\mu + np\bar{x}}{\pi + np}, \frac{1}{\pi + np}\right) \quad (6.21)$$

As this is a particularly important result, let us re-express it in the form of (6.11):

$$\left.\begin{array}{l} \text{If the prior on } M \text{ is } N(\mu, 1/\pi), \text{ then after } n \text{ observations} \\ x_1, x_2, \ldots, x_n \text{ on } X \text{ (which is } N(M, 1/p)\text{), the posterior} \\ \text{on } M \text{ is } N\left(\dfrac{\pi\mu + np\bar{x}}{\pi + np}, \dfrac{1}{\pi + np}\right) \end{array}\right\} \quad (6.22)$$

Let us interpret this important result. The first thing to note is that the posterior is normal as was the prior, irrespective of the sample size. Thus the assessment stays within the (normal) family. This is a result which you should have anticipated. The posterior mean is a weighted average of the prior mean and the sample mean, with the weights being π and np respectively. Thus, the greater is the prior precision the more weight is attached to the prior mean; and the greater is the sample size or the greater is the precision of each observation, the more weight is attached to the sample mean. This makes good intuitive sense. Finally, we note that the posterior precision is the sum of the prior precision and the product of the sample size and the precision of the observations. Again this makes good intuitive sense.

It is clear from (6.22) that the posterior mean depends on the observations x_1, x_2, ..., x_n only through their mean $\bar{x}$. Thus, the *order* of the observations is unimportant, and all the observations are given the same *weight*. Moreover, as far as our assessment of M, the population mean, is concerned, all the information contained in the observations x_1, x_2, ..., x_n is encapsulated in the sample mean $\bar{x}$. Any other information about the observations is redundant. Or, in other words, knowledge of the value of $\bar{x}$ is *sufficient* for the updating of the probability assessment about M.

One other feature revealed by (6.22) is that the posterior precision does *not* depend upon the values of the observations x_1, x_2, ..., x_n. Indeed, the precision depends solely on the parameters π, n and p. In particular, this means that any desired posterior precision can be achieved by appropriate choice of n. Equivalently, it means that any desired width for some α per cent probability interval can be achieved by appropriate choice of n. For example, consider the 95 per cent probability interval – this has a width equal to 3.92 posterior standard deviations. Suppose one wants to choose n to make this equal to some pre-specified value w. Then one chooses n to satisfy

$$w = 3.92 \sqrt{\left/\left(\frac{1}{\pi + np}\right)\right.}$$

(since the precision is the reciprocal of the variance). This equation yields the following solution for n:

$$n = [(3.92/w)^2 - \pi]/p. \tag{6.23}$$

From this it can be seen that the requisite n is larger the smaller is the prior precision, the smaller is the precision of the observations, and the smaller is the required width. As an illustration, consider the simple numerical example discussed above, in which $\pi = \frac{1}{16} = 0.0625$ and $p = \frac{1}{9} = 0.\dot{1}$. For $w = 9.408$, the solution to (6.23) is $n = 1$, which should be a reassuring result. Other examples are given in the table below (in which the value of n is the nearest integer above that given by (6.23)).

w	n
8	2
4	9
2	35
1	138
0.5	553
0.25	2213
0.125	8851

From this it can be seen that, except for low values of n (when the prior assessment dominates the sample information), the effect of a required halving of the width is a quadrupling in the requisite sample size. A glance at (6.23) shows that this is a general result whenever w is small in relation to π.

Before looking at a specific example of the use of (6.22), let us consider how we might characterize *total prior ignorance* in this context. One obvious way of doing this is to put the prior precision equal to zero. From (6.22) it is clear that the effect of this is to make the posterior assessment a function of the sample information alone. This seems sensible. Formally, we have the following result, putting $\pi = 0$ in (6.22):

> Given total prior ignorance, then after n observations $x_1, x_2, \ldots, x_n$ on X (which is $N(M, 1/p)$) the posterior on M is $N(\bar{x}, 1/np)$.   (6.24)

Alternatively, (6.24) can be expressed in the following form:

> Given total prior ignorance, then after n observations $x_1, x_2, \ldots, x_n$ on X (which is $N(M, s^2)$) the posterior on M is $N(\bar{x}, s^2/n)$.   (6.25)

This simple, but important result states that the posterior assessment of the population mean (given zero prior knowledge) is normally distributed, centred on the sample mean, and with a variance that is directly proportional to the variance of X and inversely proportional to the sample size. Posterior probability intervals for M can easily be obtained using (6.25) and Appendix A6. For example, the 95 per cent probability interval for M is $\bar{x} \pm 1.96\, s/\sqrt{n}$. The width of this interval, $3.92 \ s/\sqrt{n}$, can be made equal to any desired size by suitable choice of n.

One further feature of (6.22) and (6.25) that should be noted is that, in all cases, the posterior variance approaches zero as n approaches infinity. Moreover, the posterior mean either equals (in (6.25)), or approaches as n approaches infinity (in (6.22)), the sample mean, and this in turn approaches the population mean m as n approaches infinity. We thus get the important, and reassuring, result that, as n approaches infinity, the posterior assessment of the population mean approaches a degenerate distribution centred on the actual population mean.

Let us conclude this section with an extended illustration of the key result (6.22), and its important special case (6.25). Suppose we are interested in the weights of female students at the University of York. Suppose further that we happen to know (or are prepared to assume) that these weights are normally distributed with a known standard deviation of 14 pounds, but unknown mean M. To get information about M we can obtain a random sample of female students from the University (by selecting names from the list of students by some appropriate selection mechanism), and weigh the students in the sample. Suppose that we initially select a sample of size twenty-five, and find that the mean weight in the sample is 135 pounds. What is the assessment of M in the light of this information?

This depends upon the prior assessment. Suppose, first, that the prior knowledge is non-existent, so that prior assessment has zero precision. Using (6.25), with $\bar{x} = 135$, $s = 14$ and $n = 25$, we find that our posterior assessment of M is normal with mean $\bar{x} = 135$ and variance $s^2/n = 14^2/25 = (14/5)^2 = 2.8^2$; that is, our posterior assessment is $N(135, 2.8^2)$. This is a complete characterization, and we can obtain the various summary measures in the usual manner. For example, the posterior 95 per cent probability interval is $135 \pm 1.96 \times 2.8$, that is (129.51, 140.49). Thus, we can conclude on the basis of the sample information, that the probability is 0.95 that M lies between 129.51 and 140.49 pounds.

Suppose now that we want a more accurate assessment of M – say one for which the 95 per cent probability interval has a width of no more than 6 pounds. Using (6.23) with $w = 6$, $\pi = 0$ and $p = 1/s^2 = 1/196$, we find that the required n is 84. As we already have a sample of twenty-five students, we need to collect an additional sample of fifty-nine students to achieve the desired accuracy. Suppose that the mean of this *additional* sample is 138. What is our assessment now? There are two ways we can derive this – either by incorporating the *additional* information into the assessment reached *after* the initial sample of twenty-five students, or by combining the two samples into a large one and incorporating the information contained in this combined sample into the original (total prior ignorance) prior assessment. We consider these in turn. Recall that our assessment following the initial sample was $N(135, 2.8^2)$ and that the sample mean of the additional sample of size 59 was 138. Using (6.22) with $\mu = 135$, $\pi = 1/2.8^2$, $n = 59$, $p = 1/14^2$ and $\bar{x} = 138$, we find that our posterior assessment after the additional sample is normal with mean

$$\frac{(135/2.8^2 + 59 \times 138/14^2)}{(1/2.8^2 + 59/14^2)} = 137.1$$

and variance $1/(1/2.8^2 + 59/14^2) = 2.\dot{3}$. That is, our posterior assessment is $N(137.1, 2.\dot{3})$. The associated 95 per cent probability interval is $137.1 \pm 1.96\sqrt{2.\dot{3}}$, that is $(134.1, 140.1)$. This has a width of 6 pounds, as required.

Now suppose we combine the two samples into one large sample of size $(25 + 59) = 84$. The mean weight of this sample is $(25 \times 135 + 59 \times 138)/84 = 137.1$, since the first twenty-five students have a total weight of 25×135 and the final fifty-nine have a total weight of 59×138. Let us incorporate *this* information into our initial prior, which was one of total prior ignorance. Using (6.25) with $\bar{x} = 137.1$, $s = 14$ and $n = 84$, we find that our posterior assessment of M is normal with mean $\bar{x} = 137.1$ and variance $s^2/n = 14^2/84 = 2.\dot{3}$; that is, our posterior assessment is $N(137.1, 2.\dot{3})$. This naturally (but reassuringly!) is exactly the same as that obtained in the paragraph above by the first method.

Consider now an alternative situation in which we *do* feel able to make a (non-vague) prior assessment about M. To be specific, suppose our initial prior on M is $N(140, 9)$ (which has a 95.44 per cent probability interval of $(134, 146)$). Using (6.22) with $\mu = 140$, $\pi = 1/9$, $n = 25$, $p = 1/14^2$ and $\bar{x} = 135$, we find that our posterior assessment of M after the initial sample of twenty-five students is $N(137.33, 4.19)$. This has a 95 per cent probability interval of $(133.32, 141.34)$. It is interesting to compare this with the corresponding probability interval based on zero prior knowledge derived above – this was $(129.51, 140.49)$. The former is narrower and to the right of the latter; this reflects the influence of the prior knowledge. Finally, let us incorporate the second sample into this second assessment. Using the first of the two possible methods, we substitute $\mu = 137.33$, $\pi = 1/4.19$, $n = 59$, $p = 1/14^2$ and $\bar{x} = 138$ into (6.22). This yields a posterior assessment for *M* which is *N*(137.7, 1.853). This has a 95 per cent probability interval of (135.03, 140.37). If we compare this with the corresponding interval for the case of zero prior knowledge (134.1, 140.1), we see that they are quite similar. This reflects the increasing importance of the observations in the posterior assessment as the sample size increases (see figure 6.2).

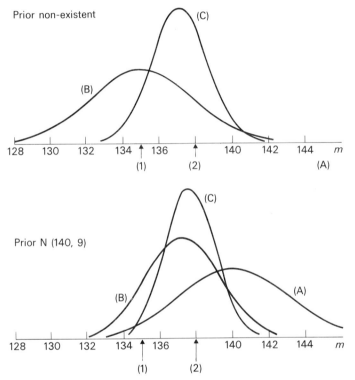

Assessments of M: (A) the prior, (B) after first sample, (C) after second sample. *Observations:* (1) the first sample mean, (2) the second sample mean.

Figure 6.2 The final example of section 6.2

This completes our analysis, for the time being, of case 2. You may have felt during this section that it is a rather strange case, in that it assumes that the mean is unknown yet the variance is known. It is difficult to think of real-life examples in which this might be the case, and clearly our example above was somewhat contrived. More realistic is case 4, in which both the mean and the variance are unknown. Before we tackle this, however, we consider case 3 in the next section. This is a case in which the mean is known and the variance is unknown. As we shall see, this case paves the way for the analysis of case 4 in section 6.4.

6.3 INFERENCE WITH AN UNKNOWN VARIANCE AND KNOWN MEAN

The two examples of inference that we have discussed so far (namely, inference about a proportion, and inference about a mean when the variance is known) have been relatively straightforward technically, and the results have all readily appealed to intuition. Accordingly, we have devoted a considerable amount of space to the derivation, discussion and interpretation of the key results. I hope that by now you are happy with the basic procedures involved, and feel confident that you can apply them yourself. From now on, our derivation, discussion and interpretation will be considerably briefer than hitherto, and to save space we will omit much of the technical detail. As long as you are happy with the basic procedures, you should not worry about this technical detail. Indeed, you are advised to take the key results on faith, and to concentrate your attention on gaining an intuitive understanding of the results and their implications.

As we proceed further into this and the succeeding chapters, the applications become more and more realistic and useful, but the underlying technical complexity also increases. In view of this, and also in view of the fact that most economic analyses that you will encounter in the literature, or carry out yourself, will assume zero prior knowledge, we will increasingly confine our attention to the special case of total prior ignorance. Even where we do explicitly consider the case of non-zero prior knowledge, it will increasingly be simply the means to the end of considering the limiting case of zero prior knowledge. Accordingly, we will devote virtually no space to justifying the particular *forms* adopted for the various prior assessments.

Let us now turn to the object of this section – namely, the question of inference with an unknown variance and known mean. The basic framework is the same as that described in the previous section: we are interested in some variable X which is normally distributed in some population. In this section, we assume that the mean of X in the population is known, but that the variance of X in the population is unknown. Accordingly, in keeping with our general notational convention, we denote the former by m and the latter by S^2. In summary, our assumptions are that

$$X \text{ is } N(m, S^2). \tag{6.26}$$

We want to show how information, in the form of observations on X, can be used to reduce our uncertainty about S^2. Alternatively, but exactly equivalently, we can express our assumptions in the form:

$$X \text{ is } N(m, 1/P), \tag{6.27}$$

where $P \equiv 1/S^2$ is the Precision of X, and state our problem as that of showing how observations on X can be used to reduce our uncertainty about P. (Note carefully that this P denotes something totally different from the P of chapter 5.) As will become apparent, the technical complexities of the derivations can be slightly reduced by using this alternative form.

Our starting point is, as usual, the statement of our prior beliefs about the unknown parameter – in this case P. As P cannot be negative but could take *any* non-negative value up to infinity, a possible candidate for the prior assessment is the gamma distribution. (The normal is ruled out since it can take negative values, and the beta is ruled out as it takes values only in the range [0, 1].) For the time being, let us simply assume that this candidate is the appropriate one: a possible justification will emerge as our analysis proceeds.

We assume, therefore, that our prior on P is gamma with parameters α and β (see section 2.4). From (2.31), we see that this implies that the prior probability density of P is given by:

$$f_P(p) \propto \begin{cases} p^{\alpha - 1} \exp(-\beta p) & p \geq 0 \\ 0 & \text{otherwise.} \end{cases} \tag{6.28}$$

Consider now the effect of a sample of size 1 on this assessment. If we continue to choose our sample randomly, then, as in the previous section, the distribution of the X-value for our sampled member will be exactly the same as the distribution of X in the population. Thus, from (6.27), our sample X is $N(m, 1/P)$. This implies that the conditional distribution of X given $P = p$ is $N(m, 1/p)$. We can therefore write:

$$g_X(x \mid p) \propto p^{1/2} \exp[-p(x - m)^2/2] \tag{6.29}$$

This is the likelihood of x given $P = p$. (Perhaps an aside is necessary at this stage. If you compare (6.3) with (6.29) you might be worried by the fact that they appear different, even though they are ostensibly expressing the same fact. Recognizing that $p \equiv 1/s^2$ removes only part of the differences; there still remains a '$p^{1/2}$' before the exp in (6.29) which does not appear in (6.3). The difference is easily explained: in the previous section we were concerned with m, and thus incorporated all terms *not* involving m into the factor of proportionality in (6.3); but in this section we are concerned with p, and thus can incorporate only those terms *not* involving p into the factor of proportionality in (6.29). Thus the $p^{1/2}$ (see (2.29)) can disappear from (6.3), but must stay in (6.29). End of aside.)

We can now apply Bayes' theorem (4.23). Using (6.28) and (6.29), this implies that the posterior distribution of P, in the light of the one observation x, is given by:

$$g_P(p \mid x)$$

$$\propto \begin{cases} p^{1/2} \exp\left[-p(x-m)^2/2\right] p^{\alpha-1} \exp\left(-\beta p\right) & p \geq 0 \\ 0 & \text{otherwise.} \end{cases}$$

This can be simplified to give:

$$g_P(p \mid x) \propto \begin{cases} p^{\alpha+1/2-1} \exp\left\{-[\beta + (x-m)^2/2]p\right\} & p \geq 0 \\ 0 & \text{otherwise.} \end{cases}$$

(6.30)

If you compare this with (2.31) you will recognize (6.30) as the probability density function of a gamma distribution with parameters $\alpha + \frac{1}{2}$ and $\beta + (x-m)^2/2$. We thus get the following important result:

> If the prior on P is $G(\alpha, \beta)$, then after an observation x on X (which is $N(m, 1/P)$) the posterior on P is $G(\alpha + \frac{1}{2}, \beta + (x-m)^2/2)$.　　　(6.31)

Once again we have a situation in which the assessment remains within the family – this time the gamma family. By now, you could be forgiven for thinking that this always happens, but this is not the case. We simply happen to have chosen our priors so that this result follows. For other priors the result would not follow: for example, if the prior on P was beta, the posterior would *not* be beta; or again, if the prior on P was normal, the posterior would *not* be normal. Similarly, if, in the previous section, the prior on M was beta (gamma), the posterior would *not* be beta (gamma). Perhaps you might like to ponder the reasons for this.

Result (6.31) is rather reminiscent of the key result of chapter 5, namely (5.8), in that the parameters are updated in a particularly simple fashion. To be specific, we see from (6.31) that the effect of the observation x is to increase the first parameter by $\frac{1}{2}$ and to increase the second parameter by $(x - m)^2/2$. The generalization to n variables $x_1, x_2, \ldots, x_n$ is thus straightforward: *each* of the observations increases the first parameter by $\frac{1}{2}$, and the ith observation increases the second parameter by $(x_i - m)^2/2$. We thus get the following important result:

If the prior on P is $G(\alpha, \beta)$, then after n observations $x_1, x_2, \ldots, x_n$ on X (which is $N(m, 1/P)$) the posterior on P is $G(\alpha + n/2, \beta + \sum_{i=1}^n (x_i - m)^2/2)$.   (6.32)

To save writing, let us introduce $\tilde{s}$, defined by:

$$\tilde{s}^2 = \sum_{i=1}^n (x_i - m)^2/n. \qquad (6.33)$$

This looks rather like the sample variance, which is $\sum_{i=1}^n (x_i - \bar{x})^2/n$, the only difference being that m, the population mean, appears in the former where $\bar{x}$, the sample mean, appears in the latter. Substituting (6.33) in (6.32) we get:

If the prior on P is $G(\alpha, \beta)$, then after n observations $x_1, x_2, \ldots, x_n$ on X (which is $N(m, 1/P)$) the posterior on P is $G(\alpha + n/2, \beta + n\tilde{s}^2/2)$.   (6.34)

Recalling from section 2.4 that a gamma distribution with parameters α and β has a mean of α/β and a variance of α/β^2, it follows from (6.34) that the prior and posterior means of P are

$$\alpha/\beta \quad \text{and} \quad (\alpha + n/2)/(\beta + n\tilde{s}^2/2) \qquad (6.35)$$

respectively, while the prior and posterior variances of P are

$$\alpha/\beta^2 \quad \text{and} \quad (\alpha + n/2)/(\beta + n\tilde{s}^2/2)^2 \qquad (6.36)$$

respectively. From (6.35) it follows that, irrespective of the values of α and β, the posterior mean approaches $1/\tilde{s}^2$ as n approaches infinity. Perhaps you would like to interpret this result. Furthermore, from (6.36) it follows that the posterior variance approaches zero as n approaches infinity. Combining these two results, we find that the posterior assessment for P approaches a degenerate distribution centred on $1/\tilde{s}^2$ as n approaches infinity.

In view of (6.34), one can 'evaluate' a given prior on P in a manner similar to that used in chapter 5. To be precise, (6.34) suggests that a prior on P of $G(\alpha, \beta)$ is 'equivalent to' having observed a sample of size 2α in which the sum of squared deviations of the observations about m was 2β. This points the way, once again, to a possible characterization of total prior ignorance – namely, by putting α and β both equal to zero. Under our interpretation, a prior of $G(0, 0)$ is 'equivalent to' having observed a sample of size zero (in which the sum of squared deviations was, tautologically, zero). Following this line of argument, we get from (6.34) the important result:

> Given total prior ignorance, then after n observations $x_1, x_2, \ldots, x_n$ on X (which is $N(m, 1/P)$) the posterior on P is $G(n/2, n\tilde{s}^2/2)$. ⎫⎬⎭　(6.37)

For reasons which will become apparent shortly, it will be helpful to express this result in a slightly different form. To do this, we first note from (2.31) that, if P is $G(n/2, n\tilde{s}^2/2)$, then its probability density function is proportional to

$$p^{(n/2) - 1} \exp{(-n\tilde{s}^2 p/2)}.$$

Now introduce temporarily a new variable Y, defined by $Y = n\tilde{s}^2 P$. Since Y is proportional to P, the density function of Y is proportional to that of P (why?), and so the density function of Y is, after simplification, proportional to

$$y^{(n/2) - 1} \exp{(-y/2)}.$$

This is the density function of a variable which is gamma with parameters $n/2$ and $1/2$. This, you may recall from section 2.4, is a special case of the gamma distribution, with a name of its own. To be specific, such a variable is said to have a *chi-square distribution with n degrees of freedom*. We thus conclude that if P is $G(n/2, n\tilde{s}^2/2)$ then the new variable $n\tilde{s}^2 P$ has a chi-square distribution with n degrees of freedom. Combining this result with (6.37) we get:

> Given total prior ignorance, then after n observations $x_1, x_2, \ldots, x_n$ on X (which is $N(m, 1/P)$) the posterior on P is such that $n\tilde{s}^2 P$ has a chi-square distribution with n degrees of freedom. ⎫⎬⎭　(6.38)

At a first glance (6.38) does not appear much of an improvement on (6.37), but the advantage of (6.38) is that it can be used in conjunction with tables of the chi-square distribution, which, unlike tables of the gamma distribution, are relatively simple to use and found at the back of virtually all statistics texts. In this book, the table of the chi-square distribution can be found in Appendix A8.

This section has been rather difficult technically. A numerical example may therefore be useful to illustrate some of the key results.

We confine attention to the case of zero prior knowledge. Consider a situation in which you are interested in the weekly expenditure of students in the local campus bar. Suppose that you know, or are prepared to assume, that X (this weekly expenditure) is normally distributed with a mean of £6 (per student per week) – a figure you have derived from the total bar receipts. Suppose, however, you do not know, but wish to learn about, the dispersion of such weekly expenditures, as measured either by their variance S^2 or by their precision P (where $P = 1/S^2$, of course). To gain information about P (or S^2) you decide to select a random sample of twelve students (*not* the first twelve people you meet in the bar that night!), and ask them to monitor their bar spending over the coming week. Moreover, you exhort them to be honest and not to let this monitoring affect their spending patterns. If they follow your advice, the reported twelve X-values should be an appropriate random sample as required by our analysis. (As you probably realize, unbiased information on expenditures on the 'naughty things in life', such as wine, women and song, is notoriously difficult to obtain. Most surveys, such as the Family Expenditure Survey, which can obtain an independent check on total spending, report consistent under-recording of such expenditures.)

Suppose the twelve observations turn out to be (in £s per week for each of the twelve students):

7.12	5.62	4.31	8.22	6.39	5.91
6.55	5.25	7.02	4.99	6.02	7.00.

These have a (sample) mean of 6.20, so we can be reasonably happy that a downward bias is not present in this sample. Substituting these observations in (6.33) with $m = 6$, we find that $\tilde{s}^2 = 1.1058$. Now let us suppose we start from a position of total prior ignorance about P. Then result (6.38) is the relevant one. This tells us that, in the light of these twelve observations our posterior assessment of P is such that

$13.2696P$ has chi-square distribution with 12 degrees of freedom, $\qquad$ (6.39)

since $n\tilde{s}^2 = 12 \times 1.1058 = 13.2696$ and $n = 12$.

This is a complete characterization of our posterior assessment, and we can summarize it in the usual ways. For example, a 95 per cent probability interval for P can be found by using (6.39) in conjunction with the table of the chi-square distribution given in Appendix A8. To use this table, note that each row refers to a different degree of freedom. The row with 12 in the left-hand margin is the relevant one for this example. If you look along this you will see that the probability that a chi-square variable with 12 degrees of freedom exceeds 4.40 is 0.975, and the probability that it exceeds 23.03 is 0.025. Thus, a (but not the minimum width) 95 per cent probability interval for a chi-square variable with 12 degrees of freedom is (4.40, 23.03). Using this in conjunction with (6.39), it follows that

$$P(4.40 \leq 13.2696P \leq 23.03) = 0.95.$$

To convert this into a statement on P itself, we simply divide each term inside the probability statement by 13.2696. We thus get

$$P(0.3316 \leq P \leq 1.7355) = 0.95. \tag{6.40}$$

(Note that the probability remains 0.95, because the statements '4.40 $\leq$ 13.2696P $\leq$ 23.03' and '0.3316 $\leq P \leq$ 1.7355' are synonymous: the second is true whenever the first is true, and vice versa. So each must hold with the same probability.) So we can conclude, on the basis of our sample information, that the probability is 0.95 that the precision of X is between 0.3316 and 1.7355. To convert this statement on the precision P into a statement on the variance S^2, we use the fact that $S^2 \equiv 1/P$. Accordingly, we take the reciprocal of each term inside the probability statement in (6.40), thus getting

$$P(0.5762 \leq S^2 \leq 3.0157) = 0.95. \tag{6.41}$$

(Note that 0.5762 is the reciprocal of 1.7355, S^2 is the reciprocal of P and 3.0157 is the reciprocal of 0.3316. Note also that the probability remains 0.95, because the statements '0.3316 $\leq P \leq$ 1.7355' and '0.5762 $\leq S^2 \leq$ 3.0157' are synonymous: the second is true whenever the first is true, and vice versa. So each must hold with the same probability.) Finally, we can, if we wish, turn (6.41) into a statement on the standard deviation S simply by taking the square root of each term inside the probability statement. This yields, using the same arguments as above,

$$P(0.7591 \leq S \leq 1.7366) = 0.95. \tag{6.42}$$

Thus, we conclude that the probability is 0.95 that the standard deviation of weekly bar expenditures is between 0.7591 and 1.7366.

Suppose now that we feel that this interval is too wide – that is, our assessment is too imprecise – and so we decide to take an additional sample of eighteen extra students. We now have a total sample of size 30. A glance at (6.38) shows that all we really need to know about the x_i values is their $\tilde{s}^2$ value. Suppose we calculate this to be 1.3260 (taking all thirty students together). Putting $\tilde{s}^2 = 1.3260$ and $n = 30$ in (6.38), we conclude that, in the light of all thirty observations, our posterior assessment of P is such that

> $39.78P$ has a chi-square distribution with 30 degrees of freedom. $\qquad$ (6.43)

(Note that we could have obtained this result by incorporating the information given by the additional eighteen students into the assessment as it existed after the first twelve, namely (6.39), using the general result (6.34). But, as we have demonstrated before, both routes lead to the same answer, and we might as well use the simpler route.)

From (6.43) we can obtain the various summary measures in the usual fashion. For example, using the table of the chi-square distribution, we find that

$P(16.79 \leq 39.78P \leq 47.0) = 0.95.$

Hence a 95 per cent probability interval for P is $(0.4221, 1.1815)$. This, in turn, implies a 95 per cent probability interval for S^2 of $(0.8464, 2.3691)$, and hence a 95 per cent probability interval for S of $(0.92, 1.5392)$. These are considerably narrower than the corresponding ones obtained after just twelve observations.

By now, you may have realized that we can avoid all reference to the precision if we so wish. Using the fact that $P \equiv 1/S^2$ we can express the key result (6.38) in the following alternative form:

> Given total prior ignorance, then after n observations $x_1, x_2, \ldots, x_n$ on X (which is $N(m, S^2)$) the posterior on S is such that $n\tilde{s}^2/S^2$ has a chi-square distribution with n degrees of freedom. $\qquad$ (6.44)

Also, if n is reasonably large (say greater than 60), we can avoid all reference to the chi-square distribution, by making use of the fact that a chi-square distribution with n degrees of freedom has a mean of n and a variance of $2n$, and is approximately normally distributed for reasonably large n, with the approximation improving as n gets larger. Thus, from (6.44), the posterior on S is such that $n\tilde{s}^2/S^2$ is approximately $N(n, 2n)$. You may like to investigate how well this approximation works in the example above (though n, at 30, is a little on the small side).

This concludes our treatment, for the time being, of case 3. Although relatively difficult technically, the underlying principles employed in this section were the same as those employed in the simpler applications of chapter 5 and section 6.2 – namely the updating of a prior assessment about some parameter by the incorporation of new information using Bayes' theorem.

6.4   INFERENCE WITH AN UNKNOWN MEAN AND UNKNOWN VARIANCE

We now consider case 4, the most general case of all within the basic framework of this chapter. In this section, we examine the case where both the mean and the variance of our variable of interest are unknown. We continue to denote the variable by X and to assume that X is normally distributed in the population of interest. As both the population mean and the population variance are unknown, we use the upper-case letters M and S^2 respectively to denote them. In summary, our assumptions are that

$$X \text{ is } N(M, S^2),\tag{6.45}$$

or, equivalently, that

$$X \text{ is } N(M, 1/P),\tag{6.46}$$

where $P \equiv 1/S^2$ is the unknown precision.

In each of our previous applications, there was only one unknown parameter. In contrast, the application considered in this section has *two* unknown parameters. Our prior and posterior assessments must therefore be *joint* probability assessments of the two parameters M and P (or, equivalently, M and S^2). In the notation of chapter 3, our prior assessment must specify $f_{MP}(m, p)$ the joint probability density function of M and P. We will specify this in a rather indirect manner, so that we can build on the material of the preceding two sections. Recall from section 3.4 that a joint probability density function can be written as the product of appropriately chosen conditional and marginal probability density functions. To be specific, we can express $f_{MP}(m, p)$ as follows:

$$f_{MP}(m, p) = g_M(m \mid p) f_P(p).\tag{6.47}$$

Drawing on the material of section 6.3, an obvious candidate for $f_P(.)$ – the prior marginal distribution of P – is the gamma distribution with parameters α and β. This is given in (6.28). Further, drawing on the material of section 6.2, a candidate for $g_M(m \mid p)$ – the prior distribution of M conditional on P equalling p – is a normal distribution with mean μ and precision πp (or variance $\sigma^2 s^2$). Formally, this is given by (see (2.29))

$$g_M(m \mid p) \propto (\pi p)^{1/2} \exp \left[-\pi p(m - \mu)^2/2 \right]. \tag{6.48}$$

(Note that the assumption, that the precision of the distribution of M given $P = p$ is a multiple of p, encapsulates the idea that the more dispersed is the distribution of X the less confident you are likely to feel about your assessment of the mean of X.)

Combining (6.28) and (6.48), we get the following prior joint assessment of M and P:

$$f_{MP}(m, p)$$

$$\propto \begin{cases} (\pi p)^{1/2} \exp \left[-\pi p(m - \mu)^2/2 \right] p^{\alpha - 1} \exp \left(-\beta p \right) & p \geq 0 \\ 0 & \text{otherwise.} \end{cases}$$

$$\tag{6.49}$$

As in the preceding two sections, our information comes in the form of observations on X which is $N(M, 1/P)$. Consider first the case of a sample of size 1. The relevant likelihood function is (6.29), reproduced here with the appropriate notational change:

$$g_X(x \mid m, p) \propto p^{1/2} \exp \left[-p(x - m)^2/2 \right]. \tag{6.50}$$

The posterior joint assessment is found as usual using Bayes' theorem, the relevant version in this case being:

$$g_{MP}(m, p \mid x) \propto g_X(x \mid m, p) f_{MP}(m, p). \tag{6.51}$$

Combining (6.50) and (6.49) in (6.51), we get

$$g_{MP}(m, p \mid x) \propto \begin{cases} \begin{aligned} &p^{1/2} \exp \left[-p(x - m)^2/2 \right] \\ &\quad \times (\pi p)^{1/2} \exp \left[-\pi p(m - \mu)^2/2 \right] \\ &\quad \times p^{\alpha - 1} \exp \left(-\beta p \right) \end{aligned} & p \geq 0 \\ 0 & \text{otherwise.} \end{cases}$$

After some considerable algebraic simplification (similar to that used in sections 6.2 and 6.3), this can be written

$$g_{MP}(m, p \mid x)$$

$$\propto \begin{cases} (\pi' p)^{1/2} \exp \left[-\pi' p(m - \mu')^2/2 \right] p^{\alpha' - 1} \exp \left(-\beta' p \right) & p \geq 0 \\ 0 & \text{otherwise,} \end{cases}$$

$$\tag{6.52}$$

where $\mu' = (\pi\mu + x)/(\pi + 1)$,

$\pi' = \pi + 1$,

$\alpha' = \alpha + \frac{1}{2}$,   (6.53)

$\beta' = \beta + \pi(x - \mu)^2/[2(\pi + 1)]$.

We thus get the following result:

> If the joint prior on M and P is such that the marginal
> distribution of P is $G(\alpha, \beta)$ and the conditional distri-
> bution of M given $P = p$ is $N(\mu, 1/\pi p)$, then after an
> observation x on X (which is $N(M, 1/P)$) the joint
> posterior on M and P is such that the marginal distri-   (6.54)
> bution of P is $G(\alpha', \beta')$ and the conditional distribution
> of M given $P = p$ is $N(\mu', 1/\pi'p)$ where α', β', μ' and π'
> are as given in (6.53).

This looks rather formidable, but basically it is simply saying that
the posterior distribution is of the same form as the prior (that is, the
assessment stays within the family) with the parameters updated as
in (6.53).

In the usual fashion, we can use this result to deduce the posterior
after n observations. However, the algebra is rather tedious, so we
omit the derivation and simply state the result. If you like algebra,
you may like to verify the result yourself. It is as follows.

> If the joint prior on M and P is such that the marginal
> distribution of P is $G(\alpha, \beta)$ and the conditional distri-
> bution of M given $P = p$ is $N(\mu, 1/\pi p)$, then after n ob-
> servations $x_1, x_2, \ldots, x_n$ on X (which is $N(M, 1/P)$)   (6.55)
> the joint posterior on M and P is such that the mar-
> ginal distribution of P is $G(\alpha', \beta')$ and the conditional
> distribution of M given $P = p$ is $N(\mu', 1/\pi'p)$ where
> α', β', μ' and π' are as given in (6.56).

$\mu' = (\pi\mu + n\bar{x})/(\pi + n)$,

$\pi' = \pi + n$,

$\alpha' = \alpha + n/2$,   (6.56)

$\beta' = \beta + \dfrac{1}{2} \displaystyle\sum_{i=1}^{n} (x_i - \bar{x})^2 + \dfrac{\pi n(\bar{x} - \mu)^2}{2(\pi + n)}$.

(If you compare (6.53) with (6.56) you will see that the expressions for
μ', π' and α' in the latter are the obvious extensions of those in the
former. The expression for β' in the latter is, however, rather less
obvious. If you wish to verify it you should try the case $n = 2$ first,
and then generalize.)

In the above expressions, the joint distribution of M and P is given in the form of the marginal distribution of P and the conditional distribution of M given $P = p$. While this is a complete characterization, it will often be useful to know in addition the *marginal distribution* of M. This can be obtained quite straightforwardly, though rather tediously, by the methods of chapter 3, particularly section 3.4. Using these methods the following result can be obtained:

If the marginal distribution of P is $G(\alpha, \beta)$ and if the conditional distribution of M given $P = p$ is $N(\mu, 1/\pi p)$, then the marginal distribution of M is such that $(\alpha\pi/\beta)^{1/2}(M - \mu)$ has a t distribution with 2α degrees of freedom. $\left.\begin{array}{l} \\ \\ \\ \\ \\ \end{array}\right\}$ (6.57)

This result can be used in conjunction with (6.55) to find the posterior marginal distribution of M.

As you will have gathered by now, the material of this section, although conceptually no different from that of previous sections, is rather tedious and clumsy algebraically. To simplify matters in this respect, we will, throughout the remainder of this section, consider only the case of total prior ignorance. How do we characterize this in this context? Recall that in section 6.2 (unknown mean, known precision) we characterized it by putting $\pi = 0$; this effectively meant that the prior density on M was constant. (This is not immediately obvious from (6.2). But consider what happens to the normal density function as σ^2 approaches infinity, that is, as π approaches zero. The function gets flatter and flatter and eventually coincides with the horizontal axis, and thus is constant.) Recall also that in section 6.3 (known mean, unknown precision) we characterized total prior ignorance by putting $\alpha = 0$ and $\beta = 0$; this effectively meant that the prior density on P was proportional to p^{-1} (see (6.28)). Combining these two results suggests that in this section (unknown mean and unknown precision), the appropriate characterization is such that the prior joint density is proportional to the product of a constant (section 6.2) and p^{-1} (section 6.3); that is, the prior joint density should be proportional to p^{-1}. Examining (6.49), we see that this requires that we put π equal to 0, α equal to $-\frac{1}{2}$ and β equal to 0. (If you are not happy with this rather difficult argument, you are advised to take it on faith. A formal, rigorous justification would take us beyond the scope of this book.)

Putting $\pi = 0$, $\alpha = -\frac{1}{2}$ and $\beta = 0$ in (6.55) we get the following result:

Given total prior ignorance, then after n observations
$x_1, x_2, \ldots, x_n$ on X (which is $N(M, 1/P)$) the joint posterior on M and P is such that the marginal distribution of P is $G(\alpha', \beta')$ and the conditional distribution
of M given $P = p$ is $N(\mu', 1/\pi'p)$ where α', β', μ' and π'
are given by   (6.58)

$$\mu' = \bar{x} \qquad \pi' = n \qquad \alpha' = (n-1)/2$$

$$\beta' = \sum_{i=1}^{n} (x_i - \bar{x})^2/2.$$

For reasons which will become apparent, let us introduce $\hat{s}$ defined
as follows:

$$\hat{s}^2 = \sum_{i=1}^{n} (x_i - \bar{x})^2/(n-1).$$ (6.59)

This is *almost* the sample variance, the only difference being that
$(n-1)$ appears in the denominator of $\hat{s}^2$, instead of n. For this
reason, we shall refer to $\hat{s}^2$ as the *modified sample variance*, and $\hat{s}$ as
the *modified sample standard deviation*. If we now combine (6.58) with
(6.57) we get the following important result:

Given total prior ignorance, then after n observations
$x_1, x_2, \ldots, x_n$ on X (which is $N(M, 1/P)$) the poste-
rior on M is such that $(M - \bar{x})/(\hat{s}/\sqrt{n})$ has a t distribu-   (6.60)
tion with $(n-1)$ degrees of freedom.

Finally, let us recall the result proved just before equation (6.38)
above to the effect that if a variable Y is $G(k/2, \beta/2)$ then the new
variable βY has a chi-square distribution with k degrees of freedom,
and combine this with (6.58) to get the following important result:

Given total prior ignorance, then after n observations
$x_1, x_2, \ldots, x_n$ on X (which is $N(M, 1/P)$) the posterior on P is such that $(n-1)\hat{s}^2 P$ has a chi-square dis-   (6.61)
tribution with $(n-1)$ degrees of freedom.

Entirely equivalently, given that $P \equiv 1/S^2$, we can write:

Given total prior ignorance, then after n observations
$x_1, x_2, \ldots, x_n$ on X (which is $N(M, S^2)$) the posterior
on S is such that $(n-1)\hat{s}^2/S^2$ has a chi-square
distribution with $(n-1)$ degrees of freedom.
$$\hspace{2cm} (6.62)$$

Results (6.60) and (6.61) or (6.62) are particularly important ones
as they completely characterize the posterior marginal distributions
of M and P or S in the case of total prior ignorance. You will note
that the only information about the sample that is used is its mean $\bar{x}$
and its modified variance $\hat{s}^2$.

This section concludes with an illustration of the use of the key
results (6.60) and (6.61) or (6.62). Suppose we are interested in X, the
IQs of students at the University of York, and suppose that we
know, or are prepared to assume, that X is normally distributed over
the population (all students at the University of York). Suppose,
however, that we do not know the mean nor the variance of X; nor,
indeed, feel capable of making any prior judgement about their possible values. To learn something about the mean and variance, we
could collect a random sample of students (selected in the manner
discussed in section 6.2) and determine the IQs of the students in the
sample. Suppose a sample size of 25 is chosen, and the following
sample values found:

111.4	118.5	117.1	115.1	102.7
108.6	113.1	115.9	113.3	110.7
111.4	117.3	116.5	118.7	123.9
109.5	122.1	123.2	110.9	114.8
116.0	115.2	114.8	118.7	119.1

We need to calculate the sample mean $\bar{x} = \sum_{i=1}^{25} x_i/25$, and the modified sample variance $\hat{s}^2 = \sum_{i=1}^{25} (x_i - \bar{x})^2/24$. Simple arithmetic
shows that these are as follows:

$$\bar{x} = 115.14 \quad \text{and} \quad \hat{s}^2 = 23.205. \quad \text{(Thus } \hat{s} = 4.817.)$$

(Most modern electronic calculators will compute these for you. But
check whether your calculator computes the sample variance – with
n in the denominator – or the modified sample variance $\hat{s}^2$ – with
$(n-1)$ in the denominator.) Substituting these sample values into
(6.60) we find that our posterior assessment of M is such that

$$\frac{M - 115.14}{0.963} \text{ has a } t \text{ distribution with 24 degrees of freedom.}$$
$$\hspace{2cm} (6.63)$$

Also, substituting the sample values into (6.62) we find that our posterior assessment of S is such that

$$\left. \frac{556.92}{S^2} \text{ has a chi-square distribution with 24 degrees of } \atop \text{freedom.} \right\} \quad (6.64)$$

Equation (6.63) is a complete characterization of our posterior (marginal) assessment of M. Equation (6.64) is a complete characterization of our posterior (marginal) assessment of S. The various summaries can be obtained in the usual manner. For example, suppose we wish to find our posterior 95 per cent probability intervals for M and for S. Then we would proceed as follows. First, we would use (6.63) in conjunction with the table of the t distribution which is given in Appendix A7. From this, we see that a variable which has a t distribution with 24 degrees of freedom lies between ± 2.064 with probability 0.95. Thus, using (6.63), we have

$$P(-2.064 \leq (M - 115.14)/0.963 \leq 2.064) = 0.95.$$

Thus, multiplying each term inside the probability statement by 0.963, we have

$$P(-1.988 \leq M - 115.14 \leq 1.988) = 0.95.$$

Thus, adding 115.14 to each term inside the probability statement, we have

$$P(113.152 \leq M \leq 117.128) = 0.95.$$

Hence, our 95 per cent probability interval for M, based on the sample information, is (113.2, 117.1) (rounded to one decimal place). We can conclude that the probability is 0.95 that the mean IQ of York University students is between 113.2 and 117.1.

To find a 95 per cent probability interval for S, the standard deviation of such IQs, we use (6.64) in conjunction with the table of the chi-square distribution which is given in Appendix A8. From this, we see that a variable which has a chi-square distribution with 24 degrees of freedom lies between 12.40 and 39.4 with probability 0.95. Thus, using (6.64), we have

$$P(12.40 \leq 556.92/S^2 \leq 39.4) = 0.95.$$

Thus, dividing each term inside the probability statement by 556.92, we have

$$P(0.0227 \leq 1/S^2 \leq 0.07075) = 0.95.$$

Thus, taking the reciprocal of each term inside the probability statement, we have

$P(14.135 \leq S^2 \leq 44.913) = 0.95.$

Finally, taking the square root of each term inside the probability statement, we have (to one decimal place)

$P(3.8 \leq S \leq 6.7) = 0.95.$

Hence, our 95 per cent probability interval for S, based on the sample information, is (3.8, 6.7). We can conclude that the probability is 0.95 that the standard deviation of IQs at York University is between 3.8 and 6.7.

Suppose we now collect a further sample of sixteen additional students, making a total of forty-one in all. Suppose the X-values of these extra sixteen are as follows:

113.1	123.7	120.8	102.9
113.2	123.1	121.5	109.5
109.3	122.6	118.1	109.3
119.8	121.2	122.9	117.7.

As usual, there are two ways we could proceed: either by incorporating this *extra* information into the assessment as it exists after the initial sample of twenty-five students using (6.55); or by combining the two samples into one and incorporating this total information into the initial (total prior ignorance) prior assessment using (6.60) and (6.62). Both ways lead to the same conclusion, but as the second is technically much simpler, we will follow it.

Simple arithmetic shows that $\bar{x}$ and $\hat{s}^2$ for the *combined* sample of forty-one students are given by:

$$\bar{x} = 115.79 \qquad \hat{s}^2 = 29.909. \qquad \text{(Thus } \hat{s} = 5.469.)$$

Substituting these sample values into (6.60) and (6.62) we find that our posterior assessments of M and S are now such that:

$(M - 115.79)/0.854$ has a t distribution with 40 degrees of freedom and $1196.38/S^2$ has a chi-square distribution with 40 degrees of freedom. $\qquad$ (6.65)

From these complete characterizations we can derive various summary measures in the usual fashion. For example, 95 per cent probability intervals for M and S can be obtained from (6.65) in conjunction with the fact that a variable with a t distribution with 40 degrees of freedom lies between ± 2.021 with probability 0.95 (from

Appendix A7) and the fact that a variable with a chi-square distribution with 40 degrees of freedom lies between 24.4 and 59.3 with probability 0.95 (from Appendix A8). Following the same procedure as above, we find that the 95 per cent probability interval for M is (114.1, 117.5) and a 95 per cent probability interval for S is (4.5, 7.0). You will notice that these are only slightly narrower than the corresponding intervals after the initial sample of twenty five students (which were (113.2, 117.1) and (3.8, 6.7) respectively). This is because the variability of the second batch was considerably larger than the variability of the first batch. Indeed, there is no *guarantee* that the intervals will get smaller as n increases. Clearly, there will be a *general tendency* for them to do so, as (6.60) and (6.62) reveal, but an increase in n could be more than offset by an increase in $\hat{s}^2$. However, in the long run (as n approaches infinity) this cannot happen – since the width of both intervals must tend to zero. One further implication of the fact that the widths of the posterior probability intervals depend upon the value of $\hat{s}$ is that it is no longer possible to be able to choose n to achieve some desired degree of accuracy (as reflected in the width of the posterior probability interval). Clearly, if one has some prior notions about S, and hence about the likely values for $\hat{s}$, one can use these to narrow down the range of possible sample sizes; but even so, a particular width cannot be guaranteed.

6.5   'CONFIDENCE INTERVALS' AND 'SIGNIFICANCE TESTS'

In Bayesian statistics, a statement of the current probability distribution of some parameter or variable of interest provides a *complete characterization* of one's current beliefs about that parameter or variable. Nothing more need or can be said. One can say *less*, of course, by simply stating certain summary measures of the current probability distribution – depending upon what aspects of the distribution one is particularly interested in. But in response to the question 'what do you currently know about this parameter (or variable)?', one simply needs to state one's current probability distribution, or certain key summary features of it. That is all there is to it.

In Classical statistics, however, they do things differently. As we discussed in section 5.6, the crucial difference between Classical and Bayesian statistics is that in the former probability statements about (fixed) parameters are not allowed, while in the latter they are not only permitted but they are mandatory.

In Classical statistics, there are two distinct, but related, aspects to the process of inference about unknown parameters using sample evidence. One is called *estimation*; the other *hypothesis testing*. As the terminology suggests, the first of these two aspects is concerned with the process of using sample data to provide estimates of unknown (population) parameters; while the second is concerned with the process of using sample data to test hypotheses about unknown parameters. We will discuss these in turn, beginning with estimation.

We have already encountered the Classical approach to estimation in section 5.6. Estimates can be of two kinds – *point estimates* or *interval estimates*; the former provides just a single number as an estimate of some unknown parameter, while the latter provides an interval, and hence some information about the accuracy of the estimate. It is not intended to explain why particular point and interval estimates are used in Classical statistics; such explanations can be found elsewhere (for example, Hey (1974)). We will content ourselves with stating what the usual estimates are, and relating them to the Bayesian analyses of sections 6.2 to 6.4.

Case 2 (section 6.2): unknown mean M and known variance s^2

In this case, the usual Classical point estimate of M is the sample mean $\bar{x}$. Thus, a Classical statistician, if asked to give one number which, in some sense, is his or her 'best estimate' of M, will respond with $\bar{x}$. Classical interval estimates, as we discussed in section 5.6, are given in the form of α *per cent confidence intervals*. In case 2, the usual α per cent confidence interval for M is given by

$$(\bar{x} - z_{(100-\alpha)/2}\, s/\sqrt{n},\ \bar{x} + z_{(100+\alpha)/2}\, s/\sqrt{n}) \qquad (6.66)$$

where z_β is defined by $F_Z(z_\beta) \equiv P(Z \leq z) = \beta/100$ where Z is a unit normal random variable. For example, the 95 per cent confidence interval for M is

$$(\bar{x} - 1.96s/\sqrt{n},\ \bar{x} + 1.96s/\sqrt{n})$$

since $P(Z \leq -1.96) = 0.025$ and $P(Z \leq 1.96) = 0.975$. The correct interpretation of the α per cent confidence interval (6.66) is as follows: 'If one always constructs α per cent confidence intervals for an unknown population mean in this fashion, then α per cent of them *will* contain the unknown mean, while the remaining $(100 - \alpha)$ per cent will *not*. Whether any particular confidence interval contains the mean, we do not know.'

Equation (6.66) may look familiar. Indeed, if you refer back to section 6.2, and in particular to equation (6.25), you will see that the *Bayesian α per cent probability interval* based on total prior ignorance is given by

$$(\bar{x} - z_{(100-\alpha)/2}\, s/\sqrt{n},\ \bar{x} + z_{(100+\alpha)/2}\, s/\sqrt{n}),$$

since

$$P(z_{(100-\alpha)/2} \le Z \le z_{(100+\alpha)/2}) = \alpha/100.$$

This is algebraically identical with (6.66). Thus, *algebraically*, the Bayesian α per cent probability interval for M based on total prior ignorance is identical with the Classical α per cent confidence interval for M. Conceptually, of course, the two are quite different.

Case 3 (section 6.3): unknown variance S^2 and known mean m

In this case, the usual Classical point estimate of S^2 is $\tilde{s}^2$ as defined in (6.33), namely $\tilde{s}^2 = \sum_{i=1}^{n} (x_i - m)^2/n$. The usual Classical α per cent confidence interval for S^2 is given by

$$(n\tilde{s}^2/y_{n,\,(100+\alpha)/2},\ n\tilde{s}^2/y_{n,\,(100-\alpha)/2}) \tag{6.67}$$

where $y_{k,\,\beta}$ is defined by $F_{Y_k}(y_{k,\,\beta}) \equiv P(Y_k \le y_{k,\,\beta}) = \beta/100$ where Y_k has a chi-square distribution with k degrees of freedom. If you consult (6.44), you should be able to show that this is algebraically identical to the Bayesian α per cent probability interval for S^2 based on total prior ignorance. Thus, once again, the Bayesian α per cent probability interval based on total prior ignorance and the Classical α per cent confidence interval are algebraically identical. (Actually, this is not a surprising result since both the Bayesian and the Classicist 'believe' under such circumstances that $n\tilde{s}^2/S^2$ has a chi-square distribution with n degrees of freedom; the difference being that the Bayesian regards this as a statement about S^2 for given $\tilde{s}^2$, while the Classicist regards it as a statement about $\tilde{s}^2$ for given S^2.)

Case 4 (section 6.4): unknown mean M and unknown variance S^2

In this case, the usual Classical point estimates of M and S^2 are $\bar{x}$ and $\hat{s}^2$ respectively, the latter being as defined in (6.59), namely $\hat{s}^2 = \sum_{i=1}^{n} (x_i - \bar{x})^2/(n-1)$. The usual Classical α per cent confidence intervals for M and S^2 are respectively (see Hey (1974), chapter 5)

$$(\bar{x} - t_{n-1,\,(100-\alpha)/2}\,\hat{s}/\sqrt{n},\ \bar{x} + t_{n-1,\,(100+\alpha)/2}\,\hat{s}/\sqrt{n})$$

and $\qquad\qquad\qquad\qquad\qquad\qquad\qquad\qquad\qquad\qquad\qquad$ (6.68)

$$((n-1)\hat{s}^2/y_{n-1,\,(100+\alpha)/2},\ (n-1)\hat{s}^2/y_{n-1,\,(100-\alpha)/2}).$$

where $y_{k,\,\beta}$ is as defined above, and where $t_{k,\,\beta}$ is defined by $F_{T_k}(t_{k,\,\beta}) \equiv P(T_k \le t_{k,\,\beta}) = \beta/100$ where T_k has a t distribution with k degrees of freedom. If you consult (6.60) and (6.62) respectively, you should be able to show that these are algebraically identical to the Bayesian α per cent probability intervals for M and S^2 respectively, based on total prior ignorance.

Thus, in all three cases, the Bayesian α per cent probability interval based on total prior ignorance and the Classical α per cent confidence interval are algebraically identical. Conceptually, of course, they are quite different, but the fact that they are algebraically identical means that it is perfectly safe for you, as a Bayesian statistician, to interpret a Classically-reported α per cent confidence interval as if it were a Bayesian α per cent probability interval based on total prior ignorance. Conversely, if a Classically-minded person wants to know the α per cent confidence interval for some parameter, you simply compute the Bayesian α per cent probability interval based on total prior ignorance.

The aspect of Classical inference known as *hypothesis testing* has no such direct counterpart in Bayesian inference, though some appropriate interpretation can be made. To avoid repetition we will confine attention to case 4, though the discussion applies equally well to the other two cases. Moreover, we will confine attention to the case of testing a hypothesis about M, though the discussion applies equally well to the case of testing a hypothesis about S^2.

Hypothesis testing about M is, as the terminology implies, concerned with using sample data to test between competing hypotheses about the (true but unknown) value of M. A typical competing pair would be hypotheses H_0 and H_1, defined by

$$H_0\colon M = m_0 \qquad H_1\colon M > m_0,$$

where m_0 is some specific value for M. The Classical procedure is to accept, in the light of the sample evidence, one of the hypotheses and to reject the other. Clearly, there will in general be a possibility that the 'wrong' hypothesis is accepted, so the test is designed in such a way that the probability of rejecting H_0 (termed the 'null hypothesis') when it is in fact true is equal to some pre-specified, satisfactorily small, value (usually 5 per cent or 1 per cent). This value is termed the *significance level* of the test. To be precise, if the test is designed so that

$$P(H_0 \text{ rejected} \mid H_0 \text{ true}) = \alpha/100,$$

then the significance level of the test is α per cent. In this particular example, it can be shown (see Hey (1974), chapter 5) that the appropriate test procedure to achieve an α per cent significance level is as follows:

$$\left.\begin{array}{l} \text{to accept } H_0 \text{ and reject } H_1 \text{ if } \dfrac{(\bar{x} - m_0)}{\hat{s}/\sqrt{n}} \le t_{n-1,\,100-\alpha}, \\[4mm] \text{to accept } H_1 \text{ and reject } H_0 \text{ if } \dfrac{(\bar{x} - m_0)}{\hat{s}/\sqrt{n}} > t_{n-1,\,100-\alpha} \end{array}\right\} \qquad (6.69)$$

where $t_{k,\,\beta}$ is as defined above. If the outcome of the test is to accept H_0 (the 'null hypothesis'), then the test is said *not to be significant at the α per cent level*, while if the outcome of the test is to reject H_0, then the test is said to be *significant at the α per cent level*. (Alternatively, it can be said that $\bar{x}$ either is not or is (as appropriate) significantly different from m_0.)

What sense can a Bayesian make of this procedure? As we shall show, the outcome of this test tells the Bayesian something about $P(M > m_0)$. First, we note that $P(M > m_0)$ can be written

$$P(M > m_0) \equiv P\left(\frac{M - \bar{x}}{\hat{s}/\sqrt{n}} > \frac{m_0 - \bar{x}}{\hat{s}/\sqrt{n}}\right)$$

(by subtracting $\bar{x}$ from each term inside the probability statement, and by dividing each term by $\hat{s}/\sqrt{n}$). Now consider the case of total prior ignorance, and recall (6.60) which states that the posterior assessment of M in this case is such that $(M - \bar{x})/(\hat{s}/\sqrt{n})$ has a t distribution with $(n - 1)$ degrees of freedom. This means we can write

$$P(M > m_0) = P\left(T_{n-1} > \frac{m_0 - \bar{x}}{\hat{s}/\sqrt{n}}\right)$$

where T_{n-1} denotes a variable which has a t distribution with $(n - 1)$ degrees of freedom. We can now use the fact that t distributions are symmetrical (so that $P(T_{n-1} > t) = P(T_{n-1} < -t)$) to deduce that

$$P(M > m_0) = P\left(T_{n-1} < \frac{\bar{x} - m_0}{\hat{s}/\sqrt{n}}\right).$$

Now suppose the test is significant at the α per cent level. This means, from (6.69) that $(\bar{x} - m_0)/(\hat{s}/\sqrt{n}) > t_{n-1,\,100-\alpha}$. Hence

$$P(M > m_0) > P(T_{n-1} < t_{n-1,\,100-\alpha}),$$

since $P(X \leq x_1) < P(X \leq x_2)$ if $x_1 < x_2$. But, by definition,

$$P(T_{n-1} < t_{n-1,\,100-\alpha}) = (100 - \alpha)/100.$$

Thus, we can conclude that

$$P(M > m_0) > (100 - \alpha)/100.$$

Similarly, if the test is *not* significant at the α per cent level, one can conclude that $P(M > m_0) \leq (100 - \alpha)/100$.

To summarize: if a Classical test of $H_0(M = m_0)$ against $H_1(M > m_0)$ results in rejection of H_0 at the α per cent significance level, then the Bayesian can interpret this as meaning that the posterior probability that H_1 is true (based on total prior ignorance) is at least $(100 - \alpha)/100$. To give a numerical example: if at the 5 per cent level H_0 is rejected, then the probability is more than 0.95 that H_1 is true, whereas if H_0 is accepted, then the probability is less than 0.95 that H_1 is true.

(Interestingly, this exposes the Classical procedure of hypothesis testing for the oddity that it is. The oddity is compounded when it is recognized that, to a Bayesian, $P(H_0$ is true$) \equiv P(M = m_0)$ is *zero*. A Bayesian is astounded by the suggestion that one should ever 'accept' a hypothesis that has a zero probability of being true. The Classicist counters, of course, by retorting that such probability statements – about constants – are meaningless.)

Be all this as it may. The crucial point for our purposes is that the Classical statement '$H_0(M = m_0)$ is rejected in favour of $H_1(M > m_0)$ at the α per cent significance level' and the Bayesian statement 'given total prior ignorance, the posterior probability that H_1 is true is more than $(100 - \alpha)/100$' are algebraically equivalent.

In conclusion, let us draw attention to the fact that all the Bayesian 'interpretations' of Classical concepts are interpretations based on total prior ignorance. This highlights the fact that Classical statistics has no role for prior information, and instead bases *all* its inference on the sample information. In this sense, Classical statistics can be regarded as an extreme special case of Bayesian statistics.

6.6 SUMMARY

This chapter has been concerned with inference about the mean and/or the variance of some variable of interest that is known to be normally distributed in some population of interest. The basic methodology employed has been exactly the same as that employed in the previous chapter (namely, the updating of prior beliefs in the light of new information), though the material has been considerably more difficult technically, particularly in section 6.4. Because of this increasing technical difficulty, we increasingly focused attention on the case of inference with total prior ignorance. The key results for this case are given in (6.25), (6.44), (6.60) and (6.62), and are summarized in table 6.1. You should study this table carefully, as it contains virtually all the results you are likely to need in practice.

Probably the most frequently used results of all are those for case 4, as given in the final row of this table. You will note that all you

Table 6.1   Inference about a mean and/or a variance with total prior ignorance

	Posterior distribution of mean M given by	Posterior distribution of variance S^2 given by
Case 2	$\dfrac{M - \bar{x}}{s/\sqrt{n}}$ is $N(0, 1)$	Known* to equal s^2
Case 3	Known* to equal m	$\dfrac{n\tilde{s}^2}{S^2}$ is $\chi^2(n)$
Case 4	$\dfrac{M - \bar{x}}{\hat{s}/\sqrt{n}}$ is $t(n - 1)$	$\dfrac{(n - 1)\hat{s}^2}{S^2}$ is $\chi^2(n - 1)$

Notation: $\bar{x} \equiv \sum\limits_{i=1}^{n} x_i/n$ (the sample mean)

$$\tilde{s}^2 \equiv \sum\limits_{i=1}^{n} (x_i - m)^2/n$$

$$\hat{s}^2 \equiv \sum\limits_{i=1}^{n} (x_i - \bar{x}^2)/(n - 1)$$

(the modified sample variance)

where $x_1, x_2, \ldots, x_n$ are the n observations on X.

Sources: Case 2:   result (6.25), which states that M is $N(\bar{x}, s^2/n)$, after transformation to unit normal (see section 2.4).
Case 3:   result (6.44).
Case 4:   results (6.60) and (6.62).
* Assumed known *a priori.*

need to calculate are the sample mean $\bar{x}$ and the modified sample variance $\hat{s}^2$. Then, in conjunction with the tables of the t distribution and chi-square distribution, you will be in a position to describe completely your posterior assessment of the population mean M and the population variance S^2. Thus, despite all the technical complexity of this chapter, the actual process of inference with total prior ignorance, even in case 4, is quite straightforward.

The chapter concluded with a brief statement of the Classical approach to inference in this context. We showed how the Classical procedures of estimation and hypothesis testing could be interpreted within the Bayesian framework. This should mean that you are now in a position to read and understand analyses of sample data based on the Classical approach, as well as those based on the Bayesian approach.

6.7   EXERCISES

6.1   Suppose income X is normally distributed with unknown mean M and known variance 100. Suppose a sample of size 9 yielded the following observations on X:

24   26   28   29   22   21   25   26   24.

Compute the posterior distribution for M, and hence a 95 per cent probability interval for M, for each of the following prior distributions for M:

(a) $N(20, 9)$ (b) $N(30, 9)$ (c) $N(20, 16)$ (d) $N(20, \infty)$.

For *two* of these four cases, compute the posterior distribution, and the implied 95 per cent probability interval, for M after the following *further* nine observations on X:

29   26   28   22   21   24   24   25   26.

For *one* of these two cases, compute the posterior in *both* of the possible two ways; namely, by considering the two samples separately and updating the assessment after each; and by combining the two samples together and updating the initial prior assessment in the light of this combined sample.

6.2   Consider the example given at the end of section 6.2. If you look at the penultimate paragraph of this section, you will see that the relevant posterior assessment, calculated '... using the first of the two possible methods ...', is $N(137.7, 1.853)$. Confirm this posterior assessment by using the second of the two methods.

6.3   If your prior knowledge about the unknown mean M of a normally distributed variable X is essentially non-existent, how large a sample size would you need to ensure that your posterior 95 per cent probability interval for M has a width less than 3.92 when the variance of X is (a) 100; (b) 25?

6.4   By using the fact (see section 2.4) that a variable which has a gamma distribution with parameters α and β has mean α/β and variance α/β^2, investigate the implications of (6.34) for the posterior mean and variance of P when m is known. In particular, explore the relative impact of prior and sample information on the posterior mean and variance.

6.5   Consider the numerical example given in section 6.3. Suppose that a further additional sample of ten students (over and above the thirty already collected) is obtained. Suppose that their X-values are as follows:

6.31	5.29	4.11	8.23	6.11
5.93	7.01	6.22	5.01	6.50.

Calculate the posterior 95 per cent probability interval for S based on total prior ignorance and the combined sample of forty students. (Be careful when calculating the value of $\tilde{s}^2$ for this combined sample. Hint: $\sum_{i=1}^{30} (x_i - m)^2 = 30 \times 1.3260 = 39.78$.)

6.6   Suppose income X is normally distributed with unknown mean M and unknown variable S^2. Suppose a sample of size 9 yielded the first set of observations listed in exercise 6.1. Compute 95 per cent probability intervals for M and for S based on total prior ignorance. What would these intervals become after the further nine observations given as the second set in exercise 6.1?

6.7   Suppose incomes in a particular region are known to be normally distributed. Suppose a sample of size 12 yielded a sample mean $\bar{x}$ of 24.4 and a modified sample standard deviation $\hat{s}$ of 10.388. In the light of this evidence, what would you feel about the claim that the mean income in this region was less than 32? How likely do you think it is that the standard deviation of incomes in the region is between 5 and 15. (You may have to interpolate the tables to approximate this.) Assume total prior ignorance.

6.8 The *logarithm* of weekly household income is approximately normally distributed. Suppose you have contacted a random sample of thirty-six households and have found that the *logarithms* of the sample incomes have a mean of 2.3 and a standard deviation of 0.5. In the light of this evidence, assess the validity of the hypothesis that the national average weekly household income is below £150. What does the sample reveal about the national dispersion of incomes? (Note: assume prior ignorance, and use logarithms to the base 10.)

6.9 Intelligence Quotients (IQs) are designed to be approximately normally distributed. Suppose you have tested a random sample of twenty-five University of York students and have found the sample IQs to have a mean of 115 and a modified standard deviation of 8. In the light of this evidence, how probable do you think it is that the average York student has an IQ above the national University average of 112? Does the spread of IQs at York appear to be unusually low (the standard deviation for the national University population as a whole is 12)? Assume total prior ignorance (on your part, of course!).

6.10 Use (6.60), and the facts that a t distribution with k degrees of freedom approaches a unit normal distribution as k approaches infinity, and that the distribution of the sample mean $\bar{x}$ approaches a degenerate distribution centred on the population mean m as the sample size approaches infinity, to determine the limiting form of the posterior assessment for M as n approaches infinity.

6.11 Use (6.62), and the facts that a chi-square distribution with k degrees of freedom has mean k and variance $2k$, and that the distribution of the modified sample variance $\hat{s}^2$ approaches a degenerate distribution centred on the population variance s^2 as the sample size approaches infinity, to determine the limiting form of the posterior assessment for S^2 as n approaches infinity.

6.12 (This is a more difficult question, and should be tackled only by the high-fliers.) Suppose the variable X is normally distributed with unknown mean M and unknown precision P. Suppose that the prior assessment of M and P is of the form specified in

(6.55) with the mean and variance of M equal to 2 and 5, respectively, and with the mean and variance of P both equal to 3. Determine the appropriate values of α, β, μ and π. Now suppose a random sample of ten observations is taken and it is found that $\bar{x} = 4.20$ and $\hat{s}^2 = 0.6$. Compute the posterior 95 per cent probability intervals for M and P. What would these be after a further ten observations for which $\bar{x} = 4.48$ and $\hat{s}^2 = 0.64\dot{6}$ (that is, $\hat{s}^2 = 5.82/9$)?

6.13 Throughout this chapter we have assumed that X is normally distributed. Would our *methods* still work if X had some other distribution? (The high-fliers might like to give an example.)

7 ELEMENTARY REGRESSION ANALYSIS

We are now in a position to apply our general methodology to the problem of most interest to economists – namely, the empirical investigation of economic relationships. As you are no doubt aware, the conclusions or predictions of virtually all economic theories are presented in the form of hypothesized relationships between economic variables. For example, the theory of demand yields the prediction that the quantity demanded of some good depends upon the price of that good, the price of other goods and the incomes of the demanders. Again, the theory of aggregate consumption predicts that consumers' expenditure depends upon income and the rate of interest. And so on. The purpose of this and the following two chapters is to show how information, in the form of observations on the relevant economic variables, can be used to improve our knowledge of such economic relationships.

Typically, economic theory is built up from a number of individual pieces of theory, each explaining the behaviour of one economic variable. These individual pieces can usually be expressed in the form of a hypothesized relationship of the form

$$Y = H(X) \tag{7.1}$$

where Y is the variable whose behaviour is being explained, and where X is a vector of explanatory variables. Usually, such a hypothesized relationship is qualified by the phrase 'ceteris paribus' to allow for the effect of any other explanatory variables whose existence has either been forgotten or ignored.

Depending upon the focus of interest, such hypothesized relationships are analysed either singly or in groups, ranging in size from 2 to several hundred. For example, a simple market model is built up from a demand curve, a supply curve and an equilibrium condition. Similarly, a simple macroeconomic model is built up from an aggregate consumption function and an income identity. More compli-

179

cated macro models contain consumption, investment, stockbuilding and import functions and equations representing wage and price inflation. Such models, consisting of two or more interrelated relationships, are called *simultaneous equation models*; they will be analysed in chapter 9. In the meantime, we examine the rather simpler problem of the analysis of single equation models – as represented by (7.1); these are the concern of chapters 7 and 8.

The general case of the single-equation model – in which X contains any number of variables, and in which the function $H(.)$ may take a variety of forms – is examined in chapter 8. Chapter 7 paves the way for this general case, by considering an important special case which introduces all the relevant conceptual ideas. This special case is when X is just a *scalar* (that is, when there is just one explanatory variable) and when $H(.)$ is *linear*. In this case, (7.1) is known as the *linear bivariate regression model*. We shall write it in the form

$$Y = A + BX, \tag{7.2}$$

where A and B are the *parameters* of the relationship (specifically, A is the intercept and B the slope, or alternatively, the coefficient of X). Thus, (7.2) specifies a hypothesized linear relationship between Y and X, such that Y equals A when X is zero, and such that an increase in X of 1 leads to an increase in Y of B. The most familiar example of this is the linear aggregate consumption function, in which Y is aggregate consumption, X is aggregate income and B is the (aggregate) marginal propensity to consume.

As we remarked above, economists tend to qualify such hypothesized relationships with the phrase '*ceteris paribus*'; this qualification is intended to signal that the relationship is hypothesized to hold only when everything else is held constant. While this is all very well and good in theory, it is rather difficult to enforce in practice. Thus, when we use data that has been generated by the workings of the economic system, rather than in a controlled experiment in which everything else has been kept constant, we must recognize that *ceteris paribus* does not hold. The usual way that this is done is by adding a 'catch-all', or residual term, to (7.2). Thus, we get, as the statement of our hypothesized relationship:

$$Y = A + BX + U \tag{7.3}$$

where U denotes this residual term. Written in the form of (7.3), we no longer need the qualification '*ceteris paribus*'.

The residual term U contains all the factors other than X which influence Y. In contrast with the part $(A + BX)$, which is referred to as the *deterministic* part of (7.3), U is *non-deterministic*. Its magnitude and relative importance in (7.3) depend partly on the importance of X in determining Y and partly on what is being held constant and what is not. More generally, the *form of the distribution* of U depends upon the particular application under consideration. A complete specification of the relationship (7.3) requires a specification of this distribution, as well as the specification of the parameters A and B. In general, therefore, there are three things about which we may wish to learn: the value of A, the value of B and the distribution of U. The purpose of this chapter is to show how observations on X and Y may be used to provide information about these three things.

As we discussed in chapter 6, the problem of learning about some distribution is considerably simplified if we know (or are prepared to assume something about) the *form* of the distribution – that is, if we know that it is uniform, or beta, or normal, or whatever. In the context of this chapter, there is an obvious candidate for the form of the distribution of U – namely, the *normal* distribution. This is the most commonly assumed form, and appears to be the appropriate form in a large number of economic applications. Moreover, theoretical justification comes in the form of the *Central Limit Theorem* (see, for example, Degroot (1970), p. 37) which states that, under certain circumstances, a variable which is the sum of a large number of independent variables will tend to have a normal distribution. Given that U captures the countless other variables which influence Y, an assumption of normality seems entirely appropriate. From now on, we will assume that U is normally distributed.

It is clearly sensible to take the mean of U as being zero (any non-zero mean could simply be incorporated into A); thus, the *mean* value of Y is $A + BX$, and so U measures the *deviation* of Y away from its mean value. The extent of the possible deviations can, as usual, be measured by the standard deviation of U. Let us denote this by S (as we shall see, in keeping with our notation of chapter 6). We can therefore summarize our assumptions about U by:

$$U \text{ is } N(0, S^2). \tag{7.4}$$

Equations (7.3) and (7.4) completely specify the *linear bivariate normal regression model*. This is the concern of this chapter.

To recapitulate: the focus of interest of this chapter is to show how observations on the variables X and Y can be used to provide information about the economic relationship between Y and X

which is assumed to take the following form (equations (7.3) and (7.4) repeated):

$$Y = A + BX + U$$
$$U \text{ is } N(0, S^2) \tag{7.5}$$

The relationship is completely specified by (7.5) and the three parameters A, B and S. Throughout this chapter it will be assumed that the specification (7.5) is correct, and thus at most all that remains to be ascertained are the values of the parameters A, B and S. To distinguish between S^2, which is the variance of U, and A and B which are the economic parameters of the relationship, we will refer to A and B as the *coefficients* of the relationship. (Clearly, B is the coefficient of X; you may like to think of A as the coefficient of a (dummy) variable which always takes the value 1.) In keeping with our previous notation, we will denote unknown parameters with upper-case letters, and known parameters with lower-case letters. Thus, the coefficients will be referred to as a and b if known, and A and B if unknown; likewise, the variance will be referred to as s^2 if known, and S^2 if unknown. As in chapter 6, there are four (main) cases to consider, as represented in the following table:

Case	Coefficients	Variance
1	known	known
2	unknown	known
3	known	unknown
4	unknown	unknown

(There are also some sub-cases: for example, in case 2, there are the two sub-cases corresponding to one of the coefficients being known and the other unknown. However, we do not consider these explicitly, since they can be treated as special cases either of the material of this chapter or of the material of chapter 6.)

As in chapter 6, case 1 is essentially trivial, and there is no problem to discuss, since everything is known about the relationship. The remaining cases are, however, non-trivial, and are examined in the next three sections; to be specific, case 2 is examined in section 7.2, case 3 in section 7.3 and case 4 in section 7.4. Then, as in chapter 6, we relate the results of these sections to the results of Classical analyses of the same problems; this we do in section 7.5. Section 7.6 then discusses the interrelated questions of the 'goodness of fit' of particular data to particular economic theories, and of the relative empirical performance of different theories purporting to explain the same variable. Some extended illustrations of regression are presented in section 7.7, while section 7.8 discusses how empirical analyses can be used to obtain predictions. Finally, section 7.9 provides a summary and section 7.10 a set of exercises.

It is important to keep in mind the ultimate purposes of the material of this chapter. First, it is to determine, in the light of observations on the relevant economic variables, the likely values of the key economic parameters A, B and S^2: a typical conclusion might be that, in the light of eighty quarterly observations on UK aggregate income and consumption, we feel that the probability is 0.95 that the aggregate mpc lies between 0.59 and 0.63; or again, in the light of observations on money and income, that the probability is 0.73 that the income-elasticity of the demand for money is at least 1. Secondly, it is to determine, in the light of observations on the relevant economic variables, the relative likelihood of competing economic theories: a typical conclusion might be that, in the light of data on inflation, the money supply and trade union membership, a monetarist explanation of inflation is deemed three times as likely as a trade-union-pressure explanation.

As you may have anticipated, the material of this chapter, although conceptually no more advanced than the material of the preceding chapters, is technically much more advanced. Accordingly, we will omit details of the derivations from the main body of the text, and confine these, where appropriate, to appendixes. Moreover, to simplify matters further, we will confine attention throughout to the case of *total prior ignorance*. References will be given for those readers who wish to explore the general case. Finally, as an aid to understanding the material of this chapter, we will draw analogies, where appropriate, with the material of chapter 6. Although not immediately obvious, the material of this chapter is the 'natural extension' of the material of chapter 6, in much the same way as the material of the next chapter is the 'natural extension' of the material of this. Thus, the drawing of analogies should ease comprehension not only of this chapter, but also of the next.

To this end, let us represent the model of chapter 6 using the notation of chapter 7. You will recall that the model of chapter 6 assumed that X, the variable of interest, was $N(M, S^2)$. Replace X by Y and M by A. We thus have, as the model of chapter 6,

Y is $N(A, S^2)$.

This can be expressed in the entirely equivalent form

$$Y = A + U$$
$$U \text{ is } N(0, S^2).$$
(7.6)

Now compare (7.5) with (7.6); as you will see, the latter is a special case of the former in that putting $B = 0$ in (7.5) yields (7.6). Thus, (7.5), the model of this chapter, is the 'natural extension' of (7.6), the model of chapter 6.

Let us now represent table 6.1 using the notation of chapter 7. This table, you will recall, contains the results of cases 2, 3 and 4 of chapter 6 for the case of *total prior ignorance* (which will be the only case considered in this chapter). Table 7.1 contains a representation of this table, with X replaced by Y, M by A and a few other notational changes as summarized in the table itself.

Table 7.1   Table 6.1 in the notation of chapter 7

	Posterior distribution† of coefficient A given by	*Posterior distribution† of variance S^2 given by*
Case 2	$\dfrac{A - \hat{a}}{s_A}$ is $N(0, 1)$	Known* to equal s^2
Case 3	Known* to equal a	$\dfrac{n\tilde{s}^2}{S^2}$ is $\chi^2(n)$
Case 4	$\dfrac{A - \hat{a}}{\hat{s}_A}$ is $t(n - 1)$	$\dfrac{(n - 1)\hat{s}^2}{S^2}$ is $\chi^2(n - 1)$

Key to notational differences

Chapter 6	Chapter 7
Model expressed as: X is $N(M, S^2)$	Model expressed as: $\begin{cases} Y = A + U \\ U \text{ is } N(0, S^2) \end{cases}$
X	Y
M	A
$X - M$	$Y - A \equiv U$
Observations $x_1, x_2, \ldots, x_n$	Observations $y_1, y_2, \ldots, y_n$
$\bar{x} \equiv \sum_{i=1}^{n} x_i/n$	$\hat{a} \equiv \bar{y} \equiv \sum_{i=1}^{n} y_i/n$
$\tilde{s}^2 \equiv \sum_{i=1}^{n} (x_i - m)^2/n$	$\tilde{s}^2 \equiv \sum_{i=1}^{n} (y_i - a)^2/n$
$\hat{s}^2 \equiv \sum_{i=1}^{n} (x_i - \bar{x})^2/(n - 1)$	$\hat{s}^2 \equiv \sum_{i=1}^{n} (y_i - \bar{y})^2/(n - 1)$
$s/\sqrt{n}$	$s_A \equiv s/\sqrt{n}$
$\hat{s}/\sqrt{n}$	$\hat{s}_A \equiv \hat{s}/\sqrt{n}$

* Assumed known *a priori*.
† Based on total prior ignorance about parameter (if unknown).

You should compare table 6.1 with table 7.1 and convince yourself that the latter is indeed the same as the former using the notation of this chapter. As will be shown in due course, the results of this chapter can be expressed in a manner entirely analogous to that of table 7.1. Let us now proceed to our analysis. We begin with case 2.

7.2 INFERENCE WITH UNKNOWN COEFFICIENTS AND KNOWN VARIANCE

In this section, we consider the case of inference with unknown coefficients and known variance. In keeping with our notational convention, we denote the former by A and B and the latter by s^2. Our model is thus (cf. (7.5)):

$$Y = A + BX + U$$
$$U \text{ is } N(0, s^2). \tag{7.7}$$

We wish to learn about the parameters A and B. Our information naturally comes in the form of pairs of observations on X and Y. Since we wish these observations to be informative about A and B, we require, as in chapters 5 and 6, that they be generated in a *random* manner; or, to use the terminology of chapters 5 and 6, that the observations be a *random sample* from the population of all such (X, Y) pairs. We will pursue the question of how we might obtain such a sample (or whether a particular sample might be considered as generated in such a fashion) in due course. For the moment, we will simply assume that our observations are so generated. We will suppose that the sample is of size n, and will denote the observations by $(x_1, y_1), (x_2, y_2), \ldots, (x_n, y_n)$.

Now, using Bayes' theorem in the manner illustrated in chapters 5 and 6, we can derive the posterior assessment of A and B for any given prior assessment and any given set of observations. Given that *two* unknown parameters are involved, these assessments will naturally be joint assessments. Apart from any technical complexity, this problem is a straightforward application of Bayes' theorem. However, we do not intend to discuss the general case (because of this technical complexity). Instead, we will confine attention to the case of *total prior ignorance*, as characterized in exactly the same manner as in section 6.2. To be specific, we will characterize total prior ignorance about A and B by assuming that the prior marginal distributions of A and B are both normal with an infinite variance. (In essence, this means that the density functions of both A and B are uniform over the range $-\infty$ to $+\infty$.) Given this prior, the posterior joint assessment of A and B can be deduced in the usual manner. Appendix A3 gives the relevant details. As is obvious, this posterior assessment takes the form of a joint probability distribution of A and B, as characterized by the joint density function

$$f_{AB}(a, b \,|\, (x_1, y_1), (x_2, y_2), \ldots, (x_n, y_n)).$$

This completely specifies the posterior joint assessment. Of the many aspects of this, one is usually most interested in the marginal distributions of A and B individually. These can be obtained from the joint distribution in the usual manner (see section 3.3). Once again, Appendix A3 gives the relevant details. From this, we obtain the following important result:

> Given total prior ignorance, then after observations $(x_1, y_1), (x_2, y_2), \ldots, (x_n, y_n)$ on (X, Y) (which is such that $Y - A - BX$ is $N(0, s^2)$), the posterior marginals on A and B are such that $(A - \hat{a})/s_A$ and $(B - \hat{b})/s_B$ are both $N(0, 1)$ where $\hat{a}, \hat{b}, s_A$ and s_B are as given in (7.9). (7.8)

$$
\begin{aligned}
&\hat{a} = \bar{y} - \hat{b}\bar{x} \qquad (\bar{y} = \sum_{i=1}^{n} y_i/n \quad \bar{x} = \sum_{i=1}^{n} x_i/n) \\
&\hat{b} = \sum_{i=1}^{n} (y_i - \bar{y})(x_i - \bar{x}) / \sum_{i=1}^{n} (x_i - \bar{x})^2 \\
&s_A = s\{\sum_{i=1}^{n} x_i^2 / [n \sum_{i=1}^{n} (x_i - \bar{x})^2]\}^{1/2} \\
&s_B = s/[\sum_{i=1}^{n} (x_i - \bar{x})^2]^{1/2}.
\end{aligned}
\qquad (7.9)
$$

Before we attempt to discuss the intuition behind this result, let us give a simple illustration of its application. As you will see from (7.8), all we need to do is to use the observations to calculate first $\bar{x}$ and $\bar{y}$ and then $\hat{a}, \hat{b}, s_A$ and s_B. These are then used to determine the posterior (marginal) assessments of A and B, from which any desired summary statements can be obtained in the usual fashion. To illustrate this procedure, suppose we have obtained the following random sample of nine observations on (X, Y):

$$
\begin{array}{lllll}
(1, 6) & (2, 9) & (3, 12) & (4, 15) & (5, 12) \\
& (6, 18) & (7, 18) & (8, 21) & (9, 24).
\end{array}
$$

From table 7.2, which sets out all the required calculations in a methodical manner, we see that $\sum_{i=1}^{9} x_i = 45$ and $\sum_{i=1}^{9} y_i = 135$, and hence that $\bar{x} = 45/9 = 5$ and $\bar{y} = 135/9 = 15$. Using these results, we obtain columns (4) and (5) – both of which sum to zero (as *must* be the case if the calculations have been carried out

Table 7.2 Background calculations for the example of section 7.2

i	(1) x_i	(2) x_i^2	(3) y_i	(4) $= (1) - \bar{x}$ $x_i - \bar{x}$	(5) $= (3) - \bar{y}$ $y_i - \bar{y}$	(6) $= (4)^2$ $(x_i - \bar{x})^2$	(7) $= (4)(5)$ $(y_i - \bar{y})(x_i - \bar{x})$
1	1	1	6	-4	-9	16	36
2	2	4	9	-3	-6	9	18
3	3	9	12	-2	-3	4	6
4	4	16	15	-1	0	1	0
5	5	25	12	0	-3	0	0
6	6	36	18	1	3	1	3
7	7	49	18	2	3	4	6
8	8	64	21	3	6	9	18
9	9	81	24	4	9	16	36
$\sum$	45	285	135	0	0	60	123

correctly). From these we obtain columns (6) and (7). Using (7.9) we thus have

$$\hat{b} = \sum_{i=1}^{9} (y_i - \bar{y})(x_i - \bar{x})/\sum_{i=1}^{9} (x_i - \bar{x})^2 = 123/60 = 2.05,$$

and hence

$$\hat{a} = \bar{y} - \hat{b}\bar{x} = 15 - 2.05 \times 5 = 4.75.$$

Now suppose the (assumed known) value of s is 1.5. Using (7.9) we thus have

$$s_A = s\{\sum_{i=1}^{9} x_i^2/[9 \sum_{i=1}^{9} (x_i - \bar{x})^2]\}^{1/2} = 1.5(285/(9 \times 60))^{1/2}$$
$$= 1.090,$$

and

$$s_B = s/[\sum_{i=1}^{9} (x_i - \bar{x})^2]^{1/2} = 1.5/(60)^{1/2} = 0.194,$$

each to three decimal places.

Finally, if we substitute these into (7.8) we find that, given total prior ignorance, and given the nine observations listed above, the posteriors on A and B are such that

$$(A - 4.75)/1.090 \text{ is } N(0, 1) \text{ and } (B - 2.05)/0.194 \text{ is } N(0, 1). \quad (7.10)$$

These are complete characterizations of the posterior (marginal) assessments. To obtain any desired summary measures, we proceed in the usual manner. For example, to find the posterior 95 per cent probability intervals for A and B, we use the fact (see Appendix A6) that a unit normal lies between ± 1.96 with probability 0.95. Thus, for A:

$$P\left(-1.96 \leq \frac{A - 4.75}{1.090} \leq 1.96 \right) = 0.95,$$

and hence (since $1.96 \times 1.090 = 2.1364$)

$$P(-2.1364 \leq A - 4.75 \leq 2.1364) = 0.95,$$

and hence (to two decimal places),

$$P(2.61 \leq A \leq 6.89) = 0.95.$$

Thus, we can conclude on the basis of the nine observations and total prior ignorance, that the probability is 0.95 that A is between 2.61 and 6.89. Similarly, for B we have

$$P\left(-1.96 \leq \frac{B - 2.05}{0.194} \leq 1.96 \right) = 0.95,$$

and hence (to two decimal places),

$$P(1.67 \leq B \leq 2.43) = 0.95.$$

Thus, on the same basis, the probability is 0.95 that B is between 1.67 and 2.43. As a further example of the use of (7.10), suppose someone asks us to assess how likely it is that the actual value of B is greater than 2. We would respond by computing $P(B > 2)$ as follows:

$$\begin{aligned} P(B > 2) &= P(B - 2.05 > 2 - 2.05) = P(B - 2.05 > -0.05) \\ &= P[(B - 2.05)/0.194 > -0.05/0.194] \\ &= P[Z > -0.25], \end{aligned}$$

where $Z \equiv (B - 2.05)/0.194$ is $N(0, 1)$ from (7.10). Hence, using the table of the unit normal distribution in Appendix A6,

$$P(B > 2) = 0.5987.$$

Thus, on the basis of the sample evidence, we would assess the probability that the actual B is larger than 2 as being almost 60 per cent.

As our illustration shows, the *use* of the key result (7.8) is straight-forward, and the way that our posterior assessments about A and B are expressed is familiar. Moreover, the key result itself is derived in a familiar manner. The only thing that remains to do is to provide some intuitive understanding of this key result.

Consider first the *means* of the posterior assessments. Since, from

(7.8) both $(A - \hat{a})/s_A$ and $(B - \hat{b})/s_B$ are unit normal, and hence both have a mean of zero, it follows that the mean of A is $\hat{a}$ and that the mean of B is $\hat{b}$. Moreover, since the unit normal is *symmetrical*, it follows that the posterior assessments of A and B are *centred* on, and *symmetrical* about, their respective means $\hat{a}$ and $\hat{b}$. It follows, therefore, that the posterior assessment of the mean relationship

$$Y = A + BX \qquad (7.11)$$

is *centred* on, and *symmetrical* about, its mean

$$Y = \hat{a} + \hat{b}X. \qquad (7.12)$$

The obvious question to ask, then, is: 'What is the meaning of $\hat{a}$ and $\hat{b}$, and hence of the relationship $Y = \hat{a} + \hat{b}X$?'

Statistically, $\hat{a}$ and $\hat{b}$ are simply the appropriate expressions resulting from the routine application of Bayes' theorem as presented in Appendix A3. Algebraically, $\hat{a}$ and $\hat{b}$ are given by the first two equations in (7.9). But neither of these facts help us very much. So let us return to our illustration, and show on a graph the nine observations and the relationship $Y = \hat{a} + \hat{b}X$ which has been computed from them. This we do in figure 7.1.

The intercept of the relationship $Y = \hat{a} + \hat{b}X$ is $\hat{a} = 4.75$, and the slope is $\hat{b} = 2.05$. Furthermore, since $\hat{a} = \bar{y} - \hat{b}\bar{x}$ (see (7.9)) it follows that the relationship $Y = \hat{a} + \hat{b}X$ passes through the mean of the observations $(\bar{x}, \bar{y})$ (in this case, the point $(5, 15)$). What else can be said? A glance at figure 7.1 suggests that this relationship is a

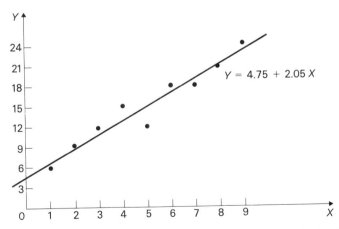

Figure 7.1 The observations and the posterior mean relationship

straight line which, in some sense, 'fits' the observations. But then lots of straight lines could, apparently equally well, be said to 'fit' the observations in some sense. What is so special about this one – the one that has been 'selected' by the application of Bayes' theorem as the mean of the posterior assessment of the relationship (7.7) based on total prior ignorance?

With the benefit of hindsight we can answer this question. Consider the (arbitrarily chosen) straight line

$$Y = a + bX,$$

and denote the vertical deviation of the *i*th observation (x_i, y_i) from this line by e_i. Thus,

$$e_i = y_i - a - bx_i. \tag{7.13}$$

Depending upon the values of *a* and *b*, some of these e_i may be positive and some may be negative. The *magnitude* of each e_i indicates how far the *i*th observation is from the line. The sum of such deviations squared $(\sum_{i=1}^{n} e_i^2)$ is therefore an aggregate measure of how far the observations are from the line. We will show below that, *of all possible a and b, the values* $\hat{a}$ *and* $\hat{b}$ *as given by (7.9) are those that minimize this sum of squared deviations*. Thus, the straight line $Y = \hat{a} + \hat{b}X$ is the line which 'best fits' the observations in the sense of minimizing the sum of squared deviations of the observations from the line. Before discussing these implications further, let us verify the above italicized assertion.

Consider the problem of choosing *a* and *b* so as to minimize $\sum_{i=1}^{n} e_i^2$ where e_i is as given in (7.13). That is, *a* and *b* are to be chosen to minimize

$$D \equiv \sum_{i=1}^{n} (y_i - a - bx_i)^2. \tag{7.14}$$

To carry out this minimization, we need to set $\partial D/\partial a$ and $\partial D/\partial b$ both equal to zero. (This is a familiar calculus condition; if, however, it is unfamiliar to you, you will lose nothing by taking the result on faith.) Anticipating somewhat, we will denote by $\hat{a}$ and $\hat{b}$ the values of *a* and *b* for which $\partial D/\partial a = \partial D/\partial b = 0$. From (7.14), these imply

$$\partial D/\partial a = -2 \sum_{i=1}^{n} (y_i - \hat{a} - \hat{b}x_i) = 0$$

$$\partial D/\partial b = -2 \sum_{i=1}^{n} (y_i - \hat{a} - \hat{b}x_i)x_i = 0.$$

After simplification, these yield

$$\sum_{i=1}^{n} y_i = \hat{a}n + \hat{b} \sum_{i=1}^{n} x_i \tag{7.15}$$

and

$$\sum_{i=1}^{n} y_i x_i = \hat{a} \sum_{i=1}^{n} x_i + \hat{b} \sum_{i=1}^{n} x_i^2. \tag{7.16}$$

These are two equations which can be solved for the two unknowns $\hat{a}$ and $\hat{b}$. From (7.15), dividing by n and re-arranging, it immediately follows that

$$\hat{a} = \bar{y} - \hat{b}\bar{x},$$

which is the first of the equations in (7.9). Finally, by using this to eliminate $\hat{a}$ from (7.16), and then solving the resulting expression for $\hat{b}$ we get

$$\hat{b} = \sum_{i=1}^{n} (y_i - \bar{y})(x_i - \bar{x}) / \sum_{i=1}^{n} (x_i - \bar{x})^2,$$

which is the second of the equations in (7.9). We have thus proved our assertion that the straight line $Y = \hat{a} + \hat{b}X$ is the line which 'best fits' the observations in the sense of minimizing the sum of squared deviations of the observations from the line. (For purists who are worried whether it is a minimum or a maximum we have found – rest assured, the *maximum* occurs when a or b is $\pm \infty$.) For obvious reasons, this line is called the *least-squares fitted line*. If you have done some statistics before, it may be familiar to you. (Many modern electronic calculators will calculate $\hat{a}$ and $\hat{b}$ for you, after you have fed in the observations.)

To summarize the discussion so far: the line $Y = \hat{a} + \hat{b}X$, where $\hat{a}$ and $\hat{b}$ are given in (7.9), is the *least-squares fitted line*. The Bayesian posterior assessment of A, the intercept of the relationship (7.7), based on total prior ignorance, is centred on $\hat{a}$, the intercept of this least-squares fitted line. Also the Bayesian posterior assessment of B, the slope of the relationship (7.7), based on total prior ignorance, is centred on $\hat{b}$, the slope of this least-squares fitted line. However, it is important to realize that *these results follow from the routine application of Bayes' theorem, and not because the least-squares fitted line has any magical properties*. The *primary* property of $\hat{a}$ and $\hat{b}$, as far as we are concerned, is that they are the posterior means of A and B respectively; the *secondary* property, that they are the intercept and slope of the least-squares fitted line, is mentioned only to help you visualize the key result (7.8).

Let us move on now to consider the factors affecting the *dispersion* of the posterior assessments of A and B. From (7.8), it can be seen that the posterior standard deviation of A is s_A, and that the posterior standard deviation of B is s_B, where s_A and s_B are as given in

(7.9). Since the posterior α per cent probability intervals for A and B are given (using (7.8)) by

$$(\hat{a} + z_{(100-\alpha)/2}\,s_A,\ \hat{a} + z_{(100+\alpha)/2}\,s_A)$$

and

$$(\hat{b} + z_{(100-\alpha)/2}\,s_B,\ \hat{b} + z_{(100+\alpha)/2}\,s_B),$$

respectively (where z_β is defined by $P(Z \le z_\beta) = \beta/100$, where Z is $N(0, 1)$), it follows that the *widths* of these intervals are directly proportional to the respective posterior standard deviations (s_A and s_B respectively). Thus, the accuracy of the posterior assessments is indicated by s_A and s_B respectively. Now, s_A and s_B are given in (7.9) and are the result of the routine application of Bayes' theorem in Appendix A3. Let us provide some intuitive understanding of the factors determining the magnitudes of s_A and s_B. We begin with the latter.

From (7.9), we see that s_B, the posterior standard deviation of B, is given by

$$s_B = s/[\textstyle\sum_{i=1}^{n} (x_i - \bar{x})^2]^{1/2}. \tag{7.17}$$

Let us express this in a slightly different form, by introducing s_X to denote the *sample standard deviation* of X; that is

$$s_X \equiv (\textstyle\sum_{i=1}^{n} (x_i - \bar{x})^2/n)^{1/2}. \tag{7.18}$$

Substituting (7.18) into (7.17), we get

$$s_B = \frac{s}{s_X\sqrt{n}}. \tag{7.19}$$

According to this, the posterior standard deviation of B is directly proportional to s (the standard deviation of U), inversely proportional to s_X (the sample standard deviation of X) and inversely proportional to $\sqrt{n}$ (the square root of the sample size). Do these properties make sense?

Consider figure 7.2, which contains three pairwise comparisons. The least-squares fitted line is the same in all six cases (since the purpose of this illustration is to discuss the factors determining the dispersions, rather than the means, of the assessments). For each pair, you should ask yourself: 'In which of the two do I feel more confident about my posterior assessment of B, the slope of the underlying relationship?' Consider first figure 7.2(a): in this pair, the number of observations (n) is the same, as is the spread in the X-direction (s_X); the only difference is the spread of the vertical devi-

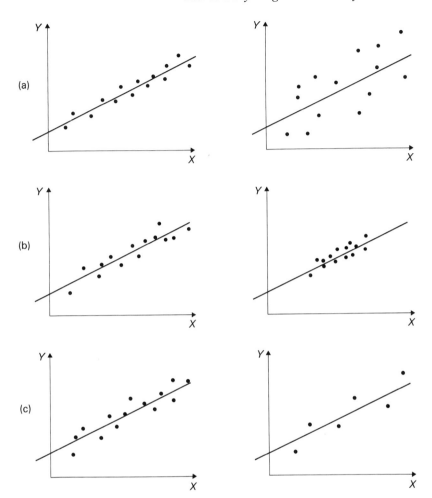

Figure 7.2 Three pairwise comparisons

ations about the line (s). In the right-hand scatter s is clearly larger than in the left-hand scatter. Now, presumably, in response to the question above, you replied: 'I feel more confident about my posterior assessment of B in the left-hand scatter.' This shows that the larger is s, the larger the spread of the posterior assessment of B (s_B). This intuitively confirms the first of the three properties given in (7.19). Consider now figure 7.2(b): in this pair, the number of observations (n) is the same, as is the spread of the vertical deviations about the line (s); the only difference is the spread in the X-direction (s_X). In the left-hand scatter s_X is clearly larger than in the right-hand scatter. Now, presumably, in response to the question posed above, you replied: 'I feel more confident about my posterior assessment of B in the left-hand scatter.' This shows that the larger is s_X, the smaller is the spread of the posterior assessment of B (s_B). This intuitively confirms the second of the three properties given in (7.19). Finally, consider Figure 7.2(c): in this pair, the spread of the vertical deviations about the line (s) is the same, as is the spread in the X-direction (s_X); the only difference is the number of observations (n). In the left-hand scatter n is larger than in the right-hand scatter. Now, presumably, in response to the question posed above, you replied: 'I feel more confident about my posterior assessment of B in the left-hand scatter.' This shows that the larger is n, the smaller is the spread of the posterior assessment of B (s_B). This intuitively firms the third and final property of (7.19). Thus the factors determining the precision of the posterior assessment of B all make good intuitive sense.

A similar interpretation of the result for s_A can be carried out, though we leave most of this to the reader. From (7.9), we see that s_A is given by

$$s_A = s\{\textstyle\sum_{i=1}^{n} x_i^2/[n \sum_{i=1}^{n} (x_i - \bar{x})^2]\}^{1/2}$$

Using s_X as defined in (7.18), and noting that $\sum_{i=1}^{n} x_i^2$ can be written as $n(s_X^2 + \bar{x}^2)$ (see exercise 7.5), we can write s_A as

$$s_A = \frac{s(s_X^2 + \bar{x}^2)^{1/2}}{s_X \sqrt{n}} \qquad (7.20)$$

Thus, as with s_B, s_A (the posterior standard deviation of A) is directly proportional to s (the standard deviation of U) and inversely proportional to $\sqrt{n}$ (the square root of the sample size). Moreover, s_A is inversely related to s_X (the sample standard deviation of X), and directly related to the magnitude of $\bar{x}$ (the sample mean of X). The intuition behind the first three of these properties is exactly the same as that behind the three properties for s_B – as illustrated in figure 7.2. The fourth property is, however, somewhat different. We leave it to you to provide an intuitive interpretation of it. (See exercise 7.4.)

To summarize: the standard deviations of the posterior assessments of A and B based on total prior ignorance are s_A and s_B respectively, as given in (7.9). As we have shown, both s_A and s_B are smaller, the smaller is s (the standard deviation of U), the larger is s_X (the sample standard deviation of X) and the larger is n (the sample size); in addition, s_A is smaller the smaller in magnitude is $\bar{x}$ (the sample mean of X). As our discussion has shown, all these properties make good intuitive sense.

The implications of the key result (7.8) have now been discussed as far as the *means* and *standard deviations* of the posterior assessments are concerned. All that remains to be mentioned is the implication for the *shape* of the posterior assessments. From (7.8) it is seen that both the posterior assessments are *normally distributed*. A glance at Appendix A3 will show that this is the inevitable consequence of the assumption that U is normally distributed. It is precisely analogous to the result of case 2 of chapter 6.

This completes our treatment, for the time being, of case 2. The key result is (7.8) which gives the posterior assessments for the unknown coefficients A and B (of the relationship $Y = A + BX + U$) based on total prior ignorance and a sample of n observations. To implement this key result, one simply calculates $\hat{a}$ and $\hat{b}$ (the intercept and slope of the least-squares fitted line) and s_A and s_B (the posterior standard deviations of A and B). These values are then substituted into (7.8), thus obtaining a complete characterization of the posterior assessments of A and B. Any required summary measures can be obtained in the usual fashion.

Throughout this section it has been assumed that s^2, the variance of U, is known. In practice, this is unlikely to be the case. Accordingly, we now proceed to investigate the situation in which S^2 is unknown. We begin in section 7.3 with the relatively simple task of inference about S^2 when a and b are known. As we shall see, this paves the way for the most general case (inference when A, B and S^2 are unknown) which is examined in section 7.4.

7.3   INFERENCE WITH KNOWN COEFFICIENTS AND
        UNKNOWN VARIANCE

In this section, we consider the case of inference with known coefficients and unknown variance. In keeping with our notational convention, we denote the former by a and b and the latter by S^2. Our model is thus (cf. (7.5)):

$$Y = a + bX + U$$
$$U \text{ is } N(0, S^2).$$
(7.21)

We wish to learn about the parameter S, using information in the form of pairs of observations on X and Y.

A moment's reflection will convince you that we have already treated this case – as case 3 of chapter 6. For essentially, since a and b are known, what (7.21) is saying is that the (known) composite variable $(Y - a - bX)$ is normally distributed (in some population) with a known mean (0) and unknown variance (S^2). Thus the results of section 6.3 are directly applicable. All we need to do is to replace the variable X of chapter 6 by the composite variable $(Y - a - bX)$, and to specify that the known mean m equals 0. The n observations are the n values of the composite variable $(y_1 - a - bx_1)$, $(y_2 - a - bx_2)$, ..., $(y_n - a - bx_n)$, and we can use these directly in the key results (6.34) or (6.44) as appropriate. Given that we are confining attention in this chapter to the case of total prior ignorance, it follows that (6.44) is the relevant result. Translated into the notation of this chapter, it implies:

> Given total prior ignorance, then after observations $(x_1, y_1), (x_2, y_2), \ldots, (x_n, y_n)$ on (X, Y) (which is such that $Y - a - bX$ is $N(0, S^2)$), the posterior assessment of S^2 is such that $n\tilde{s}^2/S^2$ has a chi-square distribution with n degrees of freedom, where $\tilde{s}^2$ is given by (7.23). $\qquad$ (7.22)

$$\tilde{s}^2 = \sum_{i=1}^{n} (y_i - a - bx_i)^2/n. \qquad (7.23)$$

Equation (7.23) is, of course, the counterpart of equation (6.33) in chapter 6.

Given that this case is essentially the same as case 3 of chapter 6, we really need not devote much space to it; the comments made in section 6.3 remain entirely appropriate. However, it may help to give a simple illustration. Consider the example of section 7.2, but 'invert' it by supposing that we know the values of a and b, and wish to use the observations to shed light on the value of S^2. To be specific, suppose that we know that a equals 5 and b equals 2. Recall that the nine observations were as follows:

(1, 6)   (2, 9)   (3, 12)   (4, 15)   (5, 12)
(6, 18)   (7, 18)   (8, 21)   (9, 24).

Figure 7.3 illustrates; on this, we have marked the nine observations and the mean relationship $Y = a + bX$; that is, $Y = 5 + 2X$. In order to apply the key result (7.22), we need to calculate $\tilde{s}^2$. Inspection of (7.23) shows that to do this, we first need to evaluate $y_i - a - bx_i$ for all i. Now, the expression $y_i - a - bx_i$ measures the vertical deviation of the observation (x_i, y_i) from the mean relationship; it will be positive if the observation is above the line, and negative if

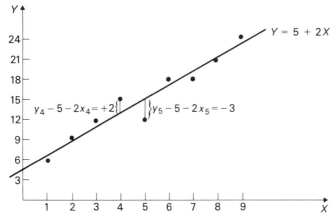

Figure 7.3 The observations and the mean relationship

the observation is below the line. Figure 7.3 illustrates this for $i = 4$ and $i = 5$. Simple arithmetic shows that the values for the nine points are as follows:

$$-1 \quad 0 \quad +1 \quad +2 \quad -3 \quad +1 \quad -1 \quad 0 \quad +1.$$

The value of $\tilde{s}^2$ is found by squaring these, summing them and finally dividing the total by 9. This yields $\tilde{s}^2 = 2$. If we now substitute this into (7.22) we find that the posterior assessment of S^2 (the variance of U), based on total prior ignorance and the nine observations, is such that $18/S^2$ is $\chi^2(9)$. This is a complete characterization of the posterior assessment. The various summary measures can be obtained in the usual way. For example, a 95 per cent probability interval for S can be found by using the fact (see Appendix A8) that a variable with a chi-square distribution with 9 degrees of freedom lies between 2.70 and 19.02 with probability 0.95. Hence, we have

$$P(2.70 \leq 18/S^2 \leq 19.02) = 0.95.$$

Taking reciprocals and then multiplying by 18 inside the probability statement, yields the following

$$P(0.9464 \leq S^2 \leq 6.\dot{6}) = 0.95.$$

Finally, taking square roots inside the probability statement, we get (to two decimal places)

$$P(0.98 \leq S \leq 2.58) = 0.95.$$

Hence, we can be 95 per cent sure that the standard deviation of U is between 0.98 and 2.58.

As a second example, suppose we are asked to judge how likely it is that the standard deviation of U is less than 2.1. We would simply compute $P(S < 2.1)$ using the result that $18/S^2$ is $\chi^2(9)$. We would do this as follows. We have

$$
\begin{aligned}
P(S < 2.1) &= P(S^2 < 4.41) && \text{(squaring both sides)} \\
&= P(S^2/18 < 4.41/18) && \text{(dividing both sides by 18)} \\
&= P(18/S^2 > 18/4.41) && \text{(taking the reciprocal of} \\
& && \text{both sides)} \\
&= P(Y_9 > 4.08),
\end{aligned}
$$

where $Y_9 \equiv 18/S^2$ has a chi-square distribution with 9 degrees of freedom. From Appendix A8 we see that $P(Y_9 > 4.08)$ is about 0.905 (interpolating between the table entries). Hence, $P(S < 2.1) = 0.905$. Thus, there is less than a 1 in 10 chance that S is greater than 2.1.

This completes our treatment of case 3 of this chapter. As we have seen, except for notational differences, it is exactly the same as case 3 of chapter 6. Thus, all the material of section 6.3 is applicable. No further analysis is necessary. We now move on to case 4 – the most general case of this chapter.

7.4   INFERENCE WITH UNKNOWN COEFFICIENTS AND UNKNOWN VARIANCE

In this section, we consider the most general case of all within the framework of this chapter; namely, the case in which all three parameters (the two coefficients and the variance) are all unknown. The model is thus

$$
\begin{aligned}
Y &= A + BX + U \\
U &\text{ is } N(0, S^2).
\end{aligned}
\tag{7.24}
$$

As in the preceding two sections, we confine attention to the case of total prior ignorance, as characterized in a fashion entirely analogous to that of case 4 of chapter 6, discussed in section 6.4. Appendix A3 gives the technical details. Again, as in the preceding two sections, we presume our information comes in the form of a random sample of observations $(x_1, y_1), (x_2, y_2), \ldots, (x_n, y_n)$ on (X, Y).

We are interested in the posterior joint assessment of the three unknown parameters A, B and S given total prior ignorance and our sample of n observations. Once again, this is a straightforward application of Bayes' theorem. However, because of the rather tedious nature of the algebra involved in this application, we confine the details to Appendix A3. In that Appendix, full details of the posterior joint assessment are presented. Here we confine attention to the marginal distributions of that joint assessment; that is, we concentrate attention on the posterior marginal assessments of A, B and S. The key results, obtained from Appendix A3, are as follows.

$$
\left.
\begin{array}{l}
\text{Given total prior ignorance, then after observations} \\
(x_1, y_1), (x_2, y_2), \ldots, (x_n, y_n) \text{ on } (X, Y) \text{ (which is} \\
\text{such that } Y - A - BX \text{ is } N(0, S^2)\text{), the posterior} \\
\text{marginals on } A \text{ and } B \text{ are such that } (A - \hat{a})/\hat{s}_A \text{ and} \\
(B - \hat{b})/\hat{s}_B \text{ both have } t \text{ distributions with } (n - 2) \\
\text{degrees of freedom, where } \hat{a}, \hat{b}, \hat{s}_A \text{ and } \hat{s}_B \text{ are as} \\
\text{given in (7.27).}
\end{array}
\right\} \quad (7.25)
$$

$$
\left.
\begin{array}{l}
\text{Given total prior ignorance, then after observations} \\
(x_1, y_1), (x_2, y_2), \ldots, (x_n, y_n) \text{ on } (X, Y) \text{ (which is} \\
\text{such that } Y - A - BX \text{ is } N(0, S^2)\text{), the posterior} \\
\text{marginal on } S^2 \text{ is such that } (n - 2)\hat{s}^2/S^2 \text{ has a chi-square} \\
\text{distribution with } (n - 2) \text{ degrees of freedom,} \\
\text{where } \hat{s}^2 \text{ is as given in (7.27).}
\end{array}
\right\} \quad (7.26)
$$

$$
\left.
\begin{array}{l}
\hat{a} = \bar{y} - \hat{b}\bar{x} \qquad (\bar{y} = \sum_{i=1}^{n} y_i/n \quad \bar{x} = \sum_{i=1}^{n} x_i/n) \\[4pt]
\hat{b} = \sum_{i=1}^{n} (y_i - \bar{y})(x_i - \bar{x})/\sum_{i=1}^{n} (x_i - \bar{x})^2 \\[4pt]
\hat{s}_A = \hat{s}\{\sum_{i=1}^{n} x_i^2/[n \sum_{i=1}^{n} (x_i - \bar{x})^2]\}^{1/2} \\[4pt]
\hat{s}_B = \hat{s}/[\sum_{i=1}^{n} (x_i - \bar{x})^2]^{1/2} \\[4pt]
\hat{s} = [\sum_{i=1}^{n} (y_i - \hat{a} - \hat{b}x_i)^2/(n - 2)]^{1/2}.
\end{array}
\right\} \quad (7.27)
$$

These results are not as formidable as they may appear at first glance. Consider first the result (7.25) for the posterior assessments of A and B, and compare this with result (7.8) for the corresponding assessments in case 2. You will note first that the posterior assessments of A and B continue to be centred on, and symmetrical about, $\hat{a}$ and $\hat{b}$ respectively (as given by the first two equations in (7.9), or, identically, by the first two equations in (7.27)). Thus, the posterior assessments continue to be centred on the intercept and slope of the least-squares fitted line. Second, note from (7.25) that the posterior α per cent probability intervals for A and B are given by

$$
(\hat{a} + t_{n-2, (100-\alpha)/2}\, \hat{s}_A, \; \hat{a} + t_{n-2, (100+\alpha)/2}\, \hat{s}_A)
$$

and

$$
(\hat{b} + t_{n-2, (100-\alpha)/2}\, \hat{s}_B, \; \hat{b} + t_{n-2, (100+\alpha)/2}\, \hat{s}_B)
$$

respectively, where $t_{k, \beta}$ is such that $P(T_k \leq t_{k, \beta}) = \beta/100$ where T_k has a t distribution with k degrees of freedom. Thus, the widths of the posterior probability intervals for A and B are proportional to $\hat{s}_A$ and $\hat{s}_B$ respectively. In case 2, when S^2 was known, these posterior probability intervals were proportional to s_A and s_B respectively. Now compare s_A and s_B with $\hat{s}_A$ and $\hat{s}_B$ respectively, as defined in (7.9) and (7.27) respectively. You will see that the only difference is that s appears in s_A and s_B where $\hat{s}$ appears in $\hat{s}_A$ and $\hat{s}_B$. (This explains the notational differences.) Now, of course, in case 4 – that considered in this section – the value of s is unknown, and so it cannot be used for the purposes of inference. You may like to think of $\hat{s}$ as some kind of estimate of s, so that $\hat{s}_A$ and $\hat{s}_B$ are some kind of estimates of s_A and s_B (since they are the same except that s is replaced by $\hat{s}$). In all other respects, however, $\hat{s}_A$ is the same as s_A, and $\hat{s}_B$ is the same as s_B. Thus, our intuitive discussion of the factors determining s_A and s_B (and hence the dispersion of the posterior assessments of A and B in case 2) applies equally well to the factors determining $\hat{s}_A$ and $\hat{s}_B$ (and hence the dispersion of the posterior assessments of A and B in case 4).

Now consider the result (7.26) for the posterior assessment of S in case 4, and compare this with the corresponding assessment (7.22) in case 3. In (7.26) $(n-2)\hat{s}^2/S^2$ has a chi-square distribution; while in (7.22) it is $n\tilde{s}^2/S^2$ that has a chi-square distribution. The difference between these two is that $\sum_{i=1}^{n}(y_i - \hat{a} - \hat{b}x_i)^2$ is the numerator in the former, while $\sum_{i=1}^{n}(y_i - a - bx_i)^2$ is the numerator in the latter. This simply reflects the fact that a and b are assumed known in case 3, but in case 4 they are unknown, and are 'therefore' replaced by their 'estimates' $\hat{a}$ and $\hat{b}$. You will also notice that the number of degrees of freedom is different: in (7.26) it is $(n-2)$, in (7.22) it is n. We will discuss the reasons for this in due course, but in the meantime you may like to think about them yourself. (A glance at table 6.1, or equivalently 7.1, may be of help; note there, the number of degrees of freedom in the assessment of S^2 goes from n in case 3 to $(n-1)$ in case 4.)

Before going into further detail on the *general* implications of (7.25) and (7.26), it may prove helpful to give a specific numerical example. Let us return to the example of section 7.2 but *let us suppose now that A, B and S are all unknown.* We recall that the nine observations were as follows:

(1, 6)   (2, 9)   (3, 12)   (4, 15)   (5, 12)
            (6, 18)   (7. 18)   (8, 21)   (9, 24).

Let us suppose, once again, that we start from a position of total prior ignorance about *A*, *B* and *S*. Then results (7.25) and (7.26) are the appropriate ones. To implement them we need to calculate the various expressions in (7.27). Some of these we have already calculated in section 7.2. To be specific, we know that

$$\hat{a} = 4.75 \qquad \hat{b} = 2.05 \qquad \sum_{i=1}^{9} x_i^2 = 285$$

$$\sum_{i=1}^{9} (x_i - \bar{x})^2 = 60.$$

A glance at (7.27) shows that the main thing that needs to be calculated is $\hat{s}$. To this end, we need to calculate the terms $(y_i - \hat{a} - \hat{b}x_i)$ which are the vertical deviations of the observations from the least-squares fitted line. Simple arithmetic shows these to be (in increasing order of *i*)

$$-0.80 \qquad 0.15 \qquad 1.10 \qquad 2.05 \qquad -3.00 \qquad 0.95$$
$$\qquad\qquad\qquad -1.10 \qquad -0.15 \qquad\quad 0.80. \qquad (7.28)$$

If we square these, sum them and then divide the total by 7 ($= n - 2$), we find $\hat{s}^2$. This yields $\hat{s}^2 = 2.55$. Hence $\hat{s} = 1.597$. If we substitute this and the earlier results into (7.27), we find the values of the remaining expressions, namely $\hat{s}_A = 1.160$ and $\hat{s}_B = 0.206$. Finally, substituting these various expressions into (7.25) and (7.26) we obtain the appropriate posterior assessments, namely:

$(A - 4.75)/1.160$ has a *t* distribution with 7 degrees of freedom,
$(B - 2.05)/0.206$ has a *t* distribution with 7 degrees of freedom
$17.85/S^2$ has a chi-square distribution with 7 degrees of freedom.

These are complete characterizations. The various summary measures can be obtained in the usual way. For example, as you can verify yourself (see exercise 7.6), the posterior 95 per cent probability intervals for *A*, *B* and *S* are given by (to two decimal places)

$$(2.01, 7.49) \qquad (1.56, 2.54) \qquad \text{and} \qquad (1.06, 3.25)$$

respectively. As a second example, consider the problem of determining the (posterior) probability that *A* is positive. We proceed in the usual way. Thus

$$\begin{aligned}
P(A > 0) &= P[(A - 4.75) > (0 - 4.75)] \\
&= P[(A - 4.75)/1.160 > (0 - 4.75)/1.160] \\
&= P(T_7 > -4.09) \text{ (where } T_7 \text{ is } t(7)) \\
&\doteq 0.998 \text{ (from the table of the } t \text{ distribution).}
\end{aligned}$$

Similarly $P(B > 0) = P(T_7 > -9.94) \doteq 1$. Therefore, we can be virtually certain that both *A* and *B* are positive.

We will generalise some of these procedures in due course, but in the meantime let us consider two features of the least-squares fitted line to which we have not yet drawn attention. Both these features relate to the (vertical) deviations of the observations from the least-squares fitted line. In our numerical example, these deviations were given in (7.28). The first and most obvious thing to note is that they sum to zero. Is this a general result? In other words, if $\hat{u}_i$ denotes the vertical deviation of the ith observation from the least-squares fitted line, namely

$$\hat{u}_i = y_i - \hat{a} - \hat{b}x_i, \tag{7.29}$$

is it always true that $\sum_{i=1}^{n} \hat{u}_i = 0$? From (7.29) we have that

$$\sum_{i=1}^{n} \hat{u}_i = \sum_{i=1}^{n} y_i - n\hat{a} - \hat{b} \sum x_i = n(\bar{y} - \hat{a} - \hat{b}\bar{x}),$$

and this is zero by virtue of the first equation in (7.27). Thus

$$\sum_{i=1}^{n} \hat{u}_i = 0. \tag{7.30}$$

(A moment's reflection should convince you that this *must* be the case: for if $\sum_{i=1}^{n} \hat{u}_i \neq 0$, the sum of $\hat{u}_i^2$ could be reduced by making $\sum_{i=1}^{n} \hat{u}_i = 0$. Thus the line could not have been the *least-squares* line.)

A rather less obvious feature of the $\hat{u}_i$ can be seen numerically as follows. Consider the $\hat{u}_i$ for our numerical example as given in (7.28) above. Multiply each of them by their respective x_i. We thus get the following $\hat{u}_i x_i$ products:

-0.80	0.30	3.30	8.20	-15.00
	5.70	-7.70	-1.20	7.20.

Now sum these; you will find the total is zero. Once again, this is a general result, which can be shown as follows. From (7.29), we have

$$\sum_{i=1}^{n} \hat{u}_i x_i = \sum_{i=1}^{n} (y_i - \hat{a} - \hat{b}x_i)x_i$$
$$= \sum_{i=1}^{n} y_i x_i - \hat{a} \sum_{i=1}^{n} x_i - \hat{b} \sum_{i=1}^{n} x_i^2,$$

and this is zero by virtue of (7.16). Thus

$$\sum_{i=1}^{n} \hat{u}_i x_i = 0. \tag{7.31}$$

You may like to ponder the reasons for this.

As you will see from (7.25) and (7.26), the posterior assessments of A, B and S depend upon $\hat{a}$, $\hat{b}$, $\hat{s}_A$, $\hat{s}_B$, $\hat{s}$ and n. It may prove useful at this stage to introduce some extra terminology to refer to these key expressions. The first two, $\hat{a}$ and $\hat{b}$, are already familiar: they are the intercept and slope of the least-squares fitted line; or, equivalently, the coefficients of the least-squares fitted line. For shorthand, we will refer to them as the *least-squares coefficients*. The next two, $\hat{s}_A$ and $\hat{s}_B$, determine the widths of the posterior probability intervals for A and B. For convenience, we will follow the Classical convention and refer to them as the *standard errors of A and B*, respectively. (As far as we are concerned, no significance need be attached to this term – clearly they are neither standard nor errors – but that is beside the point. We are simply borrowing a phrase that is commonly used in the reporting of statistical analyses.) As for $\hat{s}^2$, this is *almost* the variance of the $\hat{u}$s (the deviations of the observations from the least-squares fitted line) – the only difference being that $(n - 2)$ rather than n appears in the denominator. Accordingly, we will refer to $\hat{s}^2$ as the *modified residual variance*, and to $\hat{s}$ as the *modified residual standard deviation*. Elsewhere, you may find $\hat{s}$ referred to as the *standard error of the regression*; again no significance should be attached to this term.

To implement the key results (7.25) and (7.26), one needs to calculate the various expressions in (7.27), namely, the least-squares coefficients, the standard errors of A and B and the modified residual standard deviation. These calculations are straightforward, though rather tedious if the number of observations is at all large. Considerable effort can be saved by the use of modern calculators and computers. Most computers have a number of statistical packages which can carry out a variety of statistical calculations, including the computation of least-squares regression lines; the more sophisticated calculators also have such facilities. How one uses the computer or calculator naturally varies from machine to machine, but basically one feeds in the observations $(x_1, y_1), (x_2, y_2), \ldots, (x_n, y_n)$ and then one asks the computer or calculator to do a (least-squares) regression of Y on X. The machine will then calculate the least-squares coefficients $\hat{a}$ and $\hat{b}$, and the better ones will also calculate the standard errors, $\hat{s}_A$ and $\hat{s}_B$, and the modified residual standard deviation $\hat{s}$.

A Bayesian statistician will then substitute these values into (7.25) and (7.26) to obtain his or her posterior assessments based on total prior ignorance; from these posterior assessments the various summary measures can be obtained in the usual way. However, there are alternative ways of presenting the results of a 'regression analysis' (ways more frequently employed by Classical statisticians), and it is important that you are familiar with these ways, so that you may understand and interpret them appropriately. One of the two most popular alternative ways is to report the equation of the least-squares fitted line, with the associated standard errors placed in parentheses below the respective coefficients. Thus, the general format is as follows:

$$Y = \hat{a} + \hat{b} X. \atop (\hat{s}_A) \quad (\hat{s}_B)$$

(7.32)

The number of observations is also usually stated, and occasionally the value of $\hat{s}$ may be recorded. (Though an alternative statistic, R^2 based on $\hat{s}$, is more usually recorded; we will discuss this in section

Table 7.3   *Inference in the bivariate linear normal regression model*

	Posterior distribution† of coefficient A given by	Posterior distribution† of coefficient B given by	Posterior distribution† of variance S^2 given by
Case 2	$\dfrac{A - \hat{a}}{s_A}$ is $N(0, 1)$	$\dfrac{B - \hat{b}}{s_B}$ is $N(0, 1)$	Known* to equal s^2
Case 3	Known* to equal a	Known* to equal b	$\dfrac{n\tilde{s}^2}{S^2}$ is $\chi^2(n)$
Case 4	$\dfrac{A - \hat{a}}{\hat{s}_A}$ is $t(n - 2)$	$\dfrac{B - \hat{b}}{\hat{s}_B}$ is $t(n - 2)$	$\dfrac{(n - 2)\hat{s}^2}{S^2}$ is $\chi^2(n - 2)$

Notation: $\bar{x} = \sum_{i=1}^{n} x_i/n$ $\bar{y} = \sum_{i=1}^{n} y_i/n$

$\hat{a} = \bar{y} - \hat{b}\bar{x}$

$\hat{b} = \sum_{i=1}^{n} (y_i - \bar{y})(x_i - \bar{x})/\sum_{i=1}^{n} (x_i - \bar{x})^2$

$\hat{s}_A = \hat{s}\{\sum_{i=1}^{n} x_i^2/[n \sum_{i=1}^{n} (x_i - \bar{x})^2]\}^{1/2}$

$\hat{s}_B = \hat{s}/[\sum_{i=1}^{n} (x_i - \bar{x})^2]^{1/2}$

$\hat{s} = [\sum_{i=1}^{n} (y_i - \hat{a} - \hat{b}x_i)^2/(n - 2)]^{1/2}$

where $(x_1, y_1), \ldots, (x_n, y_n)$ are the n observations on (X, Y)

Sources: Case 2: result (7.8)
Case 3: result (7.22)
Case 4: results (7.25) and (7.26).

* Assumed known *a priori*.
† Based on total prior ignorance about parameter (if unknown).

7.6.) For example, the results of the numerical illustration of this section would be reported as follows:

$$Y = \begin{array}{cc} 4.75 & + & 2.05 \ X \\ (1.160) & (0.206) \end{array} \quad \begin{array}{l} \hat{s} = 1.597 \\ n = 9 \end{array} \tag{7.33}$$

This is clearly a useful form as it enables the main features of the analysis to be assimilated at a glance. It is also a useful form for use in conjunction with the key results (7.25) and (7.26): the Bayesian statistician can immediately 'translate' (7.33) into a statement on posterior assessments – namely that $(A - 4.75)/1.160$ and $(B - 2.05)/0.206$ both have t distributions with $7 (= 9 - 2)$ degrees of freedom, and that $7 \times (1.597)^2/S^2$ has a chi-square distribution also with 7 degrees of freedom. Equation (7.33) clearly contains all the relevant information about the regression.

There is a second, equally popular, alternative way of presenting the results of regression analyses. In appearance, it is identical to (7.33) except that, rather than standard errors being reported in parentheses below the coefficients, 't-ratios' are reported instead. We will discuss this in section 7.5, after we have explained what t-ratios are and what their significance is.

We conclude this section with a summary table of the key results of this and the preceding two sections: table 7.3 gives details of the posterior assessments of A, B and/or S, as appropriate, all based on the assumption of total prior ignorance. This table contains virtually all the results on the bivariate linear normal regression model that you are likely to need. You should study it well, and in particular, pay attention to the differences between, and the similarities of, it and table 7.1.

7.5 'CONFIDENCE INTERVALS' AND 'SIGNIFICANCE TESTS'

You will recall that, in the context of the material of chapters 5 and 6, Bayesian α per cent probability intervals for some unknown parameter based on total prior ignorance, and Classical α per cent confidence intervals for the same unknown parameter, are algebraically identical (though their interpretations are quite different). This property continues to hold in the context of the material of this chapter.

To avoid unnecessary repetition, we confine attention to case 4, though the comments and analysis below apply equally well to the other two cases, *mutatis mutandis*. From (7.25), it is clear that the α per cent probability intervals for A and B, based on total prior ignorance are

$$(\hat{a} + t_{(n-2),\,(100-\alpha)/2}\,\hat{s}_A\,,\, \hat{a} + t_{(n-2),\,(100+\alpha)/2}\,\hat{s}_A)$$

and

$$(\hat{b} + t_{(n-2),\,(100-\alpha)/2}\,\hat{s}_B\,,\, \hat{b} + t_{(n-2),\,(100+\alpha)/2}\,\hat{s}_B) \tag{7.34}$$

respectively, where $t_{k,\,\beta}$ is defined, as before, by $P(T_k \leq t_{k,\,\beta}) = \beta/100$, where T_k has a t distribution with k degrees of freedom. These are precisely the same as the Classical α per cent confidence intervals for A and B respectively (see, for example, Hey (1974), chapter 7). Likewise, from (7.26), it is clear that a α per cent probability interval for S, based on total prior ignorance, is

$$((n-2)^{1/2}\hat{s}y_{(n-2),\,(100+\alpha)/2}^{-1/2}\,,\, (n-2)^{1/2}\hat{s}y_{(n-2),\,(100-\alpha)/2}^{-1/2}), \tag{7.35}$$

where $y_{k,\,\beta}$ is defined, as before, by $P(Y_k \leq y_{k,\,\beta}) = \beta/100$, where Y_k has a chi-square distribution with k degrees of freedom. Once again, this is precisely the same as the Classical α per cent confidence interval for S. So except for the interpretation, we can safely treat Bayesian α per cent probability intervals based on total prior ignorance and Classical α per cent confidence intervals as one and the same.

Matters are slightly more complicated as regards a Bayesian interpretation of the Classical process of hypothesis testing, though, as in chapter 6, some kind of interpretation is possible. To avoid repetition, we will restrict attention to case 4, and, in particular, to the testing of a hypothesis about B, but the comments and analysis below apply equally well to other parameters and in other cases.

Among Classical statisticians, possibly the most commonly applied test about B in an economics context is a test of the (null) hypothesis

$$H_0 : B = 0$$

against the alternative hypothesis

$$H_1 : B > 0.$$

Such a test would be deemed appropriate if one was wishing to test the empirical validity of an economic theory which predicted that Y was *positively* related to X – as would be the case, say, in the theory of aggregate consumption (in which Y would be consumption and X

income). Alternatively, if the theory under test predicted a negative relationship, then '$H_1 : B > 0$' would be replaced by '$H_1 : B < 0$'. In either case, 'acceptance' of H_1 implies 'acceptance' of the theory.

As we discussed in section 6.5, the basic procedure adopted by Classical statisticians to test H_0 against H_1 is to employ a rule which determines, on the basis of sample evidence, whether to 'accept' H_0 (and 'reject' H_1) or to 'accept' H_1 (and 'reject' H_0). The rule is usually designed so there is an acceptably small chance – usually 5 per cent or 1 per cent – of 'rejecting' H_0 when it is in fact true. This small, preselected probability is referred to as the *significance level* of the test.

In the context of the test described above, the appropriate rule to achieve an α per cent significance level can be shown to be (see Hey (1974), chapter 7):

$$\begin{aligned} &\text{if } \hat{b}/\hat{s}_B \leq t_{n-2,\,100-\alpha} \text{ accept } H_0 \text{ (reject } H_1) \\ &\text{if } \hat{b}/\hat{s}_B > t_{n-2,\,100-\alpha} \text{ accept } H_1 \text{ (reject } H_0). \end{aligned} \tag{7.36}$$

If the outcome of the test is to accept H_1 (reject H_0) then the test is said to be *significant* (at the α per cent level); alternatively, $\hat{b}$ is said to be *significantly greater than zero* (at the α per cent level). We have no intention of explaining *why* the Classical approach adopts this procedure – such explanations can be found elsewhere (for example, Hey (1974), chapter 7). All we are interested in here is trying to make sense of this procedure in Bayesian terms.

As we showed in section 6.5, the way to make sense of this procedure is to think of the outcome of the test as telling us something about $P(H_1 \mid$ the observations) – that is, the probability of H_1 being true in the light of the evidence. We can show this as follows. (To save writing we take the conditioning statement '$\mid$ the observations' as read in all the following probability statements.) We have

$$\begin{aligned} P(H_1) &= P(B > 0) = P[(B - \hat{b}) > (0 - \hat{b})] = P[(B - \hat{b}) > -\hat{b}] \\ &= P[(B - \hat{b})/\hat{s}_B > -\hat{b}/\hat{s}_B] \\ &= P(T_{n-2} > -\hat{b}/\hat{s}_B), \end{aligned}$$

where $T_{n-2} \equiv (B - \hat{b})/\hat{s}_B$ has a t distribution with $(n-2)$ degrees of freedom by virtue of (7.26). Now we use the fact that a t distribution is symmetrical about zero (which implies that $P(T_{n-2} > -t) = P(T_{n-2} < t)$) to conclude from the above that

$$P(H_1) = P(T_{n-2} < \hat{b}/\hat{s}_B). \tag{7.37}$$

Now *suppose the test is significant at the α per cent level*. Then, it follows from (7.36) that $\hat{b}/\hat{s}_B > t_{n-2, 100-\alpha}$. Combining this with (7.37) shows that

$$P(H_1) > P(T_{n-2} < t_{n-2, 100-\alpha})$$

(since $P(X < x_1) > P(X < x_2)$ if $x_1 > x_2$). Finally, by definition, we have that

$$P(T_{n-2} < t_{n-2, 100-\alpha}) = (100 - \alpha)/100.$$

It follows, therefore, that *if the test is significant at the α per cent level*, then

$$P(H_1) \equiv P(B > 0) > (100 - \alpha)/100. \tag{7.38}$$

For example, if the test is significant at the 5 per cent level, then we can conclude (on the basis of total prior ignorance) that there is more than a 95 per cent chance that H_1 is indeed true.

On the other hand, if the test is *not* significant at the α per cent level, then $P(H_1) < (100 - \alpha)/100$. So the significance or otherwise of the test tell us something about $P(H_1) \equiv P(B > 0)$. (Note that the outcome of the test cannot tell us anything sensible about $P(H_0) \equiv P(B = 0)$ because this is necessarily zero, except in very unusual circumstances.)

The simplest way to summarize the above discussion is as follows: if a Classical statistician reports that '$\hat{b}$ is significantly different from zero at the α per cent level' (which is synonomous with the statement that the test is significant, or H_0 is rejected in favour of H_1, at the α per cent level) then the Bayesian statistician can interpret this as meaning that the posterior probability that B is positive (based on total prior ignorance) is at least $(100 - \alpha)/100$. For example, if '$\hat{b}$ is significantly different from zero at the 1 per cent level' then $P(B > 0)$ is at least 0.99. So statements of significance give bounds on certain probabilities.

To a Bayesian, it is much more natural and obvious to simply compute $P(B > 0)$ directly, and to report its actual value. Thus, if, for example, $P(B > 0) = 0.98$ it is more useful to give this information rather than to report rather obliquely that it is greater than 0.95 ($\hat{b}$ is significantly different from zero at the 5 per cent level') but less than 0.99 ('$\hat{b}$ is not significantly different from zero at the 1 per cent level').

In Classical statistics, it is conventional to indicate the significance or otherwise of coefficients by the use of asterisks. Typically, though not always, one asterisk attached to the coefficient indicates significance at the 5 per cent level, two asterisks indicate significance at the 1 per cent level, and no asterisks indicates significance at neither level.

If you examine (7.36), you will see that the significance or otherwise of a coefficient depends upon the magnitude of the ratio $\hat{b}/\hat{s}_B$ relative to the appropriate entry from the table of the t distribution $(t_{n-2,\,100-\alpha})$. Because of the importance of this ratio, it is given its own name – called for obvious reasons the *t-ratio* of the coefficient. Let us denote it by t_B, and the corresponding one for A by t_A. Thus,

$$t_A \equiv \hat{a}/\hat{s}_A \qquad \text{and} \qquad t_B \equiv \hat{b}/\hat{s}_B; \tag{7.39}$$

in each case, the t-ratio of the coefficient is the ratio of the least-squares coefficient to its standard error. As we remarked at the end of the preceding section, regression results are quite often reported with t-ratios (rather than standard errors) in parentheses under the coefficients. Using this convention, the results of our illustrative example of section 7.4 would be reported as (cf. (7.33))

$$\begin{aligned} Y = \quad &4.75 + 2.05 \ X \qquad n = 9 \\ &(4.09) \quad (9.94) \qquad \hat{s} = 1.597 \end{aligned} \tag{7.40}$$

(t-ratios in parentheses). (It is usual to specify which convention is being used – to avoid any possible confusion.)

With $n = 9$, the appropriate entries from the t table for carrying out the Classical test (7.36) at the 5 per cent and 1 per cent levels are 1.895 and 2.998 respectively. A glance at (7.40) reveals that both t-ratios are greater than both these entries; thus $\hat{a}$ and $\hat{b}$ are both significantly different from zero at the 1 per cent level (and hence, *a fortiori*, at the 5 per cent level). In Bayesian terms, as we have demonstrated above, this means that both $P(A > 0)$ and $P(B > 0)$ are greater than 0.99. (This is confirmed by our direct calculations of these two probabilities earlier in section 7.4.)

One advantage of presentation in the form of (7.40) is that it enables the precise values of $P(A > 0)$ and $P(B > 0)$ to be calculated directly. As should be obvious from our previous analyses, these are equal to $P(T_7 < 4.09)$ and $P(T_7 < 9.94)$ respectively, in our specific example. More generally, they are equal to $P(T_{n-2} < t_A)$ and $P(T_{n-2} < t_B)$ respectively.

7.6 COMPARISON OF THEORIES AND 'GOODNESS OF FIT'

So far the analysis of this chapter has been based on the assumption that the only potential uncertainties about the model are the values of the parameters A, B and S. In all other respects, the form of the model, as represented by (7.5), has been assumed certain and known. In particular, we have assumed certain knowledge of the relevant explanatory variable (namely, X), certain knowledge of the form of the relationship (namely, linear) and certain knowledge of the distribution of the deviation or residual term U (namely, normal). In practice, it may be the case that some, if not all, of these are not known with certainty. How does our analysis proceed in such circumstances?

In principle, there is really no additional conceptual problem: we simply list all the various possible alternatives (alternative variables and/or alternative functional forms and/or alternative distributions) and attach prior probabilities to each. We then apply Bayes' theorem in the usual fashion to obtain the respective posterior probabilities. Apart from any technical difficulties, the way of dealing with such additional uncertainties is straightforward and familiar.

In this section, we will sketch the appropriate procedures for the first of these additional uncertainties – namely, uncertainty about the relevant explanatory variable. In chapter 8, we will briefly examine the second of the additional uncertainties – namely, uncertainty about the appropriate function form. The third of the additional uncertainties – namely, uncertainty about the distribution of U – is beyond the scope of this book; however, the interested reader can find a discussion in Zellner (1971).

Let us consider, therefore, a situation in which we know that the model generating Y is of the form of (7.5), but we are unsure as to which of two potential explanatory variables X_1 or X_2 is the actual explanatory variable. There are thus two competing models under consideration, M_1 and M_2, defined as follows (cf. (7.5)):

$$\left.\begin{array}{l} M_1\colon \begin{cases} Y = A_1 + B_1 X_1 + U_1 \\ U_1 \text{ is } N(0, S_1^2), \end{cases} \\[2em] M_2\colon \begin{cases} Y = A_2 + B_2 X_2 + U_2 \\ U_2 \text{ is } N(0, S_2^2). \end{cases} \end{array}\right\} \tag{7.41}$$

To M_1 and M_2 there will be attached some prior probabilities, $P(M_1)$ and $P(M_2)$, respectively. These reflect one's prior beliefs about the validity of the competing hypotheses. If no other models are considered possible then $P(M_1) + P(M_2) = 1$, and presumably $P(M_1)$ and $P(M_2)$ will both be non-zero, for otherwise the problem would reduce to that considered earlier in this chapter. (The approach discussed below can be extended quite straightforwardly to the case of three or more competing hypotheses.) To fix ideas, you may like to think of these two models as alternative explanations of inflation (Y): M_1 could be a monetarist explanation (with X_1 equal to the rate of change of the money supply); and M_2 could be a Phillips curve type explanation (with X_1 equal to unemployment or some other indicator of excess supply).

Now, within (or given) each model some or all of A_i, B_i and S_i may be unknown and some or all known; in other words, within each model we may have one of the four cases catalogued and discussed in the earlier sections of this chapter. Obviously, the methods we are going to discuss can be applied equally well in all four cases, but, to avoid undue repetition, we will restrict attention to case 4 for both models. Thus, A_1, B_1, S_1, A_2, B_2 and S_2 will all be assumed unknown. However, we may have some prior notions about these parameters, as represented in the usual fashion in the form of a prior probability distribution. The natural way to represent these is in the form of two joint distributions conditional on the respective models. To be precise, there will be a joint distribution of A_1, B_1 and S_1 conditional on M_1 being true, and a joint distribution of A_2, B_2 and S_2 conditional on M_2 being true. Let us denote these by

$$g_{A_1B_1S_1}(a_1, b_1, s_1 | M_1) \quad \text{and} \quad g_{A_2B_2S_2}(a_2, b_2, s_2 | M_2)$$

respectively. These conditional distributions can then be multiplied by the respective marginal probabilities $P(M_1)$ and $P(M_2)$ to obtain the joint prior assessment of models *and* parameters

$$g_{A_jB_jS_j}(a_j, b_j, s_j | M_j)P(M_j) \qquad j = 1, 2. \tag{7.42}$$

Given a sample of observations on Y, X_1 and X_2, Bayes' theorem can be applied in the familiar way to obtain the joint posterior assessment of models *and* parameters. This joint assessment can be 'factored out' into the same form as (7.42) above; that is, into the product of the conditional distribution of the parameters given the model and the marginal probability of the model:

$$g_{A_jB_jS_j}[a_j, b_j, s_j | M_j; (y_i, x_{1i}, x_{2i})i = 1, \ldots, n]$$

$$\times P[M_j | (y_i, x_{1i}, x_{2i}) \quad i = 1, \ldots, n] \tag{7.43}$$

Of the various things that can be deduced from this, one of the most interesting is the posterior probabilities for the two models:

$$P[M_j | (y_i, x_{1i}, x_{2i}) \quad i = 1, \ldots, n] \qquad j = 1, 2. \tag{7.44}$$

Comparison of these with the prior probabilities, $P(M_j) j = 1, 2$, will reveal how the data have influenced the relative likelihoods of the competing models.

In general, the key expression (7.44) depends upon a whole variety of factors including the prior assessments of the parameters in the two models. Although conceptually straightforward, a general expression for (7.44) is rather tedious to obtain and algebraically somewhat clumsy. However, there is an important special case which readily appeals to intuition. Suppose, *a priori*, that M_1 and M_2 are regarded as equally likely, that is $P(M_1) = P(M_2) = \frac{1}{2}$. Suppose also that there is total prior ignorance about *all* the parameters A_j, B_j and S_j ($j = 1$, 2). Then it can be shown (see Zellner (1971) pp. 306–12) that the ratio of the posterior probabilities of the models is given by

$$\frac{P[M_1 \mid (y_i, x_{1i}, x_{2i}) \quad i = 1, \ldots, n]}{P[M_2 \mid (y_i, x_{1i}, x_{2i}) \quad i = 1, \ldots, n]} = \left(\frac{\hat{s}_1}{\hat{s}_2}\right)^{-n} \tag{7.45}$$

Here $\hat{s}_1$ denotes the modified residual standard deviation for the least-squares regression of Y on X_1, and $\hat{s}_2$ denotes the modified residual standard deviation for the least-squares regression of Y on X_2. Thus, under the postulated circumstances, M_1 is deemed more likely than M_2 in the light of the observations if $\hat{s}_1$ is less than $\hat{s}_2$, and M_2 is deemed more likely than M_1 if $\hat{s}_2$ is smaller than $\hat{s}_1$. Thus, if both models are regarded as equally likely *a priori*, then *a posteriori* the one which yields the least-squares regression with the smaller residual standard deviation is considered the most likely. This is a simple and intuitively satisfying result.

(If the prior probabilities $P(M_1)$ and $P(M_2)$ are not equal, the right-hand side of (7.45) should be multiplied by the ratio $P(M_1)/P(M_2)$. For a proof of these results, and an examination of the more general case, you could refer to Zellner (1971), pp. 306–12.)

Although $\hat{s}$ (the modified residual standard deviation) clearly plays an important role in assessing and comparing models, it is relatively rarely reported, especially in Classical analyses. More commonly reported is the value of the statistic R^2, which is related to $\hat{s}$ as follows:

$$R^2 = 1 - \frac{(n - 2)\hat{s}^2/n}{\sum_{i=1}^{n} (y_i - \bar{y})^2/n}. \tag{7.46}$$

In the term which is subtracted from 1 on the right-hand side of (7.46), the numerator is the (unmodified) residual variance from the least-square regression and the denominator is the variance of the Y observations; thus this term represents the proportion of the variance of Y that is not 'explained' by the regression. Hence, R^2

itself measures the proportion of the variance of Y that *is* 'explained' by the regression. It can range from 0 (nothing 'explained') to 1 (all the variance 'explained'). Clearly, it is an indicator of how well the least-squares fitted line fits the observations: $R^2 = 1$ indicates a perfect fit (all the observations lie on the line); $R^2 = 0$ indicates no fit whatsoever (a horizontal 'fitted line'); with values in between indicating varying degrees of goodness of fit. A closely related statistic is the 'adjusted' R^2, denoted by $\bar{R}^2$ and defined as follows:

$$\bar{R}^2 = 1 - \frac{\hat{s}^2}{\sum_{i=1}^{n} (y_i - \bar{y})^2/(n - 1)} \tag{7.47}$$

We will encounter this again in chapter 8, when we will be in a better position to explain its 'advantages' over R^2. Conventionally, either R^2 or $\bar{R}^2$ (rather than $\hat{s}$) is reported alongside the equation. For example, in our numerical illustration of section 7.4, $\hat{s} = 1.597$ and $\sum_{i=1}^{n} (y_i - \bar{y})^2/n = 30$; hence $R^2 = 0.934$ and $\bar{R}^2 = 0.924$; so the results of the regression would typically be reported in the form (cf. (7.33)):

$$\begin{align}
Y = \quad & 4.75 \quad + \quad 2.05 \ X \qquad \bar{R}^2 = 0.924 \\
& (1.160) \quad (0.206) \qquad n = 9
\end{align} \tag{7.48}$$

(standard errors in parentheses).

Clearly, R^2 (and, as we shall see in chapter 8, $\bar{R}^2$) is a useful *descriptive* statistic. It is also commonly used in Classical statistics, and, as such, you ought to be familiar with its meaning. But, as far as we are concerned, its main usefulness is that it is related to $\hat{s}$: as can be seen from (7.46) a decrease in $\hat{s}$ leads to an increase in R^2. (Similarly, as (7.47) shows, $\bar{R}^2$ and $\hat{s}$ are inversely related.) Thus when comparing two regression models (with equal prior probabilities) the relative posterior probabilities are reflected by the respective R^2 values: the equation with the higher R^2 has the higher posterior probability. This provides a justification for choosing between alternative models (with the same dependent variable) on the basis of the highest R^2. But it is a justification that should be invoked only under the appropriate circumstances.

7.7 EXAMPLES OF REGRESSION

After a large number of pages mainly devoted to theoretical issues, it is now time to give some examples of the applications of the concepts and results of this chapter. The key results are those contained in table 7.3. We illustrate their application with two examples, both of them empirical investigations of consumption functions. They differ in their level of aggregation and in the type of data used to investigate them. To be specific: the first example consists of an investigation of a UK aggregate consumption function using time-series data; the second consists of an investigation of a household consumption function using cross-section data. We consider them in turn.

You will no doubt be familiar from your macroeconomics course with the idea of an *aggregate consumption function*. Almost certainly the first such function you encountered was linear as in (7.5) where Y denotes consumption and X denotes income. (We use the notation of this chapter rather than the more familiar C and Y to avoid confusion). The coefficient B represents the aggregate *marginal propensity to consume*, and the coefficient A represents the amount of consumption if income was zero. Typically, it is postulated that A is positive and that B lies between 0 and 1. Let us investigate whether this is indeed the case, with the help of UK aggregate data.

The best source for UK aggregate economic data is undoubtedly the monthly publication *Economic Trends* and its annual companion *Economic Trends Annual Supplement*, both published by the Government Statistical Service. In the latter you will find long runs of consistent data on the main economic aggregates and sub-aggregates. At the time of the writing of this book the latest available volume of the *Annual Supplement* was the 1982 edition (number 7); this contains data on variables up to the early part of 1981. If you consult this, or any edition of *Economic Trends*, you will see that there are several possible contenders for the empirical counterparts of the theoretical concepts 'aggregate consumption' and 'aggregate data'. Theory does not help us to determine which are the appropriate counterparts, but *Consumers' Expenditure* and *GDP* (Gross Domestic Product at market prices) appear to be the most suitable contenders. We still have to choose whether to use *annual* or *quarterly* data, and, if the latter, whether it should be *seasonally adjusted* or not, and we also have to choose whether to use data in *current prices* or in *constant* (1975) *prices*. On the latter choice, theory comes to our aid as it is clear that the consumption function as normally perceived is a postulated relationship between *real* (rather than money) consumption and *real* income. Thus, data in constant prices are appropriate. As far as the choice between annual and quarterly data is concerned, however, this depends more on taste and the purpose of the investigation. Let us (rather arbitrarily) select quarterly data, and, to remove seasonal fluctuations, use seasonally adjusted data. The relevant data (Consumers' Expenditure and GDP at market prices, quarterly, seasonally adjusted in constant (1975) prices) are found in *Economic Trends Annual Supplement* (1982), pp. 17–19. You will see from these pages that such data is available from the first quarter of 1955 to the first quarter of 1981 – a total of 105 quarterly observations. Ideally, we should use as many observations as are available (if they are all generated by the same model), so that the posterior assessments are as precise as possible. But for the purposes of this illustration we will use a subset of the available observations, so that when you come to verify the calculations below you will be spared an excess of arithmetic. We restrict attention, therefore, to the ten years 1971 to 1980 inclusive, which contain a total of forty quarterly observations. (Actually, there may be good theoretical reasons for *not* using all the available data if you think that there may have been a *shift* in the underlying relationship during the observation period. Remember that the methods discussed in this chapter are based on the assumption that the relationship (7.5) has stayed constant.)

The data are graphed in the form of a scatter diagram, with Consumers' Expenditure on the *Y*-axis and GDP on the *X*-axis, in figure 7.4. (The raw data are not reproduced here: the source is noted

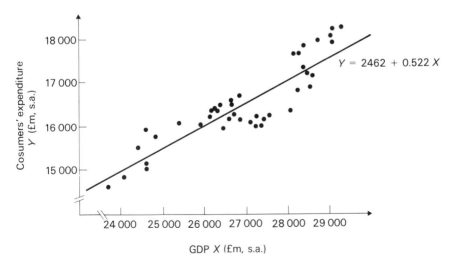

Figure 7.4 UK quarterly consumption and income 1971 to 1980

above, and you are encouraged to extract the data yourself and to verify the various calculations presented below.)

Suppose we start from a position of total prior ignorance about the values of the three parameters A, B and S in the assumed-true relationship between Y (Consumers' Expenditure) and X (GDP at market prices) given by (cf. (7.5))

$$Y = A + BX + U$$
$$U \text{ is } N(0, S^2).$$

Then, as we have shown in section 7.4, the posterior assessments in the light of a set of observations are as given in (7.25) and (7.26). To implement these we need to calculate the various expressions in (7.27). To this end, it is useful to calculate first the various sums and sums of squares and products as presented below. These are calculated directly from the raw data.

$$\sum_{i=1}^{40} x_i = 1\,074\,724 \qquad\qquad \sum_{i=1}^{40} y_i = 659\,671.$$

$$n = 40$$

$$\sum_{i=1}^{40} x_i^2 = 28\,964\,843\,682 \qquad\qquad \sum_{i=1}^{40} y_i^2 = 10\,909\,689\,009$$

$$\sum_{i=1}^{40} x_i y_i = 17\,770\,605\,111.$$

Hence $\bar{x} = 26\,868.1$ and $\bar{y} = 16\,491.775$.

Now since

$$\sum_{i=1}^{n} (y_i - \bar{y})(x_i - \bar{x}) = \sum_{i=1}^{n} y_i x_i - n\bar{y}\bar{x},$$

and

$$\sum_{i=1}^{n} (x_i - \bar{x})^2 = \sum_{i=1}^{n} x_i^2 - n\bar{x}^2$$

(see exercise 7.5), it follows that

$$\hat{b} = \frac{\sum_{i=1}^{40} (y_i - \bar{y})(x_i - \bar{x})}{\sum_{i=1}^{40} (x_i - \bar{x})^2} = \frac{17\,770\,605\,111 - 17\,724\,106\,395.1}{28\,964\,843\,682 - 28\,875\,791\,904.4}$$

$$= \frac{46\,498\,715.9}{89\,051\,777.6}$$

and so $\hat{b} = 0.52215$. Hence

$$\hat{a} = \bar{y} - \hat{b}\bar{x} = 16\,491.775 - 0.52215 \times 26\,868.1 = 2\,462.5.$$

Thus, the least-squares fitted line is $Y = 2462 + 0.522X$. This is illustrated in figure 7.4.

We now need to calculate

$$\hat{s}^2 = \sum_{i=1}^{n} (y_i - \hat{a} - \hat{b}x_i)^2/(n-2)$$

(see (7.27)). One way to calculate this is by finding each of the terms $(y_i - \hat{a} - \hat{b}x_i)$ individually and then proceeding from there; in fact, this is the method we used in section 7.4. But it is a rather tedious method. A more direct method makes use of the following result (see exercise 7.7)

$$\sum_{i=1}^{n} (y_i - \hat{a} - \hat{b}x_i)^2 = \sum_{i=1}^{n} (y_i - \bar{y})^2 - \hat{b}^2 \sum (x_i - \bar{x})^2$$

$$= [\sum_{i=1}^{n} y_i^2 - n\bar{y}^2] - \hat{b}^2 [\sum_{i=1}^{n} x_i^2 - n\bar{x}^2].$$

(7.49)

Using this, and the various results above, we find that $\hat{s}^2 = 164\,846.6$ and hence $\hat{s} = 406$. Finally, from (7.27) we find that $\hat{s}_A = 1\,158$ and $\hat{s}_B = 0.043$. Using one of the conventions discussed above, we can summarize our results as follows:

$$Y = 2462 + 0.522\,X \qquad \hat{s} = 406$$
$$ (1158) \quad (0.043) \qquad n = 40$$

(7.50)

(standard errors in parentheses).

Assuming that our prior knowledge of A, B and S was non-existent, then the appropriate posterior assessments can be found from (7.25) and (7.26). Substituting $\hat{a} = 2462$, $\hat{b} = 0.522$, $\hat{s}_A = 1158$ and $\hat{s}_B = 0.043$ in (7.25) we find that $(A - 2462)/1158$ and $(B - 0.522)/0.043$ both have t distributions with 38 degrees of freedom. Substituting $\hat{s} = 406$ in (7.26) we find that $6\,264\,171/S^2$ has a chi-square distribution also with 38 degrees of freedom. These are complete characterizations of the posterior assessments. The various summary measures can be obtained in the usual fashion. For example, 95 per cent probability intervals for A and B can be obtained from the fact (see Appendix A7) that a variable with a t distribution with 38 degrees of freedom lies between ± 2.025 with probability 0.95. Hence

$$P(-2.025 \le (A - 2462)/1158 \le 2.025) = 0.95$$

and

$$P(-2.025 \le (B - 0.522)/0.043 \le 2.025) = 0.95.$$

Thus, the 95 per cent probability intervals for A and B are (117, 4807) and (0.435, 0.609) respectively. On the basis of the evidence illustrated in figure 7.4, we can be 95 per cent sure that the UK aggregate marginal propensity to consume is between 0.435 and 0.609. That this is a fairly wide interval reflects the fact that the scatter in figure 7.4 is quite dispersed.

Economic theory hypothesises that A is positive and that B lies between 0 and 1. Do the facts agree with these hypotheses? The obvious way to check is to calculate $P(A > 0)$ and $P(0 < B < 1)$ and see if they are 'sufficiently large'. Our posterior assessment of A is such that $(A - 2462)/1158$ is $t(38)$. Hence

$$P(A > 0) = P[(A - 2462)/1158 > (0 - 2462)/1158]$$
$$= P(T_{38} > -2.13), \text{ where } T_{38} \text{ is } t(38)$$
$$\doteqdot 0.98 \text{ (interpolating in Appendix A7).}$$

Similarly,

$$P(0 < B < 1) = P[-0.522/0.043 < (B - 0.522)/0.043$$
$$< (1 - 0.522)/0.043]$$

$$= P(-12.1 < T_{38} < 11.1)$$
$$\doteqdot 1 \text{ (from Appendix A7).}$$

Thus, we can be almost certain that A is positive, and, to all intents and purposes, certain that B lies between 0 and 1.

Finally, for the record, let us calculate the t-ratios and R^2. We have $t_A = 2462/1158 = 2.13$ and $t_B = 0.522/0.043 = 12.1$. Also $R^2 = 0.795$; so almost 80 per cent of the variance of the observed Y values has been 'explained' by the regression. Using these results, we could present the outcome of our analysis using the following alternative convention:

$$Y = 2462 + 0.522X \qquad R^2 = 0.795$$
$$(2.13) \quad (12.1) \qquad n = 40 \tag{7.51}$$

(t-ratios in parentheses).

Our second example of 'regression in action' is also a consumption–income relationship, but this time we use *household* (rather than aggregate) and *cross-section* (rather than time-series) data. Such data can be obtained from the annual *Family Expenditure Surveys* (as well as the more general *General Household Surveys*). The particular data investigated below are taken from the 1979 Survey (published in 1980) and are found in Table A of Appendix 8 on page 169. The data extracted as being the appropriate empirical counterparts of consumption and income are *average weekly household expenditure* and *average weekly household income* respectively. The averages are over households in the survey in the various income

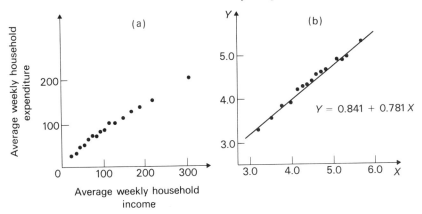

Figure 7.5 Household consumption and income 1979. Y = *the natural logarithm of average weekly household expenditure.* X = *the natural logarithm of average weekly household income.*

groups; there are sixteen such groups in the 1979 survey and so we have sixteen observations; these observations are plotted in figure 7.5(a). (We do not list the raw data: you are encouraged to find the relevant copy of the *Family Expenditure Survey* yourself, extract the relevant data, and verify the following calculations – either 'by hand' or on a computer. This will be useful practice for you.)

A careful study of figure 7.5(a) will reveal something that you may have anticipated, or that theory may have forewarned you about: namely, that the relationship does not appear to be linear. Indeed, it appears to be the case that the relationship is curved, with the slope decreasing as income increases. This accords with economic theory, which predicts that for such micro cross-sectional data the marginal propensity to consume falls as income rises. So clearly the linear form (7.5) is not *directly* appropriate to model this relationship. The question then arises: What *is* the appropriate functional form? Unfortunately, economic theory is somewhat silent on this point, so we have to answer the question without its help. Fortunately, an obvious candidate springs to mind – namely, a log-linear relationship. Let us write this in the familiar form

$$Y = A + BX + U$$
$$U \text{ is } N(0, S^2),$$

but where X and Y now denote the *logarithm* of average weekly household income and the *logarithm* of average weekly household expenditure respectively. You may know that in such log-linear relationships, the coefficients now represent *elasticities*: thus, in the equation above B now represents the elasticity of expenditure with respect to income. (If you are not familiar with this property, consult your mathematics or microeconomics lecturer or text.)

Figure 7.5(b) gives the appropriate scatter; in this we have used natural logarithms (though logarithms to any base will do equally well). As is apparent from a study of this figure, the log transformation has removed the curvature of figure 7.5(a), and yielded a relationship which can more appropriately be considered linear. We will, accordingly, use the logs of the observations throughout this example.

As in the first of our two examples, we will assume total prior ignorance. Thus (7.25) and (7.26) continue to be the relevant results, and we need to calculate the various expressions in (7.27). First we find the various sums as follows. (Remember these all relate to the natural logarithms of the observations.)

$$\sum_{i=1}^{16} x_i = 72.8518 \qquad\qquad \sum_{i=1}^{16} y_i = 70.3791$$

$$n = 16$$

$$\sum_{i=1}^{n} x_i^2 = 338.892 \qquad\qquad \sum_{i=1}^{16} y_i^2 = 313.984$$

$$\sum_{i=1}^{16} x_i y_i = 326.063.$$

Hence, from (7.27), to three decimal places

$$\hat{a} = 0.841 \qquad \hat{b} = 0.781$$
$$\hat{s} = 0.041$$

and $\quad \hat{s}_A = 0.071 \qquad \hat{s}_B = 0.015.$

These results can be summarized in the form:

$$
\begin{array}{llll}
Y = & 0.841 + 0.781\,X & \hat{s} = 0.041 & \\
& (0.071) \quad (0.015) & n = 16 &
\end{array}
\tag{7.52}
$$

(standard errors in parentheses).

The least-squares line ($Y = 0.841 + 0.781X$) is inserted on figure 7.5(b). From (7.25), we find that (given total prior ignorance) our posterior assessments of A and B are such that $(A - 0.841)/0.071$ and $(B - 0.781)/0.015$ both have t distributions with 14 degrees of freedom. Thus, the 95 per cent probability intervals for A and B are (0.689, 0.993) and (0.749, 0.813) respectively. Hence, on the basis of this *Family Expenditure Survey* evidence, we can be 95 per cent certain that the elasticity of (average weekly household) consumption with respect to (average weekly household) income is between 0.749 and 0.813.

For the record, we note that the t-ratios are 11.8 and 52.1 respectively. Also $R^2 = 0.995$. We could therefore present our results in the following alternative form:

$$Y = 0.841 + 0.781X \qquad R^2 = 0.995$$
$$(11.8) \quad (52.1) \qquad n = 16 \tag{7.53}$$

(t-ratios in parentheses).

It should be clear from the magnitude of the t-ratios that $P(A > 0)$ and $P(B > 0)$ are both 1, to all intents and purposes.

Finally, we translate our results back from the log-linear form to a form involving the original variables. Schematically, we can write the least-squares fitted line as

$$\ln(\text{consumption}) = 0.841 + 0.781 \ln(\text{income}).$$

If we take the exponential of both sides of this (noting that $\exp(\ln(k)) = k$ and that $\exp(0.841) = 2.319$) we get

$$\text{consumption} = 2.319 \text{ income}^{0.781}. \tag{7.54}$$

To give some feel for the implications of this, let us find the value of the marginal propensity to consume (mpc) at different income levels. If we differentiate (7.54), we find that the mpc is given by (since $2.319 \times 0.781 = 1.811$)

$$\text{mpc} = 1.811 \text{ income}^{-0.219}.$$

From this, we get the following table giving values of the mpc (implied by the least-squares fitted line) for different weekly household incomes.

Average weekly household income (in 1979)	Average mpc
£50	0.769
£100	0.661
£150	0.604
£200	0.568
£250	0.541

It is clear from this that mpc is not constant; this confirms that our rejection of the linear formulation was appropriate.

This completes our treatment of this second example. As this section has demonstrated, the implementation of the material of this chapter is straightforward. All that is required (if one starts from a position of total prior ignorance about A, B and S) is the calculation of $\hat{a}$ and $\hat{b}$ (the least-squares coefficients), of $\hat{s}$ (the modified residual standard deviation) and of $\hat{s}_A$ and $\hat{s}_B$ (the standard errors of A and B); these are found using (7.27). The values of these expressions are then substituted into (7.25) and (7.26) to find the posterior assessments of A, B and S. These are then summarized in any desired manner. That is all there is to it.

7.8   PREDICTION

An economist's interest in a hypothesized economic relationship does not usually end with a statement of the posterior assessments of A, B and S. Very often, an economist will also wish to use these assessments for predictive purposes; that is, for the purpose of predicting the value of Y for some given value of X. Actually, to be precise, there are two possible predictions that can be made: a prediction of the *average* value of Y corresponding to a particular value of X; and a prediction of the *actual* value of Y corresponding to a particular value of X. If we denote the specific value of X by x_0, and if we denote the average and actual values of Y corresponding to x_0 by M_0 and Y_0 respectively, then they are given by

$$M_0 = A + Bx_0 \tag{7.55}$$

and

$$Y_0 = A + Bx_0 + U_0, \tag{7.56}$$

where, of course, U_0 is $N(0, S^2)$.

You may have noted that we have used upper-case letters for *both* these values of Y; this is because both are unknown in general. (In case 3 M_0 is known, since A and B are known. But then prediction of M_0 in this case is trivial and there is no problem to discuss.)

We confine attention to case 4 (though there are corresponding results in the other cases). From (7.25) we know that the posterior assessments of both A and B are given in the form of t distributions. Moreover (7.26) implies that U_0 also has a t distribution with $(n - 2)$ degrees of freedom. (The distribution of U_0 given $S = s$ is normal; from (7.26) the marginal distribution of S is given in the form of a chi-square distribution; therefore (see chapter 6) the marginal distribution of U_0 is a t distribution.) Now there is a well-known theorem (which, however, is beyond the scope of this book) which states that a linear combination of variables with t distributions (all with the same degrees of freedom) also has a t distribution. Both

(7.55) and (7.56) satisfy the conditions of this theorem. Therefore, the posterior assessments of both M_0 and Y_0 can both be expressed in the form of t distributions. The precise results are as follows (for details of the proof, which we omit, see Zellner (1971), p. 63):

$$\left.\begin{array}{l} \text{Under the conditions of results (7.25) and (7.26) the} \\ \text{posterior assessments of } M_0 \text{ and } Y_0 \text{ are such that} \\ (M_0 - \hat{m}_0)/\hat{s}_{M_0} \text{ and } (Y_0 - \hat{m}_0)/\hat{s}_{Y_0} \text{ both have } t \\ \text{distributions with } (n-2) \text{ degrees of freedom where } \hat{m}_0, \\ \hat{s}_{M_0} \text{ and } \hat{s}_{Y_0} \text{ are as given in (7.58).} \end{array}\right\} \quad (7.57)$$

$$\left.\begin{array}{l} \hat{m}_0 = \hat{a} + \hat{b}x_0 \\ \hat{s}_{M_0} = \hat{s}\{1/n + (x_0 - \bar{x})^2/[\sum_{i=1}^{n}(x_i - \bar{x})^2]\}^{1/2} \\ \hat{s}_{Y_0} = \hat{s}\{1 + 1/n + (x_0 - \bar{x})^2/[\sum_{i=1}^{n}(x_i - \bar{x})^2]\}^{1/2}. \end{array}\right\} \quad (7.58)$$

You will see from these that the posterior assessments of M_0 and Y_0 are both centred on $\hat{m}_0$, the point on the least-squares fitted line corresponding to $X = x_0$. Also, the accuracy of the posterior assessments (as reflected in the widths of the posterior probability intervals) depend upon $\hat{s}_{M_0}$ and $\hat{s}_{Y_0}$. Thus, in both cases the accuracy is higher the smaller is $\hat{s}$, the larger is n, the nearer is x_0 to $\bar{x}$ and the larger the variance of the X observations. All these properties make good intuitive sense.

Let us illustrate the use of (7.57) in the context of our first example of section 7.7, namely the aggregate time-series consumption function. If you actually checked the relevant pages in the *Economic Trends Annual Supplement* for 1982, you will have noticed that we used the data for 1971 to 1980 inclusive, but we omitted the observation for the first quarter of 1981 which was also available. The GDP value for that quarter (as given in that publication) was £28 188 million. Let us take this as x_0 and predict the corresponding M_0 and Y_0. If we substitute the various values from section 7.7 into (7.58) we find that $\hat{m}_0 = 17\,181$, $\hat{s}_{M_0} = 85.7$ and $\hat{s}_{Y_0} = 415$. Hence, from (7.57) we find that our posterior assessments for M_0 and Y_0 are such that $(M_0 - 17\,181)/85.7$ and $(Y_0 - 17\,181)/415$ both have t distributions with 38 degrees of freedom. These are complete characterizations. The corresponding 95 per cent probability intervals are (17 007, 17 355) and (16 340, 18 021) respectively. The first is, naturally, much narrower than the latter. We cannot really 'test' the first of these two predictions as we do not know the *average* value of consumption corresponding to GDP of £28 188 million. But we do know the actual value of consumption in the first quarter of 1981, when GDP was £28 188 million. This actual value was £17 886 million. As you will see, it lies in our 95 per cent prediction (probability) interval for Y_0 given above. That is reassuring!

7.9   SUMMARY

This chapter examined the foundation-stone of all empirical analyses of economic relationships – namely, the linear bivariate normal regression model. This model is defined by (7.5) and is completely described by three parameters: A and B, the coefficients of the equation, and S^2, the variance of the residual term. We examined three cases, the first in which the coefficients were unknown but the variance was known, the second in which the coefficients were known and the variance unknown, and the third in which all were unknown. We focussed most attention on the third (and most general case) and throughout confined attention to the case of total prior ignorance. We showed that the results of this chapter were the 'natural extensions' of the results of chapter 6, in which three analogous cases appeared.

Table 7.3 contains virtually all the important results. Of these, the most important are those for case 4, as that is the case most commonly encountered in practice. As is shown in that table, the posterior assessments of both A and B are in the form of t distributions, and that of S^2 in the form of a chi-square distribution. Implementation of these key results is straightforward. All that is required is calculation of $\hat{a}$ and $\hat{b}$ (the least-squares coefficients) of $\hat{s}$ (the modified residual standard deviation) and of $\hat{s}_A$ and $\hat{s}_B$ (the standard errors of A and B).

This chapter also showed how the results of Classical analyses of the same problem could be interpreted in Bayesian terms. In particular, we showed that Bayesian probability intervals based on total prior ignorance and Classical confidence intervals coincide, and that the (Classical) significance of a test concerning a parameter gave bounds on certain probability statements about that parameter.

Two extended examples of regression were given, both based on the consumption-income relationship. One of these was also used to illustrate the material on prediction given in section 7.8.

Although technically the material of this chapter is more complex than that of the earlier chapters, the basic conceptual ideas are unchanged. In particular, statements about unknown parameters are still expressed in probabilistic terms.

7.10   EXERCISES

All these exercises assume that the basic model under consideration is

$$Y = A + BX + U$$
$$U \text{ is } N(0, S^2),$$

and that the parameters A, B and/or S are either completely known or completely unknown (as specified in the individual exercises). Moreover, the observations (x_1, y_1), (x_2, y_2), ..., (x_n, y_n) on (X, Y) are assumed to have been generated in a random manner.

7.1   Suppose six observations on (X, Y) yielded the following pairs

(20, 45)   (10, 27)   (14, 9)   (38, 75)
            (22, 21)   (16, 39).

(a) If s is known to equal 12, but A and B are unknown, find the posterior assessments of A and B in the light of the above observations. Find 95 per cent probability intervals for A and B, and find $P(A < 0)$ and $P(B > 0)$.

(b) If a and b are known to equal -4 and 0 respectively, but S is unknown, find the posterior assessment of S in the light of the above observations. Find a 95 per cent probability interval for S, and find $P(S > 12)$.

(c) If A, B and S are all unknown, find their posterior assessments in the light of the above assessment. Find 95 per cent probability intervals, and find $P(A < 0)$, $P(B > 0)$ and $P(S > 12)$.

(d) Draw a scatter diagram of the observations, and insert the least-squares fitted line.

7.2   Refer to the illustrative example consisting of nine observations introduced in section 7.2 and carried through sections 7.3 and 7.4. Without carrying out an excessive number of arithmetical calculations, determine the effects on the various posterior assessments and corresponding probability intervals of obtaining a second set of nine observations which happened to be exactly the same as the first set of nine.

7.3   Suppose the sample of n observations happened to lie exactly along a straight line. Argue that this implies that $\hat{s} = 0$. What does this imply in case 4 for the posterior assessments of A and B? Does this implication make sense?

7.4   Explain intuitively why s_A (and $\hat{s}_A$) is an increasing function of the magnitude of $\bar{x}$.

7.5   By expanding the square, and using the definition of $\bar{x}$, show that

$$\sum_{i=1}^{n} (x_i - \bar{x})^2 = \sum_{i=1}^{n} x_i^2 - n\bar{x}^2.$$

Hence show that

$$\sum_{i=1}^{n} x_i^2 = n(s_X^2 + \bar{x}^2).$$

Similarly, show that

$$\sum_{i=1}^{n} (y_i - \bar{y})(x_i - \bar{x}) = \sum_{i=1}^{n} y_i x_i - n\bar{y}\bar{x}.$$

7.6   Verify that the posterior 95 per cent probability intervals for A, B and S in the nine observation example in section 7.4 are as given in the text.

7.7   Verify (7.49). (Hint: First use the equation for $\hat{a}$ to write $y_i - \hat{a} - \hat{b}x_i$ as $(y_i - \bar{y}) - \hat{b}(x_i - \bar{x})$. Then take the square. Finally, use the equation for $\hat{b}$ to simplify the cross-product term.)

7.8   Consider the nine observation example of sections 7.2 to 7.4. Use the results given in the text to obtain 95 per cent prediction (probability) intervals for the mean and actual values of Y corresponding to an X value of 10.

7.9   Obtain some edition of the *Economic Trends Annual Supplement*. Find the table containing *annual* data on GDP and Consumer's Expenditure in constant (1975) prices. (In the 1982 edition it is on page 14.) You will find data from 1948; thus in the 1982 edition there are thirty-three annual observations. Use these observations to obtain posterior assessments of A, B and S. Hence find the 95 per cent probability interval for the UK (annual) marginal propensity to consume. How does this compare with that obtained in section 7.7? Explain any differences or similarities.

7.10   Obtain some edition of the *Economic Trends Annual Supplement*. Find the table containing quarterly data on the general index of retail prices. (In the 1982 edition it is on pages 115 to 117.) From this compute, for each quarter from the second quarter of 1963, the percentage change in the index since the previous quarter. Call this Y. Now find the table containing quarterly data on the money stock. (In the 1982 edition it is on pages 146 and 147.) From this compute, for each quarter from the second quarter of 1963, the percentage change in seasonally adjusted sterling M3 since the previous quarter. Call this X_1. Now carry out a regression of Y on X_1, focussing particular attention on $\hat{s}_1$, the modified residual standard deviation. Now, using your own ingenuity and knowledge of economics, select some other variable X_2 which you feel might be a better explanatory variable for inflation than the rate of change of the money supply. Regress Y on X_2, focussing particular attention on $\hat{s}_2$, the modified residual standard deviation for *this* regression. Finally, using the results of section 7.6, evaluate the relative plausibility of the two competing explanatory variables, assuming that you started with an open mind.

7.11 Find some edition of the *Family Expenditure Survey*. Choose some component of expenditure that interests you, and investigate the Engel curve for that component. Pay particular attention to the question of the appropriate functional form.

7.12 By finding suitable data from published government statistics, evaluate how likely it is that
   (a) aggregate investment is positively affected by the rate of interest; or
   (b) the elasticity of demand for labour is less than one; or
   (c) the interest-elasticity of the demand for money is greater than one; or
   (d) the share of profits in national income is declining; or
   (e) the rate of change of real wages is negatively affected by the rate of unemployment.

7.13 The following two equations have been adapted from Bridge (1971) Table 2.10. They both use annual US data for twenty-nine years.

$$C/Y = 0.7998 + 0.0567\ W/Y \qquad R^2 = 0.849$$
$$(0.0045)$$

$$C/Y = 0.6777 + 0.2405\ L/E \qquad R^2 = 0.571$$
$$(0.0389)$$

(standard errors in parentheses; those omitted not given by Bridge). C is aggregate consumption, Y personal disposable income, W wealth at the beginning of the year (all in constant prices), L is the labour force and E is employment. Appraise these two equations as alternative explanations of the consumption ratio C/Y.

8 FURTHER REGRESSION ANALYSIS

8.1 INTRODUCTION

Chapter 7 was exclusively concerned with the simplest type of economic relationship – namely, a linear relationship between two variables with a normally distributed residual term. It goes without saying that economists are often interested in more complex relationships, and indeed in the interactions between several such relationships. It is, therefore, the purpose of this chapter and the next to show how the methods developed in chapter 7 can be extended and generalized to cover such situations. To be specific, this chapter examines more complex single-equation relationships, while the next chapter explores the empirical investigation of several, inter-related, equations.

As we have remarked, chapter 7 was exclusively concerned with the *linear bivariate normal* regression model. Thus, within the context of single-equation models, three obvious directions for generalization spring to mind: into *non-linear* relationships; into *multivariate* relationships; and into equations with *non-normally distributed* residual terms. The third of these is beyond the scope of this book, unfortunately. However, it would also appear to be beyond the scope, or, at least, beyond the horizon, of the typical empirical economist: without exaggeration, it would be fair to say that at least 99 per cent of all published applied econometric studies (whether they are Classical or Bayesian) are based on the assumption of normally distributed residual terms. So our lack of treatment of the non-normal case is unlikely to cause you any difficulties in reading the relevant literature.

The second of the three possible directions for generalization – into multivariate relationships – will be examined in section 8.2 (though, for simplicity, we will continue to assume that the relationship is linear). The generalization to non-linear relationships will be one of the topics considered in section 8.3, which is concerned with a discussion of the various 'tricks of the trade' that the practising econometrician employs in his or her empirical investigations. Most of these 'tricks' are devices which bridge the gap between the world of the economic theorist and the 'real' world as reflected in published economic statistics. Some are devices to help the applied econometrician find empirical counterparts for theoretical concepts; others are devices which suggest the appropriate modifications to the predictions of theories whose assumptions do not hold in practice. These 'tricks of the trade' include dummy and proxy variables, the use of lagged variables of various kinds, and the modelling of adjustment processes and of the formation of expectations.

Section 8.4, examines a rather crucial issue concerning the assumptions underlying the analysis of chapter 7 and the early sections of chapter 8. You will recall that in chapter 7 we assumed that our observations were generated in a 'random' fashion – analogous to the random sampling of chapters 5 and 6. As this assumption is crucial to the validity of our results; it is clearly vital that we investigate what is meant by random sampling in this context, so that we are in a position to check whether our observations are being generated in the appropriate fashion. If they are not, then our analysis will need to be modified accordingly. Section 8.4 thus explores two related issues: the question of deciding whether these assumptions are satisfied; and the question of what alternative procedure to adopt if they are not satisfied.

As will be shown, and as you may have anticipated, if the 'random sampling' assumption of chapter 7 is not valid, but instead some other mechanism is generating the observations, then our analysis can be modified appropriately *as long as we know what this other mechanism is*. The Bayesian procedure can still be applied. Section 8.4 discusses the appropriate modifications for several alternative generating mechanisms.

In practice, of course, the situation is not as black and white as the theoretical discussion suggests. An empirical investigation tends to proceed in an iterative fashion: going from the theory to the data and back again. Whilst in theory, one lists all possible specifications *before* examining the data, in practice one partly allows the data to determine the set of all specifications under consideration. Strictly speaking, this procedure is not admissible, since it implies that the *prior* assessments are partly determined by the data – which means, in turn, that the data receive more than their 'correct' weight in the posterior assessments.

The reason why practising econometricians (and, indeed, practising statisticians of all types) employ such an iterative procedure is that it is simply too difficult, costly and time-consuming to list all possible specifications before examining the data. Also, there are good methodological reasons for attempting to find *simple* explanations first, before moving on to more complex ones. These factors suggest that the *actual practice* of econometrics must necessarily be an art rather than a science, requiring judgement and experience rather than the mechanical application of algebraic formulae. Section 8.5 discusses these issues in more detail, and illustrates them with a detailed example of 'econometrics in action'.

The chapter concludes with a summary in section 8.6 and a set of exercises in section 8.7.

8.2 THE LINEAR MULTIVARIATE NORMAL MODEL

The linear multivariate normal model is the natural extension of the linear bivariate normal model of chapter 7; whereas in the bivariate model, it is postulated that there is just one explanatory variable, in the multivariate model it is postulated that there are several such variables. In the general case, we will suppose that there are $(k - 1)$ explanatory variables, which we will denote by $X_1, X_2, ..., X_{k-1}$. Throughout this section, we will continue to assume that the relationship is linear, that the dependent variable is denoted by Y, and that there is a residual term, denoted by U. We will also continue to assume that U is normally distributed. Thus the relationship can be written as

$$Y = B_0 + B_1 X_1 + B_2 X_2 + \cdots + B_{k-1} X_{k-1} + U$$
$$U \text{ is } N(0, S^2)$$

$$(8.1)$$

(Before proceeding, an aside about notation is in order. You will have noticed that the notation in (8.1) is not the 'natural extension' of the notation in (7.5). In particular, (8.1) does not reduce to (7.5) when $k = 2$, that is, in the bivariate case: for (8.1) reduces to $Y = B_0 + B_1 X_1 + U$ whereas (7.5) is $Y = A + BX + U$. The reason for our choice of notation is clear: if '$Y = B_0 + B_1 X_1 + U$' had been used throughout chapter 7 there would have been an excess of unnecessary and confusing subscripting; but, on the other hand, there is no neat way of extending '$Y = A + BX + U$' to the general case of $(k - 1)$ explanatory variables. Perhaps we should also comment on why we have supposed there are $(k - 1)$ explanatory variables (rather than the apparently neater supposition of k such variables). This is so that the number of coefficients in the relationship, including the intercept term B_0, totals k. End of aside.)

A rather simpler way of writing (8.1) is as follows:

$$Y = \sum_{j=0}^{k-1} B_j X_j + U \qquad (8.2)$$
$$U \text{ is } N(0, S^2),$$

where X_0 is a 'variable' which always takes the value 1. Before proceeding to a statistical analysis of (8.2), let us briefly comment on its 'economic' implications. Because of the (linear) form of (8.2), it follows that the marginal effect of any one of the $(k-1)$ explanatory variables on the dependent variable is constant. Mathematically,

$$\partial Y / \partial X_j = B_j \qquad \text{for } j = 1, \ldots, k-1, \qquad (8.3)$$

that is, the marginal effect of X_j on Y is B_j irrespective of the value of any of the variables.

In this linear multivariate normal model, there are $(k+1)$ parameters, the k coefficients $B_0, B_1, \ldots, B_{k-1}$ and the residual variance S^2. Depending upon the particular application under consideration some or all of these may be known, partly unknown or completely unknown. As in chapter 7, there are four main cases: when all are known; when the coefficients are unknown but the variance known; when the coefficients are known but the variance unknown; and when the coefficients and the variance are unknown. These four cases correspond to the four cases of chapter 7. In each case, the extent of the ignorance about the unknown parameters may be partial or total.

To avoid undue repetition, we will restrict attention throughout this section to case 4 (all parameters unknown). Moreover, we will further restrict attention to the case of total prior ignorance. However, the various other cases can be analysed in the usual fashion. (If you are interested, you may like to carry out the analyses yourself.) As before, we will assume that our information comes in the form of a random sample of observations on the relevant variables $X_1, X_2, \ldots, X_{k-1}$ and Y. (Remember that the 'dummy' variable X_0 takes the value 1 always.) We will denote the ith observation on the jth explanatory variable (namely, X_j) by x_{ji}, and the ith observation on the dependent variable (namely, Y) by y_i.

Our observations are therefore as follows:

x_{11}	x_{21}	$\cdots$	$x_{k-1, 1}$	y_1	first observations
x_{12}	x_{22}	$\cdots$	$x_{k-1, 2}$	y_2	second observations
$\cdots$					
x_{1n}	x_{2n}	$\cdots$	$x_{k-1, n}$	y_n	nth observations
1st	2nd		$(k-1)$th	dependent	
explanatory variables				variable	

We will simply refer to these as 'the observations'.

Given the observations, and given total prior ignorance, we can obtain the posterior assessments of the coefficients $(B_0, B_1, ..., B_{k-1})$ and the variance (S^2) in the usual manner. However, because of the tediousness of the derivation, we confine the details to Appendix A4. As you will see there, the posterior assessment takes the form of a *joint* probability distribution over all $(k + 1)$ parameters $B_0, B_1, ..., B_{k-1}$ and S^2. As in the bivariate case, the aspects of this joint distribution on which interest is usually focussed are the *marginal* distributions of the parameters taken one at a time. These can be obtained from the joint distribution in the usual manner. Once again, details are confined to the Appendix. From that we obtain the following key result:

> Given total prior ignorance about the parameters $B_0, B_1, ..., B_{k-1}$ and S^2, then in the light of the observations (as defined above) the posterior assessments of $B_0, B_1, ..., B_{k-1}$ and S^2 are such that $(B_j - \hat{b}_j/\hat{s}_{Bj}$ has a t distribution with $(n - k)$ degrees of freedom (for $j = 0, 1, ..., k - 1$) and $(n - k)\hat{s}^2/S^2$ has a chi-square distribution also with $(n - k)$ degrees of freedom, where $\hat{b}_j$, $\hat{s}_{Bj}(j = 0, 1, ..., k - 1)$ and $\hat{s}^2$ are as given in Appendix A4.   (8.4)

You should recognize this as the 'natural extension' of (7.25) and (7.26) – the corresponding results for the bivariate case.

Thus, in the multivariate case, as in the bivariate case, the posterior assessment of each coefficient takes the form of a t distribution. As (8.4) states, the posterior assessment of the coefficient of X_j is such that $(B_j - \hat{b}_j)/\hat{s}_{Bj}$ has a t distribution with $(n - k)$ degrees of freedom. This means that the posterior assessment of B_j is centred on $\hat{b}_j$ (the meaning of which we will discuss shortly), with the widths of the various posterior probability intervals depending upon $\hat{s}_{Bj}$. To be precise, (8.4) implies that the posterior α per cent probability interval for B_j is

$$(\hat{b}_j + t_{(n-k), (100-\alpha)/2}\, \hat{s}_{Bj}, \ \hat{b}_j + t_{(n-k), (100+\alpha)/2}\, \hat{s}_{Bj}) \qquad (8.5)$$

where $t_{k, \beta}$ is defined, as usual, by $P(T_k \leq t_{k, \beta}) = \beta/100$, where T_k has a t distribution with k degrees of freedom. From (8.5) we see that the width of this interval is directly proportional to $\hat{s}_{Bj}$; moreover, since the dispersion of a t distribution decreases as its number of degrees of freedom increases, it follows that the width of this probability interval decreases with n and increases with k. Perhaps you would like to ponder the reasons for this latter result.

If you have been following the analogy with the bivariate case, you may have anticipated what the $\hat{b}_j$ are. You will recall that in the bivariate case, the posterior assessments of the coefficients were centred on the corresponding *least-squares coefficients* – these being the coefficients of the least-squares fitted line. You will also recall that the least-squares fitted line was that line which best fitted the observations in the sense of minimizing the sum of squared deviations (in the Y-direction) of the observations from the line. Consider the natural multivariate extension of this construct. As we are dealing with more than two dimensions, we can no longer talk about fitted *lines*, but must instead talk about fitted *planes*, or simply, fitted *relationships*. Consider first an arbitrary fitted relationship

$$Y = b_0 + b_1 X_1 + \cdots + b_{k-1} X_{k-1},$$

which we can write, rather more succinctly, as

$$Y = \sum_{j=0}^{k-1} b_j X_j. \tag{8.6}$$

By an *arbitrary* fitted relationship, we mean that the b_j are chosen arbitrarily. Consider now the deviations (in the Y-directions) of the observation from this fitted relationship: the deviation of the ith observation, denoted by e_j, is given by

$$e_i = y_i - \sum_{j=0}^{k-1} b_j x_{ji}. \tag{8.7}$$

Now define D as the sum of squared deviations, namely:

$$D = \sum_{i=1}^{n} e_i^2. \tag{8.8}$$

Suppose we now choose the b_j so as to minimize D. Anticipating somewhat, let us denote the value of b_j at which the minimum is attained by $\hat{b}_j$. Then the k values, $\hat{b}_0, \hat{b}_1, \ldots, \hat{b}_{k-1}$ are the solutions to the k equations

$$\partial D/\partial b_0 = \partial D/\partial b_1 = \cdots = \partial D/\partial b_{k-1} = 0.$$

The resulting fitted relationship

$$Y = \sum_{j=0}^{k-1} \hat{b}_j X_j \tag{8.9}$$

is called, for obvious reasons, the *least-squares fitted relationship* (or plane). It is the plane that 'best fits' the observations in the sense of minimizing the sum of squared deviations of the observations from the plane. As in the bivariate case, *the posterior assessment of B_j is centred on $\hat{b}_j$ the corresponding coefficient in the least-squares fitted plane* (or simply the corresponding least-squares coefficient). We must stress, once again, that this result is a consequence of the routine application of Bayes' theorem, and does *not* follow because of any magical properties of the least-squares fitted line. The *primary* property of the $\hat{b}_j$ is that they are the means of the posterior assessments of B_j; the *secondary* property, that they are the least-squares coefficients, is mentioned only to help your intuitive appreciation of the implications of (8.4).

As we have already noted, the dispersion of the posterior assessment of B_j, and hence the widths of its posterior probability intervals, depend upon $\hat{s}_{B_j}$. As in the bivariate case, we will refer to this as the *standard error* of B_j – once again borrowing a term popularly used in Classical inference. The formula for the standard errors of the B_j is given in Appendix A4. This is not so easily interpreted as in the bivariate case. However, the same properties as in the bivariate case contain to hold, as long as they are qualified by the phrase *ceteris paribus*. To be precise, $\hat{s}_{B_j}$, the standard error of B_j, is smaller, *ceteris paribus*, the smaller the standard deviation of the residuals (in the Y-direction), the larger the number of observations, and the larger the standard deviation of the X_j observations. Of course, because in the multivariate case there is more than one explanatory variable, the values taken by the observations on the *other* variables will also affect $\hat{s}_{B_j}$. A glance at Appendix A4 will reveal that this relationship (between $\hat{s}_{B_j}$ and the observations) is rather complicated, and hence rather difficult to précis. But there is one general property which emerges: the greater the association between (the observations on) X_j and (the observations on) the other variables, the larger is $\hat{s}_{B_j}$, *ceteris paribus*. Let us illustrate this property, with reference to the case $k = 3$. In this case (in which there are just two explanatory variables X_1 and X_2, in addition to the 'dummy' variable X_0), it can be shown that $\hat{s}_{B_1}$ and $\hat{s}_{B_2}$ are given by (see Hey (1974), p. 313)

$$\hat{s}_{B_j} = \frac{\hat{s}}{n^{1/2} s_{X_j} (1 - r^2)^{1/2}} \qquad (j = 1, 2). \tag{8.10}$$

In this, $\hat{s}$ is the (modified) residual standard deviation (which we will examine in more detail shortly), s_{X_j} is the standard deviation of the observations on X_j and r is given as follows:

$$r = \frac{\sum_{i=1}^{n} (x_{1i} - \bar{x})(x_{2i} - \bar{x}_2)}{\{[\sum_{i=1}^{n} (x_{1i} - \bar{x}_1)^2][\sum_{i=1}^{n} (x_{2i} - \bar{x}_2)^2]\}^{1/2}} \qquad (8.11)$$

This new expression (r) is known as the *coefficient of correlation* between X_1 and X_2 (cf. (3.43)). It is a summary measure which attempts to provide an indication of the *degree of linear association* between the observations on X_1 and those on X_2. We do not need to go into detail about r, or about the specific formula in (8.11); suffice it to say that the *sign* of r indicates the *direction* of the association, and the *magnitude* of r the *strength* of the association. More specifically, if $|r| = 1$ there is perfect linear association; if $r = 0$ there is no linear association; while if $0 < |r| < 1$ there is partial association – the higher $|r|$, the greater the degree of linear association.

It is clear from (8.10) that $\hat{s}_{B_j}$ is smaller, the smaller is $\hat{s}$, the greater is n and the greater is s_{X_j} – as we have asserted above. In addition, *the greater is r^2 the greater is $\hat{s}_{B_j}$*. If r^2 is zero, then (8.10) reduces to that applicable in the bivariate case (equation (7.19) with s replaced by $\hat{s}$); as r^2 increases, so does $\hat{s}_{B_j}$. To get some intuitive feel for this result, imagine two situations: in situation 1, the observations on our two explanatory variables X_1 and X_2 bear virtually no association to each other; in situation 2, the observations are highly associated – so that, for example, high X_1 values are associated with high X_2 values, and low X_1 values with low X_2 values. If the two situations were identical in all other respects, in which would you feel more confident about your posterior assessments of B_1 and B_2? Presumably in situation 1; for in situation 2, it is relatively difficult to disentangle the *individual* effects of X_1 and X_2 on Y, since X_1 and X_2 move together. The extreme case occurs when $r^2 = 1$ – that is, when X_1 and X_2 are perfectly linearly associated. By this we mean that if the observations on X_1 and X_2 are plotted on a scatter diagram, then all the observations lie exactly along a straight line. If this is the case, then a regression of X_1 on X_2, or of X_2 on X_1, would lead to a perfect fit, with an R^2 (see (7.46)) of 1. It is no coincidence that when $r^2 = 1$ then so is R^2: algebraically they are identical. (For a proof see Hey (1974), pp. 270–1.) Thus, you may find it simpler to think of r^2, where r is defined by (8.11), as the proportion of the variance of X_2 'explained' by a regression of X_2 on X_1, or, equivalently, as the proportion of the variance of X_1 'explained' by a regression of X_1 on X_2.

In the extreme case when $r^2 = 1$, both $\hat{s}_{B_1}$ and $\hat{s}_{B_2}$ are infinite, as can be seen from (8.10). This means that the posterior assessments for both B_1 and B_2 have an infinite variance. This can be interpreted as *total posterior ignorance*. In other words, we are no wiser about B_1 and B_2 after the observations than we were before. Why is this? Simply because when $r^2 = 1$ then the observations on X_1 and X_2 move precisely together, and thus there is no information in the observations to enable us to determine the *individual* effects of X_1 and X_2 on Y. (If you are not happy with this general argument, consider the following numerical example, which you can easily extend yourself. Suppose we have five observations on (X_1, X_2, Y) as follows

(1, 3, 12)   (2, 5, 20)   (3, 7, 28)   (4, 9, 36)   (5, 11, 44).

For these, $X_1 = 1 + 2X_1$ holds exactly for all five observations. Thus, X_1 and X_2 are perfectly linearly associated. Moreover, as you can check, the relationship between Y and X_1 and X_2 can be represented as $Y = 1 + 2X_1 + 3X_2$ or $Y = 2 + 4X_1 + 2X_2$ or $Y = 4X_2$ or $Y = 3 + 6X_1 + X_2$ or $Y = -1 - 2X_1 + 5X_2$ or indeed $Y = (1 + a) + 2(1 + a)X_1 + (3 - a)X_2$ for any of the infinite possible values of a. Thus the observations are consistent with an infinite number of possible values of B_1 and B_2, and are therefore completely uninformative about B_1 and B_2.)

This discussion also illustrates why $\hat{s}_{B_j}$ is an increasing function of r^2: as r^2 increases, the amount of information contained in the observations about the *individual* effects of X_1 and X_2 on Y decreases; accordingly the dispersion of the posterior assessments increases, *ceteris paribus*.

Although we have illustrated this phenomenon with reference to the case $k = 3$, it clearly equally well applies also to $k > 3$. This phenomenon is referred to as *multicollinearity* between the explanatory variables. As our discussion has shown, the greater the multicollinearity, that is, the greater the association between pairs of explanatory variables, the greater is the dispersion of the posterior assessments of the relevant coefficients. Multicollinearity is a 'problem' only if it is so great that it means that the dispersion of our posterior assessments is 'unacceptably' large. In such a situation, the observations do not contain enough information. In theory, the remedy is simple – obtain some more, or different, observations which contain more information; in practice, it may not always be very easy to do this – as we shall see.

We have now discussed the implications of the key result (8.4) for the posterior assessments of the coefficients B_0, B_1, ..., B_{k-1}. All that now remain to be discussed are the implications for the posterior assessment of the variance S^2. From (8.4), we see that this is such that $(n - k)\hat{s}^2/S^2$ has a chi-square distribution with $(n - k)$ degrees of freedom. In this, the numerator $(n - k)\hat{s}^2$ is the same as in the bivariate case (cf. (7.26) and (7.27)), namely the sum of squared deviations (in the Y-direction) of the observations from the least-squares fitted line. Using $\hat{u}_i$, as in chapter 7, to denote the ith such deviation:

$$\hat{u}_i = y_i - \sum_{j=0}^{k-1} \hat{b}_j x_{ji}, \tag{8.12}$$

then $(n - k)\hat{s}^2$ is given by

$$(n - k)\hat{s}^2 = \sum_{i=1}^{n} \hat{u}_i^2.$$

This yields the following expression for $\hat{s}^2$:

$$\hat{s}^2 = \sum_{i=1}^{n} \frac{\hat{u}_i^2}{(n - k)}. \tag{8.13}$$

For obvious reasons, we will once again refer to $\hat{s}^2$ as the modified residual variance, and to $\hat{s}$ as the modified residual standard deviation.

By now you may have detected a pattern in the number of degrees of freedom associated with the chi-square and t distributions in the various cases. Let us summarize the various results, and attempt an intuitive explanation of the pattern. We list below the following cases, specifying which parameters are known and which parameters, in addition to the variance, are unknown ('translating' all notation, for ease of comparison, to that of chapter 8): (1) from chapter 6, case 2 (mean b_0 known); (2) from chapter 6, case 4 (mean B_0 unknown); (3) from chapter 7, case 2 (coefficients b_0 and b_1 known); (4) from chapter 7, case 4 (coefficients B_0 and B_1 unknown); (5) from chapter 8 (coefficients B_0, B_1, ..., B_{k-1} unknown). In each case, we list the result giving the posterior assessment of S^2 based on total prior ignorance and n observations.

(1) $\displaystyle\sum_{i=1}^{n} \frac{(y_i - b_0)^2}{S^2}$ is $\chi^2(n)$

(2) $\displaystyle\sum_{i=1}^{n} \frac{(y_i - \hat{b}_0)^2}{S^2}$ is $\chi^2(n - 1)$

(3) $\displaystyle\sum_{i=1}^{n} \frac{(y_i - b_0 - b_1 x_{1i})^2}{S^2}$ is $\chi^2(n)$

(4) $\displaystyle\sum_{i=1}^{n} \frac{(y_i - \hat{b}_0 - \hat{b}_1 x_{1i})^2}{S^2}$ is $\chi^2(n-2)$

(5) $\displaystyle\sum_{i=1}^{n} \frac{(y_i - \sum_{j=0}^{k-1} \hat{b}_j x_{ji})^2}{S^2}$ is $\chi^2(n-k)$.

The pattern should now be clear: the numerator is always the sum of squared deviations of the Y-observations from the mean relationship (if known) or the fitted (least-squares) relationship (otherwise); *the number of degrees of freedom is always n* (the number of observations) *less the number of unknown* parameters (excluding S^2 itself). Thus, for each additional unknown parameter, the number of degrees of freedom is reduced by 1. This implies, as we shall demonstrate below, that, given any set of observations, the posterior assessment of S^2 is less precise the more unknown parameters there are. The intuition behind this is clear: the more unknown parameters there are, the further the information contained in any given set of observations has to be spread, and thus the smaller the reduction in uncertainty concerning S^2.

Let us now demonstrate the assertion contained in the paragraph above. The simplest way to do this is to give an illustration, and leave its generalization to you. Consider, for example, the posterior α per cent probability intervals for S^2; these are always of the form

$(N/y_{m,(100+\alpha)/2}, N/y_{m,(100-\alpha)/2})$ (8.14)

where N is the appropriate numerator, and $y_{m,(100+\alpha)/2}$ and $y_{m,(100-\alpha)/2}$ are the appropriate entries from the chi-square table. Our assertion requires that, for any given N and α, the difference

$1/y_{m,(100-\alpha)/2} - 1/y_{m,(100+\alpha)/2}$ (8.15)

decreases as m increases. Take for example $\alpha = 95$, and consider the four m-values 10, 20, 30 and 40. Then, by consulting the table of the chi-square distribution in Appendix A8, it can be shown that the respective values of the expression in (8.15) are 0.2589, 0.0751, 0.0383 and 0.0241. These are consistent with our assertion.

As (8.4) reveals, the number of degrees of freedom associated with the t distributions characterizing the posterior assessments of the coefficients is also $(n-k)$, so the arguments above apply equally well to the precision of these assessments. Indeed, it is clear that these are perfectly general arguments, which may be summarized as follows: the more things that are uncertain, the smaller is the reduction in uncertainty generated by any given set of observations.

We have spent some time discussing the general implications of the key result (8.4), and it is now time that we presented some numerical examples. To implement (8.4), we need to calculate the least-squares coefficients, $\hat{b}_0$, $\hat{b}_1$, ..., $\hat{b}_{k-1}$, the standard errors of B_0, B_1, ..., B_{k-1} (namely, $\hat{s}_{B_0}$, $\hat{s}_{B_1}$, ..., $\hat{s}_{B_{k-1}}$) and the modified residual variance $\hat{s}^2$. You may have noticed that, although we have given the formula for $\hat{s}^2$, the text has been remarkably silent on the question of the appropriate formulae for the least-squares coefficients and the standard errors. A glance at Appendix A4 will reveal the reason why: these formulae are rather nasty, to say the least. Moreover, they involve matrix manipulations – which are beyond the scope of this book. Fortunately, however, it is unlikely that you will ever find yourself in the position of actually having to calculate these various expressions: with the advent of modern computers and the widespread availability of statistical and econometric packages of various kinds, it is almost certain that you will have access to some machine that will do the calculations for you. Amongst the more commonly available statistical packages are SPSS, STATPACK and IDA, and the more specialized (but still widely available) econometric packages include TSP, ESP, GIVE, SHAZAM and TROLL. If you have access to a computer, you should check which of these are available for your use. (Appendix A5 lists some specifically Bayesian programs that are available.) All of them will calculate the least-squares coefficients, the standard errors and the modified residual variance (and a lot more besides). The results presented below were all calculated using the statistical package IDA (which stands for Interactive Data Analysis); this is an interactive program (which means that you and the computer 'talk' to each other) and is particularly simple to use. To carry out the various regressions reported below, I first typed in the relevant data, and then specified the appropriate regressions by telling IDA which was the dependent variable and which were the explanatory variables. A sample of the regression output is given in table 8.1. We will interpret this in due course.

Let us now turn to our illustration of multivariate regression. We build on the simple bivariate model of the UK aggregate consumption function presented in chapter 7. You will recall that in this model the dependent variable was Consumers' Expenditure, and there was a single explanatory variable, Gross Domestic Product at market prices (GDP). You may have felt at the time that this model was incomplete, in that it should have included other explanatory variables. Various other candidates suggest themselves, some on theoretical grounds and some on 'practical' grounds. In the latter

Table 8.1   IDA program output for regression of CE on GDP, CE_{-1} and RS

```
COMMAND> **** REGR ****
DEPENDENT VARIABLE:  COL   2  (CE     )
INDEPENDENT VARIABLE  1:  COL   1  (GDP    )
INDEPENDENT VARIABLE  2:  COL   6  (CE-1   )
INDEPENDENT VARIABLE  3:  COL   3  (RS     )

UPDATING CORR. MATRIX...
COMPUTING REGRESSION...
ANALYZING RESIDUALS...
WARNING: RESIDUAL IN ROW   34 IS  3.23 S.D. UNITS FROM 0
CHECKING AUTO CORRELATIONS...
WARNING: AUTO( 3) = 0.36


COMMAND> **** COEF ****

VARIABLE   B(STD.V)      B      STD.ERROR(B)     T

GDP        0.2611   1.5266E-01   5.1569E-02    2.960
CE-1       0.7943   7.7079E-01   1.1152E-01    6.912
RS        -0.0824  -2.0130E+01   1.9655E+01   -1.024
CONSTANT   0       -5.4354E+01   1.1263E+03   -0.048


COMMAND> **** SUMM ****

             MULTIPLE R   R-SQUARE
UNADJUSTED   0.9602       0.9219
ADJUSTED     0.9567       0.9152

STD. DEV. OF RESIDUALS = 2.4490E+02
N = 39
```

category, there is a candidate which may not be obvious to you if you have not studied, or carried out, any applied econometrics before, but which is an obvious candidate to any experienced researcher. We refer to the lagged value of the dependent variable – that is, Consumers Expenditure in the preceding period. In many time-series analyses of many economic relationships, it is found that the lagged dependent variable plays an important role; this is usually attributed to a habit, or persistence, effect in human behaviour. We shall discuss this in more detail in the next section.

A candidate suggested by theory as a possible explanatory variable for consumption is the *rate of interest;* so let us include this.

However, theory is rather silent as to which is the appropriate rate of interest. If we look at the various UK statistical sources (most notably *Financial Statistics*, the *Bank of England Quarterly Bulletin*, and *Economic Trends Annual Supplement*), we see that there is a whole spectrum of interest rates – ranging from very short-term rates, such as the rate on three-month Treasury Bills, to very long-term rates, such as the yield on $3\frac{1}{2}$ per cent (undated) War Loan. Let us suppose we are prepared to narrow down the short-list of possible candidates to just two: a short-term one (three-month Treasury Bill rate), and a long-term one (the yield on twenty-year British Government securities). As to which of these two is the appropriate one, let us suppose we have initially an open mind, and leave it to the data to determine the posterior probabilities for the two contenders. Let us suppose, also, that as a complete rival to the 'interest-rate hypothesis', we wish to investigate the 'unemployment hypothesis' – which states that the rate of unemployment is a determinant of consumption. (The theoretical reasoning behind this goes as follows: a *ceteris paribus* increase in unemployment implies an increase in the inequality of the distribution of income, 'given' that the cross-section mpc declines with income, then this re-distribution will decrease aggregate consumption.)

Let us summarize the discussion so far. We suppose that we are prepared to entertain three *rival* hypotheses concerning the determination of aggregate consumption. These are as follows:

$$
\begin{array}{lll}
\text{(a)} & CE = f_1(GDP, CE_{-1}, RS) & \\
\text{(b)} & CE = f_2(GDP, CE_{-1}, RL) & \quad\quad (8.16) \\
\text{(c)} & CE = f_3(GDP, CE_{-1}, UE) &
\end{array}
$$

where f_1, f_2 and f_3 are (different) linear functions of their arguments, and where CE stands for Consumers' Expenditure, GDP stands for Gross Domestic Product at market prices, CE_{-1} stands for Consumers' Expenditure lagged one period (which is one quarter in the subsequent analysis since we are using quarterly data), RS stands for a Short interest Rate (namely, the rate on three-month Treasury Bills), RL stands for a Long interest Rate (namely, the yield on twenty-year British Government securities) and where UE stands for the rate of Unemployment. During this example we will use this more obvious mnemonic notation, rather than the anonymous Y, $X_1, X_2, \ldots, X_{k-1}$.

Following the procedure discussed in section 7.6, we first of all investigate each relationship individually, conditional on it being the correct one. This will give us (conditional) posterior assessments of the respective coefficients and residual variances. In the light of these, we will be able to assess the posterior probabilities of the three rival hypotheses.

All the data can be obtained from *Economic Trends Annual Supplement* (*ETAS*). Here we use quarterly data from the 1982 edition, covering the ten years from 1971 to 1980 inclusive. The data on *CE* and *GDP* is the same as that used in section 7.4, namely seasonally adjusted data in constant (1975) prices from *ETAS* pp. 78–79. The data on *RS* and *RL* are obtained by taking quarterly averages of the monthly data found in *ETAS* pp. 195–7. The data on *UE* is obtained from *ETAS* pp. 107–9. Finally, the data on CE_{-1} is found from *CE* by lagging the latter by one quarter. To illustrate this procedure, we present below the relevant observations for 1971.

Quarter	CE	CE_{-1}
1	14 603	*
2	14 867	14 603
3	15 071	14 867
4	15 183	15 071

* Note that, in the absence of the *CE* figure for the final quarter of 1970, it is impossible to determine the CE_{-1} figure for the first quarter of 1971. Consequently, the number of observations is reduced from forty to thirty nine.

This data was fed into IDA, and the program was first asked to carry out the regression of *CE* on *GDP*, CE_{-1} and *RS*. (The program automatically includes a constant term; some packages allow you to suppress this if you so wish.) Table 8.1 shows the resulting output. The relevant parts of it can be displayed in the following, familiar form (all to three significant figures)

$$CE = -54.4 + 0.153GDP$$
$$(1130) \quad (0.0516)$$

$$+ 0.771CE_{-1} - 20.1RS \quad \hat{s} = 245$$
$$(0.112) \qquad (19.7) \qquad n = 39$$

(8.17)

(standard errors in parentheses).

The coefficients in (8.17) are the $\hat{b}_j$, the least-squares coefficients, and are extracted from the column headed 'B' in table 8.1. (You will note that the computer output uses a sort of 'exponential notation', with some numbers presented in the form xEy; this simply means

$x \times 10^y$. Thus $-5.4354E + 01$ is -5.4354×10^1 or -54.354; $1.5266E - 01$ is 1.5266×10^{-1} or 0.15266; and so on.) The numbers in brackets under the coefficients in (8.17) are the $\hat{s}_{B_j}$, the standard errors of the respective B_j, and are extracted from the column headed 'STD. ERROR(B)' in table 8.1. The coefficients and standard errors are given in rows preceded by the name of the variable in question; the least-squares intercept and the standard error of the intercept are given in the row preceded by the word 'CONSTANT' – this corresponds to our X_0, a dummy variable which always takes the value 1. The value for $\hat{s}$, the modified residual standard deviation, in (8.17) is given as the 'STD. DEV. OF RESIDUALS' in table 8.1. Finally, table 8.1 confirms that the number of observations was thirty nine.

We can use (8.17) in conjunction with (8.4) to describe our posterior assessments of the coefficients and residual variance of (8.16)(a) conditional on it being the correct formulation. From these posterior assessments, we can obtain the various summary measures in the usual manner. For example, we can obtain posterior 95 per cent probability intervals for the coefficients by use of the fact that a variable with a t distribution with $35 \ (= 39 - 4 = n - k)$ degrees of freedom lies between ± 2.031 with probability 0.95. Hence, using (8.17) and (8.4), the 95 per cent probability intervals for the coefficients of GDP, CE_{-1} and RS are

$$(0.153 - 2.031 \times 0.0516, 0.153 + 2.031 \times 0.0516),$$
$$(0.771 - 2.031 \times 0.112, 0.771 + 2.031 \times 0.112)$$

and

$$(-20.1 - 2.031 \times 19.7, -20.1 + 2.031 \times 19.7)$$

respectively; that is $(0.048, 0.258)$, $(0.544, 0.998)$ and $(-60.1, 19.9)$ respectively. We can also assess the probabilities that the various coefficients have the sign that is predicted by economic theory. Theory predicts that the coefficients of GDP and CE_{-1} should be positive, and that of RS negative. Using an obvious notation, we can proceed as follows:

$$P(B_{GDP} > 0) = P[(B_{GDP} - 0.153)/0.0516 > (0 - 0.153)/0.0516]$$
$$= P(T_{35} > -2.96) \quad \text{(using (8.4) and (8.17))}$$
$$= 0.997. \quad \text{(from Appendix A7)}$$

Similarly,

$$P(B_{CE_{-1}} > 0) = P(T_{35} > -6.912) = 1,$$

and

$$P(B_{RS} < 0) = P(T_{35} < 1.024) = 0.84.$$

Thus, on the basis of the evidence, we can be almost certain that GDP and CE_{-1} influence CE in the direction predicted by economic theory, but we can attach a probability of only 0.84 to the correctness of the prediction that CE is negatively related to RS. These probabilities depend, as the above calculations demonstrate, on the respective t-ratios (2.96, 6.912 and 1.024 respectively). As you will see from table 8.1, IDA calculates these t-ratios, and presents them in the column headed 'T'. This facilitates a quick calculation of the appropriate probabilities. (At this stage, it may be useful to mention a simple 'rule of thumb'. From Appendix A7, we can see that a variable with a t distribution is less than 2 with probability at least 0.975 if its number of degrees of freedom exceeds 60. Thus, if $(n - k) \geq 60$ then, if a coefficient's t-ratio is at least 2, the probability that the true coefficient has the same sign as the least-squares coefficient is at least 0.975. Thus, assuming that the least-squares coefficient has the correct sign, and that $(n - k) \geq 60$, then a t-ratio greater than 2 is 'Good News'. This is a useful 'rule of thumb'. It is also one in popular use among Classical statisticians: it means to them that the least-squares coefficient is significantly different from zero at the $2\frac{1}{2}$ per cent significance level.)

Let us now return to (8.17) and look in more detail at the least-squares coefficients themselves. (Recall that these are the means of the posterior assessments of the respective coefficients.) In particular, let us explore the economic significance of the magnitude of these least-squares coefficients. From (8.17) we see that the least-squares coefficient of GDP is 0.153, which appears to imply that the least-squares consumption function has a marginal propensity to consume of just 0.153. This seems very low – has something gone wrong? Surely an increase in income of £1 must lead to an increase in consumption of more than 15.3p? The answer is that it will, but not immediately – recall that (8.17) includes CE_{-1}, that is, consumption lagged one quarter. Thus, an increase in GDP of £1 *this* quarter will lead to an increase in CE of 15.3p *this* quarter, which will lead to an increase in CE_{-1} of 15.3p *next* quarter, and hence to an extra increase in CE of 0.771×15.3p *next* quarter, which in turn will lead to . . . And so on. The habit, or persistence, effect represented by the inclusion of CE_{-1} means that any increase in GDP will continue to be felt for many periods – the subsequent ripples take a long time to die out. Thus, the mpc of 0.153 is simply the immediate, or impact, or short-run mpc. To calculate the long-run mpc, we calculate the effect when all the ripples have died away. This is when $CE = CE_{-1}$. If we substitute this in the least-squares consumption function, we get

$$CE = -54.4 + 0.153GDP + 0.771CE - 20.1RS.$$

This implies

$$0.229CE = -54.4 + 0.153GDP - 20.1RS,$$

and hence

$$CE = 238 + 0.668GDP - 87.8RS. \tag{8.18}$$

This could be termed the long-run (least-squares) consumption function; it has an mpc of 0.668. Thus, in the long-run an increase in *GDP* of £1 leads to an increase in *CE* of 66.8p. This appears to be the appropriate order of magnitude.

Similarly, it follows from (8.17) and (8.18) that an increase of 1 percentage point in *RS* (from 8 per cent to 9 per cent, or from 12 per cent to 13 per cent) leads, in the short-run, to a decrease in *CE* of 20.1, and, in the long-run, to a decrease of 87.8. To put these numbers into perspective, it may be useful to point out that the value of *CE* in the final quarter of 1980 was 17 886 (in £m). Thus, decreases of 20.1 and 87.8 represent *percentage* decreases of 0.11 per cent and 0.49 per cent respectively. Thus, according to these figures, to stimulate consumption expenditure by 1 per cent in the long-run would require a decrease in interest rates of some 2 percentage points.

One rather odd feature of the least-squares relationship is that it has a negative intercept, which implies that there would be negative consumption if income and interest rates were zero. However, this need not concern us unduly as the standard error is very large; indeed, the probability that the true coefficient is positive is only marginally less than 0.5.

Finally, before leaving this regression, let us explain the remaining features of table 8.1. The column headed 'B(STD.V)' gives the least-squares coefficients for a fitted relationship in which all the variables have been 'standardized', by this is meant that they have been linearly transformed in such a way that their means are zero and their variances unity. This column need not detain us. The column headed 'R-SQUARE' gives R^2 (see (7.46)) in the row labelled 'UNADJUSTED' and $\bar{R}^2$ (see (7.47)) in the row labelled 'ADJUST-ED'. Finally, the column headed 'MULTIPLE R' gives R and $\bar{R}$, the square-roots of the expressions in the 'R-SQUARE' column. As we explained in chapter 7, R^2 measures the proportion of the variance of Y 'explained' by the regression, or, equivalently, 1 minus the ratio of the (unmodified) residual variance to the variance of Y. Thus, R^2 is a measure of the 'goodness of fit' of the regression. More importantly, for our purposes, R^2 is related to $\hat{s}^2$ (by (7.47)), so that the smaller is $\hat{s}^2$ the larger is R^2. The expression $\bar{R}^2$ (see (7.47)) is related to R^2, but is adjusted to allow for the number of degrees of freedom of the regression. *Ceteris paribus*, the smaller the number of degrees of freedom the smaller is $\bar{R}^2$. The idea behind $\bar{R}^2$ is to provide a measure of the 'goodness of fit' of the regression, which somehow 'corrects' for the number of variables included in the regression, so as to counteract the inevitable increase in R^2 as additional variables are included in the regression. However, $\bar{R}^2$ is essentially an *ad hoc* construct which does not appear to have a sensible interpretation from a Bayesian point of view. You are advised not to take it too seriously.

We now appear to have exhausted most of the items of interest arising out of (8.17). Let us now turn, rather more briefly, to our other two hypothesized multivariate consumption functions (as given in (8.16)(b) and (c)). The results of the relevant calculations can be summarized as follows (all to three significant figures):

$$CE = \begin{array}{c} 181 \\ (755) \end{array} + \begin{array}{c} 0.194GDP \\ (0.0489) \end{array} + \begin{array}{c} 0.716CE_{-1} \\ (0.0786) \end{array} - \begin{array}{c} 53.0RL \\ (19.6) \end{array} \qquad \begin{array}{c} \hat{s} = 226 \\ n = 39 \end{array}$$
$$(8.19)$$

$$CE = \begin{array}{c} 660 \\ (923) \end{array} + \begin{array}{c} 0.167GDP \\ (0.0611) \end{array} + \begin{array}{c} 0.693CE_{-1} \\ (0.0871) \end{array} - \begin{array}{c} 9.20UE \\ (37.7) \end{array} \qquad \begin{array}{c} \hat{s} = 248 \\ n = 39 \end{array}$$
$$(8.20)$$

(standard errors in parentheses).

In terms of the implications for the coefficients of GDP and CE_{-1}, equations (8.19) and (8.20) are broadly similar to (8.17). In particular, the least-squares coefficients of (8.19) and (8.20) imply short-run mpc's of 0.194 and 0.167 respectively (as compared with 0.153 for (8.17)) and long-run mpc's of 0.683 and 0.544 respectively (as compared with 0.668 for (8.17). But note that the standard errors of the coefficients of GDP and CE_{-1} are lowest in (8.19). Equation (8.19) also implies that the probability that the coefficient of RL is negative is almost 0.995. In contrast, equation (8.20) implies that the probability that the coefficient of UE is negative, as the theory requires, is only about 0.6.

In terms of their respective values for $\hat{s}$, the modified residual standard deviation, (8.19) has the lowest (at 226), followed by (8.17) and (8.20) (at 245 and 248 respectively). Let us now recall and generalize result (7.45) of section 7.6, which states that, if two models have equal prior probabilities, then their posterior probabilities are proportional to their respective values of $\hat{s}^{-n}$. It follows that, if our prior probabilities for the three models are equal, then our posterior probabilities for (8.16)(a), (b) and (c) are proportional to

$$245^{-39} \qquad 226^{-39} \qquad 248^{-39}$$

respectively. Carrying out the appropriate calculations (using the unrounded figures for $\hat{s}$ to avoid the accumulation of rounding error) shows that the posterior probabilities (to 3 significant figures) are

$$0.041 \qquad 0.935 \qquad 0.024$$

respectively. Thus, we can conclude that, of these three alternative explanations of Consumers' Expenditure, the probability is 0.935 that (8.16)(b) (the one with the long-term rate of interest) is the correct one.

This completes our illustration of multivariate regression. As you will have gathered, the basic procedure involved in the analysis of such relationships is a straightforward extension of the procedure involved in the analysis of bivariate relationships. The key result is (8.4), which can be easily implemented given values of the least-squares coefficients, the standard errors of the coefficients, and the modified residual variance. All of these are routinely calculated in most computer regression programs.

8.3 VARIOUS 'TRICKS OF THE TRADE'

As you are no doubt aware, the world of the economic theorist is not the same as the 'real world' as manifested in economic statistics. Thus, in any empirical investigation of any economic theory, there is a gap to be bridged. Usually, the task of bridging this gap is left to the investigator – the applied statistician or applied econometrician. It is the purpose of this section to describe some of the devices, or 'tricks of the trade', that the applied econometrician typically employs when setting about this task.

Possibly the first major problem that the applied econometrician encounters is that of finding the appropriate empirical counterparts to the variables of the theory. It is often the case that the theoretical variables are either unobservable or unobserved; in such cases *proxy variables* have to be sought. In other cases, *dummy variables* have to be introduced to allow for unmeasurable qualitative factors. We shall discuss both of these below. A second major problem concerns the empirical validity of the assumptions on which the theory is based. It is often the case that these assumptions are violated in practice. This means that the applied econometrician has to determine the appropriate way of modifying the predictions of the theory to allow for this difference between theory and practice. We shall discuss some of the commonly used modifications below. Finally, we discuss some more practical matters, including the specification of the appropriate functional form (theory is usually rather silent on such matters), and the procedure to adopt if multicollinearity is a serious problem.

We shall examine these various 'tricks of the trade' in roughly the order discussed above. To assist intuitive understanding of the various devices, and of their applicability, we will employ a rather flexible notation, using mnemonic notation where its use appears helpful. This might lead to some apparent inconsistencies *across* examples – for example, C might be used in one example to denote the variable Consumption, and in a second example to denote the Coefficient of some other variable. But the meaning will be clear from the context. Let us now turn to these 'tricks of the trade', examining them independently one at a time.

Dummy variables. These are usually used to 'quantify' qualitative effects such as sex, type of education, region, season, race, and so on. Typically, a dummy variable will take only two values, conventionally 1 and 0 – indicating possession of some characteristic and lack of it, respectively. For example, if the data relate to individual people, it may be useful to distinguish between males and females; this could be achieved by the use of a dummy variable which takes the value 1 for males and 0 for females. To illustrate the use of such dummy variables in regression models, consider the following (rather daft) example. Suppose you are investigating a simple consumption function, with income as the only explanatory variable, and you are using annual data. Suppose, further, that you think there is one consumption function

$$C = A_0 + A_1 + BY + U \tag{8.21}$$

for leap years, and a different consumption function

$$C = A_0 + BY + U \tag{8.22}$$

for non-leap years. That is, you think that the intercept is larger by the amount A_1 in leap years than in non-leap years, but in all other respects the relationship is the same. In other words, you believe that the whole relationship shifts upwards by the amount A_1 in leap years.

One obviously *bad* way to proceed would be to separate the data out into sets – one consisting of all the leap years, and the other all the other years – and to use these to investigate separately (8.21) and (8.22) respectively. This would be bad in that it ignores the fact that the two relationships have the same slope and the same residual variance. A far better way to proceed is to use *all* the data to investigate a composite equation which satisfies *both* (8.21) and (8.22). The way to do this is to introduce a dummy variable, denoted by D, which takes the value 1 in leap years and 0 in all other years. Using this new variable, (8.21) and (8.22) can be written jointly as:

$$C = A_0 + A_1 D + BY + U. \tag{8.23}$$

When D is equal to 1 (which is in leap years, by definition) (8.23) reduces to (8.21), and when D is equal to 0 (which is in non-leap years) (8.23) reduces to (8.22). Thus, (8.23) is indeed a composite relationship which includes *both* (8.21) and (8.22). To investigate (8.23), you would carry out a regression of C on D and Y in the usual fashion. The results would not only tell you about the mpc B, but also about the extent of the 'leap year shift' A_1.

The discussion above has assumed that the only change between leap years and non-leap years is in the intercept term. But the method can clearly be extended to cover a change in the slope as well. In this case, the composite equation would be

$$C = A_0 + A_1 D + B_0 Y + B_1(DY) + U, \tag{8.24}$$

where DY is a new variable formed by multiplying D and Y. As you can verify, equation (8.24) implies an mpc of B_0 in non-leap years and an mpc of $(B_0 + B_1)$ in leap years. Equation (8.24) can be investigated by carrying out a regression of C on D, Y and DY in the usual fashion. The results would tell you, *inter alia* about the extent of the change in the mpc between leap years and non-leap years.

In applied econometric studies using quarterly time-series data, a common practice is to use dummy variables to capture any seasonal variations in the relationships under study. Three dummy variables are usually employed, D_1, D_2 and D_3, defined as follows:

$$D_i = \begin{cases} 1 & \text{in } i\text{th quarter} \quad (i = 1, 2, 3) \\ 0 & \text{otherwise.} \end{cases} \tag{8.25}$$

Consider, for example, a simple bivariate relationship between Y and X, the intercept of which is thought to change from quarter to quarter. This can be expressed in the following composite form:

$$Y = A_0 + A_1 D_1 + A_2 D_2 + A_3 D_3 + BX + U. \tag{8.26}$$

As you can verify, this has an intercept of $A_0 + A_1$ in the first quarter, $A_0 + A_2$ in the second quarter, $A_0 + A_3$ in the third, and A_0 in the fourth. Equation (8.26) can be investigated by carrying out a regression of Y on D_1, D_2, D_3 and X in the usual fashion.

Dummy variables are also popularly used to 'take care' of freak observations. A familiar example is the first quarter of 1963 which was a particularly cold quarter; as a consequence the usual functioning of the economic system was distorted. As a result, many macro-economic relationships have a particularly large residual in that quarter. This explains why many applied econometric studies include a 'first-quarter-1963' dummy which takes the value 1 in that quarter, and 0 in all other quarters.

Proxy variables. Sometimes it is impossible to find an empirical counterpart of some theoretical variable. This may be because the theoretical variable is unobservable, or it may simply be because data on the variable have not been collected. In the latter case, it may be possible to remedy the situation by collecting the data oneself, but in many instances (for example if the econometric study requires time-series macro-economic data) this will not be possible. In such circumstances, it will be necessary either to resort to proxy variables, or to find some other way round the problem.

A familiar example of an unobservable variable is Friedman's concept of *permanent income*. In practice, this is usually proxied by some weighted average of actual incomes. Alternatively, Friedman's theory of consumption (which is framed in terms of permanent consumption and permanent income) is expressed in terms of its implications for *actual* income and consumption, and then investigated. This is an example of 'some other way round the problem'.

An example which is on the unobservable/unobserved borderline is that of an *expectation*. Many theories, particularly the more recent ones, include the future expected value of some variable as an explanatory variable. A very familiar example is the inclusion of an expected price inflation term in a Phillips curve (hence obtaining an 'expectations-augmented' Phillips curve). Very occasionally, such expectational data *are* collected, and may be included directly in the equation. (Though, for obvious reasons, one may have doubts about the accuracy of the data.) More usually, however, such data are not collected, and one has to resort to some kind of proxying of expectations. This process (of proxying) usually requires some kind of theory about how expectations are formed. For example, the simplest kind of proxy – namely, that of using the actual value of the variable *last* period as a proxy for its expected value *next* period – implies that economic agents form their expectations in a particularly naive fashion. Alternatively, the currently popular rational-expectations approach – which involves using the actual value of the variable *next* period as a proxy for its expected value *next* period – implies that economic agents are remarkably sophisticated in their expectations-forming ability. In between these two extremes is the adaptive expectations approach, which we shall discuss below.

It is clearly not possible to give any general advice as to what constitutes a good proxy, or a good alternative 'way round the problem'. But a general word of warning can be given: any kind of proxying may give rise to biases and distortions. One should bear the possibility of these in mind when one is assessing the results of the empirical analysis, since these are necessarily affected both by the true relationship and the nature of the proxy.

Adaptive expectations. Until recently, the most popular way of modelling expectations in applied econometric studies has been through the use of an adaptive expectations hypothesis. As the name suggests, such hypotheses relate to the way expectations are *adapted*, rather than the way they are *formed*. The simplest, and most frequently employed, adaptive expectations hypothesis takes the following form:

$$X^e - X^e_{-1} = L(X_{-1} - X^e_{-1}). \tag{8.27}$$

In (8.27) X denotes some variable of interest, and X^e the *expected value of X as viewed from the preceding period*. A suffix '-1' on a variable denotes the lagged value of that variable. Thus X_{-1} is the variable whose values are given by the corresponding values of X in the preceding period. Similarly, X^e_{-1} is a variable whose values are given by the corresponding values of X^e in the preceding period; thus, X^e_{-1} denotes the value that X was expected to take in the preceding period as viewed from the period before that. This lagging notation can obviously be generalized, so that X_{-n} denotes a variable whose values are given by the corresponding values of Xn periods previously. (Note that we continue to use our upper-case convention in denoting variables. Specific values will continue to be denoted by lower-case letters. Thus, if t denotes a specific time period, x_t denotes the value of X in period t, and x_{t-n} denotes (interchangeably, of course) the value of X in period $t - n$, or the value of X_{-n} in period t, or, more generally, the value of X_{-m} in period $t + m - n$.)

Let us now turn to an interpretation of (8.27). The left-hand side is the change in (the one-period ahead) expectations between the preceding period and the present period; it measures the amount by which expectations are revised. On the right-hand side, the term in brackets is the difference between the actual value of X in the preceding period and the value that was expected one period prior to that; this measures the amount by which the preceding period's expectation was in error. Thus, if L lies between 0 and 1 (8.27) states that expectations are revised by some fraction of the preceding error. The *direction* of the revision depends upon the sign of the error: if, in the preceding period, the expectation was too low, then the expectation is revised upwards; if, on the other hand, the expectation was too high, then the expectation is revised downwards. The *magnitude* of the revision depends upon the *magnitude* of the error, and the magnitude of L. For a given value of L, the larger the error the greater the revision; for a given error, the larger L the greater the revision. Polar cases occur when L is 0 and 1: in the former, there is never any revision at all; in the latter, expectations are revised by the full amount of the error.

Equation (8.27) is a *behavioural* hypothesis (which may or may not be true). Recall that it was introduced as one way round the problem of coping with a theory which includes an unobservable expectations variable. It is used in the following manner. Suppose that the original theory of interest is given by:

$$Y = A + BX^e + CZ + U. \qquad (8.28)$$

Thus, Y is postulated to be linearly related to the expected value of X and some other variable Z. (A familiar example is the expectations-augmented Phillips' curve, in which Y is the rate of change of money wages, X is the rate of change of prices, and Z is unemployment.) If, as we have been assuming throughout this discussion, X^e is unobservable, then it must somehow be removed from

(8.28) and replaced by something that is observable. However, simply using (8.27) to substitute for X^e in (8.28) will not work, as the resulting expression will include X^e_{-1}. What needs to be done is the following. First note that (8.27) can be written as

$$X^e - (1 - L)X^e_{-1} = LX_{-1}. \tag{8.29}$$

Now lag every term in (8.28) one period and multiply the resulting expression by $(1 - L)$. This yields

$$(1 - L)Y_{-1} = (1 - L)A + B(1 - L)X^e_{-1} + C(1 - L)Z_{-1} \\ + (1 - L)U_{-1}. \tag{8.30}$$

Now subtract (8.30) from (8.28). This yields

$$Y - (1 - L)Y_{-1} = LA + B[X^e - (1 - L)X^e_{-1}] \\ + C[Z - (1 - L)Z_{-1}] + U - (1 - L)U_{-1}.$$

The term $[X^e - (1 - L)X^e_{-1}]$ can now be replaced by LX_{-1} using (8.29), and if the term involving Y_{-1} is taken to the right-hand side, we get

$$Y = LA + (1 - L)Y_{-1} + BLX_{-1} + CZ - C(1 - L)Z_{-1} + V \tag{8.31}$$

where V is a new residual term, defined by

$$V \equiv U - (1 - L)U_{-1}. \tag{8.32}$$

Now note that equation (8.31) does not contain the unobservable variable X^e, or any of its lagged values. It can, therefore, be subjected to empirical investigation in the usual fashion – to be specific, by regressing Y on Y_{-1}, X_{-1}, Z and Z_{-1}. Note crucially though that (8.31) is a consequence of *both* (8.27) *and* (8.28), that is, of *both* the adaptive expectations hypothesis *and* the original theory. Thus, an empirical investigation of (8.31) is not simply an empirical investigation of the original theory. If the adaptive expectations hypothesis is a poor way of proxying (the adaption of) expectations then biases and distortions may have been introduced by its use. There are also two other problems with the use of this procedure. First, as a glance at (8.31) will reveal, there are five variables (including the constant term) in the equation, but only four parameters (excluding the variance). Thus, a regression of Y on Y_{-1}, X_{-1}, Z and Z_{-1} will give posterior assessments of five coefficients – the intercept, and the coefficients of Y_{-1}, X_{-1}, Z and Z_{-1}. But there are only four under-lying coefficients – namely, A, B, C and L. In other words, the straightforward application of the techniques of section 8.2 ignores the fact that the coefficient of Z_{-1} in (8.31) is the negative of the product of the coefficient of Y_{-1} and the coefficient of Z. Strictly speaking, we need to re-calculate the appropriate posteriors taking this additional information into account. In principle, this is straightforward, though the practical details are beyond the scope of this book. The second problem relates to the residual term in (8.31). As (8.32) shows, V and V_{-1} $(\equiv U_{-1} - (1 - L)U_{-2})$ both depend on U_{-1}. As we shall discuss in the next section, this might imply that our random sampling assumption is necessarily invalid.

Lagged dependent variable. We have already encountered two situations in which the lagged value of the dependent variable appears as an explanatory variable on the right-hand side of the equation. In (8.31) above, the lagged dependent variable appears because of the elimination of the expectational variable through the use of the adaptive expectations hypothesis. In our consumption function illustration of section 8.2, we found that lagged consumption played an important role in the determination of present consumption. In both these cases, the lagged dependent variable captures some kind of habit or persistence effect: a direct effect in the case of consumption, reflecting the importance of habit in determining current behaviour; an indirect effect in (8.31) above, reflecting the influence of expectations on behaviour combined with inertia in the adjustment of such expectations. This habit or persistence effect is found in many, if not most, applied econometric studies using time-series data. If carrying out such a study yourself, you should consider seriously the inclusion of the lagged dependent variable as an explanatory variable – even though the economic theory you are investigating has no role for such a variable. The rationale is usually obvious: the theory is often set in a one-period, or timeless, static framework; while the data are generated in a multiperiod, dynamic real world. We discuss these issues in more detail below.

Partial adjustment. Almost always, the predictions of economic theories are predictions concerning the *optimum* values of the relevant variables. Let us denote the optimum, or desired, value of Y by Y^*, and suppose that economic theory predicts that Y^* is related to X in the following simple fashion:

$$Y^* = A + BX + U. \tag{8.33}$$

In practice, however, because the assumptions of the theory may not be satisfied, there may be some divergence between the actual value of Y and the desired value of Y as given in (8.33). But it would seem reasonable to suppose that there might be some attempt to reduce the extent of the divergence – by partially adjusting the actual value of Y towards the desired value. Such considerations suggest appending the following *partial adjustment* scheme to (8.33):

$$Y - Y_{-1} = L(Y^* - Y_{-1}). \tag{8.34}$$

If L is between 0 and 1, equation (8.34) states that the actual adjustment of Y between two periods is some fraction of the adjustment required to take Y from its preceding value to its current desired value. The magnitude of L determines the extent of the adjustment. The polar cases are when L is 0 and 1: in the former case, there is no adjustment; in the latter case, there is complete adjustment.

The partial adjustment hypothesis (8.34) can be used to eliminate the unobservable variable Y^* from (8.33). First, we have from (8.34) that

$$Y = (1 - L)Y_{-1} + LY^*.$$

We can now substitute for Y^* from (8.33) to get

$$Y = (1 - L)Y_{-1} + LA + LBX + V, \tag{8.35}$$

where V is a new residual term defined by

$$V = LU. \tag{8.36}$$

Equation (8.35) can now be investigated in the usual manner – by regressing Y on Y_{-1} and X. Once again, we have an equation which includes the lagged dependent variable as an explanatory variable; and, once again, because of some kind of habit or persistence effect.

Note that (8.35) contains none of the additional problems that (8.31) contains. In particular, there are the same number of underlying coefficients as coefficients in the final equation. (Information on L is obtained from the coefficient of Y_{-1}; information on LA and LB is obtained from the intercept and coefficient of X; and finally this information is combined to give information on A and B themselves.) Moreover, there is no particular extra reason to suppose that the random sampling assumption is invalid (see section 8.4).

Lagged independent variables. In time-series analyses there is also often a case for the inclusion of lagged values of some of the explanatory variables as additional explanatory variables. The justification is straightforward: the influence of some explanatory variable on the dependent variable may persist for several periods, and it will therefore be necessary to include the appropriate number of lagged independent variables to capture the full effect. Thus an appropriate formulation may be as follows:

$$Y = A + B_0 X + B_1 X_{-1} + \cdots + B_j X_{-j} + CZ + U. \qquad (8.37)$$

In this, the variable Z influences Y for just the current period (so the value of z_t influences y_t but has no effect on y_{t+i} for $i \neq 0$), whereas the variable X influences Y not only in the current period, but also in each of the succeeding j periods. A simple example is the role of income in the consumption function: income in any given period not only affects consumption in that period, but also in several subsequent periods.

In principle, no additional problem is raised by the inclusion of lagged values of explanatory variables as additional explanatory variables. The empirical investigation of an equation such as (8.37) can be carried out in the usual fashion – by regressing Y on X, X_{-1}, ..., X_{-j} and Z. There might, however, be a practical problem raised by the presence of multicollinearity; almost certainly with economic data, X and its lagged values will be associated with each other. As we discussed earlier, this implies that the posterior assessments of the coefficients B_0, B_1, ..., B_j will be relatively imprecise, in that they will have relatively large dispersions. The way round such a problem is, as we discussed earlier, the incorporation of additional information. This may take the form of extra observations, or it may take the form of additional information about the coefficients. In the latter category, a common 'trick of the trade' is to assume that j is infinite (which is not much of an improvement in itself!), and that the coefficients B_0, B_1, B_2, ... form a geometrically declining series. That is,

$$B_j = BL^j \qquad j = 0, 1, 2, \ldots. \qquad (8.38)$$

If (8.38) is substituted into (8.37), we get

$$Y = A + B(X + LX_{-1} + L^2 X_{-2} + \cdots) + CZ + U, \qquad (8.39)$$

which does not look much of an improvement. However, note that, in addition to A, C and the residual variance S^2, there are now only two unknown parameters, B and L, rather than an infinite number B_0, B_1, B_2, ... Note also the following rather ingenious trick. First, lag each term in (8.39) and then multiply the resulting equation by L. This yields

$$LY_{-1} = LA + B(LX_{-1} + L^2 X_{-2} + L^3 X_{-3} + \cdots) \\ + LCZ_{-1} + LU_{-1}. \qquad (8.40)$$

Now subtract (8.40) from (8.39), noting that all the lagged values of X disappear. We thus get

$$Y - LY_{-1} = A(1 - L) + BX + CZ - LCZ_{-1} + U - LU_{-1}.$$

Finally, taking the lagged dependent variable over to the right-hand side, we get

$$Y = LY_{-1} + A(1 - L) + BX + CZ - LCZ_{-1} + V, \qquad (8.41)$$

where V denotes the new residual term, and is given by

$$V = U - LU_{-1}. \qquad (8.42)$$

Equation (8.41) is clearly much easier to investigate than (8.39), from which it was derived: while (8.39) has an infinite number of explanatory variables, (8.41) has just 5, including the constant term. Equation (8.41) can be straightforwardly investigated empirically, by regressing Y on Y_{-1}, X, Z and Z_{-1} in the usual fashion. However, we encounter the same problems that we met in the adaptive expectations model: in (8.41) there are five coefficients, but only four underlying coefficients A, B, C and L. Strictly speaking, therefore, our posterior assessments should be derived using the additional information that the negative of the coefficient of Y_{-1} equals the ratio of the coefficients of Z_{-1} and Z. As we remarked before, the appropriate modifications are conceptually straightforward, though technically beyond the scope of this book.

Distributed lags. Assumption (8.38), that the coefficients of the X variables in (8.37) form a geometrically declining series, is known as the *Koyck distributed* lag assumption. It is one of several, commonly invoked assumptions concerning the appropriate *distributed lag scheme* – that is, concerning the pattern of the B_j. An alternative assumption is to postulate that the B_j form a polynomial series; that is, are given by

$$B_j = P_0 + P_1 j + P_2 j^2 + \cdots + P_k j^k \qquad (j = 0, 1, 2, \ldots) \quad (8.43)$$

where k is the degree of the polynomial. This *polynomial distributed lag scheme* is clearly more flexible than the Koyck scheme; for example, it can encapsulate a situation in which B_j first increases, and then decreases, with j. You may like to consider economic examples in which this would be an appropriate formulation. If k, the degree of the polynomial, is less than the number of lagged variables in the equation, then there will be fewer coefficients to estimate, and hence greater precision in their posterior assessments. The implementation of a polynomial distributed lag scheme is straightforward. Suppose, for example, k is 2, and that the original equation included lagged values of X up to the fifth. Then the appropriate substitution of (8.43) into (8.37) yields:

$$Y = A + P_0 X + (P_0 + P_1 + P_2)X_{-1} + (P_0 + 2P_1 + 4P_2)X_{-2}$$
$$+ (P_0 + 3P_1 + 9P_2)X_{-3} + (P_0 + 4P_1 + 16P_2)X_{-4}$$
$$+ (P_0 + 5P_1 + 25P_2)X_{-5} + CZ + U.$$

After simplification, this yields

$$Y = A + P_0 W_0 + P_1 W_1 + P_2 W_2 + CZ + U, \tag{8.44}$$

where W_1, W_2 and W_3 are given by

$$W_0 \equiv \sum_{j=0}^{5} X_{-j} \qquad W_1 = \sum_{j=0}^{5} jX_{-j} \qquad W_2 = \sum_{j=0}^{5} j^2 X_{-j}. \tag{8.45}$$

Clearly, equation (8.44) can be straightforwardly investigated by a regression of Y on W_0, W_1, W_2 and Z. This leads to posterior assessments of A, P_0, P_1, P_2 and C (in addition to S^2), and hence to posterior assessments of A, B_0, B_1, B_2, B_3, B_4, B_5 and C_1. No additional problems are involved.

There are a number of other distributed lag schemes which are used in applied econometrics, but we do not have the space to consider them here. The interested reader could refer to (the classical text) Kmenta (1971), section 11.4.

Non-linear equations. The general methods for regression developed in chapters 7 and 8 assumed that the basic relationship was *linear in the coefficients.* We have already encountered two situations in which equations non-linear in the coefficients have resulted from the application of certain 'tricks of the trade'. In both these situations, we have noted that our general methods need to be modified to take account of these non-linearities. However, there are other situations where we can *modify the relationships* instead, and thereby obtain relationships linear in the parameters which we can investigate in the usual manner. A good example is the 'Cobb-Douglas' type of relationship:

$$Y = CX_1^{B_1} X_2^{B_2}, \ldots, X_{k-1}^{B_{k-1}} V. \tag{8.46}$$

If you have not encountered this type of equation before, note that if we partially differentiate Y with respect to X_j, we find that

$$\frac{\partial Y/\partial X_j}{Y/X_j} = B_j. \tag{8.47}$$

This states that the elasticity of Y with respect to X_j is B_j, and hence a constant. This is the reason why (8.46) is often called the *constant-elasticity form*.

Although non-linear in the coefficients (the B_j), (8.46) can be converted into an equation which *is* linear in the coefficients by the simple device of taking logarithms. This yields

$$\ln Y = B_0 + B_1 \ln X_1 + B_2 \ln X_2 + \cdots + B_{k-1} \ln X_{k-1} + U,$$

(8.48)

where $U = \ln V$ and $B_0 = \ln C$.

Equation (8.48) can be investigated in the usual manner by regressing $\ln Y$ on $\ln X_1$, $\ln X_2$, ..., and $\ln X_{k-1}$. This is what we did in our cross-section consumption function example of section 7.7.

Note that the equation need not be linear in the *variables*. For example, the quadratic equation

$$Y = A + BX + CX^2 + U,$$

is linear in the coefficients, and can be investigated in the usual manner by regressing Y on X and X^2.

Multicollinearity. We have already commented that the way round the problem of multicollinearity is the incorporation of additional information in one form or another. We have also given a number of examples of how this might be implemented in practice. A further example is the combination of time-series and cross-section data. For instance, suppose we are interested in the demand function

$$Q = A + BP + CY,$$

where Q is quantity demanded, P is price and Y is income. If we were to use only time-series data, we would almost certainly find that P and Y were highly collinear, since both tend to rise steadily through time. As a consequence our posterior assessments of B and C would be relatively imprecise. To improve the precision of these assessments, we could first use cross-section data (in which P is effectively constant) to get a reasonably precise view of C, and then we could use time-series data to get a reasonably precise view of B. Perhaps you might like to consider other such ways round the multicollinearity problem.

This completes our partial survey of the 'tricks of the trade' that are used by applied econometricians. Some of these will be illustrated in section 8.5. Others you will encounter in the literature, and in your own empirical research. Indeed, as you gain experience with the empirical investigation of economic relationships, you will probably develop some of your own 'tricks of the trade'.

8.4   THE VALIDITY OF THE ASSUMPTIONS

We now return to the assumptions underlying our analysis of the bivariate and multivariate regression models contained in chapter 7 and in sections 8.1 to 8.3. You will recall that we assumed throughout this discussion that our observations had been generated by an appropriate 'random sampling' mechanism. It is now time to look in detail at what is meant by this assumption, and to examine the modifications to our analysis that are necessary if this assumption is not satisfied in practice.

For expositional purposes, we will restrict attention throughout this section to the case of the bivariate regression model. However, as will become apparent, the analysis of this section can be straightforwardly generalized to the multivariate case.

Our basic model is as follows (cf. (7.5))

$$Y = A + BX + U$$
$$U \text{ is } N(0, S^2).$$
(8.49)

Furthermore, we have assumed that our observations (x_1, y_1), (x_2, y_2), ..., (x_n, y_n) have been generated in a 'random manner'. To get some intuitive feel of what is meant by this, it helps to consider the observations as having come from n pairs of realizations on X and U; these latter can be denoted by (x_1, u_1), (x_2, u_2), ..., (x_n, u_n). Of course, the following relationship must hold:

$$y_i = A + Bx_i + u_i \qquad (i = 1, 2, \dots, n). \tag{8.50}$$

Thus, we can think of a particular Y value as being generated from a particular X value and a particular U value, combined through (8.50). Of course, what we actually observe is y_i, and not u_i; nor can we work out what u_i is, since we do not know the values of A and B. But it is x_i and u_i that are the 'primitives', not x_i and y_i.

We can, therefore, think of the requirement that our observations be generated in a 'random manner' as equivalent to the requirement that $(x_1, u_1), (x_2, u_2), \dots, (x_n, u_n)$ be generated in a 'random manner'. This requirement can be stated as follows:

(1) The X values $(x_1, x_2, \dots, x_n)$ are either fixed or generated from some distribution;

(2) The U values $(u_1, u_2, ..., u_n)$ are generated randomly from a normal distribution with mean 0 and variance S^2 (see (8.49));
(3) The X values and U values are generated independently of each other.

Before proceeding, we ought to qualify (1) slightly, by adding the restriction that the distribution which generates the X values should not depend on A, B or S. For if it did, then the X values themselves would contain information about A, B or S. We also ought to draw attention to the fact that the X values need *not* be generated randomly. Our analysis would still be valid even if there was extreme non-randomness as implied, for example, by the generating mechanism

$$X_{i+1} = X_i + 1 \qquad (i = 1, 2, ..., n - 1).$$

However, *it is crucial that the U values be generated randomly from* $N(0, S^2)$ (so that the observations accurately reflect the underlying model (8.49)), *and that the X and U values be independent.*

Since (1) above is relatively harmless, let us focus attention on (2) and (3). To clarify what is implied by (2), let us subdivide it into its four component parts:

(2a) the U values are generated from a distribution with mean 0;
(2b) the U values are generated from a distribution with variance S^2;
(2c) the U values are generated from a normal distribution;
(2d) the U values are generated independently of each other.

(Recall, from chapter 5, that (2d) is what is implied by a *random* generating mechanism.) Let us now consider each of (2a) to (2d) and (3) separately, and, for each of these assumptions, explore how our analysis may need to be modified if we believe that the assumption is not valid in a particular application. As we shall see, the basic procedure in each case is to transform the model in such a way that the transformed model *does* obey assumptions (1), (2) and (3). Then we carry out the usual regression analysis on the transformed relationship.

Assumption (2a): that the U values are generated from a distribution with mean 0. If this is not true, then the U values must be generated from a distribution with some other mean. If this other mean is constant, equal to M say, then there is no problem – the relationship (8.49) is simply re-written

$$Y = (A + M) + BX + (U - M),$$

or, more succinctly,

$$Y = A' + BX + U', \tag{8.51}$$

where $A' \equiv A + M$ and where U', the new residual term, equals $U - M$. It is clear that U' has a zero mean, and therefore we can apply our usual regression analysis to the transformed relationship (8.51). If, on the other hand, the mean of U is not constant, but instead is given by

$$U = CZ + U',$$

say, where Z is some observable variable, and U' is a new residual term with a zero mean, then the original relationship (8.49) can be re-written

$$Y = A + BX + CZ + U', \tag{8.52}$$

which can be investigated in the usual fashion by regressing Y on X and Z.

Thus, treatment of the violation of assumption (2a) is straightforward as long as one knows the factors influencing the (non-zero) mean of U.

Assumption (2b): that the U values are generated from a distribution with variance S^2. This assumption essentially means that the variance of the residual term is constant, and therefore does not vary with X or with any other factor. This assumption is usually referred to as the assumption of *homoscedasticity* of the residuals. If it is violated, then the residuals are said to be *heteroscedastic*. Once again, if the form of the violation, that is, the form of the heteroscedasticity, is known, then the appropriate procedure is straightforward. Consider, for example, a situation in which you know that the standard deviation of U is proportional to X – so that the larger is X, the larger is the dispersion of the X values. This is a case quite frequently encountered in economic applications. We can express it as follows

$$\text{sd } X = SX, \tag{8.53}$$

where S is the (known or unknown) factor of proportionality. Equivalently, (8.53) can be expressed as

$$\text{var } X = S^2 X^2. \tag{8.54}$$

It is clear that if (8.54) holds, then assumption (2b) is violated. However, we can easily rectify the situation as follows. Divide the original relationship (8.49) throughout by X (for reasons which will become apparent shortly). This yields

$$Y/X = A/X + B + U/X.$$

This can be written, rather more succinctly, as

$$Y' = AX' + B + U', \tag{8.55}$$

where $Y' \equiv Y/X$, $X' \equiv 1/X$ and $U' \equiv U/X$.

The standard deviation of U', the residual term in the transformed relationship (8.55), is now constant, a fact which can be shown as follows:

$$\text{sd } U' = \text{sd } (U/X) = (\text{sd } U)/X = SX/X = S.$$

(In this, the first equality is an identity; the second follows from the fact that if a variable is multiplied by a constant, then its standard deviation is multiplied by the same constant; the third equality uses (8.53); and the fourth equality is an identity.) Thus, the variance in (8.55) is a constant, and so assumption (2b) is satisfied as far as (8.55) is concerned. Thus, our usual methods can be used to investigate (8.55) – by carrying out a regression of Y' on X'. This provides posterior assessments of A, B and S, as desired. (Note that the intercept in (8.49) is the slope in (8.55) and *vice versa*.)

Thus, treatment of the violation of assumption (2b) is straightforward as long as one knows the form of the heteroscedasticity.

Assumption (2c): that the U values are generated from a normal distribution. If this is violated, then the U values must be generated from some other distribution. If the form of this other distribution is known, so that the distribution can be characterized in terms of one or more parameters, then Bayes' theorem can be applied, and the posterior assessments derived, in the usual manner. Clearly, the posterior assessments depend critically on the particular form taken by the U distribution; thus, no *general* conclusions about these assessments can be made. Each case would have to be treated individually. However, as we have remarked before, most econometric studies assume normality (and justify this assumption by recourse to the Central Limit Theorem). So we do not feel that we are letting you, the reader, down unduly by not giving details of alternative specifications. Except for special models (such as those involving limited dependent variables), you are unlikely to need results relating to non-normal residual terms.

Assumption (2d): that the U values are generated independently of each other. This assumption implies that each of the n observations constitutes a separate, individual item of information. If, in contrast, the U values were not independent, then the information contained in one observation would partly overlap with the information contained in some other observation(s). We would have to take this into account when deriving our posterior assessments. Moreover, the *form* of these posterior assessments would depend crucially on the particular *form* that the dependence between the U values took. However, as before, if we know the form of the dependence, we can, in principle, make the appropriate modifications to our analysis. Consider, for example, the following type of dependence, which is frequently encountered when using economic time series:

$$U = rU_{-1} + U'. \tag{8.56}$$

This equation states that the residual in some period is partly determined by the residual in the preceding period and partly by some new residual term U'. Let us suppose that the values of U' *are* generated independently of each other. Equation (8.56) therefore states that there is partial dependence between successive values of the residual term in the original relationship (8.49); the particular form specified in (8.56) is termed a *first-order autoregressive scheme*. (More generally, an nth-order autoregressive scheme states that U is dependent on all its lagged values up to and including U_{-n}.) For the time being, we shall assume that the coefficient of U_{-1} in (8.56) is known.

Clearly, if (8.56) holds, then the U values are *not* generated independently of each other, and so assumption (2d) is violated. Accordingly, we cannot apply our usual inference procedures directly to (8.49). However, as we have done before, we can transform the original relationship in such a way that the transformed relationship *does* satisfy all the usual assumptions. (Before reading on, you may like to think yourself about how this may be done.) The original relationship is

$$Y = A + BX + U. \tag{8.57}$$

If we lag each term one period, and then multiply the resulting expression by r, we get

$$rY_{-1} = Ar + BrX_{-1} + rU_{-1}. \tag{8.58}$$

Let us now subtract (8.58) from (8.57); this yields

$$Y - rY_{-1} = A(1 - r) + B(X - rX_{-1}) + (U - rU_{-1}). \tag{8.59}$$

Equation (8.56) can now be used to simplify the residual term, giving

$$Y' = A' + BX' + U', \tag{8.60}$$

where $Y' \equiv Y - rY_{-1}$, $A' \equiv A(1 - r)$ and $X' \equiv X - rX_{-1}$.

By our supposition above, the residual term in (8.60) *does* satisfy assumption (2d). We can, therefore, investigate the transformed relationship (8.60) in the usual fashion by regressing Y' on X'. (Note that both Y' and X' are known functions of the original variables.) This provides posterior assessments of A', B and the variance of U', from which can be derived posterior assessments of A, B and S^2 (since $A' \equiv A(1 - r)$ and var $U' = (1 - r^2)S^2$). Once again, we have got round the problem of a violated assumption by transforming the original relationship in such a way that the transformed relationship *does* obey all the assumptions.

The above discussion has assumed that the value of r in (8.56) is known. In practice this may well not be the case, so we would have to express (8.56) as

$$U = RU_{-1} + U'. \tag{8.61}$$

We can, however, carry out the same steps as before, thereby deriving an equation which is the appropriate counterpart of (8.59), namely

$$Y - RY_{-1} = A(1 - R) + B(X - RX_{-1}) + (U - RU_{-1}). \tag{8.62}$$

Again, we can use (8.61) to simplify the residual term in (8.62), but we cannot introduce new variables $Y' \equiv Y - RY_{-1}$ and $X' \equiv X - RX_{-1}$, since R is unknown. (In other words, it is now impossible to calculate the observed values of (X', Y') corresponding to the observed values of (X, Y).) However, we can write (8.62) as follows:

$$Y = A(1 - R) + RY_{-1} + BX - BRX_{-1} + U'. \tag{8.63}$$

At first glance, it appears that we can investigate this empirically by carrying out a regression of Y on Y_{-1}, X and X_{-1}. However, we encounter once again a problem we met twice in section 8.3: in (8.63) there are four variables (including the dummy constant variable), and so the regression analysis will provide posterior assessments of the four coefficients – namely, $A(1 - R)$, R, B and $-BR$. But, there are only three underlying coefficients A, B and R. The conventional regression analysis ignores the fact that the four coefficients in (8.63) are inter-related.

This is not to say that our general methodology cannot be applied to (8.63). Of course it can; and it will take into account the important extra information that the four coefficients in (8.63) are inter-related. Unfortunately, the technical details are beyond the scope of this book. Moreover, the actual results (which can be found in Zellner (1971) section 4.1) concerning the posterior assessments of A, B and R cannot be stated in terms of familiar distributions. Indeed, as Zellner shows, one needs to resort to numerical integration to determine these posterior assessments. However, with the advent of modern computers, numerical integration is now relatively straight-forward, and there are several programs which will do the necessary calculations. One such program is *B34T* (a stepwise regression program which was developed under the supervision of Professor Zellner); general information about this and other Bayesian pro-grams can be found in Zellner (1980) chapter 27 ('Bayesian Com-puter Programs', S. James Press). If you do not have any such Bayesian programs on your computer, you are strongly advised to obtain one or more. (See Appendix A5 for more details.)

Assumption (3): that the X values and U values are generated indepen-dently of each other. In contrast to assumption (2), the role of which in the statement of the relationship (8.49) is immediate, the signifi-cance of assumption (3) is not obvious. It may therefore be useful, before discussing the consequences of its violation, to illustrate its importance in the inference process. Our illustration will be deliber-ately extreme. Suppose the relationship between Y and X is given by

$$Y = X + U,$$
$$U \text{ is } N(0, 1) \tag{8.64}$$

that is, $A = 0$, $B = 1$ and $S^2 = 1$.

Suppose we have ten observations, and that the U values are gener-ated randomly from $N(0, 1)$ as required by assumption (2); suppose they are as follows (I took these from a table of unit normal random numbers):

0.250	1.265	−0.927	−0.227	−0.577
−0.291	−2.828	0.247	−0.584	0.446.

Finally, suppose crucially that, in flagrant violation of assumption (3), the X values are completely dependent on the U values as speci-fied in the following equation:

$$X = 4 + 2U. \tag{8.65}$$

Then the X values corresponding to the above U values are

| 4.500 | 6.530 | 2.146 | 3.546 | 2.846 |
| 3.418 | −1.656 | 4.494 | 2.832 | 4.892. |

Of course, we do not observe the U values, but instead the Y values as jointly generated by the X values and U values through (8.64). These Y values are as follows:

| 4.750 | 7.795 | 1.219 | 3.319 | 2.269 |
| 3.127 | −4.484 | 4.741 | 2.248 | 5.338. |

Now examine the (X, Y) observations. (Plotting them on graph paper may help.) You will see that *all* ten lie *exactly* along the following straight line

$$Y = -2 + 1.5X.$$

Thus, if you were unaware of the dependence between X and U, your posterior assessments of A, B and S^2 would be degenerate at the values -2, 1.5 and 0 respectively. In other words, you would believe with certainty that A, B and S^2 were -2, 1.5 and 0 respectively, when, in fact, they were 0, 1 and 1. *You would be very badly mistaken.*

This example, although extreme, does make the point that the validity of assumption (3) is crucial for the validity of the inferences drawn in chapter 7 and sections 8.1 to 8.3. Of course, as before, if we know the *form* of the violation of this assumption, we can make the appropriate modifications to our analysis. We will give an example in chapter 9.

This concludes our discussion of the consequences of the violation of the assumptions underlying our earlier analysis. As we have shown, the basic procedure is straightforward: we simply transform the original relationship in such a way that the transformed relationship *does* obey the assumptions. Then we carry out the usual regression analysis on the transformed relationship, 'translating' if necessary the conclusions of this analysis into statements about the original relationship. In many cases, this procedure works well – as long as we know the form of the violation.

In theory, therefore, there is no real problem if the assumptions underlying our earlier analysis are replaced by some other assumptions: we simply modify the posterior assessments appropriately. Given any set of assumptions, we can, in principle, always apply the general methodology of Bayesian inference propounded in this book.

In practice, however, we often encounter two problems. First, there may be a *technical* problem – in that the mathematical analysis is excessively complex. But this problem is increasingly being circumvented by the use of computers to solve the mathematics numerically. The second problem is more serious, and concerns the correct specification of the underlying model and of the mechanism generating the observations. In theory, there is no problem: one simply adopts the most general set of assumptions that one thinks necessary. In practice, this may not be feasible, since it might imply an unnecessarily complicated analysis. So in practice, one must always keep in mind the possibility that one's underlying assumptions are incorrect. Classical statisticians face a similar problem. To that end, they use a series of 'test statistics' which are designed to detect possible violations of the assumptions. We cannot go into detail here, though we should mention one of the most popular of these test statistics – namely, the *Durbin-Watson statistic*. This is designed to detect the violation of assumption (2d) – particularly a violation in the form of a first-order autoregressive scheme (see (8.56)). It takes values in the range 0 to 4: a value around 2 is expected if assumption (2d) is not violated; a value nearer 0 or 4 suggests violation. For further details, the reader could consult any classical text (for example, Kmenta (1971)).

8.5   AN EXAMPLE OF ECONOMETRICS IN ACTION

Most of the material of this book has been concerned with the empirical investigation of a *given* model using a *given* (or, at least, pre-specified) set of data. In practice, this constitutes only part of the art of applied econometrics; the other, possibly the major, part is concerned with *model specification* and *data selection*. Any discussion of econometrics in action is necessarily concerned with these wider issues; this section is no exception.

We use as our illustrative example the empirical investigation of the determinants of the *demand for money*. A glance at any economic theory text will reveal that the theoretical specification is apparently straightforward: the theory states that the demand for money is a function of income and the rate of interest. However, a glance at any applied econometrics text will soon dispel this illusion of simplicity – most estimated equations seem to include many other explanatory variables. What are the reasons for this apparent discrepancy?

One obvious reason is that discussed in section 8.3 above – namely, the gap between the world of the theory and the real world (at least as evidenced by the economic data at our disposal). Let us look at this in more detail. We may write our simple theoretical proposition as

$$M = f(Y, R), \tag{8.66}$$

where M is the demand for money, Y is income, R is the rate of interest and $f(.,.)$ is some function. Before we can begin our empirical investigation, we need to decide what are the appropriate empirical counterparts of M, Y and R, and we need to determine the appropriate functional form (or set of forms) for f. Let us look at each of these in turn. Presumably, M is the *desired* demand for money. However, in practice it is difficult to observe this; instead, one observes the *actual holding* of money, which may well be different from the desired demand. To reconcile the two, we need to specify the relationship between actual holdings (the M of the real world) and desired holdings (the M of the theory). One way of doing this is to use the *partial adjustment hypothesis* which we introduced, and justified, in section 8.3. Similarly, it would appear that the Y of the theory is *expected* income, while the Y of the real world is *actual* income. To reconcile the two, some kind of expectations scheme is required, such as the *adaptive expectations* scheme, introduced in section 8.3. It could also be argued that the R of the theory is also an expectations variable, which should be treated in a similar fashion, but let us disregard this possiblity at this stage. The question of the appropriate functional form is always a difficult one, and theory does little to guide us. Let us, therefore, adopt the simplest formulation for the moment, and assume that the relationship is linear.

We can summarize the above discussion as follows. We first write the theoretical specification (8.66) more precisely as

$$M^* = A' + B'Y^e_{+1} + C'R \tag{8.67}$$

where M^* denotes the desired demand for money and Y^e_{+1} denotes (next period's) expected income. These variables are related to M (the actual holding of money) and Y (actual income) through the partial adjustment scheme and the adaptive expectations scheme respectively, as follows:

$$M - M_{-1} = L(M^* - M_{-1}) \quad \text{or} \quad M = LM^* + (1 - L)M_{-1}$$

$$\tag{8.68}$$

and

$$Y^e_{+1} - Y^e = K(Y - Y^e) \qquad \text{or} \qquad Y^e_{+1} = KY + (1 - K)Y^e.$$
(8.69)

(cf. (8.34) and (8.27).)

We now 'solve' equations (8.67) to (8.69) to get a model specification which contains only observable variables. We do this by first eliminating M^* between (8.67) and (8.68), which yields

$$M = A'L + B'LY^e_{+1} + C'LR + (1 - L)M_{-1}.$$
(8.70)

We now eliminate Y^e_{+1} from (8.70) using (8.69) (in exactly the same way as X^e was eliminated from (8.28) using (8.27) to yield (8.31)). This gives

$$M = A + BY + CR + DR_{-1} + EM_{-1} + FM_{-2},$$
(8.71)

where $A \equiv A'LK$, $B = B'LK$, $C = C'L$, $D = -(1 - K)C'L$, $E = (2 - K - L)$ and $F = (1 - K)(1 - L)$.

(An aside is necessary at this stage. You will note that (8.71) has six coefficients, namely A to F. These are, in turn, defined in terms of the five 'primitive' coefficients A' to C', K and L. Therefore, there is a dependence between the six coefficients of (8.71), and, strictly speaking, we ought to take this dependence into account when investigating (8.71). However, to do so properly would take us beyond the scope of this book. Accordingly, we shall ignore this dependence. End of aside.)

Equation (8.71) is an 'investigable' version of (8.67). If we now include a residual term U, we can now subject it to empirical investigation using the tools developed earlier in this chapter. If you compare (8.71) with specifications adopted by other researchers (see, for several examples, Mayes (1981), chapter 5) you will see that it is a fairly typical form. Variations on the theme include log-linear specifications, the addition of the price level as an additional explanatory variable (an issue which we shall discuss shortly) and the inclusion of extra lagged terms. On this latter point, it is increasingly common practice amongst applied econometricians to include a large number of lagged variables (both dependent and independent) as additional explanatory variables. In principle, this is a satisfactory procedure, as it is more important that the model specified errs on the side of excessive generality rather than excessive particularity. After all, if we have included too many variables, the data can convey that fact by implying that their associated coefficients are close to zero; but if we have omitted some key variables, there is no (mechanical or obvious) way that the data can warn us of the omission. Having said that, we should remember that a given data set contains only a given amount of information, and we would be foolish to squander it by using it to tell us something we should have known already.

Let us now return to the question of whether the price level should be included as a separate explanatory variable. To answer this, we first need to specify rather more carefully whether M and Y in (8.71) are in *nominal* or *real* terms. The published data on M are, of course, in nominal terms, but we could deflate it by some suitable price index if we so wished. In looking to theory for some guidance, we find a measure of ambiguity. Some interpretations suggest that both M and Y should be in real terms, and some suggest that both should be in nominal terms. Some others suggest that while M should be in nominal terms, the (nominal) Y on the right-hand side should be split up into its two components X and P, real income and the price level (where nominal $Y = PX$, of course). This apparently would allow for the presence of money illusion.

Let us remain agnostic on this issue, and include as an alternative specification to (8.71) the following:

$$M = A + B_1 X + B_2 P + CR \\ + DR_{-1} + EM_{-1} + FM_{-2}, \quad (8.72)$$

in which real income and the price level appear as separate explanatory variables.

We now turn to the more specific question of data selection. (For obvious reasons I use UK data, with which I am most familiar. If you are more familiar with another country's data, you should consider what would be the relevant counterparts.) First M; as you are no doubt aware, there is continuing (and inevitable) controversy over what precisely money is. Consequently, there are a variety of candidates, ranging from very narrow definitions, such as M1, to very broad definitions, such as PSL2. (These abbreviations are now fairly generally accepted internationally; you should check with your own domestic monetary statistics as to what they stand for, and how they are defined.) For each, presumably, there is an appropriate demand function. Let us, rather arbitrarily, select just two of these for the purposes of our illustration – namely, M1 and sterling M3. These are, respectively, a narrowly and a fairly broadly defined measure.

For income, we select the 'obvious candidate' GDP (Gross Domestic Product), though possibly you may prefer some other candidate (such as Personal Disposable Income, or Total Final Expenditure). For (nominal) Y, we take GDP in *current* prices, and for (real) X, we take GDP in *constant* prices. The price level P is simply calculated as the ratio of Y to X. When we come to R, the rate of interest, we are confronted with an embarrassingly large choice – ranging from very-short-term interest rates (such as Treasury Bill rate) to very-long-term interest rates (such as the yield on undated government stock). Some guidance is offered by economic theory, but this is not conclusive – unless one has overwhelming faith in certain of the various schools of thought. However, we can narrow down the choice somewhat, and restrict the range of possibilities under consideration to just two – a short-term rate and a long-term rate. But let us remain agnostic as to which is the correct one. We take as our representatives of these two possibilities the three-month Treasury Bill rate and the yield on British Government long-dated (twenty years) stock; we denote these by R^S and R^L respectively. Finally, we need to decide the periodicity of the data, and the data period. As quarterly data is available in the UK we use that, and since *Economic Trends Annual Supplement 1982* contains all the data we require for the period from the third quarter of 1970 to the first quarter of 1981, we use that as our data period. This gives us a total of forty-three observations. We use seasonally adjusted data where available (on M, Y, X and P), though clearly this is a matter of taste. (The data on X and Y is from *ETAS 1982*, pp. 7–8, that on M1 and sterling M3 from pp. 146–147, and that on R^S and R^L from pp. 195–197.)

To summarize: for each of our two independent variables (M1 and sterling M3) there are four possible specifications – equations (8.71) and (8.72) each with either R^S or R^L as R. As we have already noted, we assume that we regard all four of these specifications as being equally likely. Within *each*, we shall follow the practice of chapter 7 and sections 8.1 to 8.4 in assuming total prior ignorance about the parameters, though, in principle, the analysis can equally well be conducted with alternative priors. (For example, a more sensible prior on E and F would assume that they were between 0 and 1.) We report below the results of the empirical investigation (standard errors are in parentheses).

Dependent variable M1

(1) $\quad M = 978 + 0.0623\ Y - 106\ R^S$
$\qquad\ \ \ (388)\quad (0.0393)\qquad (42.3)$
$\qquad\qquad + 6.23\ R^S_{-1} + 0.906\ M_{-1} + 0.0326\ M_{-2}$
$\qquad\qquad\ \ (52.4)\qquad\quad (0.193)\qquad\quad (0.172)$

$$\hat{s} = 324.66 \qquad n = 41.$$

(2) $\quad M = 780 + 0.0589\ Y - 97.3\ R^L$
$\qquad\ \ \ (693)\quad (0.0486)\qquad (75.2)$
$\qquad\qquad + 74.4\ R^L_{-1} + 1.16\ M_{-1} - 0.256\ M_{-2}$
$\qquad\qquad\ \ (83.9)\qquad\quad (0.165)\qquad\quad (0.164)$

$$\hat{s} = 399.31 \qquad n = 41.$$

(3) $\quad M = -4471 + 0.256\ X + 1534\ P - 116.6\ R^S$
$\qquad\ \ \ (1707)\ (0.0843)\qquad\ (779)\qquad\ (38.2)$
$\qquad\qquad - 7.49\ R^S_{-1} + 0.727\ M_{-1} + 0.190\ M_{-2}$
$\qquad\qquad\ \ (47.3)\qquad\quad (0.184)\qquad\quad (0.166)$

$$\hat{s} = 296.51 \qquad n = 41.$$

(4) $\quad M = -3514 + 0.219\ X + 1909\ P - 117.3\ R^L$
$\qquad\ \ \ (2455)\quad (0.133)\qquad (1130)\qquad (74.7)$
$\qquad\qquad + 51.3\ R^L_{-1} + 1.06\ M_{-1} - 0.206\ M_{-2}$
$\qquad\qquad\ \ (83.6)\qquad\quad (0.176)\qquad\quad (0.163)$

$$\hat{s} = 392.44 \qquad n = 41.$$

Dependent variable sterling M3

(1) $\quad M = 688 + 0.0890\ Y + 33.0\ R^S$
$\qquad\ \ \ (457)\quad (0.0652)\qquad (73.7)$
$\qquad\qquad - 27.0\ R^S_{-1} + 1.27\ M_{-1} - 0.333\ M_{-2}$
$\qquad\qquad\ \ (76.9)\qquad\quad (0.169)\qquad\quad (0.186)$

$$\hat{s} = 650.43 \qquad n = 41.$$

(2) $\quad M = 1846 - 0.0753\ Y - 190\ R^L$
$\qquad\ \ \ (607)\quad (0.0767)\qquad (132)$
$\qquad\qquad - 60.5\ R^L_{-1} + 1.04\ M_{-1} + 0.085\ M_{-2}$
$\qquad\qquad\ \ (131)\qquad\quad (0.196)\qquad\quad (0.239)$

$$\hat{s} = 591.23 \qquad n = 41.$$

(3) $M = -2102 + 0.121\ X + 2283\ P + 29.1\ R^S$
      $(4351)\quad (0.209)\qquad (1894)\qquad (79.4)$
      $\qquad\quad -\ 22.4\ R^S_{-1} +\quad 1.29\ M_{-1} -\ 0.363\ M_{-2}$
      $\qquad\qquad (85.0)\qquad\quad (0.181)\qquad\quad (0.212)$

$$\hat{s} = 663.07\qquad n = 41.$$

(4) $M =\quad 871 + 0.0514X - 1783\ P - 200\ R^L$
      $(3715)\quad (0.171)\qquad (1979)\qquad (136)$
      $\qquad\quad -\ 35.4\ R^L_{-1} +\quad 1.08\ M_{-1} + 0.0317M_{-2}$
      $\qquad\qquad (134)\qquad\quad (0.199)\qquad\quad (0.242)$

$$\hat{s} = 597.78\qquad n = 41.$$

We will keep our discussion of these results brief, leaving amplification to the reader. First consider the results for M1. A comparison of $\hat{s}$ (the modified residual standard deviation) in (1) with that in (2), and a comparison of $\hat{s}$ in (3) with that in (4) shows clearly that the data favour the hypothesis that R^S is the relevant interest rate as far as M1 is concerned. (Using result (7.45) of section 7.6 the posterior probabilities of specifications (1) and (2) are in the ratio 2117 to 1 ($\equiv 324.66^{-41}$ to 399.31^{-41}), while the corresponding ratio for specifications (3) and (4) is almost 10 000 to 1. Note, however, that result (7.45) cannot be used to compare the posterior probabilities of (1) and (3) (or (2) and (4)) since these specifications differ in the number of explanatory variables.) Within specification (1), the above empirical results imply the following mean effects:

| | Leads to an increase in M of | |
An increase:	(in the short run)	(in the long run)
of Y by £1 million	£0.0623 million	£1.015 million
of R^S by 1 (percentage point)	−£106 million	−£1625 million

(To put these figures in perspective it may be useful to note that M1 ranged from £10 210 million to £31 850 million during the observation period, and R^S ranged from 4.37 to 16.72.) The long-run income effect is clearly of a sensible order of magnitude, and the interest-rate effect is economically quite significant. Obviously, there is some margin of uncertainty attached to these mean effects, as the standard errors indicate. The following 95 per cent probability intervals are implied:

for the coefficient of Y: $(-0.0175, 0.1421)$
for the coefficient of R^S: $(-192, -20)$
for the coefficient of R^S_{-1}: $(-100, 112)$
for the coefficient of M_{-1}: $(0.514, 1.298)$
for the coefficient of M_{-2}: $(-0.317, 0.382)$

Thus the coefficients of Y, R^S and M_{-1} are the most precisely determined. Additionally, they have the signs and the orders of magnitude required by economic theory – which is reassuring. A comparison of (8.71) with the empirical findings indicates that one can be reasonably confident that K is close to 1. This implies (from (8.69)) that expected income equals actual income, or that the appropriate income variable in the original specification was actual income. Indeed, if we investigate the model specified by (8.71) with K put equal to 1, we get the following result:

$$M = 1003 + 0.0667\ Y - 98.6\ R^S$$
$$(275)\quad (0.0283)\quad (19.3)$$
$$+ 0.930\ M_{-1}. \qquad \hat{s} = 316.20$$
$$(0.0520)$$
$$\tag{8.73}$$

This is clearly satisfactory. Indeed, it is probably the 'best' of all the specifications. Though note that it is just a special case of specification (1) – with K put equal to 1, and hence the coefficients of R^S_{-1} and M_{-2} put equal to zero. (An aside for the purists: strictly speaking, our prior specification should have attached a non-zero probability to K being 1. Then the emergence of (8.73) as the 'best' specification could be formally justified by its having the largest posterior probability. However, this formal justification takes us beyond the scope of this book. End of aside.)

The results for sterling M3 are less satisfactory. Superficially, the results do suggest that R^L is the more appropriate interest rate. However, the signs of the mean coefficients on Y in (2) and on P in (4) disagree with economic theory. Many of the coefficients are very imprecisely determined (as indicated by the widths of their posterior probability intervals), with the exception of the coefficient on M_{-1}. One is tempted to conclude that other specifications of the demand for sterling M3 need to be sought.

This rather negative conclusion for sterling M3 highlights a continuing problem for the (Bayesian as well as Classical) econometrician. While, strictly speaking, one ought to specify all the possible models in advance (and, therefore, not allow them to be influenced by the data), in practice this is not always possible. But if the data determines the model, then the data is 'counted twice'. Possible ways round this seemingly intractable problem (which takes us beyond the scope of this book) can be found in the splendid book by Leamer (1978).

8.6 SUMMARY

We have covered a lot of ground in this chapter, starting on the relatively solid foundation of the multivariate extension of the linear bivariate regression model of chapter 7, and finishing on the relatively shifting sands of econometrics in action.

As we saw in section 8.2, the multivariate regression model is the natural extension of the bivariate model. Given total prior ignorance, the posterior assessments of the parameters are in familiar forms: to be specific, in the form of t distributions for the coefficients, and in the form of a chi-square distribution for the residual variance. The key results concerning these posterior assessments, given in (8.4), are easily implemented given the values of the least-squares coefficients, the standard errors of the coefficients and the modified residual variance. All these are routinely calculated by many computer packages.

We then moved on to discuss, in section 8.3, various 'tricks of the trade' that are typically employed by applied econometricians. Most of these are devices which help bridge the gap between the world of economic theory and the 'real world' as manifested in economic statistics. The fact that these devices need to be employed is one of the reasons why applied econometrics is an art as well as a science.

Section 8.4 then returned to the assumptions underlying the analyses of the earlier sections, and asked how the analyses would need to be modified if some of these assumptions were violated. We showed that, in principle, there was no problem as long as we knew the form of the violation. Bayesian analysis could still proceed. Indeed, we saw that in many cases, a simple transformation of the original problem was all that was required. However, in certain circumstances it may not be clear what the appropriate alternative assumptions are; in such cases, the researcher necessarily needs to exercise his judgement.

We tried to give some insights into this art (of applied econometrics) in section 8.5, when we gave an example of econometrics in action. But the only real way to get genuine insights is to carry out an investigation of your own. I hope you are sufficiently inspired to do so.

8.7 EXERCISES

8.1 Investigate empirically an aggregate consumption function of your own design, using the data on consumption described in section 8.2 (if you live in the UK) or the equivalent data for your own country (if you live outside the UK). Obtain a 95 per cent probability interval for the (short-run) marginal propensity to consume.

8.2 By use of the 'tricks' described in section 8.3 or otherwise, investigate empirically an expectations-augmented Phillips curve using appropriate economic data for your country.

8.3 Investigate empirically a cross-sectional consumption function for a consumption good of your choice using data from a copy of the *Family Expenditure Survey* (if you live in the UK) or the equivalent data for your own country (if you live outside the UK).

8.4 By referring to the discussion in section 8.2, speculate as to the form of the posterior assessment for S^2 in a situation in which the coefficients $b_0, b_1, \ldots, b_{k-1}$ are *known*. What would be the assessment if some of the coefficients were known (say $b_0, \ldots, b_m$) and the rest unknown?

8.5 In the illustrative example of section 8.2, the posterior probability of formulation (8.16b) was considerably greater than that of the other two formulations. Does this (statistical) finding make sense in *economic* terms?

8.6 Refer to the discussion of dummy variables in section 8.3. What equation would you investigate empirically if you thought that the 'leap-year effect' changed the slope but not the intercept of the consumption function?

8.7 Suppose an empirical investigation of equation (8.23) led to the following result:

$$C = \;\; 523 \;\; + \;\; 32.1 \, D + \;\; 0.692 \, Y \qquad \hat{s} = 22.9$$
$$\quad\;\; (21.3) \quad (66.6) \quad\;\; (0.111) \qquad n = 43$$

(standard errors in parentheses).
Assess the importance of the 'leap-year effect'.

8.8 Refer to section 8.4. Suppose that, in a particular application, you know that assumptions (1), (2) and (3) are all true except for assumption (2b). Moreover, suppose you know that the variance of U is given by

$$\text{var } U = S^2 X.$$

Discuss how you should transform the original relationship so as to obtain a transformed relationship for which *all* the assumptions *are* valid.

Repeat this exercise for the case when the variance of U is given by

$$\text{var } U = S^2/X^2.$$

8.9 Refer to section 8.4. Suppose that, in a particular application, you know that assumptions (1), (2) and (3) are all true except for assumption (2d). Moreover, suppose you know that the U values are dependent upon each other as described in the equation:

$$U = r_0 U_{-1} + r_1 U_{-2} + V,$$

where the V values are independent of each other, and where (as the notation indicates) r_0 and r_1 are known. Discuss how you should transform the original relationship so as to obtain a transformed relationship for which *all* the assumptions are valid.

Repeat this exercise for the case when the dependence takes the form

$$U = rU_{-4} + V.$$

8.10 By referring to section 7.8, speculate as to the *means* of the posterior assessments for predictions of the actual and the mean values of Y for a given set of X values (say, $x_{10}, x_{20}, \ldots, x_{k-1, 0}$) in the multivariate model. Discuss *intuitively* the factors which determine the dispersion of these assessments.

8.11 Choose an area of economics that particularly interests you. Express the alternative theories (including your own) in testable form. Find the appropriate data and investigate which theory best explains the evidence.

8.12 Select, from the reading list for your macroeconomics course, a reference on applied econometrics. Write a concise summary of the main findings addressed to a reader unfamiliar with statistics and econometrics.

8.13 The following consumption functions (quoted from Bridge, 1971), were fitted by (ordinary) least squares, using annual data for the US from 1929–41 and 1947–62.

$$C = 4.95 + 0.6640\ Y + 0.2752\ C_{-1} \qquad R^2 = 0.998$$
$$\quad (1.71) \quad (0.0631) \qquad (0.0736)$$

$$C = 0.5834 + 0.3875\ C_{-1} \qquad\qquad R^2 = 0.998$$
$$\quad (0.0640) \quad (0.0706)$$

$$C/Y = 0.6777 + 0.2405\ L/E \qquad\qquad R^2 = 0.571$$
$$\qquad\qquad (0.0389)$$

$$C/Y = 0.5697 + 0.2062\ L/E$$
$$\qquad\qquad (0.0610)$$
$$\quad + 0.1542\ (C/Y)_{-1} \qquad\qquad R^2 = 0.564$$
$$\quad (0.2102)$$

(standard errors in parentheses; those omitted were not given by Bridge),

where C is total consumption (at constant prices)
Y is personal disposable income (at constant prices)
L is labour force
E is employment,
and the suffix '-1' indicates a lagged value.

Comment on the significance and meaningfulness of these results.
What additional information might be of use in interpreting them?

8.14 Repeat exercise 8.13 with respect to the following wage inflation equations (quoted from Wynn and Holden, 1974) which were fitted by (ordinary) least squares using annual data for the UK for the fourteen years from 1953 to 1966 inclusive.

$$\dot{W} = -0.27 + 6.69\ U^{-1} + 0.50\ \dot{P} \qquad \bar{R}^2 = 0.822$$
$$\quad (1.03) \quad (2.33) \qquad\quad (0.20)$$

$$\dot{W} = 0.12 + 6.26\ U^{-1} + 0.55\ \dot{P}$$
$$\quad (1.11) \quad (2.38) \qquad\quad (0.20)$$
$$\quad - 0.09\ \dot{P}_{-1}$$
$$\quad (0.09) \qquad\qquad\qquad \bar{R}^2 = 0.788$$

$$\dot{W} = -0.19 + 6.21\ U^{-1} + 0.56\ \dot{P}$$
$$(0.83)\quad (1.89)\qquad\quad (0.16)$$

$$-\ 0.018\ \dot{U}$$
$$(0.007)\qquad\qquad\qquad\qquad \bar{R}^2 = 0.863$$

$$\dot{W} = 0.03 + 6.00\ U^{-1} + 0.59\ \dot{P}$$
$$(0.92)\quad (1.97)\qquad\quad (0.17)$$

$$-\ 0.05\ \dot{P}_{-1} - 0.017\ \dot{U}$$
$$(0.08)\qquad\quad (0.007)\qquad\quad \bar{R}^2 = 0.854$$

(standard errors in parentheses)

where W is an index of hourly wage rates
$\quad\quad P$ is an index of retail prices
$\quad\quad U$ is the percentage of the total labour force unemployed
and a *dot* over a variable indicates its rate of change.

9 ANALYSIS OF SIMULTANEOUS EQUATION MODELS

9.1 INTRODUCTION

In the previous two chapters, we have explored in some detail the empirical investigation of economic theories whose conclusions can be presented in terms of a *single-equation* model. It is now time to turn our attention to the empirical exploration of *simultaneous-equation* models. Such models occur frequently in economics, both in microeconomics and in macroeconomics. In the former, familiar examples include demand and supply models for single markets, and systems of demand equations covering many markets; in the latter, a familiar example is the macro model, describing the functioning of the economy as a whole. The essential feature of such simultaneous-equation models is that they allegedly describe the *simultaneous* determination of several economic variables. Thus, in contrast with the single equation models of chapters 7 and 8, there is not just one dependent variable, but several inter-dependent variables.

Nevertheless, a simultaneous-equation model is necessarily constructed by combining several single-equation models. For example, a supply and demand model for a single market is usually composed of three equations: a demand equation, a supply equation and an equilibrium (or market clearing) condition. The natural question to ask, therefore, is whether our single-equation methods, as described in chapters 7 and 8, can be used to investigate simultaneous models simply by applying them to each equation in the model individually. Unfortunately, the answer is no. The reason why this is so is that one of the key assumptions underlying the analysis of chapters 7 and 8 (namely assumption (3), as listed in section 8.4) cannot hold in a simultaneous model, except in rather unusual circumstances. We illustrate this violation in section 9.2, in the context of a simple two-equation macro model, and show that it is the simultaneity itself which leads to the violation. The question then arises, particularly in view of the material of section 8.4, whether we can somehow transform the original relationship in such a way that the transformed

281

relationship does not suffer from the violated assumption. The answer is that we can; indeed, the appropriate transformation makes good sense from an economic point of view. From a statistical point of view, the intuition behind the transformation is appealing – effectively what is being done is to change the model from a genuinely simultaneous model into a set of independent single-equation models. We can then apply our familiar techniques to these single-equation models, thus obtaining posterior assessments of the parameters of these models.

So far so good. The question then arises: can we 'translate' these posterior assessments of the parameters of the transformed relationships into posterior assessments of the parameters of the original relationships? The answer is that it all depends upon the structure of the model under consideration: sometimes we can do this translation; other times, we cannot.

Although a full treatment of these issues is beyond the scope of this book, it is important that you are aware of some of the main problems involved with the empirical investigation of simultaneous models. Accordingly, this chapter explores in superficial detail some of the issues raised above. We begin, in section 9.2, with an examination of the implications of the use of 'single-equation' methods in the context of simultaneous models. In this section, we discuss the appropriate transformation to remove the violation referred to above, and discuss the economic meaning of the transformed relationship. Then, in section 9.3, we discuss the 'identification problem', which is the question of whether we can translate assessments concerning the parameters of the transformed relationship into assessments concerning the original relationships. Section 9.4 then goes on to explore, albeit very briefly, the issues raised by the identification problem in particular, and the problems of simultaneous models in general. The Bayesian approach to the solution of these problems is sketched. A simple illustration of the methods discussed in sections 9.2 to 9.4 is presented in section 9.5. Finally, section 9.6 gives a summary and section 9.7 provides a set of exercises.

9.2   THE USE OF 'SINGLE-EQUATION' METHODS

Most of the main issues involved with the analysis of simultaneous equation models can be illustrated through the use of simple illustrative examples. Let us begin by considering one of the simplest of such models – namely a two-equation ('Keynesian cross') macro model, of the type familiar from first-year macroeconomics. Using an obvious mnemonic notation, we can write this as:

(a) $C = A + BY + U$
$\hspace{9cm}$ (9.1)
(b) $Y = C + G$

In this, C is aggregate consumption, Y is aggregate income and G is government expenditure. Equation (9.1a) is a linear consumption function with parameters A and B; the former being the intercept and the latter the slope or mpc. Equation (9.1b) is the income identity; implicit in it is an assumption that consumption and government spending are the only two components of aggregate expenditure. As a whole, the model described by (9.1) is familiar, except for the inclusion of the residual, or deviation, term U in the consumption function. We need to include such a term when we are carrying out an empirical investigation, for the reasons discussed earlier – namely, the inevitable violation in practice of the *ceteris paribus* assumption of the theory. If you like, you can think of U as an addition to the intercept A. Thus, an increase in U is 'equivalent to' an increase in the intercept; so variations in U shift the consumption function upwards and downwards.

Now recall how this simple macro model is used. Normally, the Keynesian cross illustrated in figure 9.1 is employed as a visual aid.

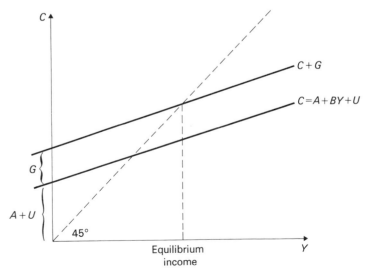

Figure 9.1 A simple macro model

On this, the consumption function is first drawn; then the amount G is added everywhere, to yield an aggregate expenditure function $C + G$. Then the point where this crosses the 45° line is located: the Y-value corresponding to this in the *equilibrium* level of income. The diagram can then be used to show how variations in G (or, entirely equivalently, in A or U) affect the equilibrium level of income.

Now let us suppose that (9.1) is indeed an accurate representation of the workings of the macroeconomy, and therefore that the published data on C and Y have been generated by this two-equation model. Can we use this data to provide posterior assessments of the parameters A and B in the manner described in chapters 7 and 8? Unfortunately not – since one of the key assumptions underlying the analysis of chapters 7 and 8 is necessarily violated as far as equation (9.1a) is concerned. We refer to assumption (3) as described in section 8.4. As translated into the notation of this chapter, this assumption requires that the so-called independent variable in the equation (namely, Y) and the residual term (namely, U) are independent of each other. But this clearly cannot be so – an increase in U (being equivalent to an upward shift in the consumption function) leads to an increase in equilibrium income Y, as can be demonstrated using figure 9.1. Thus, U and Y are quite clearly (positively) related to each other.

In section 8.4, we gave a numerical example of a similar violation of assumption (3), and showed how one could be led astray quite badly if one ignored the violation. Let us give a similar numerical example here. Consider an extreme situation in which G has remained unchanged at the value 100 throughout the observation period. Suppose that A is 100 and that B is 0.75. Suppose finally that we have ten observations and that these were generated by U values of

2.50	12.65	-9.27	-2.27	-5.77
-2.91	-28.28	2.47	-5.84	4.46.

(To obtain these, I took ten values from a unit normal random number table, and multiplied each value by 10; thereby obtaining ten observations on a variable which is $N(0, 100)$.) This information is sufficient to determine the corresponding ten equilibrium values of Y and C. Using either figure 9.1, or otherwise (see later), you should be able to verify that the appropriate values of Y are

810.00	850.60	762.92	790.92	776.92
788.36	686.88	809.88	776.64	817.84

Hence, from (9.1a), or otherwise, the appropriate values of *C* are

| 710.00 | 750.60 | 662.92 | 690.92 | 676.92 |
| 688.36 | 586.88 | 709.88 | 676.64 | 717.84. |

Do you notice anything odd about these *C*- and *Y*-values? They are *exactly* related by the relationship

$$C = -100 + Y.$$

This has an intercept of -100 and a slope of 1, and bears precious little relationship to the underlying consumption function

$$C = 100 + 0.75Y + U.$$

Thus, if you used the methods of chapters 7 and 8 in conjunction with the data given above, you would conclude that *A* was exactly -100, that *B* was exactly 1 (and that *S*, the standard deviation of *U*, was exactly 0), when, in fact, *A* was 100, *B* was 0.75 (and *S* was 10). In other words, you would be seriously led astray.

The reason, of course, is that the methods of chapters 7 and 8 assume that *Y* and *U* are independent, but in this example they clearly are not. Let us demonstrate this explicitly, by finding the solution to the simultaneous model (9.1). This model consists of a pair of equations which jointly determine the values of the variables *C* and *Y*. We can solve the equations for *C* and *Y* by eliminating *Y* and *C* respectively. First, eliminate *C* from (9.1b) by using (9.1a); this yields

$$Y = (A + BY + U) + G.$$

Taking the term in *Y* to the left-hand side we get

$$Y(1 - B) = A + G + U.$$

Finally, dividing through by $(1 - B)$, we get

$$Y = A/(1 - B) + G/(1 - B) + U/(1 - B). \tag{9.2}$$

Similarly, by eliminating *Y* from (9.1a) using (9.1b) and re-arranging, we get

$$C = A/(1 - B) + BG/(1 - B) + U/(1 - B). \tag{9.3}$$

Equation (9.2) shows how equilibrium income *Y* is determined by *G* and *U* (in addition to *A* and *B*, of course). In particular (9.2) shows that an increase of government spending by ΔG leads to a (multiplied) increase in income of $\Delta G/(1 - B)$, the multiplier being the familiar $1/(1 - B)$. A similar multiplier effect applies to changes in U; this is not surprising since a change in U is equivalent to a shift in the consumption function. Thus, equation (9.2) makes explicit the (positive) dependence of Y on U.

At this stage, it may be useful to distinguish between those variables (namely C and Y) whose values are determined *within* the model (9.1), and those variables (namely G and U) whose values are determined *outwith* the model. The former are called the *endogenous* variables of the model and the latter the *exogenous* variables. (We should make clear that, although both G and U are exogenous, they differ in that Z is observable while U is unobservable.)

Equations (9.2) and (9.3) present the solution to the simultaneous model (9.1) in the sense that for each endogenous variable there is an individual equation showing how *it* is determined by the values of the exogenous variables. The pair of equations (9.2) and (9.3) is termed the *reduced form* of the model, as compared with the *structural form* as given by (9.1).

To clarify our subsequent discussion, let us rewrite the reduced form (9.2) and (9.3), as follows:

$$Y = D + EG + V \tag{9.4}$$

$$C = D + (E - 1)G + V, \tag{9.5}$$

where the reduced form coefficients, D and E, are related to the structural coefficients, A and B, by

$$D = A/(1 - B) \quad \text{and} \quad E = 1/(1 - B), \tag{9.6}$$

and where the reduced form residual V, is related to the structural form residual U by

$$V = U/(1 - B). \tag{9.7}$$

Consider equation (9.4), the reduced form equation for Y. The form of this is familiar – it is a straightforward bivariate linear relationship between Y and G. Moreover, if U, the residual of the consumption function is normally distributed, then so will V, the residual of (9.4), as can be seen from (9.7). Therefore, equation (9.4) is a familiar bivariate linear normal regression model. Hence, if all the relevant assumptions hold for equation (9.4), we can apply the standard procedure of chapter 7 to investigate it empirically. Clearly, if all the assumptions relevant to U hold (see section 8.4), then they will also hold with respect to V. The only remaining assumption concerns the independence of G (the independent variable in (9.4)) and V (the residual term of (9.4)); *if we know that G and V are independent, then we can straightforwardly apply the methods of chapter 7 to investigate equation (9.4) empirically.* By so doing, we can obtain posterior assessments of the reduced form coefficients D and E, from which we may be able to obtain posterior assessments of the structural coefficients A and B. This appears to be a promising line of enquiry.

Let us therefore turn to the question of the independence or otherwise of G and V. On economic grounds, there would appear to be good reasons for supposing that they are independent. V is related to U, which captures those factors which influence consumption other than income; and there is no particular reason to suppose that government expenditure G is one of those factors. True, G will influence Y and hence influence C *indirectly*, but it is unlikely that G will influence C *directly*. (Remember that G is *net* of all transfer effects.) Equally, it is unlikely that G will be influenced by the value of V. (Though it is possible that the government, if operating an anti-cyclical fiscal policy, may vary G in the light of variations in consumption expenditure. But this effect may be small, and, in any case, would probably operate with a lag.) Thus, it would seem reasonable to assume that G and V *are* independent; certainly they do not suffer from the obvious dependency between Y and U that is the *inevitable* implication of the model itself. So let us proceed on this assumption. (Though we should note that our methods can be modified if it is known that G and V are dependent – as long as we know the form of the dependence. We would then extend the model, by including the appropriate additional equations, and apply the methods discussed here to the extended model.)

To summarize: if we are prepared to assume that G and V are independent (and there would appear to be strong economic grounds for so doing), and if the usual 'random sampling' assumptions (detailed in section 8.4) apply to U, and hence to V, we can empirically investigate the reduced form equation for Y using the methods discussed in chapter 7. We can therefore obtain posterior assessments of the reduced form coefficients D and E. Now it may be the case that our interest stops there; in other words, we may solely and simply be interested in the reduced form equations. This would be the case if we were interested only in the comparative static implications of the macro model (9.1), and in predicting the values of Y (and C) corresponding to any given values of G. All these, by no means trivial, matters can be explored in the light of posterior assessments of the reduced form coefficients D and E. We will give an example in section 9.5. However, it may also be the case that we want to learn more about the structural coefficients A and B. The question then is

– can we 'translate' assessments on D and E into assessments on A and B?

To answer this question, let us recall equation (9.6) which shows how the reduced form coefficients D and E are related to the structural coefficients A and B. Simple algebra reveals that these relationships can be inverted to show how A and B are related to D and E. As you will be able to verify, these inverse relationships are as follows:

$$A = D/E \quad \text{and} \quad B = (E - 1)/E. \tag{9.8}$$

From these it is clear that, in principle, we can translate probability assessments about D and E into probability assessments for A and B.

Consider first the equation for B in (9.8) above; this is slightly simpler than that for A in that it involves only one of the reduced form coefficients. It is clear from this that, since B is a simple, completely specified and known function of E, the distribution of B corresponding to any given distribution of E can be straightforwardly derived. The easiest way to see this is by use of the respective distribution functions, $F_B(.)$ for B and $F_E(.)$ for E. We have

$$
\begin{aligned}
F_B(b) &\equiv P(B \le b) && \text{(by definition)} \\
&= P[(E - 1)/E \le b] && \text{(from (9.8))} \\
&= P[E \le 1/(1 - b)] && \text{(since } (E - 1)/E \le b \Leftrightarrow E \\
&&& \le 1/(1 - b)) \\
&= F_E[1/(1 - b)] && \text{(by definition).}
\end{aligned}
$$

Thus, if we can specify $F_E(e)$ for all values of e, it follows that we can determine $F_B(b)$ for all values of b. In other words, if we can specify the distribution of E, we can determine the implied distribution of B. So the 'translation' is indeed possible.

In particular, we can derive probability intervals for B from the corresponding probability intervals for E. Suppose, for example, that $(e_{\alpha 1}, e_{\alpha 2})$ is an α per cent probability interval for E. Then we can write

$$P(e_{\alpha 1} \le E \le e_{\alpha 2}) = \alpha/100.$$

Thus,

$$P(e_{\alpha 1} \le 1/(1 - B) \le e_{\alpha 2}) = \alpha/100.$$

Hence, since $e \le (\ge)1/(1 - B)$ if and only if $(e - 1)/e \le (\ge)B$, we can write

$$P[(e_{\alpha 1} - 1)/e_{\alpha 1} \le B \le (e_{\alpha 2} - 1)/e_{\alpha 2}] = \alpha/100.$$

Thus, an α per cent probability interval for B is $[(e_{\alpha 1} - 1)/e_{\alpha 1}, (e_{\alpha 2} - 1)/e_{\alpha 2}]$. (Note that we say *an* α per cent probability interval, and not *a minimum width* α per cent probability interval, since, in general, it will not be – even if $(e_{\alpha 1}, e_{\alpha 2})$ was a minimum width α per cent probability interval for E. Perhaps you might like to ponder the reasons for this.)

We have therefore demonstrated that probability assessments about D and E can be translated into a probability assessment about B. The same is true for A, but the procedure is slightly more complicated. Examine the equation for A in (9.8) above; this shows how A is determined in terms of D and E. If we know the joint distribution of D and E, we can use this equation to find the distribution of A. This can be seen as follows. Let $F_A(.)$ denote the distribution function of A, and let $f_{DE}(.,.)$ denote the joint probability density function of D and E. (This assumes that D and E are continuous variables, as will usually be the case; there is a corresponding derivation if D and E are discrete variables.) We have

$$
\begin{aligned}
F_A(a) &\equiv P(A \leq a) &&\text{(by definition)} \\
&= P(D/E \leq a) &&\text{(from (9.8))} \\
&= P(D \leq aE) \\
&= \int_{e=-\infty}^{\infty} \int_{d=-\infty}^{ae} f_{DE}(d, e) \, \mathrm{d}d \,.\, \mathrm{d}e.
\end{aligned}
$$

(This last step simply states that the probability that D is less than aE is determined by 'adding up' the total probability corresponding to values of D and E such that d is less than ae.) Thus, if we can specify $f_{DE}(d, e)$ for all values of d and e, it follows that we can determine $F_A(a)$ for all values of a. In other words, if we can specify the joint distribution of D and E, we can determine the implied distribution of A. So, once again, the 'translation' is indeed possible.

(Actually, we can do even more than this. We can derive the *joint distribution* of A and B from knowledge of the joint distribution of D and E. The formal derivation is beyond the scope of this book, though the intuition should be reasonably apparent.)

Let us summarize the discussion so far. First, we have shown that the methods of chapter 7 *cannot* be applied directly to investigate empirically the consumption function as part of the simultaneous model (9.1), for the simple reason that the so-called independent variable Y and the residual term U are *necessarily* dependent. Secondly, we have shown that we *can* use the methods of chapter 7 to investigate empirically the *reduced form equations* of the model. By so doing, we can obtain posterior assessments of the reduced form coefficients D and E. Finally, we have shown that these assessments can be 'translated' into posterior assessments for the structural coefficients A and B.

The obvious question to ask is, how general are these findings? Clearly, the first finding is perfectly general: in any simultaneous model, any endogenous variable appearing on the right-hand side of any equation of the model *must* be dependent on the residual term in that equation (except possibly in some extremely unusual circumstances). The proof of this is left as an exercise. The second finding is also perfectly general – as long as all the exogenous variables in the model are generated independently of all the residual terms in the model. This would seem to be a reasonable assumption; indeed, it is an almost tautological implication of true exogeneity. (Though this is not to deny that it might not be difficult in practice to decide whether a particular variable is truly exogenous or not. As a general rule, one should always err on the safe side – by specifying a variable as endogenous if one is in any doubt about its status.) Once again, the proof of this is left as an exercise to the reader.

However, the third finding is, unfortunately, not general. As we will show in the next section, there are cases in which this translation is not possible. The key question is whether the equations specifying the reduced form coefficients in terms of the structural coefficients can be 'inverted' to obtain equations specifying the structural coefficients in terms of the reduced form coefficients. This is known as the identification question (or problem). We shall consider it in the next section.

Before doing so, we ought to conclude this section with two small footnotes. The first is a relatively minor technical point concerning the translation of a probability assessment on E into one on B. If this assessment ascribes a positive probability density to E taking the value 0, then, since $B = (E - 1)/E$, the implied probability assessment for B ascribes a positive probability density to B taking the value ∞. This would create a number of technical difficulties, not least being the fact that the mean and variance of B would therefore be infinite. This problem can be overcome by ascribing a zero *prior* probability density to E equalling 0, which would imply a zero posterior probability density for E equalling 0.

The second footnote relates to the numerical example presented in this section: you will recall that the ten observations on C and Y lay exactly along the line $C = -100 + Y$ which had nothing whatsoever to do with the actual consumption function $C = 100 + 0.75Y + U$. As our discussion showed, the reason for the observations not reflecting the consumption function was the dependence between Y and U. What our discussion did not point out was that the reason for the lack of *any* connection between the real and fitted consumption functions was the constancy of G throughout the observation period. One of several ways of illustrating this is by considering the posterior assessments of the reduced form coefficients implied by the ten observations, and the consequent posterior assessments of the structural coefficients. If we start from a position of total prior ignorance about D and E, then the relevant posterior assessments are given by (7.25). Consider the standard errors of D and E. Since G was constant throughout the observation period, it is clear from (7.27) that $\hat{s}_D$ and $\hat{s}_E$ are *both infinite* (since '$\sum_{i=1}^{n} (x_i - \bar{x})^2$' $= \sum_{i=1}^{10} (g_i - \bar{g})^2 = 0$). This implies that the observations are totally uninformative as far as D and E are concerned. The intuition behind this is immediate: if the ten observations on Y and G are plotted in (Y, G) space, they all lie on a vertical line at the constant value of G. Since it is apparent that this cannot be the actual reduced form equation for Y, it follows that the observations tell us nothing about where this equation actually is. We are thus in a position of total *posterior* ignorance about D and E. It follows that the same must be true for A and B. In other words, if G is constant throughout the observation period, no set of observations can tell us anything about A and B. That is why the 'fitted' line between C and Y has nothing to do with the actual consumption function.

An obvious corollary of this argument is that, if G *does* vary in the observation period, then the observations *can* tell us something about D and E (and hence A and B). Moreover, the more G varies, the more the observations tell us about D and E (and hence A and B).

9.3 THE IDENTIFICATION PROBLEM

The easiest way to describe the identification problem is to present a few simple illustrative examples. From these, a general pattern will be seen to emerge. The examples that follow are all single-market supply and demand models consisting of two equations – a supply equation and a demand equation. The examples differ in their specifications of these two equations. We will let P denote the price of the good, and, since we will assume that the market always clears (so that, *ex post*, quantity supplied and quantity demanded are always equal) we will use the single letter Q to denote the quantity of the good. We will introduce other variables as and when required. Throughout the following discussion we will ignore (and hence omit) the residual terms, since the identification problem (at least in the form considered in this book) concerns the coefficients of the variables, rather than the residual terms.

Consider first the simplest supply and demand model:

$$Q = A + BP \quad \text{(supply)}$$
$$Q = C - DP \quad \text{(demand).} \tag{9.9}$$

This model assumes that both equations are linear: A and B are the coefficients of the supply equation and C and $-D$ are the coefficients of the demand equation. (Note that we have followed convention in writing our equations as if to imply that the demand curve is downward sloping; but there really is no such implication since the data may well convince us that D is negative, and hence that the demand curve is upward sloping.)

The model (9.9) simultaneously determines the (market-clearing) price and quantity of the good. Thus (9.9) is a simultaneous model with two endogenous variables, P and Q, but no exogenous variables (other than the unobservable residual terms, which we are ignoring throughout this section). To find the solution to the model, we first eliminate Q by equating the right-hand sides of the two equations. This yields

$$A + BP = C - DP,$$

which solves for P to give

$$P = (C - A)/(B + D). \tag{9.10}$$

This is the reduced-form equation for P. We can similarly find the reduced-form equation for Q by eliminating P from (9.1). This yields

$$Q = (AD + BC)/(B + D). \tag{9.11}$$

Let us now follow section 9.2 in simplifying the appearance of the reduced form equations by introducing some notation for the reduced form coefficients. We therefore get

$$P = G \quad \text{and} \quad Q = J, \tag{9.12}$$

where

$$G \equiv (C - A)/(B + D) \quad \text{and} \quad J \equiv (AD + BC)/(B + D). \tag{9.13}$$

Thus, A, B, C and D are the structural coefficients of the model (9.9) and G and J are the reduced form coefficients. Let us now investigate the question: can we 'translate' a probability assessment about G and J into a probability assessment about A, B, C and D? As we saw in section 9.2, the answer depends on whether we can 'invert' the equations specifying G and J in terms of A, B, C and D into equations specifying A, B, C and D in terms of G and J. Simple intuition suggests that, in this instance, this is not possible – since, in general, two equations in four unknowns cannot be uniquely solved. This can easily be confirmed: for any given values of G and J there are an *infinite* number of possible sets of A, B, C and D that satisfy (9.13). For example, if $G = 10$ and $J = 20$, then each of the following sets are consistent with (9.13).

A	B	C	D
10	1	30	1
10	1	40	2
0	2	30	1
0	2	10	-1
$20 - 10b$	b	$20 + 10d$	d

Thus, in the model given by (9.9) it is impossible to convert probability assessments about the reduced form coefficients into probability assessments about the structural coefficients. To describe this situation, we say that the supply and demand equations in (9.9) are *not identified* or are *under-identified* (or, perhaps better but less widely used, *not identifiable*). Intuitively, it is easy to see the reason why: given the model (9.9), there is a unique pair (P, Q) which satisfies it. Thus, in the absence of any residual terms, only one pair (P, Q) will ever be observed. Now ask yourself: given one point in (P, Q) space can you uniquely determine the supply and demand curves which gave rise to this point? Clearly not – since there are an infinite number of possible supply and demand curves that intersect at a given point.

Consider now a slightly different model, specified as follows:

$$Q = A + BP \qquad \text{(supply)}$$
$$Q = C - DP + EY \qquad \text{(demand).} \qquad (9.14)$$

In this, income Y is an additional determinant of demand. The model still contains two endogenous variables P and Q, but now also includes an exogenous variable, namely Y. As you should be able to verify the reduced form equations of the model are given by:

$$P = G + HY \qquad \text{and} \qquad Q = J + KY, \qquad (9.15)$$

where the reduced form coefficients, G, H, J and K are related to the structural coefficients A, B, C, D and E by:

$$G = (C - A)/(B + D) \qquad H = E/(B + D)$$
$$J = (AD + BC)/(B + D) \qquad K = BE/(B + D). \tag{9.16}$$

Let us now ask the same question as before: can we 'invert' (9.16) so as to obtain equations for A, B, C, D and E in terms of G, H, J and K. Once again, intuition suggests that this is not possible, since we have five unknowns (A to E) and only four equations (those in (9.16)). However, all is not lost: from (9.16) we see that

$$A = J - BG \qquad \text{and} \qquad B = K/H, \tag{9.17}$$

and hence the coefficients of the supply equation *can* be expressed in terms of the structural coefficients. However, the same is not true for the coefficients of the demand equation; indeed, as before, for any given values of G, H, J and K, there are an infinite number of sets of C, D and E consistent with (9.16). (You should verify this yourself.) In this model, therefore, the supply curve is *identified* (or identifiable) while the demand curve is not. Once again, the intuition behind this property is immediate. Envisage the model portrayed in (P, Q) space: the supply curve is fixed, but the demand curve shifts with changes in Y. Consider the set of intersection points generated as Y varies; clearly, these all lie along the supply curve. Thus, the observations trace out the supply curve (which is therefore identified); but there are an infinite number of sets of demand curves consistent with the observations. Entirely analogously, if the model was given by

$$Q = A + BP + EW \qquad \text{(supply)}$$
$$Q = C - DP \qquad \text{(demand)}$$

then the demand curve would be identified, but not the supply curve; this you could verify yourself. Furthermore, if the model was given by

$$Q = A + BP + EW \qquad \text{(supply)}$$
$$Q = C - DP + FY, \qquad \text{(demand)}$$

then *both* supply and demand curves would be identified. Once again, you should verify this yourself. There is clearly a general pattern here, which we can summarize as follows: in the context of two-equation models, *an equation is identified if it omits a variable which appears in the other equation*. Actually, this result can be generalized, though a proof takes us beyond the scope of this book: *in a k-equation model, an equation is identified* (except under most unusual circumstances) *if it omits* $(k - 1)$ *variables which appear in the other equations of the model.*

There is one other case to consider. This is one in which we have an 'embarrassment of riches', and which we describe by saying that an equation is *over-identified*. We can illustrate this case with the following example. Suppose our supply and demand model is:

$$Q = A + BP$$
$$Q = C - DP + EY + FZ. \tag{9.18}$$

The reduced form of this model is given by

$$P = G + HY + IZ \quad \text{and} \quad Q = J + KY + LZ, \tag{9.19}$$

where the reduced form coefficients G to L are related to the structural coefficients A to F by

$$\begin{aligned}
&G = (C - A)/(B + D) &&H = E/(B + D) \\
&I = F/(B + D) &&J = (AD + BC)/(B + D) \tag{9.20} \\
&K = BE/(B + D) &&L = BF/(B + D).
\end{aligned}$$

From (9.20), we can see that

$$A = J - BG \quad \text{and} \quad B = K/H,$$

but also $B = L/I$.

Thus, if we derived the posterior assessments of the reduced-form parameters G to L *without taking into account the fact that K/H and L/I are equal*, then we would probably find ourselves with two conflicting posterior assessments of B – one obtained from the ratio of K to H and the second from the ratio of L to I. This would further imply (since $A = J - BG$) that we would have two conflicting posterior assessments of A. In this situation, the supply curve is said to be *over-identified*. As you might be able to infer, the condition for an equation in a k-equation linear simultaneous model to be overidentified is that it omits *more* than $(k - 1)$ variables that appear elsewhere in the model.

Actually, to a Bayesian, overidentification is not really a problem. If one knows that there are certain relationships between the reduced form coefficients implied by the structural form, then one simply takes these into account when deriving one's posterior assessments of the parameters. For example, in the model specified by (9.18) above, the Bayesian econometrician would *not* derive the posterior assessments of G and L in the reduced form (9.19) by investigating each equation *on its own*; rather he or she would look at the reduced form as a whole, and derive the posterior assessments of G to L

taking into account the fact that K/H and L/I are equal. Such issues will be explored in a little more detail in the next section.

9.4 INFERENCE IN SIMULTANEOUS EQUATION MODELS

So far in this chapter we have discussed whether the single-equation methods described in chapters 7 and 8 can be appropriately adapted for the empirical investigation of simultaneous models. We can summarize our findings as follows:

(1) it is *not* appropriate to use these single-equation methods on the *structural* equations of the model; however
(2) it *may* be appropriate to use these single-equations methods on the *reduced form* equations of the model; moreover
(3) if all the equations of the model are exactly (as distinct from over- or under-) identified, then the posterior assessments of the reduced form coefficients can be translated into posterior assessments of the structural coefficients; though
(4) if an equation is under-identified, then it is impossible to carry out this translation; while
(5) if an equation is over-identified, there will be several ways of carrying out this translation, unless the posterior assessments of the reduced form coefficients are derived taking into account the implied relationships between them.

It is therefore only when equations are under- or over-identified that single-equation methods do not yield the desired assessments of the structural coefficients. In the former case (under-identification), there is nothing that can be done about it, since it is the inherent nature of the model that implies that observations cannot be informative about certain aspects of the structure. In the latter case (over-identification), there is obviously something that can be done about it – namely, deriving the posterior assessments taking the restrictions into account.

But, you might well ask, why bother with trying to adapt single-equation methods for use in a simultaneous model? Why indeed? Why not simply apply the standard Bayesian inference procedure directly to the simultaneous model as it stands?

Well, clearly, the only reasons for trying to adapt single-equation methods are that they are familiar, easy to understand and easy to apply. But if we have to twist and adapt them significantly, these virtues disappear; it might, therefore, be simpler to start from scratch, and build up a new set of methods specifically for dealing with simultaneous models. In principle, this is straightforward. It simply requires the application of the standard Bayesian procedure that we described in chapter 4, and which we applied, in different contexts, in chapters 5, 6, 7 and 8.

In principle, this *is* straightforward. In practice, as you might have anticipated, it requires rather a lot of tedious algebraic manipulation, of a complexity which takes us beyond the scope of this book. However, we can sketch the basic procedure, and provide a reference for those readers who wish to pursue the issues further.

Consider a general simultaneous model consisting of k equations in which there are k endogenous variables (note that there must always be the same number of equations as endogenous variables, as there must be an equation 'explaining' each endogenous variable). Let us denote these variables by Y_1, Y_2, ..., Y_k, or, rather more neatly, by the vector $\mathbf{Y} \equiv (Y_1, Y_2, ..., Y_k)$. Suppose that the model contains a total of j exogenous variables, denoted by X_1, X_2, ..., X_j, or, rather more neatly, by the vector $\mathbf{X} \equiv (X_1, X_2, ..., X_j)$. We can express a general linear simultaneous model in the form

$$\mathbf{BY} = \mathbf{AX} + \mathbf{U}. \tag{9.21}$$

In this, $\mathbf{U}$ is a vector of residual terms U_1, U_2, ..., U_k (one for each of the k equations). The matrices $\mathbf{B}$ and $\mathbf{A}$ are matrices of structural coefficients – $\mathbf{B}$ being the coefficients of the endogenous variables and $\mathbf{A}$ being the coefficients of the exogenous variables. To avoid indeterminacy, we shall assume that all the diagonal elements in B take the value 1 (so that the ith equation is the equation 'relating to' the ith endogenous variable). Note that (9.21) contains k equations, so that the dimensions of the matrices B and A are $k \times k$ and $k \times j$ respectively. (If you are not familiar with the use of matrices, do not worry; you should be able to follow the subsequent discussion since it is essentially an appeal to intuition.) Suppose, finally, for illustrative purposes, that $\mathbf{U}$ is (multivariate) normally distributed, such that $\mathbf{U}$ is $N(\mathbf{0}, \mathbf{S})$ where $\mathbf{S}$ is the variance (-covariance matrix) of $\mathbf{U}$.

The solution to, or reduced form of, the model (9.21) is obtained by multiplying throughout by $\mathbf{B}^{-1}$, the inverse of $\mathbf{B}$. This yields

$$\mathbf{Y} = \mathbf{CX} + \mathbf{V} \tag{9.22}$$

as the reduced form of the model, where the reduced form coefficients are related to the structural coefficients by

$$\mathbf{C} = \mathbf{B}^{-1}\mathbf{A}, \tag{9.23}$$

and where the reduced form residuals are related to the structural residuals by

$$\mathbf{V} = \mathbf{B}^{-1}\mathbf{U}. \tag{9.24}$$

From (9.22), (9.23) and (9.24), it can be seen that the conditional distribution of $\mathbf{Y}$ given specific values for the parameters of the model, $\mathbf{A}$, $\mathbf{B}$ and $\mathbf{S}$, can be derived. (Indeed, if the $\mathbf{X}$ vector values are taken as given, it can be shown that this conditional distribution of $\mathbf{Y}$ is (multivariate) normal, given our assumptions.) We can thus specify

$$g_{\mathbf{Y}}(\mathbf{y} \mid \mathbf{a}, \mathbf{b}, \mathbf{s}), \tag{9.25}$$

the conditional probability density function of $\mathbf{Y}$. (Strictly speaking, we ought also to make explicit that this distribution is also conditional on a given set of $\mathbf{X}$ values or a given $\mathbf{X}$ distribution. This additional conditioning will be taken as given throughout the following discussion; its inclusion would simply clutter the exposition.)

Let us now suppose our prior assessments of the parameters $\mathbf{A}$, $\mathbf{B}$ and $\mathbf{S}$ can be represented in the form of a joint probability density function $f_{\mathbf{ABS}}(., ., .)$ so that we can specify

$$f_{\mathbf{ABS}}(\mathbf{a}, \mathbf{b}, \mathbf{s}) \tag{9.26}$$

for all values of $\mathbf{a}$, $\mathbf{b}$ and $\mathbf{s}$. Then, we can straightforwardly derive the posterior assessment of $\mathbf{A}$, $\mathbf{B}$ and $\mathbf{S}$ in the light of one observation on $\mathbf{Y}$ by using Bayes' theorem. This yields

$$g_{\mathbf{ABS}}(\mathbf{a}, \mathbf{b}, \mathbf{s} \mid \mathbf{y}) \propto g_{\mathbf{Y}}(\mathbf{y} \mid \mathbf{a}, \mathbf{b}, \mathbf{s}) f_{\mathbf{ABS}}(\mathbf{a}, \mathbf{b}, \mathbf{s}), \tag{9.27}$$

in the familiar fashion. Furthermore, if we have a random sample of n observations $\mathbf{y}_1$, $\mathbf{y}_2$, ..., $\mathbf{y}_n$, then we can derive the posterior assessment of $\mathbf{A}$, $\mathbf{B}$ and $\mathbf{S}$ in the light of these n observations. This yields

$$g_{\mathbf{ABS}}(\mathbf{a}, \mathbf{b}, \mathbf{s} \mid \mathbf{y}_1, \mathbf{y}_2, \dots, \mathbf{y}_n)$$

$$\propto \prod_{i=1}^{n} g_{\mathbf{Y}}(\mathbf{y}_i \mid \mathbf{a}, \mathbf{b}, \mathbf{s}) f_{\mathbf{ABS}}(\mathbf{a}, \mathbf{b}, \mathbf{s}), \tag{9.28}$$

the generalization of (9.27). Thus, in principle, we have solved the 'problem' of inference in a simultaneous model. As we have shown, the standard Bayesian inference procedure can be employed to derive posterior assessments of the parameters of the model.

The key step in this derivation is, of course, the specification of the likelihood function (9.25). As should be clear, this takes into account any restrictions on the reduced form coefficients implied by the model; thus, the problem of over-identification can never arise. Of course, under-identification must necessarily remain a problem: in terms of the discussion of this section, under-identification of certain coefficients manifests itself in equation (9.28) in the form of total posterior ignorance for the relevant coefficients, irrespective of the number and value of the observations.

As we have remarked earlier, the practical implementation of (9.28) is beyond the scope of this book. The interested reader could, however, refer to Zellner (1971) for an excellent treatment.

9.5 A SIMPLE EXAMPLE

We conclude this chapter with an empirical implementation of the methods discussed in section 9.2. To be specific, we re-explore the aggregate consumption function investigated in section 7.7 in the light of the discussion of this chapter. We will continue to use the mnemonic notation of section 9.2.

As we now know, it is not appropriate to apply the methods of chapter 7 directly to the consumption function (cf. (9.1))

$$C = A + BY + U.$$

Instead, we should first investigate the reduced form equation of Y (or, interchangeably, that for C), and then 'translate' our posterior assessments back. The reduced form equation for Y is (see (9.4))

$$Y = D + EG + V,$$

where D, E and V are given by (9.6) and (9.7). Using the data from *Economic Trends Annual Supplement* described in section 7.7, deriving G by subtracting C from Y (see (9.1b)), and employing the methods described in chapter 7, we get the following results relating to the reduced form equation for Y:

$$Y = 10\,267 + 1.5999G \qquad R^2 = 0.7645$$
$$(1499) \quad (0.144) \qquad n = 40 \tag{9.29}$$

(standard errors in parentheses).

Hence, starting from a position of total prior ignorance about the reduced form parameters D and E, our posterior assessments are such that $(D - 10\,267)/1499$ and $(E - 1.5999)/0.144$ both have t distributions with 38 degrees of freedom. Thus, for example, 95 per cent probability intervals for D and E are given by

$$(10\,267 \pm 2.025 \times 1499) \qquad \text{and} \qquad (1.5999 \pm 2.025 \times 0.144)$$

respectively; that is, by

$$(7232, 13\,302) \qquad \text{and} \qquad (1.3083, 1.8915)$$

respectively. As we discussed in section 9.2, the latter of these can straightforwardly be converted into a 95 per cent probability interval for B. Since $B = (E - 1)/E$, the implied 95 per cent probability interval for B is

$$[(1.3083 - 1)/1.3083, (1.8915 - 1)/1.8915];$$

that is,

$$(0.236, 0.471).$$

Thus, on the basis of this evidence, we can be 95 per cent certain that the UK aggregate marginal propensity to consume is between 0.236 and 0.471. Note that this interval is below the corresponding interval (0.435, 0.609) which was (incorrectly) obtained in section 7.7. Perhaps you might like to ponder the reasons for this.

9.6   SUMMARY

This chapter has discussed some of the issues involved in the empirical investigation of simultaneous models. As we showed in section 9.4, there are no additional conceptual *problems* raised by the analysis of such models; indeed, the standard Bayesian procedure can be applied in the usual fashion. However, the move from single equation models to simultaneous equation models does inevitably increase the level of algebraic and computational complexity of the analysis. For that reason, we spent some time discussing whether single-equation methods can be employed or adapted for use in a simultaneous context. Our first finding was that we could not employ single-equation methods directly on the structural equations of a simultaneous model for the simple reason that the endogenous variables on the right-hand sides of the equations are necessarily dependent on the residual terms. This means that one of the assumptions underlying the single-equation methods of chapters 7 and 8 is necessarily violated. However, our second finding was that we could employ these single-equation methods on the reduced form equations of the model, as long as the exogenous variables of the model and the residual terms are independent. By so doing, we can obtain posterior assessments of the reduced form parameters. These assessments can be translated into assessments on the structural parameters if the relevant equations are identified. However, the model may be such that some equations are under-identified, which means that this translation cannot be achieved; in Bayesian terms, this simply means that the observations are necessarily uninformative about the equations in questions. On the other hand, some equations may be over-identified; this means that the model is such that certain relationships amongst the reduced-form parameters exist. These must be taken into account to obtain unique posterior assessments of the structural parameters. In principle, the standard Bayesian procedure can take such relationships into account. In practice, the algebraic and computational complexities take us beyond the scope of this book. We hope that this book has stimulated your interest sufficiently for you to pursue such issues further.

9.7 EXERCISES

9.1 Demonstrate that in any simultaneous model, any endogenous variable appearing on the right-hand side of any structural equation must (almost) inevitably be dependent on the residual term.

9.2 Demonstrate the rather trivial result that if, in a simultaneous model, all the exogenous variables and residual terms are independent, then the independent variables in all the reduced-form equations and the residual terms in those equations are independent.

9.3 Show that, in the model given by (9.14), there are an infinite number of sets of C, D and E consistent with (9.16) for any given G, H, J and K.

9.4 Show that, in the model given by

$$Q = A + BP + EW \quad \text{(supply)}$$
$$Q = C - DP \quad \text{(demand)},$$

the demand curve is identified, but not the supply curve.

9.5   Show that, in the model given by

$$Q = A + BP + EW \qquad \text{(supply)}$$
$$Q = C - DP + FY \qquad \text{(demand)},$$

both supply and demand curves are identified.

9.6   Suppose two variables Y and X are exactly related by $Y = g(X)$ where $g(.)$ is a strictly increasing function. Show that if (x_1, x_2) is a (minimum width) α per cent probability interval for X, then $[g(x_1), g(x_2)]$ is an α per cent probability interval for Y. Using a simple example, show that it is not necessarily a *minimum width* α per cent probability interval.

9.7   Consider the simple example of section 9.5. Discuss *intuitively* why the 95 per cent probability interval for B is below that obtained in section 7.7.

9.8   Consider the supply and demand model given by (9.14). Suppose you are given the following data from twenty observations:

$$\sum_{t=1}^{20} (p_t - \bar{p})^2 = 50 \qquad \sum_{t=1}^{20} (p_t - \bar{p})(y_t - \bar{y}) = 10$$

$$\bar{p} = 5 \qquad \bar{y} = 42.5. \qquad \sum_{t=1}^{20} (y_t - \bar{y})^2 = 100$$

Assuming total prior ignorance, obtain posterior assessments of the coefficients of the reduced form equation for P. Suppose you know that $E = 0.2$, find a 95 per cent probability interval for B, the coefficient of P in the supply equation.

9.9   Consider the following simple macro-model:

$$C = A + BY + U$$
$$I = D + ER + V$$
$$Y = C + I$$

C is aggregate consumption, I aggregate investment, Y aggregate income and R is the rate of interest. R is exogenous. Suppose you are given the following data from twenty observations:

$$\sum_{t=1}^{20} (c_t - \bar{c})^2 = 16 \qquad \sum_{t=1}^{20} (y_t - \bar{y})^2 = 20$$

$$\sum_{t=1}^{20} (c_t - \bar{c})(r_t - \bar{r}) = -12 \qquad \bar{c} = 55$$

$$\sum_{t=1}^{20} (y_t - \bar{y})(r_t - \bar{r}) = -16 \qquad \bar{y} = 60$$

$\sum_{t=1}^{20} (r_t - \bar{r})^2 = 4$ $\qquad$ $\bar{r} = 3.$

Assuming total prior ignorance, obtain posterior assessments of the coefficients of the reduced form equations for C and Y. How might these be used to obtain a posterior assessment for B? Are the consumption and investment functions identified?

9.10 A simultaneous model is said to be *recursive* if it can be written in such a way that, of the k endogenous variables Y_1, Y_2, ..., Y_k, only the first i (namely Y_1, Y_2, ..., Y_i) appear in the first i equations of the model (for $i = 1, 2, ..., k$). How might one investigate empirically such a model?

APPENDIX

A1 NOTATION FOR SUMS AND PRODUCTS

To save space, the shorthand expression $\sum_{i=1}^{n} x_i$ is often used to represent the sum $x_1 + x_2 + \cdots + x_n$ of the n values $x_1, x_2, \ldots, x_n$. Similarly, the shorthand expression $\prod_{i=1}^{n} x_i$ is often used to represent the product $x_1 x_2 \ldots x_n$ of the n values $x_1, x_2, \ldots, x_n$. As should be apparent, the expressions $_{i=1}^{n}$ attached to the $\sum$ or $\prod$ indicate the set of x-values which are to be included in the sum or product. If this set is obvious from the context, then the expressions $_{i=1}^{n}$ are usually omitted, and the sum and product written simply as $\sum x_i$ and $\prod x_i$, or even $\sum x$ and $\prod x$ if the subscript i can be omitted without fear of confusion.

As the reader can easily verify (by writing all the expressions in longhand) the following 'rules' apply to the use of this notation.

Sums

$$\sum_{i=1}^{n} a = na$$

$$\sum_{i=1}^{n} (ax_i) = a\sum_{i=1}^{n} x_i$$

where a is a constant

$$\sum_{i=1}^{n} (x_i + y_i) = \sum_{i=1}^{n} x_i + \sum_{i=1}^{n} y_i.$$

Products

$$\prod_{i=1}^{n} a = a^n$$

$$\prod_{i=1}^{n} (x_i^a) = \left(\prod_{i=1}^{n} x_i\right)^a$$

where a is a constant

$$\prod_{i=1}^{n} (x_i y_i) = \left(\prod_{i=1}^{n} x_i\right)\left(\prod_{i=1}^{n} y_i\right)$$

304

A2 CALCULUS: SOME IMPORTANT NOTATION AND RESULTS

Suppose the two variables Y and X are related by the function $F(.)$ so that $y = F(x)$. Then the *derivative of y with respect to x*, denoted interchangeably by dy/dx, $dF(x)/dx$ or $F'(x)$, is defined as the *slope of the function* $F(.)$ *at the point* x (which, in turn, is defined as the slope of the tangent to the function at the point x).

Suppose the two variables Y and X are related by the function $f(.)$ so that $y = f(x)$. Then the (definite) *integral* of y *between* $x = x_1$ *and* $x = x_2$, denoted by $\int_{s=x_1}^{x_2} f(s)\, ds$, is defined as the *area bounded* (vertically) *by the function* $f(.)$ *and the x-axis, and* (horizontally) *by the values* $x = x_1$ *and* $x = x_2$.

An important theorem of the calculus states that derivatives and integrals are the 'reverse' of each other, in the following sense:

$$\frac{dF}{dx}(x) = f(x) \Leftrightarrow F(x) = \int_{s=-\infty}^{x} f(s)\, ds. \qquad (A.1)$$

This explains the relationship between the distribution function and the probability density function for continuous variables (see chapter 2): the latter is the slope of the former and the former is the area under the latter.

The notion of derivatives and integrals can be extended to the bivariate and multivariate cases. For our purposes, extension of the notion of derivatives to the bivariate case is sufficient. Suppose the variable Z is related to the two variables X and Y by the function $F(.,.)$ so that $z = F(x, y)$. Then the *partial derivative of z with respect to x* (y), denoted interchangeably by $\partial z/\partial x$ or $\partial F(x, y)/\partial x$ $(\partial z/\partial y$ or $\partial F(x, y)/\partial y)$, is defined as the *slope of the function* $F(.,.)$ at the point (x, y) *as measured in the x-direction* (y-direction), that is, holding y (x) constant. In other words, for the purpose of finding the partial derivate of z with respect to x, the function $F(.,.)$ is taken to be a function of x alone – and the univariate definition of a derivative applied. It follows, therefore, from (A.1) above, that

$$\frac{\partial F}{\partial x}(x, y) = f(x, y) \Leftrightarrow F(x, y) = \int_{s=-\infty}^{x} f(s, y)\, ds.$$

A3 SKETCHES OF PROOFS OF RESULTS OF CHAPTER 7

Result (7.8). This is the result for case 2 (unknown coefficients and known variance) starting from a position of total prior ignorance.

Thus the relevant prior is $f_{AB}(a, b) \propto 1$. From (7.7), it follows that the likelihood of observing the single observation (x, y) is proportional to

$$s^{-1} \exp \left[-(y - a - bx)^2/2s^2 \right],$$

(cf. 2.29). Hence the likelihood of observing the n observations $(x_1, y_1), \ldots, (x_n, y_n)$ is proportional to

$$s^{-n} \prod_{i=1}^{n} \exp \left[-\frac{(y_i - a - bx_i)^2}{2s^2} \right]$$

$$\equiv s^{-n} \exp \left[-\sum_{i=1}^{n} \frac{(y_i - a - bx_i)^2}{2s^2} \right]. \tag{A.2}$$

It follows, therefore, that the posterior assessment of A and B, $f_{AB}(a, b \,|\, (x_1, y_1), \ldots, (x_n, y_n))$, based on total prior ignorance, is also proportional to the expression in (A.2). Now note that the term

$$\sum_{i=1}^{n} (y_i - a - bx_i)^2$$

can be written in the algebraically identical form

$$\hat{s}^2(n - 2) + (a - \hat{a})^2 n + 2(a - \hat{a})(b - \hat{b}) \sum_{i=1}^{n} x_i + (b - \hat{b})^2 \sum_{i=1}^{n} x_i^2,$$

where $\hat{a}$ and $\hat{b}$ are as given in (7.9) and $\hat{s}^2$ is as given in (7.27). Hence, (ignoring scaling factors not involving a and b) it follows that the posterior assessment of A and B is given by

$$f_{AB}(a, b \,|\, (x_1, y_1), \ldots, (x_n, y_n))$$

$$\propto \exp \left\{ -\frac{\left[(a - \hat{a})^2 n + 2(a - \hat{a})(b - \hat{b}) \sum_{i=1}^{n} x_i + (b - \hat{b})^2 \sum_{i=1}^{n} x_i^2 \right]}{2s^2} \right\} \tag{A.3}$$

This is the form of a bivariate normal distribution (see Degroot (1970), section 5.4). It is a complete characterization of the posterior joint assessment of A and B. The marginal distributions of A and B can be found in the usual manner (see section 3.3). This yields

$$f_A(a \,|\, (x_1, y_1), \ldots, (x_n, y_n)) \propto \exp \left[-(a - \hat{a})^2/2s_A^2 \right]$$

and

$$f_B(b \,|\, (x_1, y_1), \ldots, (x_n, y_n)) \propto \exp \left[-(b - \hat{b})^2/2s_B^2 \right],$$

respectively, where s_A and s_B are as given in (7.9). Thus, the posterior assessments of A and B are $N(\hat{a}, s_A^2)$ and $N(\hat{b}, s_B^2)$, respectively. After standardization, this yields the result stated in (7.8).

Results (7.25) and (7.26). These are the results for case 4 (unknown coefficients and unknown variance) starting from a position of total prior ignorance. Thus, in this case, the relevant prior is

$$f_{ABS}(a, b, s) \propto 1/s.$$

(Compare section 6.4, particularly the material preceding equation (6.58), and note that if the density of $p \equiv 1/s^2$ is proportional to $1/p$, then the density of s is proportional to $1/s$ – this being a result which uses the 'change of variable technique', a technique outwith the scope of this book. See Degroot (1970), section 3.7.)

The likelihood of observing the n observations $(x_1, y_1), \ldots, (x_n, y_n)$ remains as in case 2, namely proportional to the expression in (A.2). It follows that the posterior assessment of A, B and S, $f_{ABS}(a, b, s \,|\, (x_1, y_1), \ldots, (x_n, y_n))$, based on total prior ignorance, is proportional to

$$s^{-n-1} \exp\left[-\sum_{i=1}^{n} \frac{(y_i - a - bx_i)^2}{2s^2} \right]$$

Once again, the algebraic identity noted above can be used to rewrite this expression. This yields

$$f_{ABS}(a, b, s \,|\, (x_1, y_1), \ldots, (x_n, y_n))$$

$$\propto s^{-n-1} \exp\left\{ -\left[\hat{s}^2(n-2) + (a - \hat{a})^2 n \right.\right. \tag{A.4}$$

$$\left.\left. + 2(a - \hat{a})(b - \hat{b})\sum_{i=1}^{n} x_i + (b - \hat{b})\sum_{i=1}^{n} x_i^2 \right]\middle/ 2s^2 \right\}.$$

This is a complete characterization of the posterior joint assessment of A, B and S. The marginal distributions of A, B and S can be found in the usual manner (see section 3.3). This yields

$$f_A(a \,|\, (x_1, y_1), \ldots, (x_n, y_n)) \propto \left[(n-2) + \left(\frac{a - \hat{a}}{\hat{s}_A}\right)^2 \right]^{-(n-1)/2},$$

$$f_B(b \,|\, (x_1, y_1), \ldots, (x_n, y_n)) \propto \left[(n-2) + \left(\frac{b - \hat{b}}{\hat{s}_B}\right)^2 \right]^{-(n-1)/2},$$

308   *Appendix*

and

$$f_S(s \mid (x_1, y_1), \ldots, (x_n, y_n)) \propto s^{-n+1} \exp\left[-\frac{(n-2)\hat{s}^2}{s^2} \right]$$

respectively, where $\hat{s}_A$, $\hat{s}_B$ and $\hat{s}$ are as given in (7.27). Using (2.33) the first two of these yield the result stated in (7.25), and the third yields the result stated in (7.26).

Full details of these proofs can be found in Zellner (1971), section 3.1.2, pp. 60–3. You will note that our concentration in the main body of the text on the *marginal* distributions of A, B and S necessarily ignores some of the information contained in the posterior *joint* assessment. In particular, our treatment ignores the dependence between the assessments of A, B and S. As can be seen from (A.3) and (A.4) above, these assessments *are* dependent, so one needs to be careful if one wishes to make some probability statement involving two or more of A, B and S. Such a statement can *not* be made on the basis of the marginal assessments alone – one needs to return to the joint assessment. Unfortunately, this takes us beyond the scope of this book, though, in principle, the appropriate procedure is straightforward.

A4 SKETCHES OF PROOFS OF RESULT (8.4) OF CHAPTER 8

To avoid excessive algebraic complexity, we find it useful to use matrix notation at this point. We denote the n observations on the dependent variable Y by the $n \times 1$ vector $\mathbf{y} \equiv (y_1, y_2, \ldots, y_n)'$. We denote the n observations on the k explanatory variables X_0, X_1, $\ldots, X_{k-1}$ by the $n \times k$ matrix $\mathbf{x}$ given by

$$\mathbf{x} \equiv \begin{pmatrix} 1 & x_{11} & x_{21} & \cdots & x_{k-1,1} \\ 1 & x_{12} & x_{22} & \cdots & x_{k-1,2} \\ \vdots & \vdots & \vdots & & \vdots \\ 1 & x_{1n} & x_{2n} & & x_{k-1,n} \end{pmatrix}$$

(Recall that the 'dummy' variable X_0 always takes the value 1.) We denote the coefficients by the $k \times 1$ vector $\mathbf{B} \equiv (B_0, B_1, B_2, \ldots, B_{k-1})'$. From (8.2) we can express the relationship between the observations by

$$\mathbf{y} = \mathbf{x}\mathbf{B} + \mathbf{u} \tag{A.5}$$

where $\mathbf{u} \equiv (u_1, u_2, \ldots, u_n)'$ is an $n \times 1$ vector of residuals. By assumption, these *us* are a random sample from a normal distribution with mean 0 and variance S^2. It follows that the likelihood of **y** given **x**, $\mathbf{B} = \mathbf{b}$ and $S = s$ is given by

$$f_\mathbf{Y}(\mathbf{y} \mid \mathbf{x}, \mathbf{b}, s) \propto s^{-n} \exp\left[-(\mathbf{y} - \mathbf{xb})'(\mathbf{y} - \mathbf{xb})/2s^2\right].$$

(Compare this with (A.2), the equivalent expression in the bivariate case. The multivariate extension is apparent.)

Now suppose that we start from a position of total prior ignorance about **B** and *S*. Then the appropriate prior (cf. Appendix A.3) is given by

$$f_{\mathbf{B}S}(\mathbf{b}, s) \propto 1/s.$$

Hence the posterior assessment of **B** and S, $f_{\mathbf{B}S}(\mathbf{b}, s \mid \mathbf{x}, \mathbf{y})$, based on total prior ignorance, is proportional to

$$s^{-n-1} \exp\left[-(\mathbf{y} - \mathbf{xb})'(\mathbf{y} - \mathbf{xb})/2s^2\right]. \tag{A.6}$$

Now note that $(\mathbf{y} - \mathbf{xb})'(\mathbf{y} - \mathbf{xb})$ is algebraically identical to

$$(n - k)\hat{s}^2 + (\mathbf{b} - \hat{\mathbf{b}})'\mathbf{x}'\mathbf{x}(\mathbf{b} - \hat{\mathbf{b}}), \tag{A.7}$$

where $\hat{\mathbf{b}}$ and $\hat{s}$ are given by

$$\hat{\mathbf{b}} \equiv (\mathbf{x}'\mathbf{x})^{-1}\mathbf{x}'\mathbf{y} \tag{A.8}$$

and

$$\hat{s}^2 = (\mathbf{y} - \mathbf{x}\hat{\mathbf{b}})'(\mathbf{y} - \mathbf{x}\hat{\mathbf{b}})/(n - k) \tag{A.9}$$

respectively. Thus, the posterior assessment of **B** and S is given by

$$f_{\mathbf{B}S}(\mathbf{b}, s \mid \mathbf{x}, \mathbf{y}) \propto s^{-n-1} \exp\left\{-\left[(n - k)\hat{s}^2 + (\mathbf{b} - \hat{\mathbf{b}})'\mathbf{x}'\mathbf{x}(\mathbf{b} - \hat{\mathbf{b}})\right]/2s^2\right\}. \tag{A.10}$$

This is a complete characterization of the posterior assessment. The marginal assessments of (the vector) **B** and S can be found in the usual manner (see section 3.3). This yields

$$f_\mathbf{B}(\mathbf{b} \mid \mathbf{x}, \mathbf{y}) \propto \left[(n - k)\hat{s}^2 + (\mathbf{b} - \hat{\mathbf{b}})'\mathbf{x}'\mathbf{x}(\mathbf{b} - \mathbf{b}')\right]^{-n/2}$$

and

$$f_S(s \mid \mathbf{x}, \mathbf{y}) \propto s^{-n+k-1} \exp\left[-\frac{(n - k)\hat{s}^2}{2s^2}\right],$$

respectively. The first of these is in the form of a multivariate *t* distribution (see Degroot (1970), section 5.6), while from the second, it can be deduced that the posterior assessment of S is such that

$(n - k)\hat{s}^2/S^2$ has a chi-square distribution with $(n - k)$ degrees of freedom. This latter is one of the results stated in (8.4).

The posterior marginal assessments of the individual Bs can be obtained from the posterior joint assessment of **B** in the usual manner. This yields (for $j = 0, 1, \ldots, k - 1$)

$$f_{B_j}(b_j \mid \mathbf{x}, \mathbf{y}) \propto \left[(n - k) + \left(\frac{b_j - \hat{b}_j}{\hat{s}_{B_j}} \right)^2 \right]^{-(n - k + 1)/2}$$

where $\hat{s}^2_{B_j}$ is the jth diagonal element of the matrix $\hat{\mathbf{s}}_B$ defined by

$$\hat{\mathbf{s}}_B \equiv \hat{s}^2(\mathbf{x}'\mathbf{x})^{-1}. \tag{A.11}$$

From this it follows that (for $j = 0, 1, \ldots, k - 1$) the variable $(B_j - \hat{b}_j)/\hat{s}_{B_j}$ has a t-distribution with $(n - k)$ degrees of freedom. This is the remaining result stated in (8.4).

Full details of these proofs can be found, once again, in Zellner (1971), pp. 65–8. Once again, you should note that the marginal posterior assessments (as stated in (8.4)) omit a great amount of the information contained in the joint posterior assessment (A.10). Our remarks at the end of Appendix A.3 therefore remain relevant.

A5   BAYESIAN COMPUTER PROGRAMS

A useful listing of generally available Bayesian computer programs can be found in Zellner (1980), chapter 27 ('Bayesian Computer Programs' by S. J. Press). Of the fifteen programs summarized in this chapter, four are particularly relevant to the material discussed in this book. These are BRAP, BRP, CADA and SEARCH. Their main features are listed below. (The prices given are those quoted to me in November 1982.)

BRAP (Bayesian Regression Analysis Program). This is written in FORTRAN IV H and is available for $50 from Professor Arnold Zellner, Graduate School of Business, University of Chicago, 1101 East 58th Street, Chicago, IL 60637, USA. This program performs Bayesian analysis of the multivariate normal linear regression model (as dicussed in chapters 7 and 8), either under total prior ignorance or under an informative prior. It provides detailed analysis (both tabular and graphical) of the posterior assessment. The input to the program is similar in format to the (classical econometric) programs TSP and ESP, thus facilitating both Bayesian and classical analyses of the same problem.

BRP (Bayesian Regression Program). This is written in FORTRAN (both IV and 77 versions are available) and is available for 3000 Belgian Francs from Professor Luc Bauwens, Center for Operations Research and Econometrics, 34 Voie du Roman Pays, 1348 Louvain-la-Neuve, Belgium. This program performs Bayesian analysis of various standard econometric models, including the multivariate normal linear regression model (as discussed in chapters 7 and 8) and several others beyond the scope of this book. (Such models encompass block heteroscedasticity, errors in variables, limited and full information analysis and seemingly unrelated regressions.) This is a more sophisticated program than the other three, but it looks more difficult to use (though I do not speak from experience).

CADA (Computer-Assisted Data Analysis). This is written in BASIC and is available for $600 (plus 10 per cent for non-US delivery less a discount for some non-profit educational and research institutions) from the CADA Research Group, 348 Lindquist Center, The University of Iowa, Iowa City, IO 52242, USA. This is a multipurpose interactive package, and is particularly suited to general (that is, non-specialist) use. It performs all the Bayesian analyses discussed in chapters 5 to 8 inclusive of this book, and a lot more besides. It is not sophisticated in an econometric sense (as, for example, BRP is), but it is very 'user-friendly'. It is easy to use, particularly by non-specialists, and is therefore an ideal introduction to Bayesian computing.

SEARCH (Seeking Extreme and Average Regression Coefficient Hypotheses). This is written in FORTRAN and is available for $150 from Professor Edward E. Leamer, Department of Economics, UCLA, Los Angeles, CA 90024, USA. This performs Bayesian analysis of the multivariate normal regression model (as discussed in chapters 7 and 8 of this book) as well as other things. Its main distinguishing feature is (as its name rather elliptically implies) its ability to carry out Extreme Bounds Analyses. This enables the researcher, who may be unsure as to which variables to include as explanatory variables, to evaluate the sensitivity (of the coefficients of the variables he is sure ought to be included) to the inclusion or exclusion of the other variables. This Extreme Bounds Analysis should become fairly widely accepted in the future.

I recommend that you check details of installation, compatibility, etc., before parting with any money.

A6 TABLE OF THE UNIT NORMAL DISTRIBUTION

An entry in the table is the proportion under the entire curve which is between $z = 0$ and a positive value of z. Areas for negative values of z are obtained by symmetry.

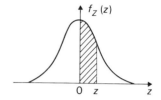

z	0.00	0.01	0.02	0.03	0.04	0.05	0.06	0.07	0.08	0.09
0.0	0.0000	0.0040	0.0080	0.0120	0.0160	0.0199	0.0239	0.0279	0.0319	0.0359
0.1	0.0398	0.0438	0.0478	0.0517	0.0557	0.0596	0.0636	0.0675	0.0714	0.0753
0.2	0.0793	0.0832	0.0871	0.0910	0.0948	0.0987	0.1026	0.1064	0.1103	0.1141
0.3	0.1179	0.1217	0.1255	0.1293	0.1331	0.1368	0.1406	0.1443	0.1480	0.1517
0.4	0.1554	0.1591	0.1628	0.1664	0.1700	0.1736	0.1772	0.1808	0.1844	0.1879
0.5	0.1915	0.1950	0.1985	0.2019	0.2054	0.2088	0.2123	0.2157	0.2190	0.2224
0.6	0.2257	0.2291	0.2324	0.2357	0.2389	0.2422	0.2454	0.2486	0.2517	0.2549
0.7	0.2580	0.2611	0.2642	0.2673	0.2704	0.2734	0.2764	0.2794	0.2823	0.2852
0.8	0.2881	0.2910	0.2939	0.2967	0.2995	0.3023	0.3051	0.3078	0.3106	0.3133
0.9	0.3159	0.3186	0.3212	0.3238	0.3264	0.3289	0.3315	0.3340	0.3365	0.3389
1.0	0.3413	0.3438	0.3461	0.3485	0.3508	0.3531	0.3554	0.3577	0.3599	0.3621
1.1	0.3643	0.3665	0.3686	0.3708	0.3729	0.3749	0.3770	0.3790	0.3810	0.3830
1.2	0.3849	0.3869	0.3888	0.3907	0.3925	0.3944	0.3962	0.3980	0.3997	0.4015
1.3	0.4032	0.4049	0.4066	0.4082	0.4099	0.4115	0.4131	0.4147	0.4162	0.4177
1.4	0.4192	0.4207	0.4222	0.4236	0.4251	0.4265	0.4279	0.4292	0.4306	0.4319
1.5	0.4332	0.4345	0.4357	0.4370	0.4382	0.4394	0.4406	0.4418	0.4429	0.4441
1.6	0.4452	0.4463	0.4474	0.4484	0.4495	0.4505	0.4515	0.4525	0.4535	0.4545
1.7	0.4554	0.4564	0.4573	0.4582	0.4591	0.4599	0.4608	0.4616	0.4625	0.4633
1.8	0.4641	0.4649	0.4656	0.4664	0.4671	0.4678	0.4686	0.4693	0.4699	0.4706
1.9	0.4713	0.4719	0.4726	0.4732	0.4738	0.4744	0.4750	0.4756	0.4761	0.4767
2.0	0.4772	0.4778	0.4783	0.4788	0.4793	0.4798	0.4803	0.4808	0.4812	0.4817
2.1	0.4821	0.4826	0.4830	0.4834	0.4838	0.4842	0.4846	0.4850	0.4854	0.4857
2.2	0.4861	0.4864	0.4868	0.4871	0.4875	0.4878	0.4881	0.4884	0.4887	0.4890
2.3	0.4893	0.4896	0.4898	0.4901	0.4904	0.4906	0.4909	0.4911	0.4913	0.4916
2.4	0.4918	0.4920	0.4922	0.4925	0.4927	0.4929	0.4931	0.4932	0.4934	0.4936
2.5	0.4938	0.4940	0.4941	0.4943	0.4945	0.4946	0.4948	0.4949	0.4951	0.4952
2.6	0.4953	0.4955	0.4956	0.4957	0.4959	0.4960	0.4961	0.4962	0.4963	0.4964
2.7	0.4964	0.4966	0.4967	0.4968	0.4969	0.4970	0.4971	0.4972	0.4973	0.4974
2.8	0.4974	0.4975	0.4976	0.4977	0.4977	0.4978	0.4979	0.4979	0.4980	0.4981
2.9	0.4981	0.4982	0.4982	0.4983	0.4984	0.4984	0.4985	0.4985	0.4986	0.4986
3.0	0.4987	0.4987	0.4987	0.4988	0.4988	0.4989	0.4989	0.4989	0.4990	0.4990

A7 TABLE OF THE *t*-DISTRIBUTION

Example:
for $k = 10$ degrees of freedom
$P[T_k > 1.812] = 0.05$
$P[T_k < -1.812] = 0.05$

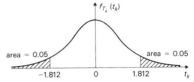

P \ k	0.25	0.20	0.15	0.10	0.05	0.025	0.01	0.005	0.0005
1	1.000	1.376	1.963	3.078	6.314	12.706	31.821	63.657	636.619
2	0.816	1.061	1.386	1.886	2.920	4.303	6.965	9.925	31.598
3	0.765	0.978	1.250	1.638	2.353	3.182	4.541	5.841	12.941
4	0.741	0.941	1.190	1.533	2.132	2.776	3.747	4.604	8.610
5	0.727	0.920	1.156	1.476	2.015	2.571	3.365	4.032	6.859
6	0.718	0.906	1.134	1.440	1.943	2.447	3.143	3.707	5.959
7	0.711	0.896	1.119	1.415	1.895	2.365	2.998	3.499	5.405
8	0.706	0.889	1.108	1.397	1.860	2.306	2.896	3.355	5.041
9	0.703	0.883	1.100	1.383	1.833	2.262	2.821	3.250	4.781
10	0.700	0.879	1.093	1.372	1.812	2.228	2.764	3.169	4.587
11	0.697	0.876	1.088	1.363	1.796	2.201	2.718	3.106	4.437
12	0.695	0.873	1.083	1.356	1.782	2.179	2.681	3.055	4.318
13	0.694	0.870	1.079	1.350	1.771	2.160	2.650	3.012	4.221
14	0.692	0.868	1.076	1.345	1.761	2.145	2.624	2.977	4.140
15	0.691	0.866	1.074	1.341	1.753	2.131	2.602	2.947	4.073
16	0.690	0.865	1.071	1.337	1.746	2.120	2.583	2.921	4.015
17	0.689	0.863	1.069	1.333	1.740	2.110	2.567	2.898	3.965
18	0.688	0.862	1.067	1.330	1.734	2.101	2.552	2.878	3.922
19	0.688	0.861	1.066	1.328	1.729	2.093	2.539	2.861	3.883
20	0.687	0.860	1.064	1.325	1.725	2.086	2.528	2.845	3.850
21	0.686	0.859	1.063	1.323	1.721	2.080	2.518	2.831	3.819
22	0.686	0.858	1.061	1.321	1.717	2.074	2.508	2.819	3.792
23	0.685	0.858	1.060	1.319	1.714	2.069	2.500	2.807	3.767
24	0.685	0.857	1.059	1.318	1.711	2.064	2.492	2.797	3.745
25	0.684	0.856	1.058	1.316	1.708	2.060	2.486	2.787	3.725
26	0.684	0.856	1.058	1.315	1.706	2.056	2.479	2.779	3.707
27	0.684	0.855	1.057	1.314	1.703	2.052	2.473	2.771	3.690
28	0.683	0.855	1.056	1.313	1.701	2.048	2.467	2.763	3.674
29	0.683	0.854	1.055	1.311	1.699	2.045	2.462	2.756	3.659
30	0.683	0.854	1.055	1.310	1.697	2.042	2.457	2.750	3.646
40	0.681	0.851	1.050	1.303	1.684	2.021	2.423	2.704	3.551
60	0.679	0.848	1.046	1.296	1.671	2.000	2.390	2.660	3.460
120	0.677	0.845	1.041	1.289	1.658	1.980	2.358	2.617	3.373
∞	0.674	0.842	1.036	1.282	1.645	1.960	2.326	2.576	3.291

Source: This table is abridged from table III of Fisher and Yates *Statistical Tables for Biological, Agricultural and Medical Research* London, Longman Group Ltd. (previously published by Oliver & Boyd, Edinburgh) and is reproduced by permission of the authors and publishers.

A8 TABLE OF THE CHI-SQUARE DISTRIBUTION

Example:
for k = 10 degrees of freedom
$P[Y_k > 15.99] = 0.10$

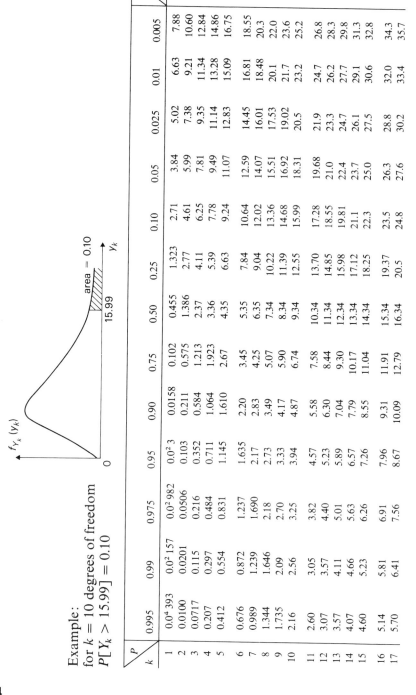

k	0.995	0.99	0.975	0.95	0.90	0.75	0.50	0.25	0.10	0.05	0.025	0.01	0.005	k
1	0.0^4393	0.0^2157	0.0^2982	0.0^23	0.0158	0.102	0.455	1.323	2.71	3.84	5.02	6.63	7.88	1
2	0.0100	0.0201	0.0506	0.103	0.211	0.575	1.386	2.77	4.61	5.99	7.38	9.21	10.60	2
3	0.0717	0.115	0.216	0.352	0.584	1.213	2.37	4.11	6.25	7.81	9.35	11.34	12.84	3
4	0.207	0.297	0.484	0.711	1.064	1.923	3.36	5.39	7.78	9.49	11.14	13.28	14.86	4
5	0.412	0.554	0.831	1.145	1.610	2.67	4.35	6.63	9.24	11.07	12.83	15.09	16.75	5
6	0.676	0.872	1.237	1.635	2.20	3.45	5.35	7.84	10.64	12.59	14.45	16.81	18.55	6
7	0.989	1.239	1.690	2.17	2.83	4.25	6.35	9.04	12.02	14.07	16.01	18.48	20.3	7
8	1.344	1.646	2.18	2.73	3.49	5.07	7.34	10.22	13.36	15.51	17.53	20.1	22.0	8
9	1.735	2.09	2.70	3.33	4.17	5.90	8.34	11.39	14.68	16.92	19.02	21.7	23.6	9
10	2.16	2.56	3.25	3.94	4.87	6.74	9.34	12.55	15.99	18.31	20.5	23.2	25.2	10
11	2.60	3.05	3.82	4.57	5.58	7.58	10.34	13.70	17.28	19.68	21.9	24.7	26.8	11
12	3.07	3.57	4.40	5.23	6.30	8.44	11.34	14.85	18.55	21.0	23.3	26.2	28.3	12
13	3.57	4.11	5.01	5.89	7.04	9.30	12.34	15.98	19.81	22.4	24.7	27.7	29.8	13
14	4.07	4.66	5.63	6.57	7.79	10.17	13.34	17.12	21.1	23.7	26.1	29.1	31.3	14
15	4.60	5.23	6.26	7.26	8.55	11.04	14.34	18.25	22.3	25.0	27.5	30.6	32.8	15
16	5.14	5.81	6.91	7.96	9.31	11.91	15.34	19.37	23.5	26.3	28.8	32.0	34.3	16
17	5.70	6.41	7.56	8.67	10.09	12.79	16.34	20.5	24.8	27.6	30.2	33.4	35.7	17

k														k
18	6.26	7.01	8.23	9.39	10.86	13.68	17.34	21.6	26.0	28.9	31.5	34.8	37.2	18
19	6.84	7.63	8.91	10.12	11.65	14.56	18.34	22.7	27.2	30.1	32.9	36.2	38.6	19
20	7.43	8.26	9.59	10.85	12.44	15.45	19.34	23.8	28.4	31.4	34.2	37.6	40.0	20
21	8.03	8.90	10.28	11.59	13.24	16.34	20.3	24.9	29.6	32.7	35.5	38.9	41.4	21
22	8.64	9.54	10.98	12.34	14.04	17.24	21.3	26.0	30.8	33.9	36.8	40.3	42.8	22
23	9.26	10.20	11.69	13.09	14.85	18.14	22.3	27.1	32.0	35.2	38.1	41.6	44.2	23
24	9.89	10.86	12.40	13.85	15.66	19.04	23.3	28.2	33.2	36.4	39.4	43.0	45.6	24
25	10.52	11.52	13.12	14.61	16.47	19.94	24.3	29.3	34.4	37.7	40.6	44.3	46.9	25
26	11.16	12.20	13.84	15.38	17.29	20.8	25.3	30.4	35.6	38.9	41.9	45.6	48.3	26
27	11.81	12.88	14.57	16.15	18.11	21.7	26.3	31.5	36.7	40.1	43.2	47.0	49.6	27
28	12.46	13.56	15.31	16.93	18.94	22.7	27.3	32.6	37.9	41.3	44.5	48.3	51.0	28
29	13.12	14.26	16.05	17.71	19.77	23.6	28.3	33.7	39.1	42.6	45.7	49.6	52.3	29
30	13.79	14.95	16.79	18.49	20.6	24.5	29.3	34.8	40.3	43.8	47.0	50.9	53.7	30
40	20.7	22.2	24.4	26.5	29.1	33.7	39.3	45.6	51.8	55.8	59.3	63.7	66.8	40
50	28.0	29.7	32.4	34.8	37.7	42.9	49.3	56.3	63.2	67.5	71.4	76.2	79.5	50
60	35.5	37.5	40.5	43.2	46.5	52.3	59.3	67.0	74.4	79.1	83.3	88.4	92.0	60
70	43.3	45.4	48.8	51.7	55.3	61.7	69.3	77.6	85.5	90.5	95.0	100.4	104.2	70
80	51.2	53.5	57.2	60.4	64.3	71.1	79.3	88.1	96.6	101.9	106.6	112.3	116.3	80
90	59.2	61.8	65.6	69.1	73.3	80.6	89.3	98.6	107.6	113.1	118.1	124.1	128.3	90
100	67.3	70.1	74.2	77.9	82.4	90.1	99.3	109.1	118.5	124.3	129.6	135.8	140.2	100
Z_α	-2.58	-2.33	-1.960	-1.645	-1.282	-0.674	0.000	0.674	1.282	1.645	1.960	2.33	2.58	Z_α

For $k > 100$ take $\chi^2 = \frac{1}{2}(Z_\alpha + \sqrt{(2k - 1)})^2$

Z_α is the standardized normal deviate corresponding to the α level of significance, and is shown in the bottom of the table.

Source: This table is abridged from Table 8 of *Biometrika Tables for Statisticians*, vol. 1, 3rd edition (1966).

FURTHER READING

As the reader may already have deduced, the key reference for those who wish to pursue the study of Bayesian econometrics is Zellner (1971). This masterly book, although technically quite advanced, contains a wealth of results and insights. Some flavour of developments since 1971 can be found in Leamer (1978), Zellner (1980) as well as in the other volumes in North-Holland's Studies in Bayesian Econometrics and Statistics series. Readers interested in pursuing the decision-making implications of Bayesian statistics could consult Degroot (1970), while those interested in examining the Classical approach to the statistical problems discussed in this present volume could refer to Hey (1974) or Kmenta (1971). Bridge (1971), Mayes (1981) and Wynn and Holden (1974) examine empirical applications of these statistical tools.

Bridge, J. L. (1971) *Applied Econometrics*, North-Holland, Amsterdam.

Degroot, M. H. (1970) *Optimal Statistical Decisions*, McGraw-Hill, New York.

Hey, J. D. (1974) *Statistics in Economics*, Martin Robertson, Oxford.

Kmenta, J. (1971) *Elements of Econometrics*, Macmillan, New York.

Leamer, E. E. (1978) *Specification Searches*, Wiley, New York.

Mayes, D. G. (1981) *Applications of Econometrics*, Prentice-Hall, New Jersey.

Wynn, R. F. and Holden, K. (1974) *An Introduction to Applied Econometric Analysis*, Macmillan, London.

Zellner, A. (1971) *An Introduction to Bayesian Inference in Econometrics*, Wiley, New York.

Zellner, A. (ed.) (1980) *Bayesian Analysis in Econometrics and Statistics: Essays in Honor of Harold Jeffreys*, North-Holland, Amsterdam.

Index

(**Bold** page numbers give the most
important reference for the entry

Adaptive expectations, **251–4**, 269
Addition symbol ($\sum$), 305
Area (under probability density
    function), **15**, 26–7, 29, 125
Arithmetic mean; *see* Mean, arithmetic
Association, Measure of; *see* Correlation
Assumptions about regression model,
    260–1
Autoregression (of residuals), 264–6
Average; *see* Measures of central
    tendency

Bank of England Quarterly Bulletin, 241
Bayes' theorem, 2, 38, **83–8**, 88–105, 119,
    139, 154, 161, 185, 232, 306–9
Bayesian analysis of simultaneous
    equation models, **296–9**
Bayesian statistics (as compared with
    Classical statistics), 129–30, 168–73,
    205–9
Behavioural equation, 252
Beta distribution, **27–9**
    as representative of beliefs about
      proportion, 99–102, 106, **112–6**
    mean, **28**
    variance, **28**
Bibliography, 316
Bivariate case, **43–66**
Bivariate distribution function, **44–50**
Bivariate normal regression model; *see*
    Linear bivariate normal regression
    model
Bivariate probability distribution, **44–50**
BRAP, 310
BRP, 311

CADA, 311
Calculus, **305**
Central limit theorem, **181**
Certainty, 11
Ceteris paribus assumption in theory,
    180
Characteristic of interest, 98, 111
Chi-square distribution, **33**
    as representation of beliefs about
      variance/precision, 156, 238
    as representation of beliefs about
      variance of residuals of relationship,
      196, 199–200, 232, 238, 310
    table, **314–5**
Classical statistics, 129–30, 168–73,
    205–9
Coefficient of correlation *see* Correlation
    coefficient
Coefficient of relationship, **182**
    learning about, **185–6, 198–9, 232**
    specific formulae for, **186, 199, 204**, 232
Comparison of theories, **209–13**, 247,
    274–6
Complete characterization, 17, 71, 149
Computer programs, 239, 266, 310–1
Conditional distributions, **58–66**, 139
Conditional probability, **35–8**, 84
Confidence intervals, **129–30, 168–77,**
    205–6
Consumption function
    estimated using cross-section data,
      219–22
    estimated using time-series data,
      214–9, 239–47, 299–300
Continuous variables, 10
Correlation coefficient, **74**, 235
Covariance, **74**
Cumulative probability, 8; *see also,*
    Distribution functions

317

Decision-making, 1, 316
Degrees of freedom
  of chi-square distribution, 33
  of t distribution, 33
Demand for money, 268–76
Dependence, 65
Description of probabilistic views, 1, 2, **5–78**
Deterministic part (of regression), **181**
Differentiation, 305
Discrete variables, 10
Dispersion, Measures of; *see* Measures of dispersion
Distributed lags, **255–8**
Distribution functions, **7–12, 44–50**
Dummy variables, **248–50**
Durbin–Watson statistic, **268**

Econometrics, 268–76
Economic relationships, 3, 179
Economic theory, 3
Economic Trends, 214
Economic Trends Annual Supplement, 214, 223, 226, 241, 242, 272, 299
Endogenous, 286
Estimation, 169
Events, 6
Events, Mutually exclusive, **34**
Events, independent; *see* Independent events
Exhaustive, **83**, 88
Expectations, **251–4**
Expected value, 21; *see also* Mean, arithmetic
Exogeneity assumption, 287
Exogenous, 286

Family Expenditure Survey, 218, 220, 227
Financial Statistics, 241
Fitted line; *see* least-squares fitted line

Gamma distribution, 33, 109
  as representation of belief about variance, 153, 161
General Household Survey, 218
Goodness of fit, 209–13

Heteroscedasticity, 262–3
Homoscedasticity, 262–3
Hypothesis testing, 130, 169, 171–3, 206–9

IDA, 239–40
Identification, **291–6**
Improper density function, 125
Independent events, **37**, 85–6
Independent variables, **62–3, 69**, 82
Information, 5, 58, **79–109**, 118–24
Informativeness, **37**, 82
Integration, 305
Isoquants, **72–3**

Joint probability distribution; *see* Bivariate probability distributions
Jointly normal variables, **73**

Knowledge in economics, 1
Koyck distributed lag, **257**

Lagged dependent variable, 254
Lagged independent variables, **255–8**
Lags, 242, 251–8
Least-squares coefficients, **203, 233–4**
Least-squares fitted line, **191**
Least-squares fitted relationship, **233**
Left-triangular distribution, 27, 113
Likelihood, **84**, 86, 90, 96, 161
Limiting distribution, 124, 149
Limiting probability, 95
Linear bivariate normal regression model, **180** *ff*
Linear multivariate normal regression model, **230** *ff*
Location, Measures of, **19–22**
Lower-case letters, 7, 111, 136–7

Marginal distributions, **50–8**
  relationship with joint distribution, **52–8**
Marginal propensity to consume, 5, 214, 217–21, 244
Mean, arithmetic, **20–2**
  learning about, 3, 102–5, **135–78**
  specific formulae for, **140, 148, 162, 163, 164**
Measures of association, 74
Measures of central tendency, **19–22**
Measures of dispersion, **22–4**
Median, **20**
Minimum area probability regions; *see* Probability regions
Mode, **19–20**

Modified residual standard deviation, **203**, 234, 274
Modified residual variance, **203**
Modified sample standard deviation, **164**, 212, 237
Modified sample variance, **164**
Mpc; *see* Marginal propensity to consume
Multicollinearity, 259–60
  effect on precision of posterior, **235–6**
  extreme, **236**
Multiple regression, **230** *ff*
Multivariate case, **43**, **66–71**
Mutually exclusive events, 34, **83**, 88

Non-deterministic part (of regression), **181**
Non-existent prior information, 105–6, 125–6; *see also* Total prior ignorance
Non-linear equations, **258**
Normal distribution, **29–32**, 136, 181
  as distribution of residual of relationship, **263**, 306
  as representation of belief about coefficients of economic relationship, 185, 306–8
  as representation of belief about mean, 103, 105–6, **138**, 161
  table of unit, **312**
  unit, **29–32**
  see also Jointly normal variables
Normality assumption (in regression), **263–4**
Null hypothesis; *see* Hypothesis testing

'Objective' probability, 129
Overidentification, 295
Overidentified (equation), 295

Parameters of the reduced form; *see* Reduced form parameters
Parameters of the structure; *see* Structural parameters
Partial adjustment, **254–5**, 269
Poisson distribution, 109
Polynomial distributed lag, **257**
Population mean, 102, **135–78**; *see also* Mean, arithmetic

Population proportion, 98, 111; *see also*, Proportion
Population variance; *see* Variance
Posterior beliefs, **79**, 84
Precision, 141, 153
Prediction, **222–4**
Prior beliefs, **79**, 84
  Sample equivalence of, **120**, 155
Probability, 2, **5–78**
Probability density function
  univariate, **14–17**
  bivariate, **48–9**
  multivariate, **68**
Probability function
  univariate, **12–3**
  bivariate, **47**
  multivariate, **68**
Probability intervals, **17–9**, 123, 129–30, 147, 169–71, 192, 199, 206, 232, 243, 288–9
Probability laws, 34, **37**, 38
Probability regions, **72–3**
Product ($\prod$) notation, 304
Proofs, 305–10
Proportion, 3, 98, 111
  learning about, 98–102, **110–34**
  specific formulae for, **118**, **119**, **126**
Proportionality form, **26–7**, 90
Proxy variable, **250–1**

Quarterly dummies, 250

R^2, **212–3**, 245–6
$\bar{R}^2$, **213**, 245–6
Random sampling, 117, 139, 185, 260–1
Rational expectations, 251
Rationality, 5, 83
Reduced form, 286
Reduced form equations, 286
Reduced form parameters, 286
Regression, **179–301**; *see also*, Linear bivariate normal regression model, and Linear multivariate normal regression model
Regression coefficients; *see* Coefficient of relationship
Residual, 180
Revision of probabilistic views, 1, 2, **79–109**
Right-triangular distribution, **27**, 113

Sample mean, 147
Sample proportion, 120, 122
Sample variance; *see* Modified sample variance
Sampling with and without replacement, 124
SEARCH, 311
Sigma ($\sum$) notation, 304
Significance, **172–3**, 207–9
Simultaneous models, 4, 180, **281–303**
Single equation models (as compared with simultaneous models), 281
Single-equation methods, **282–91**
Skewness, 24
Smallest width probability intervals; *see* Probability intervals
Spread; *see* Measures of dispersion
Standard deviation, **23–4**; *see also,* Variance
Standard error, **203**, 234, 243
Standard error of regression, 203
Statistics, 1
Step-function, 9, 45
Structural form, 286
Structural parameters, 286
Structure; *see* Structural form
Subjective probability, 5
Sufficiency, 147
Summaries, **17–24**, 71–4
Summation ($\sum$) notation, 304
Surprise, 94–5

t-distribution, 33
    as representation of beliefs about coefficients of relationship, **199–200**, **232**, 309–10
    as representation of beliefs about mean, 163, 164
    as representation of beliefs about predicted values, 223
    table of, 313

t-ratio, **209**, 244
Total posterior ignorance, **236**
Total prior ignorance, 105–6, 125–6, 128, 130, 148, 156, 159, 163–4, 185, 196
Transformation of relationship, 262–5
'Tricks of the trade', **247–60**

Uncertainty, 1
Unconditional probabilities (as compared with Conditional probabilities), 35
Underidentification, 293, 294
Underidentified (equation), 293
Uniform distribution, **25–7**, 113
    mean, **27**
    variance, **27**
Upper case letters, 7, 111, 136–7

Validity of assumptions, **260–8**
Variable of interest, 102, 135
Variables, 6
Variance, **23–4**
    learning about, 3, **152 78**
    specific formulae for, 154, 155, 156, 159, 162, 163, 164, 165
    see also, Variance of residuals of relationship
Variance of residuals of relationship, **180–2**
    learning about, **195–8**, **198–9**, **232**
    specific formulae for, **196**, **199**, **204**, **232**
    see also, Variance
Vector notation, **66–71**
Violation of assumptions, 260–8

Zero prior probability, 88; *see also,* Total prior ignorance